GARDEN SECRETS

A guide to understanding how your garden grows and how you can help it grow even better

DOROTHY HINSHAW PATENT
& DIANE E. BILDERBACK

Rodale Press, Emmaus, Pennsylvania

To our families, whose patient
understanding during our long working hours
made this book possible.

Printed in the United States of America on recycled paper, containing a high percentage of de-inked fiber.

Book design by Linda Jacopetti
Illustrations by Kathi Ember

Library of Congress Cataloging in Publication Data

Patent, Dorothy Hinshaw.
    Garden secrets.

    Bibliography: p.
    Includes index.
    1. Vegetable gardening. I. Bilderback, Diane E.
II. Title.
SB321.P375   635   82-5420
ISBN 0–87857–420–4 hardcover AACR2

    4 6 8 10 9 7 5 3   hardcover

Contents

Acknowledgments

First and foremost, we both wish to thank David Bilderback, Diane's husband, for reading and commenting on the entire manuscript, even when it meant staying up until two in the morning to meet a deadline. His scientific training as a Ph.D. in botany and his experience as a fellow gardener have been invaluable to us. Besides lending a hand with the editing and playing the devil's advocate, he helped find sources of information, assisted as our scientific advisor, and took care of the Bilderback children while Diane was off writing and researching.

In the process of working on the book, Diane phoned and talked to scientists with various specialties. She would like to thank them for their time and patience in answering her questions: Dr. Robert Dwelle, University of Idaho, Branch Experiment Station, Aberdeen, Idaho (potatoes); Dr. H. J. Mack, Department of Horticulture, Oregon State University, Corvallis, Oregon (beets); Dr. Edward J. Ryder, United States Agricultural Research Station, Salinas, California (lettuce); Dr. William L. Sims, Extension Vegetable Specialist, University of California, Davis, California (tomatoes); Dr. Paul G. Smith, Department of Vegetable Crops, University of California, Davis (peppers); and Dr. Ronald E. Voss, Vegetable Crops Specialist, Cooperative Extension, University of California, Davis (onions). In addition, special thanks are due to Dr. Dwelle and Dr. Sims for reading and commenting on the potato and tomato chapters respectively. We would also like to thank Dr. Sherman Preece and the Department of Botany at the University of Montana for their encouragement and support.

And finally, we wish to thank our editors, Suzanne Nelson and Anne Halpin, for helping get the book into final form with their thoughtful comments and questions and for their patience in working with us.

Introduction

This is a gardening book very different from any other you've ever read. Instead of merely giving you instructions on how, when, and where to plant your vegetable crops, we will usher you into the exciting world of your garden to help you see things you've never noticed before and to show you how your plants function and why they sometimes behave in strange or frustrating ways. We strongly believe that when you really understand the biology of your plants, you will be a far better gardener than if you were to blindly follow the instructions in a book without understanding the *whys* behind the *hows*. And when you know something about the factors that can influence your crops for good or ill, you'll be able to deal more effectively with gardening problems and to experiment more creatively with gardening methods.

Unfortunately, there are many gaps in our knowledge of garden plants. We would like to be able to tell you why radishes get hot when temperatures rise and what chemical makes lettuce bitter. It is frustrating not to be able to state exactly what daylengths will make some popular onion varieties bolt. But these and many other aspects of vegetable crops remain mysterious and will stay that way until someone chooses to investigate them. You will see as you read this book that we know the most about crops such as corn and potatoes, which are grown extensively on a commercial scale. Plants like kale, kohlrabi, peppers, and radishes, which are not of great economic importance, have been slighted by researchers. For this reason, our book is necessarily uneven in its coverage; we can only explain the phenomena which have been studied!

Our sources of information are varied. We combed scientific literature for writings illuminating the biology of vegetable plants, and much of our information on major crops came from government publications based on research carried out at state universities such as the University of California, Davis. Several books summarizing scientific information about specific crops were also utilized, as were more general works such as *Evolution of Crop Plants* (see the Bibliography).

In this book we'll start by talking about plants in general, examining how they awaken to life from seed and how they develop into full-fledged, mature,   1 productive plants. Next, we'll turn our attention to the garden itself and show you what goes on in the soil at root level and how you can create the best possible environment in which your plants can thrive. A chapter on the most effective cultural techniques for you to follow all season long (and *why* they're effective) will help you sidestep the common mistakes that are the downfall of many a gardener.

With all that background information in mind, we'll go on to consider each of more than 20 common garden crops in turn. We'll give you pointers on: choosing varieties; specific growing conditions (in terms of temperature, light, daylength, nutrients, and water) that will hinder or help your crop to form; growing and storing the crop; how to save your own seed (where applicable); certain pest and disease problems you're likely to encounter and how to prevent and control them; and finally, we'll provide a glimpse at what sort of breeding research is being done for each crop to give you a preview of what new kinds of varieties to expect in the seed catalogs of the future. By the time you've finished the book, you will have a new appreciation of your plants as living things as well as a better understanding of how to make them do their best for you, the gardener. We hope you enjoy yourself in the process.

To set the stage for what follows in *Garden Secrets*, we'd like to start out by explaining a few key concepts that will be referred to throughout the book.

Days to Maturity

When a seed catalog advertises that a particular variety of corn or radish takes only 68 days or 25 days to mature, what does that really mean? Where we live, in Missoula, Montana, we average slightly over 90 days of continuously frost-free weather in the growing season. But that doesn't mean we can have success with every crop that's listed in catalogs as taking fewer than 90 days to mature. Unfortunately, many of our frost-free days are quite cool, averaging less than 50°F over the 24-hour period. In the case of a crop like corn, temperatures below 50°F will call a halt to growth, while temperatures above 50°F will allow the corn to grow. Up to a point, the higher the temperature, the faster the corn will grow.

Some scientists and some seed catalogs use a measurement called degree days for determining days to maturity of certain crops such as corn. Since 50°F is the critical point for corn growth, any daily temperature average above this point will earn degree-day units, one unit for each degree that the average temperature is over 50°F. For instance, if the average temperature for 4 days was 60°F, this would count as 40 degree-day units (10 units for each day). Just how many units a corn plant must amass to reach maturity varies a bit among varieties, but to give you some idea, scientists have calculated that Golden Cross Bantam sweet corn takes about 1,875 degree-day units to reach maturity. You can see that corn will mature faster under warm temperatures than under cool ones—just 2 days averaging 80°F will count for 60 degree-day units, whereas 4 days at 60°F would only produce 40 degree-day units. This simple phenomenon accounts for the difficulty we have in growing sweet corn varieties that are rated at more than 68 days to maturity, even though there are more than 90 frost-free days here. There just isn't enough heat on many of those days to make the corn grow.

With all crops, seed sellers have to assume particular climatic conditions when they calculate days to maturity, whether they use degree days as a measure or not. If you have cool summers with average temperatures below 65° to 70°F, your crops will generally mature more slowly than the catalog's predictions lead you to believe. To guarantee that you'll be able to harvest a crop, you must select the most quickly maturing varieties. Remember that we are talking about *average* daily temperature, not maximum. Our average temperature here in a mountain valley can be low even on a day when the maximum reaches 95°F. The 95°F temperature only lasts a couple of hours, and the nighttime temperature almost always drops below 60°F, even in the height of summer. A coastal area with less difference between daily maximum and minimum temperatures may allow crops to grow faster than they do here, even if the maximum never exceeds 85°F. And if you have very hot weather—temperatures in the 90s or above 100—crops that do well in the heat may mature more rapidly than the catalogs predict.

Because they may not be calculated in the same way, listings of days to maturity in catalogs from different companies are not necessarily comparable. Before you order your seeds, do a little comparing among the seed catalogs you have on hand. Find a common variety that most catalogs offer, and check the days to maturity given for this variety in each catalog. You may be surprised at the wide range you find given for the same variety. You might want to cross-check a few more common varieties to get a feel for which catalogs tend to give a shorter time to maturity than others. Also, be sure to note whether the time given is from direct seeding in the garden or from transplanting; some crops, such as carrots and radishes, are always given from seeding whereas others, including broccoli and peppers, are generally given from transplanting.

Varieties and Microclimates

Wherever possible in this book, we recommend particular varieties of crop plants for different regions of the country. However, each broad geographic area has its own climatic variations, and even within a small area, like our mountain valley, the variations among microclimates can be quite significant. This concept can even extend into the garden itself—one area of the garden may be protected from the wind by a fence, for example, or another part may be shaded by a large tree for part of the day. Since frost tends to settle in low spots, you may find that some parts of your garden will become frosted, while just a foot away the plants are untouched.

For all these reasons, variety recommendations must be taken with a grain of salt. Early Cascade Hybrid tomato, which is an early variety with a supposedly sweet flavor, was sour and tough when grown in more than one Missoula garden. Dutch Treat pepper, however, grows beautifully here but was panned by a midwestern gardener in a gardening magazine article. The two of us have found that crops or varieties that grow well for one may be a real problem for the other. For example, Diane grows beautiful cucumbers, squash, and corn, while Dorothy has trouble with all three. When Dorothy is happily eating her way through a mound of peppers, Diane may be carefully rationing out a few ripe fruits. But then, there are always the exceptions to the general trend, as in the year Diane was the one whose pepper plants were loaded with Colorado chilis while Dorothy's crop was modest! Early Girl Hybrid tomatoes consistently ripen first and taste best in Dorothy's garden, while Burpeeana Early Hybrid is Diane's star tomato crop. We could go on and on, but the point is that the best recommendation for a particular variety is that it grows best for you in your own garden. But even a year with unusual conditions can result in a disappointing crop or no crop at all. For this reason, we always plant more than one variety of almost every crop we grow. Since there is no such thing as a typical growing season in our valley, we always hope that by planting different varieties, we will at least have good success with some of them.

Warm and Cool Places

Here and in other books, you are often directed to place germinating seeds or to store harvested crops in a warm or a cool place. What exactly do these terms mean? For our purposes, a warm place should stay as much as possible between 75° and 85°F. You can probably find some warm spots like this in your home without much trouble. For instance, if your water heater is in a closet, the temperature there is likely to be warm. A cupboard above a wall oven, especially a gas oven with a pilot light, is another place that's often warm, in part because the oven is frequently on but also because warm air rises, making a high cupboard warmer than a low one in the same room.

If you lack these warm places in your home, you can resort to the space on top of the water heater, but you must be careful. Many water heaters get quite hot on top, as friends of ours can testify. They lost all their newly planted seeds because the water heater got so hot that it cooked them all! To be safe, place the containers holding your newly sown or just-germinating seeds on cake racks on top of the heater; keeping this buffer zone between the heat source and the seeds should ensure that it won't get hot enough to kill them.

Those of you with wood stoves know that it is toasty warm in the vicinity of the stove. You could locate your germinating seeds near the stove (not *on* it), but only after measuring the temperature to determine the best distance. Since wood stoves produce dry heat, be especially careful about keeping the soil moist if you are relying on this heat source.

If you have a window that gets sunny and hot during the daytime, you can place your containers full of freshly sown seeds by the window during the day and move them to the warmest part of the house at night.

Spinach and lettuce are two crops that germinate best under cool conditions (60° to 65°F). Cool germinating locations can be found in an unheated closet or cupboard which shares an outside wall. Basements also tend to be cool, as long as you are careful not to put the seeds near a furnace or water heater.

When we talk about cool storage conditions for harvested crops, we're referring to the 32° to 40°F temperature range. Many of the crops you'll be carrying through the winter, such as acorn squashes, beets, cabbage, carrots, onions, and turnips, require a cool, but not freezing, location for the longest storage life. A root cellar, of course, is the ideal location. Those of you who aren't lucky enough to have access to one can improvise by storing your vegetables in a basement window well that has a 6-inch layer of insulating leafy mulch strewn on the bottom and a board set over the top to keep out the elements and hungry animals. An attic, breezeway, or unheated room are other possible options. In a house that's heated by a wood stove, check the closets on the north side of the house—they may be just the right temperature. Dorothy has had good results storing her onions in her unheated garage, along the wall that's attached to the house. Following these suggestions, you should pull on your detective's cap and sleuth around your house to find the nooks and out-of-the-way crannies that will provide nice, cool storage conditions.

Chapter 1

The Secret Life of Seeds

Have you ever picked up all your garden seed packets and realized that you are holding an entire garden in your hands? The seed is one of nature's greatest miracles, for it stores the essence of its kind in the smallest of spaces. Seeds from related crops often look very much alike. You probably could not tell the difference between cauliflower, broccoli, or cabbage seeds, if you mixed them together in your palm, for they are very similar in size, shape, and color, resembling so many tiny, deep brown to black pebbles. But what differences you see when these members of the Cabbage family have grown up!

The dissimilarity between seeds of unrelated plants, however, is usually quite obvious. Tawny carrot seed, with the characteristic deep ridges running lengthwise along its oval shape, is certainly easy to distinguish from the khaki green, wrinkled, roughly spherical seed of the pea plant. Corn seed, which looks like shrunken, wizened pieces of ambergris, is a striking contrast to the small, angular, matte black bits of onion seed. Beet seeds, with their brownish coloring and crinkly surface, may remind you of vermiculite and appear downright dowdy when you compare them with smooth-as-ivory, jet black bean seeds.

Despite the vast array of seed shapes, colors, and sizes, in terms of actual growth habit there are just two basic types of seeds produced by two quite different sorts of plants: dicots and monocots. Most garden crops are dicots. If you look closely at a large dicot seed such as a shelled peanut, you can see that it can be split into two halves. These two halves are the cotyledons (also called seed leaves). They contain nourishment for the young plant as it germinates. Hidden between the seed leaves is a tiny plant embryo that will grow into the mature plant. The seed leaves and the embryo are surrounded by the seed coat, which protects them from environmental extremes such as drying out and from mechanical damage to their delicate tissues.

The other basic type of seed is exemplified by a corn seed, which cannot be split in two. Corn, onions, and grasses are monocots and have only one cotyledon. Most monocots store food for the young growing plant as endosperm tissue, which lies outside the embryo, rather than entirely within the cotyledon itself. Corn stores almost all the nourishment for the young plant as protein and carbohydrate (sugar and starch) in its endosperm. This sugar

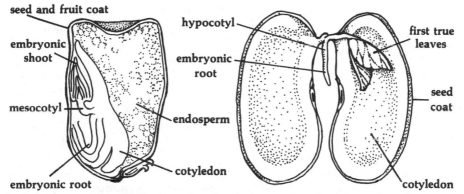

Seed Structure: *The seed of a dicot plant like the bean seed on the right can be easily separated to reveal the embryo nestled between two seed leaves (cotyledons). The corn seed on the left, a monocot, has only one cotyledon, along with a large endosperm containing stored food, which is used to fuel the germination process.*

in the endosperm is what gives corn its delightful sweetness. Onions have much less endosperm than corn and store food both there and in the cotyledon. As you'll see in this chapter and the one that follows, there are other important differences between monocots and dicots besides their seeds.

The Best Way to Store Seeds

Within each seed is all the information it needs to develop into a productive garden plant—if you treat it right and plant it properly. And treating seeds right begins with proper seed storage. So many of us just stow our seeds haphazardly in a box or bag and leave them in the basement for the winter. Diane, too, has been guilty of using this method, but as a result of an experience she had this year, she has resolved to mend her ways. For years her long-lasting seeds, like tomatoes and peppers, survived just fine in the basement. But her luck ran out this past spring, and she was very disappointed when all her stored seeds germinated very poorly. Something was different about last winter, probably the weather, and thus the basement was significantly more damp than in previous years. But whatever the reason, her stored seeds simply did not deliver. Diane had to replant many crops, losing valuable time and money in the process.

If you've ever had an experience like that, you've already learned the hard way that the most important factor in the survival of stored seeds is moisture. Your seeds will last much longer the drier they are kept. Ideally, storage humidity should be only about 4 to 6 percent. Cool temperatures also help, but dryness is the real key to success. Increases in humidity and temperature lead to more rapid degeneration of the stored food and genetic information within the seeds. This in turn decreases the chances that the seeds will successfully complete their complex germination process.

A reliable way to store your seeds is to enclose them in an airtight container with some silica gel or other type of drying crystals, and set the whole container in a cool (but not humid) place like an unheated attic. Most hobby shops sell kits for drying flowers which include an airtight container and crystals. For a less expensive setup, use recycled glass jars with screw top lids and add a tiny packet of powdered milk to act as the desiccant. Making these packets is easy; just layer four tissues on top of each other and heap 2 tablespoons of powdered milk in one corner. Roll up the tissues, draw the long ends together, and secure them with a rubber band. If your seeds will be in storage for a while, replace the packet every six months or so.

How long seeds last in storage depends not only on storage conditions but also on seed type. Tomato seeds will remain viable for five or more years under favorable conditions, while onion seeds rarely survive more than a year even under the best of circumstances. Sometimes old seeds will germinate all right but will produce inferior plants. One friend of ours grew Yellow Globe onions two years in a row from the same seeds. Both years she started the seeds indoors, so their early growing conditions were similar each year. The first year the plants grew quickly, but the second year they grew very slowly. The seeds apparently had been weakened in storage although they were still capable of germinating. Perhaps the stored food inside the seeds had deteriorated and thus the young plants did not get that vital early boost to their growth.

Testing for Germination

If you read your seed packets carefully, you will see that some seed companies give germination information for the seeds they sell. A well-labeled packet should give the year the seeds were packaged and give the expected percent of germination. Companies germination-test their seeds by placing them between layers of dampened absorbent paper and leaving them in special germination chambers for a specified number of days. Then they count the number of germinated and ungerminated seeds to arrive at a percentage. Germinating the seeds on paper is much easier than planting them in soil, and besides, the paper method usually gives a higher percentage of germinated seeds for the company to advertise. When seeds are planted in the ground, the young plants must push their way through the soil. The weaker seedlings may not make it in the garden, but they can usually germinate between damp paper.

It is easy to test your own seeds for germination. Just place at least ten of them between layers of moist paper toweling, and keep them damp. (Be careful not to waterlog them, however.) Wait a few days after the first seeds

Germinating Seeds between Paper Towels

In several chapters of this book, we recommend germinating seeds between layers of paper towels; here are some tips for doing it successfully.

• Use only white or off-white towels; there is always the possibility that dyes in colored towels may kill the seeds.

• Use a brand of towel that is advertised as being strong when wet; you don't want towels that will disintegrate before the seeds have germinated!

• Using a ballpoint pen, label each towel (before wetting it) in one corner with pertinent information such as the variety and the date.

• Just dampen the towels thoroughly; they should be wet but not dripping. The fine spray from a plant mister does a good job of providing just enough but not too much moisture. If they get too wet, gently squeeze out any excess water.

• Sprinkle the seeds on one-half of the labeled towel which you have dampened, then fold the other half over to make a seed "sandwich."

• Layer several of these "sandwiches" in a casserole or glass pie plate over which you drape a loose covering. Alternate the position of the corners of the "sandwiches" as you layer them, so that you can easily get to one layer at a time by lifting up a corner.

• Place the container in a location where you can expect the temperature to stay within the germination range for the crop you are sprouting. Be sure to check every two days to make sure the towels haven't dried out and to see if the seeds have begun to germinate. If the towels are getting dry, bring out the plant mister again and remoisten them, or sprinkle a tablespoon of water at a time over the pile (to avoid inadvertently saturating the seeds to the point of no return).

germinate and then count them. If seven out of ten seeds germinate, your germination rate is 70 percent. If less than 50 percent germinate, you should scrap that batch and get new seeds.

Other conditions can also make the germination rate of seeds planted in your garden considerably lower than the rate given on the packet and the rate your home test shows. Seed companies often sort out the larger seeds for selling. These seeds give better results in germination tests but may have a harder time pushing through the soil because of their larger cotyledons. Bacteria, insects, and fungi present another hazard—all can attack seeds before they break through the soil. A friend of ours was very puzzled when bean seeds which germinated perfectly well for her in damp paper towels never sent shoots above the soil when planted in the garden. Finally, after her second or third try, she couldn't resist digging some of them up to see what had gone wrong. She discovered, to her dismay, that the seeds had rotted before the cotyledons had appeared, victims of harmful organisms in the soil.

What Seeds Need to Germinate

There are many theories about determining the best time to plant. Some gardeners go by the phases of the moon, while others gear their planting to coincide with the blooming or budding of certain key plants in the local landscape. But the most foolproof method is to plant when the soil temperature is right for germination of the crop you wish to grow. Many garden supply companies offer soil thermometers which are definitely a worthwhile investment. They are simple to use; just plunge the thermometer into the soil to the depth at which the particular seed is to be planted, and compare the temperature that registers to the best temperature for germination of that seed. (Germination temperature is listed in the Vital Statistics box at the beginning of each crop chapter, later in this book.) If you start your seeds indoors, try to keep them at the optimum temperature. Some crops, such as onions and peas, will germinate over a wide temperature range. But others, like beans, are very particular and must be given the right temperature within a very narrow range.

The seeds of some cool-weather crops, such as lettuce and spinach, will refuse to germinate at high temperatures. The warmth actually induces dormancy in the seeds rather than stimulating germination as it would with eggplant or pepper seeds. Last summer Diane planted spinach seeds during the hot August weather and mulched them with only a light covering of grass clippings. She also piled up her old bolted-and-gone-to-seed spinach plants in a shady corner for future composting. She waited and waited for her planted seeds to germinate, but only two seeds in the entire 100-foot row pushed their way up! But when she got around to lifting the old spinach plants to add them to the compost pile, she found hundreds of tiny spinach plants beneath them. The seeds she had so carefully planted under the hot sun with their shallow mulch cover had gone dormant, but those which fell under the cool pile of plants germinated perfectly. For this reason, if you want to start lettuce, spinach, or parsley during the summer, plant the seeds indoors or in a cool, shady corner of the garden to ensure that they will germinate properly.

The temperature at planting time not only affects germination of the seed; it also can affect later stages of the plant's development. If you sow peas or lettuce seeds in cold soil, the resulting plants will flower and form their own seeds earlier than if the original seeds had been planted in warm soil. Of course, this is fine for peas, for earlier flowering means earlier peas for picking. But you don't want your lettuce to bolt and go to seed early if it can be avoided.

Light can also affect seed germination. Most vegetable seeds germinate best in darkness, but some (including many varieties of lettuce and some celery) may actually require light for germination. Light not only affects the garden seeds you plant so carefully; it also affects weed seeds. Many weed seeds will only germinate in light. This is why your garden may sprout into a lush weed patch after you have so painstakingly tilled it; your tilling brings the weed seeds to the soil surface where they germinate in the light. Temperature affects weeds too—they may go dormant like spinach if the weather gets too hot. Then, when the soil cools again, you can end up with a fresh crop of weeds. Another "trick" used by some weeds, such as the British weed called fat hen and the American pigweed, is to produce two kinds of seeds. One sort has a normal seed coat and will germinate easily. The other sort has a hard seed coat which must be weakened by a scratch before it will come to life. Every time you conscientiously cultivate your garden, some of those hard-coated seeds are scratched by small rocks in the soil and then germinate. No wonder weeds are so hard to get rid of!

Another necessity for seeds to germinate is oxygen. If they are planted in water-logged soil or are planted so deeply that sufficient oxygen cannot reach them, seeds will just sit there and rot. One year that very thing happened to Dorothy's cucumber seeds. She planted them too deeply in heavy clay soil, in valleys rather than on hills and then watered them much too abundantly. Not a single seed germinated. In the Vital Statistics box at the beginning of each crop chapter, you will find the proper planting depth for each sort of seed; be sure to follow this guide carefully.

Although temperature, light, and oxygen are all important to seed germination, the most vital factor is adequate moisture. Water-logged and drowned seeds will not germinate, but neither will sun-baked, dried-out ones. A lettuce seed planted at the proper temperature near the soil surface where it receives the right amount of light and oxygen will not germinate if it does not get enough moisture. That's why it is sometimes difficult to germinate lettuce seeds and others with similar requirements. They need light (so they should be planted shallowly), but they also must not be allowed to dry out. This often can be a tricky combination to achieve during a warm, sunny spring. In the garden, a light mulch such as grass clippings can help keep these seeds moist while still letting in the necessary amount of light. In the house, seeds such as those of lettuce, snapdragons, and runnerless strawberries can be successfully germinated by sprinkling them on top of the soil, watering them gently, and placing the container in a plastic bag on a bright windowsill. The plastic cover will act as a miniature greenhouse, letting in light but retaining plenty of moisture.

The Seed Coat's Role in Germination

The seed coat which surrounds the living seed sometimes does more than just protect the seed. The seed coats of many plants contain chemicals which inhibit germination of the seeds. This keeps them from germinating too early or when only briefly exposed to moisture. But gardeners are most interested in rapid germination, not slow germination. To get around these germination inhibitors, soaking and washing the seeds is often effective. Some sorts of peppers, such as Jalapeños, may germinate faster if soaked in a couple of changes of lukewarm water before planting. Beet seeds also benefit from soaking. The strange-looking lumpy seeds of beets and chard are not actually seeds at all. They are the dried-up fruits of the plant, and each one contains several seeds. (That's why beets and chard always need to be thinned.) The hard fruit covering contains a germination inhibitor which can be removed by soaking the seeds overnight.

Seed coats play other important roles in the lives of plants, too. They regulate how much oxygen, water, and light are received by the seeds. Because of the importance of even water uptake, some gardeners make it a practice to soak large seeds such as peas or beans overnight before planting to ensure that all the seeds take up enough water and will germinate evenly.

How Seeds Germinate

The uptake of water by seeds is actually the first stage in germination. But just because your seeds swell with water does not necessarily mean they are alive. Water uptake is purely a passive process which even dead seeds will undergo. So don't think you can determine if your peas or beans are still alive just by soaking them and seeing how many swell up. This water absorption can generate a surprising amount of force. A friend of ours was sprouting some wheat seeds for eating and put too many seeds in the jar, which she covered with a screw-on lid. The next day, when she went to rinse the seeds, she found that the force of their swelling had cracked the jar!

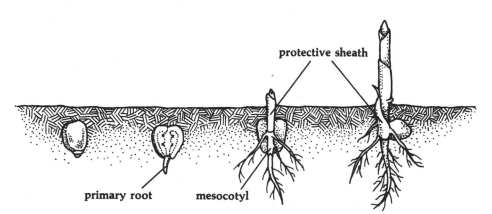

Corn Germination: *The leaves of the developing corn plant emerge from the soil in a protective sheath, leaving the old seed behind in the soil.*

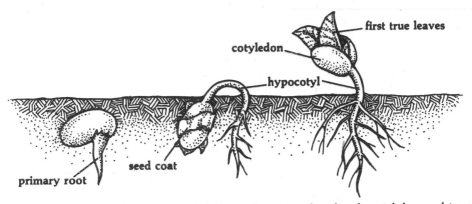

Bean Germination: *The new stem of the bean elongates and pushes the cotyledons and true leaves to the surface of the soil. The stem and leaves, bent like an upside-down J, break through the surface of the soil and are drawn to an upright position by the sun.*

After the seed has swollen with water, the tiny embryo inside begins to grow. It sends a chemical message (a hormone) to the part of the seed where the food is stored (endosperm in monocots like corn; cotyledons in beans and other dicots), which directs cells in the storage area to produce enzymes. These enzymes digest the stored food and make it available to the developing embryo.

The tiny, delicate embryonic root is the first part of the new little plant to break through the seed coat. It grows straight down, guided by the force of gravity, into the soil. It makes no difference which way the seed is planted, the root will always grow downward. Then the stem and leaves begin to grow. Once the life inside a corn seed is roused, the leaves, covered by a protective sheath, grow straight up towards the surface, leaving the old seed behind in the soil. With beans, the stem elongates, pushing the cotyledons and true leaves to the surface of the soil. The young bean stem is bent when it breaks through the soil and looks like an upside down J, with the cotyledons and true leaves pointing downward as part of the hook. As soon as the seedling breaks through into the sunlight, the stem straightens out, exposing the leaves to the sunlight.

You can easily distinguish the cotyledons from the true leaves on beans and on any other seedlings. The cotyledons are thick and spongy with stored food. Their shape is different from the first true leaves, which are miniature versions of the leaves that will be produced by the plant throughout its life. Although bean cotyledons do photosynthesize to produce some food for the young plant, they continue to nourish it primarily with their stored food.

The seed leaves of peas remain in the soil as the young plant grows, while tomatoes send their cotyledons up into the sunlight to manufacture

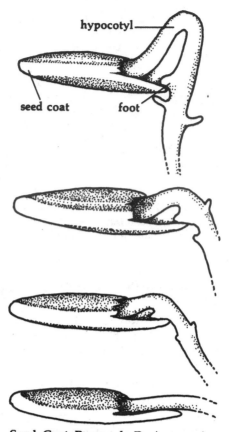

hypocotyl

seed coat   foot

Seed Coat Removal: *During germina-*
tion, the cucumber produces a unique foot
on its stem that catches onto the seed coat
and pulls it away from the emerging co-
tyledons. The removal process begins in the
bottom illustration and progresses as the
foot becomes fully developed, top.

food for the plant before the first true leaves are even visible. As you can see, with all seedlings it is important to leave the seed leaves alone and not pinch them off since in one way or another they are providing food for the young plant.

Some young seedlings must discard the hard old seed coat from the cotyledons. This occasionally presents a problem, especially with peppers, when the seed coat will not come off and holds the tips of the cotyledons together. The small true leaves become imprisoned between the cotyledons and cannot expand. When this happens, you can very carefully try to remove the old seed without damaging the seed leaves or the true leaves. Cucumber seedlings will rarely need assistance from you in unfurling their leaves. The embryonic plants have a special little foot which develops on the stem to push off the old seed coat. As the cotyledons bend out of the seed coat, this foot catches on the coat and levers it off.

When an onion seed germinates, the old seed is carried aloft on top of the single, long green cotyledon. The tip of the cotyledon is actually buried in the endosperm of the seed, gleaning nutrients from it. For this reason you should leave the onion seedling with its hard black head alone for fear of pinching off its supply of early nourishment.

What Makes Hybrid Seed So Special?

It seems that more and more varieties of garden vegetables every year are called hybrids. Have you ever wondered just what hybrid seeds are, anyway? You may have also questioned what makes them so expensive and whether they are really worth the extra cost. Gardening books caution against saving seed from hybrid plants, but do you know why?

Hybrid seed is produced by crossing two different strains of a particular plant species. Each of the parent strains has been bred to itself for so many generations that it is very uniform genetically. These two uniform strains, which are quite different from each other, are cross-pollinated to produce the hybrid seed. Growers experiment with different crosses to find out which ones result in good crop plants, for not all hybrids are winners. Hybrids are very consistent in their characteristics, such as size and time of maturity, because the genetic makeup of each hybrid plant is almost identical to that of every other plant resulting from the same cross.

It takes a lot of time, space, and labor—all of which cost money—to maintain the parent strains which are crossed to obtain hybrid seed. In addition, the flowers of one parent strain must generally be hand-pollinated with the pollen of the other strain in order to ensure uniform hybrid seed. This can be a very laborious process. For example, when hybrids of vegetables with perfect flowers (containing both male and female organs) are wanted, the anthers (pollen-producing parts) of the flowers that will be the female parents may need to be carefully removed. Doing this guarantees that the plant won't pollinate itself but will instead receive only the pollen from the male parent to complete the desired cross.

Before the advent of corn plants that don't produce pollen, hybridizing corn offered summer employment for many teenagers who lived near big seed growers. Each corn plant has its own male flower (the tassel) and female flower (the ear with its silks). The normal course of events is for pollen from the tassel to drift down and find its way to the silks or to be carried by the

The Making of a Hybrid Variety

All plants carry two units of inheritance, called genes, for each genetic trait, one derived from the female parent and one from the male parent. The genes determine the flavor of the produce, the height of the plant, the time to maturity, and all the other characteristics that make up the plant. This chart shows what happens when hybrids are produced. Each set of letters—AA, Bb, Cc, and so on—represents one pair of genes.

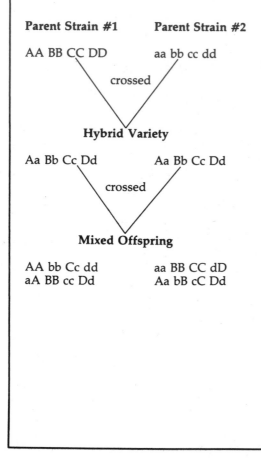

Parent Strain #1

AA BB CC DD

Parent Strain #2

aa bb cc dd

crossed

Hybrid Variety

Aa Bb Cc Dd   Aa Bb Cc Dd

crossed

Mixed Offspring

AA bb Cc dd   aa BB CC dD
aA BB cc Dd   Aa bB cC Dd

Parent strains are inbred for generations so that they are genetically uniform. The individual plants within each strain have an almost identical genetic makeup, and both genes for each trait are also identical (AA, aa).

When plant breeders cross the parent strains, the hybrid offspring receive one gene for each trait from each parent (Aa, Bb). Since plants of each parent strain are essentially identical, all the offspring are almost identical.

When hybrid plants are allowed to go to seed, the pollination that occurs as a matter of course introduces an incredible variety of combinations of genes, and thus of traits. This diagram shows only some of the potential combinations of only four gene pairs. There are actually thousands of genes in each plant, so you can see that the variety of possible combinations is almost infinite. That's why when you sow seeds taken from hybrid plants you can never be quite sure what will come up.

wind to silks on nearby plants. Seed growers intent on making a cross needed to control which pollen did the pollinating, so they had their hired helpers cover each set of tassels on the female parent plants with a paper bag so that the tassels could not spread their pollen and pollination would be done by the male parent plants.

Hybrid varieties are often worth the extra cost, for they offer several advantages that may help you in your particular gardening situation. Hybrids of many crops mature earlier than do the standard, open-pollinated varieties. For example, there are hybrid varieties of corn and tomatoes which mature several days earlier and yield more consistently than the standard ones. If you live in the north and want to grow corn or tomatoes, you may have no choice but to plant early-maturing hybrid varieties. The quality and quantity of the harvest might also convince you to buy hybrid seed, for many hybrids have a better flavor and a higher yield than standard varieties. Disease resistance is another important trait built into many hybrids that is a boon to organic gardeners.

But if a hybrid variety does not offer any overwhelming advantage over a more traditional strain, you should seriously consider buying nonhybrid seed. With nonhybrid varieties you can save your own seeds and not have to depend each year on commercial sources. If you save seed from hybrids, the genetic traits from the two parent strains will be mixed up in the second generation, and you will end up with a variable and unreliable bunch of plants. Seeds from nonhybrid plants produce a more predictable crop, and if you carefully save seeds over the years from the best individual plants in the garden, you will, bit by bit, select seeds which are especially adapted to your own growing conditions. In the long run, you could end up with strains that are even more reliable and more productive in your garden than hybrids which you must buy from a seed company or off the rack in a store, year after year.

Chapter 2

Understanding Plant Structure

Each part of a plant—root, stem, leaf, flower—plays its own unique role in the life of the plant. It stands to reason that understanding the special functions of the different plant parts can make you a better gardener, for you will be better able to meet the needs of your crops. We'll start from the bottom up and examine each part of the plant to find out just what is going on as our plants grow, mature, and provide us with tasty and satisfying food.

Roots

Plant roots may be hidden in the soil where you can't see them, but this doesn't mean you can afford to ignore them and their needs. Many gardeners have an out-of-sight-out-of-mind philosophy toward roots, especially non-edible ones. This is too bad, for the roots are tremendously important. They provide most of the mineral nutrition, water uptake, and support for the rest of the plant. Roots are vital to the nutritional content of our food, too, for they mine the soil and bring important minerals into the plant, and hence into the food chain.

The Many Shapes of Roots

Just like leaves and flowers, roots come in different shapes and sizes. Many plants send one fleshy primary root deep into the soil with only a few insignificant roots branching off the sides. Beets, carrots, rutabagas and turnips all have these big, succulent taproots, which we enjoy eating so much. Taproots enable plants to probe deep within the ground for minerals and water. Since the fat root acts as a storage organ for moisture, plants with taproots can withstand drought better than plants with shallower, fibrous roots. Taproots also store food to fuel the plant's growth. When you bite into a crunchy carrot stick, the delicious, sweet flavor comes from the sugars the plant has stowed away in the taproot. The long taproot also anchors the plant deeply in the soil so that it isn't easily uprooted. If you've ever been harvesting carrots and had the tops break off when you tried to pull them up, you already know how well taproots function as anchors. Because their roots extend so far down, carrots and other taprooted plants should be planted in the part of the garden where the loose, crumbly topsoil is deepest.

Other plants, such as beans, cabbages, and peas, have a shallower, more branched root system. Since the surface of the soil dries out first, these plants need more frequent watering than do those with deep taproots. Corn and potatoes have a somewhat different sort of branched root system. These plants have underground stems from which many small roots grow. Like cabbages and peas, corn and potatoes need plenty of water, for their roots are shallow. These plants sometimes have problems remaining upright, for the underground growth may not be extensive enough to stabilize the part of the plant that extends above the ground. Corn plants have special prop roots which are supposed to help the plant stand up straight, but they don't always do the job. One hot summer day Diane had watered her corn very heavily in the morning, and that afternoon her area experienced a very gusty thunder storm. When the storm was over, Diane and her husband were alarmed to

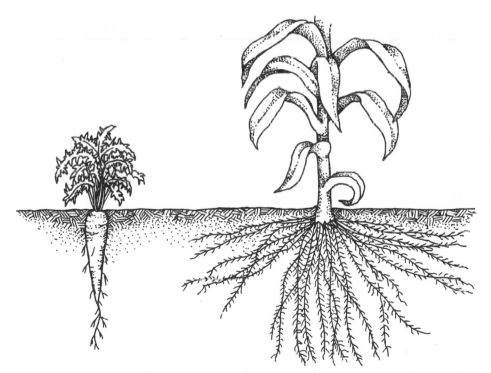

Root Types: *Carrots (left) develop one large, swollen, fleshy taproot with a few secondary roots. The corn plant on the right has a branched, fibrous root system with many small roots growing from the underground stem.*

see all their corn plants lying flat on the ground. They rushed out and carefully straightened up each stalk, giving it a stronger anchor by heeling the soil up against it. It was tedious work, but it paid off when the corn produced a delicious, abundant crop.

Proximity to other plants is an important factor that affects how the root system of a plant develops. Competition with other nearby plants will force the plant to send its root downward instead of sideways, or will inhibit root growth altogether. Since the topsoil is richer in minerals than the deeper subsoil, such crowded, deep-probing plants will be smaller and will yield less than if they were not spaced so close together. If you've ever grown your garden near the edge of the lawn, you've probably seen firsthand a good example of root competition among plants. Crop plants growing near the lawn's edge will be weaker than those situated in the center of the plot because the very vigorous grass roots ramble underground quite a ways and will absorb nutrients and water, "stealing" them right out from under your crop plants.

Branching plant roots can cover an amazingly large area. This is to the plant's advantage, for the more extensive the root surface area, the more minerals and water will be absorbed to fuel growth. One patient scientist grew a rye plant in a box of soil 12 inches square and 22 inches deep and measured the roots when the plant was four months old. He found that the total length of the roots, not counting the tiny root hairs, was 387 miles. When he added in the lengths of the root hairs, he estimated that the grand total was 7,000 miles! This provided the modest little rye plant with a root surface area of 7,000 square feet.

When a plant grows uncrowded in loose, organically rich soil, its roots can spread out naturally to develop plenty of surface area for the absorption of water and minerals. But if the roots have to force their way through heavy clay or compacted hardpan or if they have to compete with invasive roots of weeds or grass, they cannot grow to their natural size and will not be able to nourish the plant adequately. Another characteristic to remember about roots is that they will grow toward the source of water. Thus, if plants are sprinkled lightly but often, their roots will be concentrated near the surface and won't be able to bring enough water to the stem and leaves when this top layer of soil dries out. Less frequent but thorough watering will allow the water to soak down deeper into the ground, encouraging deeper roots that will be able to extract water from the lower levels of the soil even when the top few inches are dry.

How Roots Do Their Job

If you've ever tested your seeds to find their germination rate, you've seen how delicate a seedling's first little root looks. But appearances are deceiving, for this tiny, pale appendage is incredibly strong and resilient. It breaks out of the seed coat and thrusts its way down, down, down into even the heaviest clay or roughest rocky soil, pushing aside soil particles and even small pebbles or probing its way around the more resistant obstructions it encounters. How can such a tender-looking bit of tissue accomplish this arduous task? First of all, the delicate tip of the root is protected by a tough group of cells called the root cap which shields the growing cells from damage by stones or hard dirt particles. The root cap cells often produce a slimy lubricating substance which helps the growing root ease its way through the soil. These cells also play a role in orienting the growth of the root. They contain tiny starch grains which respond to gravity and settle to the lowermost side of the cells. This buildup of grains tells the root to grow toward gravity.

Behind the cap cells is the actively growing region of the root. Here the cells divide very quickly. After dividing, the new root cells in a region a few millimeters long just behind the dividing tip begin to elongate. These elongating cells help propel the tip through the soil. After they lengthen, the root

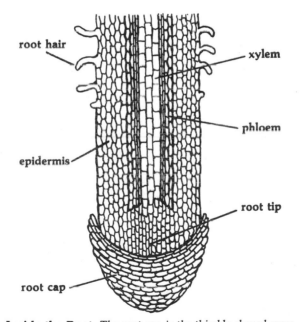

Inside the Root: *The root cap is the thimble-shaped mass of cells that direct growth and protect the actively dividing cells in the root tip. The epidermal cells, with the aid of the root hairs, function to extract from the soil minerals and water that will be transported to larger roots and the shoot by the xylem. The phloem cells are located to the outside of the xylem.*

cells begin to specialize to fulfill various functions. The outer or epidermal cells absorb minerals and water from the soil. Many of them form tiny extensions called root hairs which probe between soil particles to extract water and minerals. Because these root hairs are so delicate and their job so important, you must make every effort when transplanting not to disturb the soil around the roots. Each individual root hair functions for only a few days to a few weeks, then its job is taken over by newly formed hairs closer to the growing tip. Besides careless transplanting, any setback which slows root growth, such as allowing the soil to dry out or not replenishing soil nutrients, will decrease the number of root hairs and thus the capacity of the root to absorb water and minerals. This can hinder your plant's growth considerably.

Locked within the central part of the root are the vital plant transport systems, the xylem and the phloem. Like the circulatory systems of animals, the xylem and phloem carry nutrients and fluids throughout the plant. The xylem exists in many plants as an X-shaped cluster of tubes in the center of the root. It carries minerals and water to the rest of the plant from the roots. The phloem consists of bundles of tubes nestled between the arms of the "X." The phloem carries food manufactured in the leaves to root cells for maintenance and storage.

Between these transport tubules and the outermost layer of root cells are various other kinds of cells. Some of these cells divide to enlarge the root or to form other roots. Others store food and are able to concentrate the very dilute minerals found in the soil and pass these nutrients on to the xylem and thereby the rest of the plant.

Most plants can count on help from some friends in the soil when it comes to gathering the nutrients necessary for growth. Bacteria and fungi growing in tandem with the roots assist by extracting minerals from the soil. In the case of bean and pea roots, the bacteria actually convert nitrogen gas into a form which the plant can use. While scientists already know a great deal about the beneficial bacteria associated with legumes such as beans and peas, they are just beginning to learn about many other fascinating associations of bacteria and fungi with plant roots. Surprisingly, fungi can, for some plants, substitute entirely for the root hairs. The plant provides the fungus with food, and the fungus sends its filaments great distances into the soil to extract minerals and water for the plant. Bacteria associated with the roots of corn and tomatoes may actually receive vitamins and other nutrients from the plant roots and in turn manufacture plant hormones which stimulate growth of the corn and tomatoes!

As research uncovers more and more information about such interactions between soil microorganisms and plants, the importance of building and maintaining a healthy soil becomes readily apparent. When you conscientiously replenish the organic matter content of your soil, you create an environment conducive to the growth and proliferation of the soil microorganisms that are important partners for your crops.

Stems

Gardeners often regard stems as mere hat poles; they are just there to hang the leaves on. But stems are actually the indispensable main arteries of the plant; they carry vital substances between the roots, leaves, and flowers. Stems also grow in such a way that they ensure that the leaves get their share of vital sunlight. When a plant is shaded, the stem responds by developing long internodes (the stem lengths between the leaves), and it continues to lengthen in this manner until it reaches sunlight. With some crops, such as asparagus and kohlrabi, the stem is the relished edible portion. In order to fully appreciate the importance of the stem, we'll take a closer look at the structures that make up a stem and how they help the plant to grow and develop.

The Stem Tip and How It Grows

All plants have a region of actively growing cells at the tip of the stem. This apical tip is actually the main part of the plant aboveground where cell divisions take place and new stem and leaves are formed. This tip is usually protected within a small bud of developing leaves. If you carefully expose the stem tip and examine it closely, you will see a tiny, rounded dome with minute bumps budding off around its edge. These bumps are the very be-

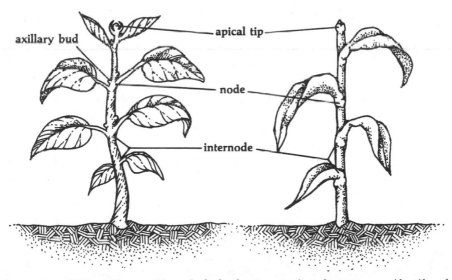

Monocot and Dicot Shoots: *If you look closely at a growing plant, you can identify a few of its parts. The node is the place where leaves and buds arise and is distinctively swollen in monocots (right). The internode is the area between two adjacent nodes, and on the dicot shown at left, you can spot axillary buds tucked in the leaf axils. The apical meristem can be found in the terminal bud at the tip of the shoot and is accountable for the elongation of the shoot.*

ginnings of leaves which form at regular intervals below the dome. When the apical tip grows and leaves are produced, new secondary growth centers are spawned along the way above each leaf. These potential growth sites are called axillary buds. Just below the leaf-forming area of the dome is the region where cells divide to form more of the stem and then elongate to lengthen the stem.

The young plant, before true leaves and axillary buds form, depends entirely on this tiny, delicate tip for its present and future growth. For this reason, you must always be careful not to damage the growing tip of a young plant. Diane has had the unfortunate experience of observing firsthand what happens when the stem tip is disturbed. One spring her inquisitive two-year-old son got into her tomato seedlings and carefully pinched off only the cotyledons from some plants and removed the first true leaves and stem tips from the rest. She kept the poor plants to see what would happen. The plants stripped of their cotyledons recovered after a while and grew to be normal plants while those with no true leaves and no stem tips withered away to nothing. The reason why some grew back and some didn't is easy to see: when her son nipped off the stem tips and the first true leaves, he doomed those plants to a speedy demise by removing their growth centers. On the other hand, the plants with stem tips and true leaves were able to keep right on growing since their critical growth center was still intact.

There are other menaces to vulnerable growing tips besides two-year-old boys. In the course of transplanting, it's very easy to do irreversible damage to your seedlings through careless handling. Never pick them up by their stems. Instead, gently hold one cotyledon between your thumb and first finger and support the plant with your hand or a spoon nestled under the roots. Also try to keep as much soil around the roots as possible. Even if you are careful in your handling, factors in the environment like frost, drought, or insects can damage the growing tip. You can sidestep these spoilers by not planting out too early, sheltering your young plants from any late frosts, keeping them well watered, and keeping close tabs on the insect population in your garden. Tend your young transplants carefully at this vulnerable stage so their growing stems remain healthy and vigorous and can develop unimpeded.

Why Stem Length Is Crucial

The length of stem between the leaves is called an internode. How a plant looks is actually determined by the length of its internodes. A plant with long internodes will be tall and thin like corn or long like winter squash vines. If the internodes are very short, the plant will be short, like beets or spinach. Each type of plant has an optimal length for its internodes. But conditions in your garden, such as too little light, too high temperature, or improper nutrition, can interfere with normal growth and cause the inter-

---

A Few Words on Axillary Buds

If you look closely at a plant, you can see the axillary buds as tiny bumps just above the spot where the leaves join the stem (the leaf axil). Most axillary buds remain tiny and untested, their potential for growth untapped. This is because the apical tip of the plant produces a hormone that inhibits their growth. But once you remove the apical tip, you remove the inhibiting factor, and the axillary buds spring into action and sprout forth with growth of their own. Diane saw this happen in her cold frame early one season when a cutworm snuck inside and ate the tops of some of her tomato seedlings. Luckily, the hungry invader left the first set of true leaves untouched, and new stems eventually grew from the angles between the leaves and the stem. What the worm did, of course, was destroy the apical tips. But because the leaves with their axillary buds were left on the plant, the removal of the inhibiting hormone freed them to grow, resulting in tomato plants with two main stems. When you pinch back your flower plants or houseplants to make them bushier, you are doing the same thing the cutworm did—removing the apical tips so that the axillary buds can grow.

The effect of the apical tip is different in different plants. The axillary buds of a naturally bushy plant grow because the stem tip does not have a strong influence on the axillary buds. In indeterminate-type tomato plants, the axillary buds begin to grow when the main stem is about a foot long. By then, not enough hormone can reach the axillary buds to have an effect. In Brussels sprouts, the inhibiting effect of the apical tip disappears as the plant matures, allowing the axillary buds to develop into tasty sprouts.

---

nodes to be much longer than usual. A plant in this condition is spindly and likely to fall over in a high wind.

Although you might not expect it, the length of a plant's internodes can also affect its fruit. For example, if you grow your tomato plants under low light conditions and they grow too tall too quickly, the roots cannot keep pace with the tops, and will not develop enough surface area to provide the large amounts of nutrients and water that the plant will need later when it fruits. When the root system is inadequate, the plant responds by producing fewer flowers than it would if the stem were not so long. The result? Fewer tomatoes for you, the gardener. Because sun-loving plants grown in low light yield less, it is important when you start such plants indoors to always give them as much light as possible.

You may never have received this bit of advice before, but if you watch some of your plants' internodes carefully, you'll know when to harvest. When a beet or spinach plant is ready to flower, a hormone causes the plant to form long internodes, so the stem between the newly forming leaves lengthens. If you want to harvest your beets or spinach before they bolt and flower, watch the length of the internodes, and when they start to get longer, harvesttime has come. The same hormone that causes the internodes of some plants to lengthen before flowering also affects other plants during normal growth. Bush beans, dwarf peas, and bush squash produce less of this key hormone so that their internodes are short, producing bushy plants. If you were to spray such bush varieties with a hormone solution, they would grow long and viney, just like their full-sized relatives.

A Look inside the Mature Stem

If you cut across the stem of a dicot and look at the exposed surface, you can see that the outer ring of tissue appears quite different from the center. The central pith is a food storage area, while the outer vascular area transports nutrients and water throughout the plant. Enveloping this ring of tissue is the cortex which contains photosynthetic, storage, and support cells. The outermost covering of the stem is the epidermis which may be waxy, as in cabbage, or hairy, as in tomatoes. The main functions of the epidermis are to slow water loss, prevent infections, and reduce mechanical injury to the important transport system in the stem.

The pith is the tender and succulent portion of the stem of many plants; its cells have thin, delicate walls and are packed with stored food. The vascular area is tougher than the pith due to the thick-walled transport cells and fibrous support cells it contains. Next time you enjoy a succulent piece of broccoli, remember that it is the enlarged pith that makes every bite so delectable. Cookbooks that tell you to peel away the outer layers before preparing this vegetable are actually instructing you to peel away the tough vascular area, leaving the tender pith for you to enjoy at the dinner table.

The vascular area around the pith actually has three parts to it. The xylem shuttles water and minerals to the plant from the roots while the phloem transports nutrients from the leaves to the rest of the plant. Both of these tissues have special cells which help support the upright stems. Between the xylem and phloem is the third part, the vascular cambium, which gives rise to new xylem and phloem cells. The older a stem, the more of these transport and support cells it has, and the tougher it is. This explains why the succulent stems of your tomato seedlings become tough and woody by season's end. Some of the cells of the cortex clustered around the outside of the vascular tissue have chlorophyll in them and perform photosynthesis. This accounts for the green color of the stem. Other outer cells form fibrous strands of tissue which help support the stem.

After all this talk about dicots, what could you expect to find inside the stem of monocots like corn or onions? Right away you'd notice that there's no neat arrangement of pith and vascular area into rings. Monocot stems contain the same kind of tissues as dicots, they're just arranged differently. Instead of seeing the xylem and phloem concentrated in an area surrounding

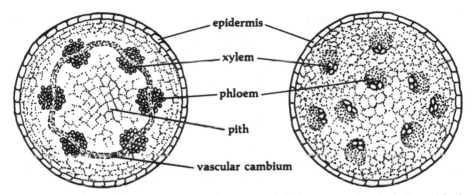

epidermis

xylem

phloem

pith

vascular cambium

Stem Cross Section: *The tissues in a dicot stem (left) have a concentric design with the vascular bundles arranged in a circle around the pith. Monocots (right) have a random distribution of their vascular tissue and lack a vascular cambium, which lies between the xylem and phloem in each bundle of a dicot.*

the pith, you would find them scattered throughout the pith itself, in structures called vascular bundles. Although they're organized differently, the xylem and phloem in both types of plants perform the same important role in transporting water and nutrients.

The Stem's Transport System

In an ironic twist on the usual order of affairs, xylem cells are only able to function as transport channels once they have died. While they are living, the cells lengthen and develop especially thick, sturdy walls with tiny holes through which water and minerals penetrate. When they die, the ends of many xylem cells disappear, leaving behind tiny hollow tubes. You can think of these little tubes, connected to one another end to end, as microscopic water pipes.

For a long time, scientists didn't understand how water defied gravity and moved all the way from the roots to the leaves of plants. After all, some sequoia redwood trees are over 350 feet tall! Now we know that the evaporation of water from the leaves provides the pulling power which brings the water up through the stem. The leaves of one plant, when added all together, have an enormous surface area from which water is always evaporating. The suction force produced by this constant evaporation is estimated to be minus 30 times the pressure of the atmosphere (minus because it is a pulling power, like a vacuum, as opposed to the push exerted by the atmosphere) and can result in water being pulled up through the stems of some plants as fast as 30 inches per minute.

The structural support the xylem gives the plant is also vital, for it keeps the plant upright so that its leaves can be exposed to sunlight. Plants grown indoors where the wind never blows produce fewer xylem cells and are less sturdy than plants grown outdoors. As a matter of fact, the stems of wind-blown plants are actually thicker than those of protected plants. Plants jostled by the wind also have shorter internodes, which is an asset since stocky plants are sturdier than spindly ones. You can take advantage of these particular plant features in your garden by growing your seedlings in a cold frame. There the young plants can be exposed to the wind which will help them develop into strong, sturdy plants which are not likely to topple over in a storm. Seedlings grown indoors will have a harder time adjusting to the weather conditions in the garden and will be more likely to suffer damage from winds or heavy rain.

The phloem, which differs from the xylem in several important ways, carries the nutrients manufactured in the leaves (during photosynthesis) throughout the rest of the plant. The photosynthetic process produces carbohydrates (sugar), and thus, the sap which flows through the phloem is a 10 percent to 25 percent sugar solution. Some plant pests have found ways to tap into the phloem, much as people tap the phloem of the sugar maple tree in the springtime. The champion phloem feeder is the aphid. Aphids have long, hollow, needlelike mouths which they use to penetrate the stem of a plant and pierce the phloem. The sap is under pressure so the aphid doesn't even need to suck. It just sits there as the sap flows into its body!

Scientists have used aphids in some studies of phloem tissue. As soon as the aphid's mouth is imbedded, they cut the rest of the insect off, leaving only the tiny hollow stylet (piercing mouthpart) through which the phloem flows. Then the scientists collect and analyze sap samples and use radioactive tracers to find out where and how fast materials circulate in the phloem. From such studies it appears that nutrients can move up or down within the phloem, but usually the lower leaves produce food that is transported to the roots, while the upper leaves make food for the stem tip and young leaves. Fluid moves through the phloem much more slowly than in the xylem. Its rate of speed is generally less than an inch a minute.

Phloem transport cells are long and narrow and have end walls pitted with tiny holes. The phloem cells are butted up one against the other to form transporting tubes, but unlike the disappearing ends of xylem cells, the end walls in the phloem cells remain intact and all materials must pass through the holes found in the end walls. If you cut through a stem, special microscopic fibers block the holes in the end walls, preventing the plant from "bleeding" to death. This reaction can save a plant's life, but it makes it difficult for scientists to study phloem in action, since this transport channel must be cut to get a good look at it.

Partly for this reason, scientists still don't know exactly how transport in the phloem occurs. They do know that the sugars manufactured in leaves first move into spaces between the cells, then into specialized transfer cells next to the phloem. From there, they move into the phloem cells themselves. The transfer process requires energy and is quite selective. For example, in sugar beets, the sugar, sucrose, is given preferential transfer over other sugars, and the minerals nitrogen, phosphorus, and potassium are transported while calcium, iron, and boron aren't.

Certain environmental factors can adversely affect the phloem, and the telltale signs that this is happening are easy to spot in the garden. One reason beans only grow well during warm weather is that cold inhibits movement of materials through the phloem. If the temperature dips a bit too low, fewer nutrients will be moving, and without adequate nutrients, your bean plants will grow slowly at best or not at all. On the other hand, the phloem of other plants, such as sugar beets, is not affected by the cold, and the plants will grow even in cool weather. Your plants can be damaged or even killed off when bacteria, fungi, or viruses block the phloem. This is how damping-off disease strikes down your young seedlings—a fungus blocks the phloem, usually resulting in a girdled stem and a dead plant. One strange potato disease is caused by a fungus that restricts nutrient flow through the phloem. Sugars accumulate in the aboveground portion of the stem, and the plant responds by producing potatoes there instead of underground.

Aphids, squash bugs, and other sap-feeding insects can transfer diseases from one plant to another through their feeding activities. If a squash bug feeds on an infected plant and then moves to an uninfected one, it will transmit the disease-causing organisms to the healthy plant when it inserts its stylet. Once this happens, the disease can spread throughout the plant by way of the phloem.

Anything you do that restricts the flow of material in the phloem, such as tying tomatoes or cucumbers too tightly to stakes, will slow the plant's growth or stop it altogether. To avoid this problem, use soft, cushiony materials like strips of cloth or pieces of old nylon stocking to tie up your plants instead of using string or wire.

Leaves

Leaves are vital to plants and equally important to gardeners. Structures called chloroplasts located in leaves manufacture food for the plant, and when we pluck tender greens from the garden, leaves also provide nourishment for our bodies. In addition to being a source of sustenance for plant and human alike, leaves give signals to the attentive gardener, acting as a handy gauge of the plant's health. If they are wilted, we assume that the plant needs water.

If the plant lacks nutrients, we'll notice the symptoms first in the leaves. However, there's a lot more going on inside these structures than meets the eye, so let's take a closer look.

Leaf Development

As we have seen, leaves first form as tiny bumps on the growing tip of the stem. They grow by cell divisions which first make them longer, then wider. At this stage, they are still very small and may be hidden by the larger leaves surrounding the stem tip. But soon the leaves undergo a growth spurt and the cells get larger as each develops into a specialized structure to perform its specific function. This early stage of leaf growth and development can be severely affected by environmental conditions. Here's an example. Diane's grandmother's garden was hit by a light frost in May. All her green beans had just two or three leaves at the time. After the frost, the next two leaves to appear were very long and narrow, like shoestrings! Her grandmother feared that a terrible virus must be attacking the beans, but when the next leaves were normal, she realized that the frost had stopped the development of the leaf margins. Diane's tomato plants were hit like that last year, and the next few leaves were very twisted and strange looking. However, after that the next leaves grew normally. So don't despair if you find a few strangely shaped leaves after a cold snap. If the plants aren't obviously damaged, it's more than likely that only a few leaves will be affected and the rest will be all right.

Leaf development can also be affected by nutritional stress. With a potassium deficiency, young tomato leaves become wrinkled and carrot leaves curl. If the leaves on your young plants look strangely misshapen and there has been no cold weather, you should check for a mineral deficiency in your soil or call your county extension agent and enlist his aid.

Examining the Leaf Surface

The upper and lower surfaces of a leaf are covered by a waxy coating called the cuticle, which is produced by the outer layer of leaf cells. (This outer cell layer is called the epidermis, just like our skin.) The cuticle helps slow the loss of water from the leaf. Some plants, like cabbage, have a very prominent cuticle. This is why water will bead up into droplets on a cabbage rather than soak the leaves. If you rub a cabbage leaf, you can sometimes remove the waxy layer. Then water will wet the leaf instead of beading up. Recently, we've begun to learn that air pollution can damage this important waxy layer. For example, scientists found that table beets grown in Los Angeles have widely separated bumps of wax instead of waxy sheets covering the leaf surface. Cabbage plants grown in a polluted environment can be damaged through the increased loss of moisture from the unprotected parts of the leaves.

Many plants, such as tomatoes and turnips, have tiny hairs on their leaves. These hairs can have very different functions on different plants. The hairs on some leaves are dense enough to create a dead air space against the leaf, slowing water loss, especially on windy days. The hairs of sunflowers and possibly other plants reflect ultraviolet light, helping prevent too many of the damaging rays from entering the leaves. You'll be glad to know, too, that leaf hairs can frustrate insect pests. Some varieties of wheat are resistant to the cereal leaf beetle because their leaf hairs deter the female beetles from laying their eggs. If the females do persist, the eggs dry out and die easily. And even if some eggs hatch, the dense hairs make it difficult for the larvae to get at the leaves to feed. Some leaf hairs have glands associated with them. These glands manufacture chemicals that affect insects in various ways. Some tobacco leaf hairs secrete poisons which paralyze the legs of aphids and kill them. The leaves and stems of wild potatoes have a thick covering of hairs. If one is touched by an aphid, it releases a clear liquid. On contact with the oxygen in the air, this liquid is transformed into a black, insoluble substance that coats the aphid's legs. As the aphid explores the plant, it triggers more and more hairs until it is so covered with the black material that it cannot move. Eventually, it starves to death.

How Leaves Monitor Water Loss

The epidermal cells which cover the leaf are flat and translucent so that light can penetrate into the leaf interior. These cells have tough walls that resist injury. Scattered among the epidermal cells are tiny openings called stomata. The stomata are vital to the leaf, for they regulate the amount of water lost to the atmosphere and allow carbon dioxide to enter the leaf to be transformed into sugars during photosynthesis. There are many more stomata on the lower, shaded leaf surface than on the sunnier upper side. This helps minimize unnecessary water loss.

If you look at the lower surface of a leaf with a hand lens, you can see the stomata as tiny mouthlike openings. The "lips" are two specialized guard cells which are shaped like sausages attached to each other at both ends. The stomata open and close in response to the amount of water present in the leaf. The inner side of each guard cell is thicker than the outer side. When the cells are full of water, the pressure pushes against the more flexible outer wall and makes the guard cells bow outwards, causing the stomate (singular of stomata) to open. When there is not enough water in the guard cells, they become deflated and lie flat. This closes the stomate, keeping water inside the leaf but also keeping the important carbon dioxide out.

Since plants need carbon dioxide for photosynthesis and photosynthesis is absolutely vital to growth, it's easy to see that a plant with closed stomata won't grow very well. If a plant is water-stressed and starts to wilt, the stomata will close, slowing water loss. But photosynthesis and thus growth will also slow down, producing less food for the plant . . . and ultimately less for you.

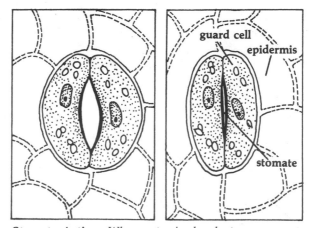

Stomate Action: *When water is abundant, pressure on the elastic outer wall of the guard cells forces the stomate open (left). When the guard cells dry out they will deflate and cause the pore to close (right), preventing any further loss of water.*

Potatoes provide a dramatic example of what water stress can do to a plant. Potatoes grown with an erratic water supply will be irregular in shape with constrictions along their length marking the parts of the tuber which were forming during water stress to the plant.

It is important that you regularly provide your garden with adequate water so that plant growth never slows down due to wilting. Don't wait until your plants wilt before you water, for their growth will already have slowed down or stopped by then. Be vigilant in checking the soil moisture level and be sure to give a deep, thorough soaking when the top four inches have dried out.

What Goes On inside the Leaf

Underneath the upper leaf epidermis in dicot plants is a layer of tall, rectangular cells. These palisade cells are packed with chlorophyll-laden chloroplasts and are very active in photosynthesis. The palisade layer is very sensitive to environmental conditions. Leaves of many kinds of plants will produce two layers of palisade cells when grown in bright light. In shade, leaves have only one layer of palisade cells. This is why, in general, leaves that grow in shade are thinner than those that grow in the sun. Potato leaves vary a bit from this general rule. Leaves on plants grown in sun have only one palisade layer, but the cells are longer and have more chloroplasts than the palisade cells in shade-grown leaves.

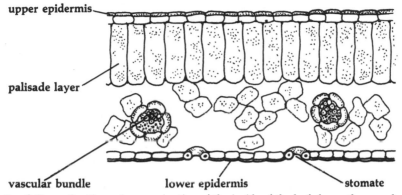

upper epidermis

palisade layer

vascular bundle   lower epidermis   stomate

Leaf Cross Section: *An examination of the inside of the leaf shows the vascular bundles in a layer of loosely arranged, spongy cells and the rectangular-shaped palisade cells sandwiched between the upper and lower epidermis. The stomata are located in the lower epidermis in this example, although they can appear on both epidermal surfaces.*

Even after the leaf is fully formed, it can still respond to the level of sunlight it receives. If there is not much light, the chloroplasts will line up so that their broadest surfaces are facing the sun. If the sun is very bright, they will move so that their narrow surfaces face the sun so less light hits them. They can even flatten against the side walls of the cell to further decrease their exposure to even brighter sunlight.

Because the leaves are so responsive to light conditions, it is important for you to grow your seedlings in the strongest possible light. Leaves which develop only one palisade layer under weak light levels can never produce another after they have formed. These leaves will die and fall off when you move the plant into a sunnier location. You can minimize damage to plants grown in low light, however, by gradually exposing them to the sun. Even though the job of chlorophyll is to absorb sunlight, too much sun will destroy it. This explains why the leaves of plants you may have moved outside abruptly will turn white. In effect, these leaves are "sunburned," and this overexposure is as great a shock to their system as too much sun is to yours. But when you take care to expose your plants gradually to the sun, pigments called carotenoids will form in the leaf. These pigments protect the chlorophyll from the bright sun and keep it from breaking down all at once. This in turn gives the chlorophyll level time to adjust and decrease gradually. This decrease is necessary since a plant grown in full sun needs less chlorophyll to do the job than one raised in the shade.

It's interesting to note that cells aren't the only structures that play a part in the activity inside the leaf. Air spaces turn out to be just as important as

What Is Photosynthesis?

Without photosynthesis, life on Earth wouldn't last very long. Photosynthesis provides the stored energy which, along with oxygen, most living things need for survival. Plants are the ultimate solar energy converters, using the energy from the sun to manufacture energy-rich carbohydrates which are a form of food for the plant. Several plant pigments are capable of trapping the sun's energy and using it to fuel chemical reactions, but the most commonly encountered ones are forms of chlorophyll, the green pigment responsible for the most familiar of plant colors.

Just how the plant captures the energy of the sun is a very complex, fascinating process, which is not yet entirely understood. What we do know is that when light hits pigment molecules within the plant chloroplast, these molecules become excited. Chlorophyll molecules and other yellow, red, or orange pigments (called carotenoids) collect the solar energy and pass it on to particular chlorophyll molecules, providing those reactor molecules with enough energy to cause some of their electrons (extremely tiny, negatively charged particles) to escape. When that happens, the reactor molecules must replace their electrons, and they do so by splitting water molecules into hydrogen and oxygen, picking up stray electrons in the process.

The splitting of water into oxygen and hydrogen requires light energy, but the next step in photosynthesis can occur in the dark. (Don't be fooled into thinking that your plants shut down shop when the sun goes down!) The hydrogen from the water is combined with carbon dioxide to form sugars and other carbohydrates, while the oxygen from the water is released into the atmosphere through the stomata in the leaves. This release of oxygen is a very significant step, for almost all the oxygen in the air came originally from the photosynthetic activities of plants. During this same stage of photosynthesis, the open stomata let in the carbon dioxide necessary to keep the whole process going.

cells. Within the lower part of the leaf are widely scattered, irregularly shaped cells (which also contain chloroplasts). The spaces between these cells are filled with air which allows for the crucial exchange of carbon dioxide and oxygen that occurs during photosynthesis. The area above a stomate is clear of cells, providing another air space in which the vital exchange of gases can take place.

Besides the photosynthetic cells, leaves of many plants contain other sorts of specialized cells. Spinach leaves have cells which contain crystals of calcium oxalate. This is the substance that makes your teeth feel coated when you eat a lot of spinach. Bolted lettuce leaves have specialized cells containing bitter chemicals which impart a bad flavor, while corn leaves have bubble-shaped cells that make the leaves fold when they are under water stress. If you ever see your corn leaves folded in half the long way, water the plants immediately to relieve the water stress.

If you examine a leaf closely, the pattern formed by the veins is usually visible. While you can often see the veins, you must use your imagination to see the xylem and phloem that lie within the veins themselves. In monocots such as corn and onions, the veins are parallel, while those of dicots branch out into a fine network much like the blood capillaries in our bodies. As the veins branch, they get smaller and smaller until they can hardly be seen. Cells that are photosynthesizing often have a vein running right beside them, and no active cell is very far from one of these fine vein branches. These ultimate branches of the vascular system transfer water and other nutrients from the xylem to the cells while the phloem picks up the food produced by photosynthesis, largely the sugar sucrose, and distributes it to other parts of the plant.

The Bridge between Stem and Leaves

Next time you're in the garden, pause for a minute and examine a plant closely to see how the leaves are attached to the stem. If the plant is a dicot, the leaves will be attached by a stalk called the petiole. Monocot leaves are attached directly to the stem and thus, lack petioles. Some plants, such as celery and rhubarb, have very large petioles which we eat. The petiole carries the vascular system to the leaf (some of the "strings" you find in a celery stalk are nothing more than bundles of xylem and phloem) and helps orient the leaf towards the sun. A hormone manufactured by the leaf moves to the darker side of the petiole and makes that side grow faster than the light-exposed side. This results in the elongation we see as the leaf grows towards the light.

Leaves may also move in response to the daily light-dark cycle. One night Diane ventured into her garden to catch cutworms in the act and was upset to see all the leaves of her bush beans hanging down. She thought they needed water badly, but the next morning the leaves had perked up and were back in their normal position. Since that episode, she has learned that bean leaves undergo especially dramatic movements, drooping down at night and rising up during the day. No one knows for sure why this happens, but one appealing idea is that leaves which are drawn closer to the stem at a vertical angle will lose less water than those held up in a horizontal position.

Flowers

You may find, like many vegetable gardeners, that you have developed a love-hate relationship with flowers. At the same time you are watching anxiously for the first female squash or cucumber blossom that announces the fruit to come, you are cringing at the sight of a flower stalk developing on a spinach or lettuce plant, for that signals the end of the edible harvest and the onset of seed production. Many factors affect flowering and the setting of fruit and seed from those flowers. When you understand some of the things that influence flowering you will be far ahead of the game, for there is much you can do to take advantage of nature.

But you must keep in mind that the whole question of flowering is quite complex and varies from crop to crop. Although there's been much research on the phenomenon of flowering, scientists are often discouraged to find that the more they uncover, the more there remains to be uncovered! As a gardener, you can help in this area by keeping your own records of how the different varieties you grow respond to environmental conditions such as daylength and then communicating that information to other gardeners through magazines such as *Organic Gardening,* or through exchanges with members of garden groups. Sometimes seed companies have information available concerning the varieties they carry, so queries to them can also be helpful.

What Makes a Plant Flower?

Many factors affect plant flowering. Nutrition is one cultural characteristic that often plays a role. For example, tomatoes grown in soil deficient in nitrogen or phosphorus will flower much later than plants with adequate mineral supplies. Potatoes, on the other hand, will be slow to flower and form tubers if grown in nitrogen-rich soil. Tilth is another factor to be reckoned with. Radish plants grown in compacted, heavy soil are likely to flower without first producing radishes.

Many garden plants must reach a certain stage of maturity before they flower. Beans, peas, and corn grow quickly in warm weather and will reach the blooming stage earlier during an uninterrupted stretch of warm weather than they would if their growth had been held in check by a brief cold spell. And plants grown in rich soil will be bigger and stronger when they get to that critical flowering stage than ones grown in poor soil. For example, indeterminate tomatoes will generally flower when they have twelve to fourteen internodes. That's why it is important for you to get your tomatoes off to a good start so that they are vigorous and strong when they reach the flowering stage.

Environmental factors affect the flowering time of some crops more than stage of maturity does. Many gardeners, especially those in northern areas where spring is often cold but the daylength increases rapidly as summer approaches, have had the discouraging experience of watching their tiny spinach plants bolt and flower when they have only a few small leaves. Like wild animals which only produce their young at certain times of year, plants such as spinach have certain times of year which are best for flowering and producing seed. These sensitive plants have ways of perceiving daylength and respond to it by flowering when daylight lasts a particular number of hours. While this can be very frustrating for you, the gardener, from the plant's point of view the system has its advantages. The length of day is one environmental cue that does not vary from year to year, while temperatures can fluctuate widely. A plant which responds to temperature can be thrown off by a mild winter and bloom too early.

As you can see, temperature and daylength can conspire against your best efforts in the garden. In order to be able to work around these two environmental factors and raise a good crop, you need to understand what you're up against. The next three sections will tell you in detail how your garden crops respond to these stimuli and how you can outsmart them.

How Temperature Affects Flowering

Plants react to warm temperatures because all of their metabolic processes are dependent on enzymes. Up to a point, the higher the temperature, the faster the enzymes work and the faster the plants grow. Conversely, at lower temperatures most enzymes slow down and so does plant growth. Through this basic effect on growth rate, temperature influences the flowering time of almost all plants. However, each enzyme has its own optimum temperature at which it works best. Enzymes of cool weather crops like broccoli and radishes have lower optimum temperatures than those of warm weather crops like beans and corn. Above the optimum temperature, enzyme activity slows down again.

But temperature can also affect flowering in other ways. For example, most tomatoes flower when they have twelve or more internodes. But if a young seedling is exposed to night temperatures of 43° to 50°F, it will begin to flower when it has only four to ten internodes. Not only will the plant bloom earlier, all its flower clusters will have more blossoms than they would have had without the cold treatment. So if you want early tomatoes you should expose your young tomato plants to low nighttime temperatures (but not so low that your plants freeze!). If you grow your tomato plants in a heated greenhouse with nighttime temperatures of 80°F, it will actually increase the time to flowering!

Cold temperatures can also influence flowering in other ways. When swollen and just germinating beet, lettuce, or pea seeds remain in cold soil for a couple of weeks, the plants that eventually emerge will flower sooner than they would normally. This might be an advantage with peas, especially if you have a short spring followed by a hot summer, but it is a distinct disadvantage in growing beets and lettuce. (For more details on these crops, refer to chapters 5, 8, and 10.) Onion sets will also be affected by cold temperatures. If the sets are kept in cold storage (below 35°F), they will bolt rather than form bulbs once they are planted.

The name for this process in which cold stimulates early flowering is vernalization. The Russian word for this process means "making-like-spring-grain," for it was first discovered by Russian researchers in winter rye and wheat. They found that by planting these crops in the fall, the farmer gets a head start since his crops will grow quickly the next spring to the stage where they produce their grain.

Cabbages, Brussels sprouts, carrots, celery, and some varieties of beets require two growing seasons before they flower. Plants with a life cycle that spans two seasons are called biennials. Like wheat and rye, these plants are vernalized by cold temperatures and will flower during the next growing season. Sugar beets that have never been exposed to a cold winter and are kept warm will keep growing and never flower. If you garden in the extreme south, you'll have a frustrating time trying to grow your own seeds of plants like sugar beets. Because it never gets cold enough in the winter for vernalization, your plants will never flower. You might want to experiment with lifting your biennials and storing them for some weeks in a cool location to see if the plants can be "fooled" into blooming when you plant them out again.

The apical tip of the plant is especially sensitive to cold temperatures. In areas where the mercury dips down low in the winter, the apical tip may be killed by the cold temperatures. This would keep the plant from blooming the following spring, even though the rest of the plant may survive the cold. If you garden in a cold-winter area, you will have to buy commercially grown seed for biennial plants unless you can devise a way to prevent your plants from freezing. One way to get seed from your biennials is to lift the plants before the ground freezes, store them in a root cellar or other cool location, and replant them in the garden come spring. Or, you can "put them to bed" in the fall by covering them deeply with leaves and adding a layer of plastic to anchor the leafy mulch. When it warms up in the spring, just uncover them and watch for signs of flowering. An especially cold winter, however, might kill the apical tips of even such protected plants. A word of warning to northern gardeners who store their eating carrots in the ground over winter under a thick cover of leaves: you must dig out all the carrots by spring, for if the apical tips survive, you will find yourself with a row full of bolting plants whose roots have gone bitter and woody and are no longer fit to eat.

How Daylength Affects Flowering

Let's go back to the problem of small spinach plants forming flower stalks instead of leaves. Spinach blooms under long days and short nights. But how does the plant keep track of daylength? Spinach and many other plants perceive the length of night and day through a pigment in their leaves called phytochrome. Phytochrome changes chemically in response to light, and the changes in the phytochrome result in the production of plant hormones that are involved in initiating flowering. The whole process is very complicated and has different results in long-day and short-day plants.

To affect the phytochrome of spinach plants, light doesn't have to be as strong as the sun. Those of you who garden in the city or other areas lighted at night may have had trouble growing spinach, radishes, beets, turnips, and lettuce without their bolting. If the lights are strong enough, they can affect the light-sensitive pigment in the leaves of short-day plants and make them flower much faster than they ordinarily would.

Bolting of dill, radishes, and spinach actually requires two conditions. First, the plants must have been growing for a certain number of days. After that, exposure to just one long period of light will trigger the flowering hormone. For example, many spinach varieties require about thirteen days of growth before they will respond to a long day/short night period. Once the plants have been exposed to one twelve-hour day, there is nothing you can do to stop them from flowering. Many of our fellow gardeners in Montana wait until May 1 or later to plant their spinach. By the time it comes up, the days are already almost twelve hours long. All those plants need to bolt is their thirteen days of growth, then they are goners! Hapless spinach plants like these may bolt when they have as few as three or four true leaves. The gardeners complain that "you just can't grow spinach here" and give up. But if these neighbors as well as other northern gardeners planted their spinach and radishes earlier, around April 1, as do more southerly gardeners, they could harvest a reasonable crop in mid-June. Another alternative is to plant such crops in late July or early August when the days are getting shorter. Or, they can wait until mid-August and plant one of the spinach varieties designed for overwintering. Southern gardeners who plant spinach in the fall don't need to worry about the effect of daylength on their crop.

Certain varieties of beets, lettuce, peas, and turnips have a somewhat different reaction to daylength. They must be exposed to a particular total number of daylight hours before flowering. This could mean many short days or fewer long days. And, in order to respond at all, they must have reached a certain stage of maturity. This sort of situation has different consequences for the gardener. If you're a northerner who plants beets, lettuce, or turnips in the early spring (late March or early April) you risk having these crops bolt when they are fairly small in response to the long days of May and June. However, if you wait until June to plant these crops, you will find that they are too immature to respond to the long days and will thus grow bigger and yield more before bolting than would April-planted seed. If you frequently run into trouble with these plants, keep an eye out for varieties listed in catalogs as being "slow to bolt."

Since you want peas to bloom early and beat the heat, the whole situation is reversed with them. Plant your late-flowering varieties early so they will respond to the long days of May and June by flowering and producing before the hot weather hits.

Just as there are plants that flower during long day/short night conditions, there are those which bloom during short days and long nights. Some varieties of corn, soybeans, sugar cane, and sunflowers fit into this category. Varieties of many short-day crops have been developed which have different daylength requirements. This can be very significant for gardeners in certain regions. For example, some soybean varieties flower best when they receive about twelve hours of daylight. If they get more than that, flowering decreases in proportion to the increasing hours of light until no flowers at all are produced in twenty hours of light. A northern gardener would reap a poor harvest from these soybeans! Plant breeders have come to the rescue and have developed soybean varieties adapted to the north, although some of these varieties are very specific, growing well only over an area within 50 miles of a particular latitude. The point to remember if you want to grow soybeans is to be sure that the variety you select is bred to produce at your particular latitude.

Not all garden plants are as temperamental as those we've just discussed. In fact, some are not the least bit sensitive to daylength. Some varieties of corn, cucumbers, Jerusalem artichokes, kidney beans, peas, and tomatoes are unaffected by hours of light and dark. These varieties are known as day-neutral.

Daylight and Temperature Combined

Daylength and temperature sometimes act together to influence flowering. Low temperature vernalization of the spinach variety Nobel, for example, will shorten the daylength requirement for flowering from 14 to about 8 hours. Planting this variety in the north in early spring, when the seeds might take a long time to germinate in cold ground, would result in young plants that bolt very quickly. Obviously, Nobel should not be grown for a spring crop in the North. It is much more suitable as a fall crop in the South.

Some varieties of lettuce grown at low temperature are unaffected by daylength. But when exposed to high temperatures, they will respond to long days by sending up seed stalks. This accounts for the shorter than usual spring lettuce-growing season northern gardeners experience if there are hot days in May or June. Beets, on the other hand, are more subject to bolting when it is cool than when it is warm. You'll harvest a better crop if you grow them in July and August rather than in May and June in the cool north.

Even though temperature and daylength can have these profound effects on garden crops, you'll find very little specific information as to which varieties fit into which categories in gardening guides or seed catalogs. This is where home gardeners can help out. By keeping good records of how your crops respond to different conditions each year, you can share valuable information

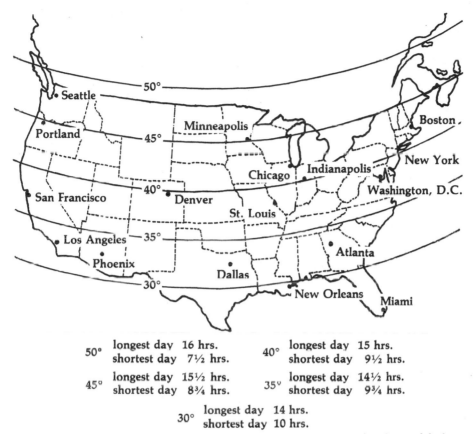

50°	longest day 16 hrs. shortest day 7½ hrs.	**40°**	longest day 15 hrs. shortest day 9½ hrs.
45°	longest day 15½ hrs. shortest day 8¾ hrs.	**35°**	longest day 14½ hrs. shortest day 9¾ hrs.
		30°	longest day 14 hrs. shortest day 10 hrs.

Longitudinal Map of Daylengths: *This map provides you with a rough estimate of the hours of daylight in the longest and shortest day of the year for each latitude. The longest day occurs at the summer solstice (June 21 or 22) and the shortest day occurs at the winter solstice (December 21 or 22).*

with your fellow gardeners. For example, if you plant several varieties of lettuce and one consistently bolts before the others, it is probably reacting to the temperature and daylength conditions of your area.

To help you get a rough idea of what your area's daylengths are at different times of year, we have provided a map that shows daylengths at the summer solstice (June 21 or 22) for different latitudes. At the spring (March 21 or 22) and fall (September 21 or 22) equinoxes, day and night are just about twelve hours long at all latitudes. For more exact daylength information, consult your local newspaper or weather bureau.

Flowers and Their Variety

The visually pleasing variety of flower color, size, and shape is certainly easy to spot in the garden. But flowers vary in other ways that aren't as visible to the eye, although they are more important to the vegetable gardener. Some flowers are perfect, that is, they have both male and female parts combined within the same flower. Tomatoes and peas, for example, have perfect flowers. Some garden crops have flowers which have only the male or female parts; these are known as imperfect flowers. In some cases, as with spinach or asparagus, the male and female flowers are on separate plants. One year when Diane was slow in pulling up her bolted spinach, she noticed that some plants had lots of seed and others none. The reason for this, of course, is that only the female plants had produced seed. Other crops with imperfect flowers, such as squash and corn, have male and female flowers on the same plants.

If you examine a perfect flower such as a buttercup closely, you can easily distinguish the different parts. Underneath the familiar petals is a circle of green petallike sepals. The sepals protect the flower bud before it opens. In the center of the flower is a cluster of pistils, or one large pistil; these are the female parts of the flower. The pistil has a long stalk called the style topped by a rounded end called the stigma. The stigma has a sticky surface to which pollen adheres when the flower is pollinated. Around the pistil or pistils is a circle of stamens. The stamens are the male parts of the flower. Each stamen is made up of a stalk called the filament, and the oval structure sitting atop the filament is called the anther. The anthers contain the pollen.

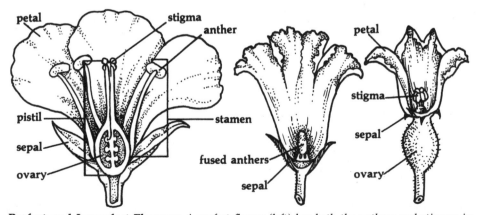

Perfect and Imperfect Flowers: *A perfect flower (left) has both the anthers and stigmas in the same flower. Plants with imperfect flowers, such as squash (right), have separate male and female flowers on the same plant. A female squash flower is shown far right, with a male flower next to it.*

The flowers on the crops in your garden are modified from this simple type represented by the buttercup. In tomato flowers, the anthers are all fused together so that they form a tube around the pistil. Peas and beans have perfect flowers, but the petals on each flower are not all the same. All the flowers on a squash or cucumber plant look much alike at first glance, but you can tell the male and female flowers apart by examining them closely. The female flower has a nubbin that resembles a miniature cucumber or squash at its base, while the male flower has only a small stem. Also, the female flower has a stigma in the center, while the male flower has a fat tube with a convoluted top; this consists of the fused filaments and anthers.

Pollination and Fertilization

While flowers come in different colors and shapes, the processes of pollination and fertilization are basically the same in all garden plants. Pollen grains are transported from the anthers by wind or pollinating animals such as bees or hummingbirds onto the sticky surface of the stigma. This transfer of pollen from anther to stigma signals that pollination has occurred. Once they've alighted, these grains begin to grow, forming long microscopic tubes which push their way down through the style. At the base of the style is the ovary, where the egg cells lie. A growth hormone (auxin) from the pollen grains causes the ovary to begin to enlarge once it is pollinated, even before actual fertilization occurs. For this reason, a heavily pollinated tomato fruit will grow faster than a lightly pollinated fruit (one that hasn't been visited by bees or jostled by the wind).

When a pollen tube approaches an egg, its tip bursts open, releasing two sperm cells. One of these fuses with the egg cell to produce the beginnings of the embryo. The other fuses with a cell next to the egg. The resulting cell develops into the endosperm which nourishes the seedling during germination. The twin action of these sperm cells fusing with female cells to form the embryo and the endosperm means that fertilization has taken place.

Many things can go wrong with pollination and fertilization that will affect your crops. If the temperature is low (below 55°F), for example, tomato pollen tubes grow so slowly that the flowers sometimes drop off before fertilization has occurred. On the other hand, too-high temperatures can also cause flowers to drop. Water stress can affect pollen so that it won't germinate and grow when it lands on the stigma, so you must be sure that your plants are getting enough water while flowering and setting fruit.

Fruit Growth and Ripening

The fruits we so look forward to eating from our vegetable plants—squash, cucumbers, tomatoes, peppers, and eggplants—are actually the thickened ovary walls which develop around the seeds. At first, the fruit develops by cell division with little discernible growth, so you don't actually see the

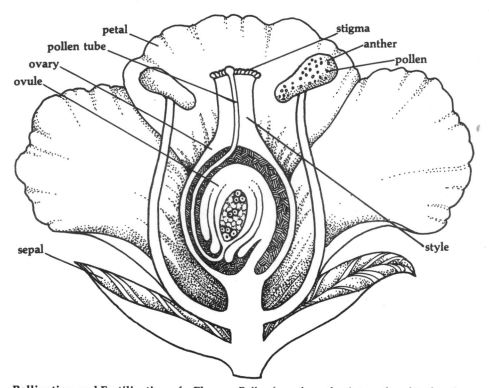

petal
pollen tube
ovary
ovule
stigma
anther
pollen
sepal
style

Pollination and Fertilization of a Flower: *Pollen from the anther is transferred to the stigma where it will germinate and form a pollen tube. The pollen tube grows down the style to the embryo sac where it releases two sperm cells. One sperm will unite with the egg to form the zygote, which develops into the embryo, and the other fuses with two polar nuclei to form the endosperm.*

fruit enlarge very much. But the rest of the growth process is accomplished by cell expansion, which can happen very rapidly—so rapidly, in fact, that during this period your zucchini can swell to the size of a giant club almost overnight. After the cells expand to their final size, they specialize into their ultimate roles as the fruit ripens. In tomatoes that are ripening, for example, several changes take place. The fruit changes from green to red, it softens, the seed develops, and most importantly, the flavor changes dramatically.

While plants in your garden are developing fruits, you should keep them well watered and well nourished. The fruit is almost completely dependent on the rest of the plant for its food and water. Fruit that lacks a specific nutrient may take it from the rest of the plant, weakening it. Don't crimp or bend the area where the fruit is attached to the stem, for this could damage the phloem and xylem which transport food, minerals, and water to the fruit. This point of attachment is highly specialized for rapid and efficient transport of materials to the developing fruit.

Toward the end of their ripening phase, most fruits undergo a dramatic rise in their respiration rate. Because cold slows respiration, putting fruits in the refrigerator will slow their ripening. Some fruits, such as tomatoes and peppers, will also ripen more slowly in a plastic bag than when exposed to air. This is because the plastic keeps out oxygen and holds in carbon dioxide, thus slowing respiration. Each fruit has its optimal storage conditions. For example, some especially long-lasting cucumber varieties will only last 15 days at 41°F but will store for 65 days at 55°F. At room temperature, their storage time is about 50 days. With each of the crops we discuss later in the book, we will give information about storage conditions.

Chapter 3

The Care and Feeding
of Your Garden Soil

Garden soils are a little bit like thumb prints—no two gardeners' will be exactly alike. It's important for you to understand the characteristics of the soil you've got to work with, for its physical composition determines to a large degree how early in the season you can plant and whether your growing crops will receive enough water and air at root level. It's a good idea to remember the maxim that healthy plants mirror a healthy soil—and you do have a say in the state of health of your soil.

Basic Soil Types

All soil is made up of three basic sorts of particles—sand, silt, and clay—in varying proportions. A given soil will generally have more of one component than another, and the presence of this particle in such large quantities determines the characteristics of the soil.

Take a stroll out to your garden and pick up a handful of soil, look at it critically and rub it between your fingers. If it's a sandy soil, you'll be able to distinguish the sand particles with your naked eye. Sandy soil feels grainy and gritty and falls apart when you try to squeeze it into a ball. Gardening in sandy soil is a challenge, for the large sand particles encourage water and soluble nutrients to flow through rapidly, often before the roots have a chance to absorb them. This nutrient leaching means that sandy soils are often deficient in nitrogen, phosphorus, potassium, and calcium. On the plus side, this soil does dry out and warm up early in the season, so it's possible to get started earlier with spring crops. You should be aware though, that later into the hot stretch of the season, there will be little water held in reserve for the plants to draw upon.

A soil laden with silt particles will have a fine, powdery texture like flour and will have the silky feel of talcum powder between your fingers. Silt

46 particles are much smaller than sand particles so you won't be able to see

them with the unaided eye. Although silt is an important component of a good textured soil, too much silt can be too much of a good thing. A predominantly silty soil is considered a light soil and will exhibit some of the characteristics of a sandy soil.

If your soil inspection reveals rock-hard lumps under dry conditions or sticky, rubbery, greasy clumps under moist conditions, your soil is composed mostly of clay particles. When you squeeze a ball of this soil together in your palm, it forms a sticky, dense mass that won't fall apart easily. Clay soil is slow to absorb water, but once it becomes wet, it is very slow to dry out. It usually stays too cold and wet in early spring for the gardener to hope for much luck with early-season crops. But clay can be a boon at the other end of the season, when it stays warmer longer than lighter soils, encouraging good fall crops. You must be careful not to work clay soil when it is still very wet, for rocklike clods will form that are nearly impossible to break apart. There is little nutrient leaching in this type of soil.

If your soil looks like it's made of various-sized crumbs that mold together in a ball when you squeeze them, but fall apart easily when you poke the ball with your finger, you've got a loamy soil. In general, loam consists of approximately 40 percent sand, 40 percent silt, and 20 percent clay. This ideal soil retains water well but is loose enough to allow the excess to drain away. There's seldom a problem with nutrient loss through leaching.

How Soil Texture Affects Plant Growth

Each of these soils behaves differently and a look at what goes on underground will point out differences in their functioning. The particles of sand, silt, and clay, along with any organic matter that is present, form the texture of a soil. These components, plus rocks and pebbles incorporated in the soil, also determine the pore size of the soil. Pores, or empty spaces, between the soil particles are essential to provide channels for water and air to reach plant roots. Actually, plant roots don't grow *in* soil; they grow in the spaces between soil particles. In order for roots to have room to grow and access to air and water, about half the soil volume should consist of these pores.

The size of the spaces as well as their number is important also, for this determines how well the soil will store water and how efficiently it can conduct water up from the lower soil levels as the upper layer dries out. If the pores are too large, as in a very sandy soil, water will run through quickly and be lost to your garden. If the pore size is too small, as in clay soils, the water will move slowly because of the strong attraction between the water molecules and the narrow walls of the pores. Clay soils can store as much as eight times more water than sandy soils, but a lot of this water can't do the plants any good, for it is stuck to the walls of the tiny pores. As the surface soil dries out, water from below can move upward only very slowly, which explains why clay soil takes so long to dry out. In a loamy soil, with the proper balance of sand, clay, and silt, the pore spaces are of a number and size that facilitate the movement of moisture through the soil. Water in a loamy soil is available as the plants need it, with little delay. The water can be pulled toward the surface even from quite deep down, much as water is pulled up through plant stems by the evaporation of water from the leaves.

Soil pores do more than regulate the movement of water, of course; they also hold air, which is probably the most critical element for plant growth. The amount of oxygen in the soil controls how fast the roots respire. This respiration is very important, for it provides the roots with the energy they need for growth and mineral uptake. Finely textured soils with tiny pores will not come close to providing the amount of oxygen a growing plant needs, and the consequences can be alarming. If the roots are starved for oxygen, their growth slows, upsetting the well-being of all parts of the plant. In addition, insufficient oxygen slows down the production of hormones within the plant, further disrupting the plant's functioning. In waterlogged soil where oxygen is scarce, microorganisms that produce toxic substances can multiply and cause your plants to wilt and slow down their growth rates.

Since pore size plays such a critical role in determining how much water and air your plants' roots receive and, hence, how well they grow, you should take steps to remedy a soil with extremely small or extremely large pores. The key to balancing pore size is organic matter. If your garden soil is predominantly clay, the addition of organic matter will loosen it up and increase the pore size, enhancing both air and water circulation. You can also work in some sand to help unlock the tiny clay particles and create more spaces. In a sandy soil, organic matter will work its magic by improving the water-holding capacity. The spongy bits will soak up and hold water in the root zone, where it's needed. Pieces of organic matter will also decrease the pore size by filling in some of the large spaces between the sand grains.

Nutrient Availability

All of the nutrients in the soil aren't free-floating, amorphous bodies just waiting to be sucked in by a hungry plant root. There's an intricate choreography going on all the time in which nutrients are changed from forms that are unacceptable to plants into forms that can be readily assimilated. For example, soil phosphorus is locked up in insoluble compounds, and soil potassium is bound up in mineral form. As is, neither of these nutrients are in forms that allow them to be taken up by plant roots and put to use. Organic matter is the key that unlocks both of these nutrients and makes them available. In the case of phosphorus, the organic matter promotes active colonies of soil bacteria to secrete acids that spur the breakdown of the insoluble phosphorus compounds into a form that the plants can use. Some soluble potassium is available in the soil for the plants to draw upon, but most is locked away in a mineral form. The soluble nutrient is not a dependable supply, for it can be leached away quickly. Organic matter acts as a sponge and holds the soluble potassium right where the roots can get to it and helps transform mineral potassium into a form acceptable to the plants.

Soil type and texture will dramatically affect how available nutrients are to plants. Clay particles and organic particles act like magnets, holding minerals on their surfaces so they aren't washed away. When plant roots absorb some of the soluble minerals from the soil water, minerals attached to the clay or organic particles are released to replenish the mineral content of the water. If your soil is lacking in organic matter and/or in clay content, it won't hold onto minerals very well and will be low in fertility. Overall, organic matter is better at holding onto minerals than clay, and it will release the minerals back into the soil water more readily than clay will.

Using Fertilizers in the Garden

Many organic gardeners shy away from using chemical fertilizers because they know these materials don't contribute to the structure and overall health of the soil, but they aren't entirely sure just what their shortcomings are. We are convinced that overdependence on chemical fertilizers leads the unwitting gardener into a self-defeating cycle that can be described in the following way. When you use chemical fertilizers, nutrients are available to your plants for only a short time. Only a portion of the minerals are held by the soil particles, while the rest are washed away. If you continue to use *only* chemical fertilizers year after year, the natural processes of erosion, water movement, and plant growth use up whatever organic matter was in the soil to start with. Each season there are fewer organic particles in the soil to retain the minerals you add, so you have to add more and more fertilizer each year to sustain the plants' growth. As the organic material decreases, your soil becomes subject to erosion, because there are fewer microorganisms producing cementing materials. You find that you have to water more frequently because there's less organic matter to absorb water and hold it in the root zone. Perhaps worst of all, chemical fertilizers make the soil more and more acid and promote salt buildup to the point where your plants may actually have trouble growing.

Organic gardeners avoid this unpleasant scene by turning to rock powders, compost, manure and other organic materials to boost the soil's fertility. There is a possible drawback to organic fertilizers, however, in that most of them are very slow acting. If you are starting out with poor soil, most organic fertilizers simply will not get your plants off to a fast start. You can make up for this pause between application and availability by planning ahead and adding slow-acting fertilizers to the soil well before you plan to plant so the nutrients will be there when needed. For example, slow-release potassium fertilizers like granite dust and greensand are best applied in the fall for spring crops or in the spring for crops that will be grown later in the season. This rule of thumb also applies to the application of slow-release phosphorus fertilizers like phosphate rock and bone meal.

There are some organic fertilizers that release their nutrients at a relatively faster rate. These should not be applied too early, or all the nutrients will be leached away and wasted. Apply these quick-release fertilizers right before planting for best results. Relatively fast-acting potassium sources include green plant residues, seaweed, and wood ashes. (A word of warning: On contact, wood ashes burn seeds, stems, and root hairs of young plants. To avoid any mishaps, work the ashes thoroughly into the top 8 inches of soil before planting.) Fast-acting nitrogen sources include dried blood and fish emulsion. If you take the time to understand the mechanics of nutrient availability and apply organic fertilizers so that they will be releasing nutrients when needed, you'll seldom have to make supplemental feedings through the season, since there won't be any nutrient deficiencies to remedy.

What's the Big Deal about pH?

We've all heard it a thousand times—keep the soil pH between 6.5 and 7.0 for most common vegetable crops. But what are the consequences if our garden soil strays outside those boundaries? Here are a few answers to that question that should help you see why it's important to monitor pH.

A soil that's too far to the alkaline side of the pH scale (above 7.5) will corral most of the trace elements and keep them locked up and unavailable to the growing plants. Acutely alkaline soil will even go so far as to break apart humus and cause a salt concentration to build to toxic levels.

An overly acid soil (below 5.0) is not a pleasant prospect either. Under these conditions phosphorus is no longer in a form amenable to uptake by plant roots. Calcium, potassium, and magnesium tend to leach out of this type of soil. Soil bacteria stage a work slowdown so less humus is being formed. Even earthworms are turned off by too high an acid level and will move on to a more agreeable pH environment. And the crowning blow, if you're growing any members of the Cabbage family, is that there's a higher incidence of the disease clubroot in acid soils.

Soil tests (done with home-style kits or by a soil laboratory) are a sure-fire way to assess your pH status. To combat alkaline soil, add pine needles, cottonseed meal, peat moss, leaf mold, sawdust, or wood chips. To remedy an overly acid soil, add dolomitic limestone, bone meal, ground eggshells, clamshells, oyster shells, or wood ashes. Work in a pound of material at a time, test the pH in several weeks, and keep adding material as needed until you've arrived at the desired range. Different crops have different pH preferences and these are noted in the Vital Statistics box accompanying each of the crops we will discuss later.

Chapter 4

Nurturing Plants throughout the Season

When we first began to garden, most of us learned the basics from a knowledgeable friend or from a gardening book. We simply accepted what we were told or read without much question. We didn't ask why things were done a certain way; we did them like that because we were told to. But after gaining some experience (or thinking we have gained some!), gardeners often become daring and want to experiment. Our experiments can, however, get us into big trouble when we don't understand the "whys" of the basic gardening practices we've been following so faithfully. Without this knowledge, we don't know which of our methods can be changed without bringing disastrous results.

When Diane first began to garden, she was told to harden off her indoor-grown tomato plants before setting them outside. She decided that since the plants had been grown in a very sunny west-facing window, two days of hardening off, with two hours outside the first day and four hours outside the second day would be enough. She proceeded to give the plants their abbreviated hardening-off period, then planted them out in the garden and congratulated herself on her efficiency. She was horrified when all her tomatoes soon lost every single leaf! If she'd been told why gradual hardening off is so important, she would never have made such a foolish mistake.

In this chapter, we'll discuss the reasons behind hardening off and some other common garden tasks like indoor seed starting, transplanting, watering, fertilizing and mulching, so you will understand why some things must be done in a certain way.

Getting a Head Start

There are lots of reasons to start some of your crops indoors. Because of a limited outdoor growing season, few of us have the luxury of seeding all our crops directly in the garden. Crops like tomatoes and peppers wouldn't **51** have a long enough period of warm weather to mature if we direct-seeded them.

Even some of those crops which you might be able to grow easily during your regular outdoor growing season will do better if started inside, away from summer heat and from bugs that would eat them. If a fall crop of lettuce is what you're after, you'll get better germination indoors in a cool place than you would in the hot, dry soil found in most gardens in midsummer. In our gardens here in Montana, we find that starting our broccoli inside allows it time to grow big enough to withstand the annual onslaught of flea beetles before being planted outside. Our direct-seeded broccoli often has a hard time, and some years the flea beetles will demolish young seedlings before they can grow very large. Southern gardeners may also gain ground on insect pests by starting their especially vulnerable crops inside.

But whatever your reasons for planting seeds indoors, you must give your plants the right conditions, or they will be sickly and will never yield well. Factors like soil, planting depth, moisture, temperature, and light must all be carefully monitored if you want to end up with sturdy, healthy transplants.

Choosing the Right Container

The first critical decision you have to make about planting seeds indoors is what sort of containers you are going to use. Your choice of containers may be governed primarily by cost, for commercial pots can be very expensive. Cut-off milk cartons, yogurt cups, Styrofoam egg cartons, and other such household containers which can be recycled work just as well as anything you can buy. There are some disadvantages to such found containers, however, that you should be aware of. Most recycled containers come with no drainage holes, so before you start planting you must add your own by puncturing the bottoms. If egg cartons are your choice, use only Styrofoam ones, never the cardboard kind. After a few waterings, you'd have a soggy mass of disintegrating cardboard on your hands and be faced with the prospect of starting your seeds all over again. Another point to remember is that the compartments in egg cartons are so small that they are only useful for starting crops such as tomatoes and peppers which are transferred into larger individual containers while still very small.

While purchased containers add to your gardening expenses, they do offer some advantages. Square plastic pots and peat cube planters are designed to fit closely together so they take up a minimum of space. They often come with trays to hold them all together as a unit. This setup is especially useful when you start to harden off the seedlings and are shuttling them outside and back every day.

Before you settle on a certain kind of container, you should be aware of some "hidden" character traits they possess that can affect how your indoor garden grows. Pots that breathe, like those made from peat and fiber, do well in an enclosed area like a greenhouse or on a windowsill, but we've found that they do not work well in an open cold frame because they dry out much too quickly. Clay pots also breathe, but they do not dry out quite so fast. If you plan to grow your plants in a cold frame that is open on sunny days, plant your seeds in clay, plastic, Styrofoam, or waxed containers (such as milk cartons or yogurt cups), or in wooden flats. This will cut down on water lost through evaporation, so you won't have to hover over your seedlings with a watering can.

With paper containers such as fiber pots, you will need to use a soil richer in nitrogen than if you planted in plastic pots. The microbes that break down wood products like paper need extra nitrogen, in addition to carbon, to fuel their work. The wood fiber provides them with a carbon source but has little nitrogen. So, the microbes will pull nitrogen from the soil into the container, leaving less for the growing plants.

Many gardening experts recommend starting crops which are especially sensitive to transplanting, such as squash and cucumbers, in biodegradable peat pots so that the pot can be planted in the garden right along with the plant, disturbing the roots very little in the process. But in our gardens we've found that setting peat pots right into the soil retards the growth of these temperamental crops, for their roots often have a hard time breaking through the pot. We've had much better luck using plastic, Styrofoam, or waxed containers. Before transplanting, water the seedlings so that the soil in the pot is slightly damp and will, therefore, not crumble away from the roots. Then tap the pot lightly to loosen the mass of roots and soil, gently slide the plant and soil out of the container, and carefully place them into a watered, prepared hole. The roots are hardly disturbed and can grow right into the soil without having to first struggle their way through a tough layer of peat.

There are gardeners who use peat pots with good results, but they have a few secrets that ensure their success. Right before planting they make a couple of vertical tears in the sides of each pot so that the roots can easily grow through. When they set the pots in place they make sure the rims are completely buried, or they trim off the part of the pot that protrudes. If this top portion sticks out above the soil it acts like a wick, carrying water up out of the ground and away from the plant's roots. Individual peat cubes bound by plastic netting can also restrict root growth when they're set in the garden, so if you use these, be sure to clip off the netting just before you transplant so the roots can grow freely.

If you start your seeds in a small container such as the cavity of an egg carton or one of those compressed peat pellets that swell with water, you must be sure to transplant your seedlings before their growth is slowed by the cramped quarters. If this happens, the future harvest is affected for they will not produce as big a crop as they would have if their growth pattern hadn't been upset. When a plant's roots are crowded, the shoot, or above-ground portion, outgrows them. This creates a situation where the root system is not large enough to supply nutrients or water to the whole plant. When you water, the small root system will absorb all the water it is capable of, but this will not be nearly enough to satisfy the requirements of the aboveground growth. The shoot will quickly use up all the available water from the roots and start to droop unless you add more water soon.

The necessity of frequent waterings makes the whole situation worse by leaching nutrients out of the soil. Plants with crowded roots will be in double jeopardy—prone to water stress and to nutrient deficiencies. What's worse, both problems will persist after you transplant the seedlings into the garden. The roots will have a hard time catching up to the top growth, so these top-heavy plants will always be more susceptible to problems, especially when they begin to bear and there are heavy nutrient and water demands placed on the roots. One way to avoid this whole situation and grow sturdy, problem-free transplants is to follow this basic rule: keep plants in containers as deep as the plants are tall, especially during the first six weeks of growth.

Potting Soils for Seedlings

Choose your potting soil as carefully as you choose your containers. Soil for seedlings must be very light and loose so that their small, fine roots can grow freely and get off to a good start. A planting mixture that drains well is vital in the limited confines of a container, yet at the same time it must be able to hold enough water and air to keep the plant roots healthy.

The soil that works so well out in your garden isn't necessarily the best choice to fill your containers. Just plain garden soil is too heavy a medium to use in the confined space of a pot or flat, and seedlings will be hampered by a lack of air spaces and inadequate drainage. To lighten it up and increase its porosity, you will have to add vermiculite or peat moss in large quantities, even if your garden soil is in good shape. In addition, you will have to heat it to kill the damping-off fungus and its spores, which are an ever-present menace to young seedlings. Spread your soil in a shallow layer in a foil baking pan and set it in a 140°F oven for half-an-hour. This heat treatment will kill damping-off spores and other disease organisms but will leave beneficial microorganisms unharmed.

Once you've pasteurized your soil, it's ready to be blended with soil conditioners like peat moss, perlite, builder's sand, and vermiculite. While there are almost as many home potting soil formulas as there are gardeners, one simple, successful mix contains 1 to 2 parts pasteurized garden soil, 1 to 2 parts organic matter (fine compost or peat moss), 1 part vermiculite or sand, and a little steamed bone meal (a good source of phosphorus).

The process of pasteurizing soil for blending into growing mixes is fine for small batches, but if you do much indoor planting, you'll find yourself spending a lot of time and energy preparing enough garden soil. And besides, the hot soil can really smell up your house! To save time, many gardeners forego this procedure and buy their potting soil at the local garden center.

In some areas, organic potting soil that's rich in crumbly humus and devoid of chemical fertilizers is available. In other areas, gardeners may be able to purchase premixed bags of potting soil already containing conditioners like peat moss or vermiculite. All these gardeners have to do is pour the mix into containers and plant their seeds. But most of us, unfortunately, do not have much choice when it comes to purchasing this product. In a given geographic area, only a few brands of potting soil will be available, and you must buy what you can get. Most of the potting soils on the market are too heavy to use alone, so you must lighten them up, just as you do with soil from your garden.

There are some other problems with commercial soil too, so keep your eyes carefully on your young plants as they grow. While just about all brands claim to be sterilized, many still contain viable damping-off spores and weed seeds. Some commercial potting soils contain harsh chemical fertilizers, while others are deficient in basic nutrients. The most common problem is a lack of phosphorus. You can neatly sidestep this problem by adding bone meal or phosphate rock to the soil at the same time you are blending in soil conditioners like sand or vermiculite. If you don't add any extra phosphorus to the soil, and you notice that the undersides of your seedlings' leaves are turning a reddish-purple, that's a sure sign that there's a deficiency. A good dose of fish emulsion at the concentration recommended on the container will quickly restore your plants to health. Likewise, if your plants have an anemic, pale green tone to their leaves instead of a deep green, healthy glow, they're showing the effects of nitrogen deficiency. You can remedy the situation by administering a dose of manure tea. If you keep your seedlings in the same soil for more than four weeks, you should feed them with fish emulsion or manure tea anyway to keep them well nourished. Any nutrient deficiency that develops while the plant is young can seriously affect its ultimate yield. But if you correct a deficiency as soon as you notice it and give seedlings a nutrient boost at the four-week mark, your plants won't disappoint you at harvesttime.

Starting the Seeds

A general rule for planting seeds indoors is to plant them as deep as they are wide. Some crops, such as lettuce, require light for germination and you should press the seeds into the soil surface with a very light touch. After planting your seeds, moisten the soil with lukewarm water and put the container in a place where the temperature is as close as possible to the ideal for germination of that particular seed. The best germination temperature is listed in the Vital Statistics box at the beginning of each crop chapter.

If your planted seeds are at the right temperature and they haven't begun to germinate in the amount of time listed for that crop, your seeds could be too old, and you may need to replant with a fresh batch of seeds. (The way to find this out of course, before you go to the trouble of planting, is to pre-test the seeds for germination as described in chapter 1.) Sometimes, older seeds take longer to germinate, however, so don't give up right away. Old pepper and eggplant seeds are notorious for taking their time to germinate; they may delay a week or more beyond the expected time before breaking through the soil. With most other crops, however, if no seedlings have emerged by three days after the maximum germination time, you should replant to play it safe. Also, if the temperature is lower than ideal, the seeds may take quite a bit longer to sprout.

Be sure to keep your seeds moist but not sopping wet while they are germinating. If they are too dry, the embryos will not be able to break out of the seed coats. If they are too wet, they won't be able to "breathe" and consequently won't grow. Many gardeners create a sort of incubator by covering their flats or pots loosely with plastic while the seeds are germinating, taking care that the plastic doesn't rest directly on the soil surface. If the seeds have been adequately watered, the plastic will hold in enough moisture for successful germination. Be on the alert for any signs of mold or fungus growing in these covered containers, and be sure not to overwater and create soggy soil. If any problems do develop, prop open the cover to allow air to circulate and dry out the soil a bit. After the young plants push their way up, remove the plastic and place the flat or pot where there is bright light. While the containers still have their plastic covers on, never place them in the sun, or their contents will fry.

If you do not use a plastic cover, you will probably have to water your seeds more often while you wait for them to come to life. Water very gently so you don't disturb the delicate germinating seeds, and use warm but not hot water. Water that is too hot can kill the embryos, and water that is too cold will cool the soil, slowing germination.

The Best Environment for Growing Seedlings

The most common mistake gardeners make when growing seedlings indoors is to give them too little light and too much warmth. Outdoors, when the temperature increases, so does the intensity of the sunlight. Most plants grow best under these increasing proportions of light and heat, for that is what they are adapted to. When you grow your plants in a heated house, however, you can upset the balance between increase in temperature and increase in light intensity, and your plants can become spindly. For example, if you have seedlings in a sunny window, the combination of heat from the house and of solar radiation coming through the window can bring the air temperature around the plants up to 80°F. Outdoors at this temperature the plants would be in full sunlight. But on the windowsill, they are only getting a portion of the sunlight which passes through the glass, considerably less than the full amount. Under these conditions not only does the top of the plant grow too fast, but the roots, which grow best in cool soil, grow too slowly, and the balance between roots and the rest of the plant is upset. In addition, the leaves, which are receiving less than maximum light, produce many chloroplasts which are packed with chlorophyll. When a plant grown this way is planted outside in the garden, the leaves absorb so much sunlight that they actually self-destruct; the chlorophyll is destroyed and the leaves turn white and fall off.

If windowsills are such iffy places to get seedlings off to a good start, why do so many gardeners plunk their growing plants down there? The most likely answer is for the sake of convenience. But for gardeners ultimately concerned with the health and well-being of their plants, we recommend using a cold frame. A cold frame provides the best possible growing conditions for seedlings. Unlike a greenhouse, it allows you to gradually expose them to the sun, wind, and temperature extremes they will encounter when planted out in the garden. You can set your seedlings in the cold frame as soon as they are up. During sunny days, you should raise the top so that your plants receive the natural ratio of temperature to sunlight. In the colder parts of the country, you will have to protect your plants from freezing nights with a heat source of some kind. We run an electric soil heating cable under pots and flats containing our frost-sensitive plants. Not only does this protect them

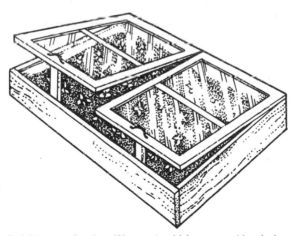

Cold Frame for Seedlings: *A cold frame provides the best environment for growing seedlings, as it allows them to adapt naturally to the conditions they will be exposed to when transferred to the garden. Raise the lid on hot days to prevent the buildup of heat in the frame.*

from frost, but it also keeps the roots from getting too cold at night, and it doesn't cost very much.

A variation on the cold frame that harnesses the heat from the sun to protect plants from low temperatures is the solar growing frame. This super-insulated structure is designed to collect the solar energy available during the day and with the help of a folding shutter, release this stored heat to the growing plants steadily throughout the night. The solar growing frame is a real boon to gardeners who live in cold-winter regions, for it allows them to grow greens throughout the winter, as well as to start their seedlings in spring. Do-it-yourselfers can find plans for building one of these frames in the book *Solar Growing Frame* (see the Bibliography).

A cold frame of any sort offers several advantages at this early stage of the gardening season. For one thing, your garden plants are out of the house so they don't occupy all your window space and compete with your house plants. When you open the frame on sunny days, the plants will be exposed to unfiltered sunlight and to the fresh air. Every time the breeze shakes the plants, it helps stimulate the stems to grow stronger and thicker. And all that air circulation also causes the plants to lose water more quickly, placing a demand on the roots which stimulates them to grow. Plants grown in an open cold frame for at least the last couple of weeks before they are trans-planted need no hardening-off period either, so you are relieved of the chore of hauling your plants out of and back into the house.

If you are lucky enough to have a greenhouse, you can easily provide better lighting for your plants than they would get inside the house. But if you can't open up the greenhouse to let unfiltered sunlight shine on your plants, you will still have to harden them off, although it should take less time than for house-grown seedlings. One problem with a greenhouse is the heat that can build up inside on sunny days. Excessive heat can stimulate spindly growth, so if you don't have a good venting system in your green-house, you may end up with a whole crop of leggy, inferior seedlings.

House-grown plants and some greenhouse-grown plants may need sup-plemental light beyond the sunlight they receive. If your plants are growing tall and spindly, with long internodes, it's a sign that they need more light. Fluorescent fixtures provide the most natural light and are cheaper to operate than incandescent ones. Special grow light tubes are available for fluorescent fixtures, too, although you may find that a combination of the less expensive cool white and warm white tubes works just as well.

When you set your plants under artificial lights, don't keep the light on for more than fourteen hours. Plants need darkness as well as light to grow properly. Timer switches that turn the lights off and on for you are inexpen-sive, easy to install, and save you the bother of having to remember yourself. Hang the light fixture 3 to 4 inches above the tops of the plants and check the plants daily to make sure no leaves are perilously close to the hot bulbs.

Raise the fixture as necessary to keep the leaves from getting scorched (a task made easier by an adjustable fixture).

Although a windowsill is not the best environment for raising transplants, many gardeners make do with such a location year after year with good results. If you don't have access to a cold frame or a greenhouse, just keep the following tips in mind, and you'll still be able to grow good sturdy seedlings. Give them as much light as possible, and if for some reason you can't provide supplemental light as described above, lower the temperature in the room and keep it around 65°F. Never let it go above 75°F, or your plants will grow so spindly they'll look like they're on stilts. You should also turn the heat down further at night, if possible, to between 50° and 55°F. The plants won't grow as fast, but they will be stronger and better balanced. A sturdy plant on the small side with a strong root system that is large enough to support the top growth will outproduce a larger, but spindly plant whose top outgrew its roots.

Seedlings grown in a sheltered environment like a windowsill or a greenhouse need to be acclimated gently to the vagaries of the outdoors. They need to toughen up a bit so that they can withstand the increased light exposure, buffeting winds, and dipping and rising temperatures that will be their lot in the garden. This gradual process of hardening off is a crucial one, akin to the slow but steady way we brace our entry into a chilly lake in summer. Jumping in all at once is a shock to our system, but if we start by sticking a toe in and slowly wading in from there, the total immersion is not nearly as stressful!

What Happens during Hardening Off?

Hardening off young plants is really a process of increasing their resistance to drought and decreasing their efficiency at gathering sunlight. As they are slowly exposed to increasing amounts of sunlight and cooler air, the plants' older leaves, which are adapted to the filtered light of the indoor environment, gradually decrease their chlorophyll content. This diminished efficiency is necessary so they won't absorb light at such a high rate outdoors; too much sunlight would actually destroy the leaves. At the same time, the new leaves that form grow thicker, with two layers of sunlight-gathering palisade cells to make good use of the extra light. As your carefully tended indoor plants are given more outdoor exposure, the waxy cuticle of their leaves thickens, affording them more protection from the drying wind and generally drier conditions they'll be exposed to out in the garden. Decreasing the amount of water you give the plants stimulates their roots to grow so they won't be water stressed after transplanting. Exposure to the wind also induces structural cells to grow in the stem; these help the plant to endure heavy winds without falling over or snapping.

Timetable for Hardening Off

	First Day	Second Day	Third Day	Fourth Day	Fifth Day	Sixth Day
In Full Sunlight						
Spindly plants	½ hour	¾ hour	1 hour	1½ hours	2¼ hours	3½ hours
Sturdy plants	1½ hours	2½ hours	3½ hours	5 hours	6 hours	7 hours
In Light Shade*						
Spindly plants	1 hour	1½ hours	2¼ hours	3½ hours	5 hours	3 hours in sun
Sturdy plants	2½ hours	3½ hours	5 hours	6 hours	7 hours	7 hours in sun

*Receiving reflected or indirect sunlight only for the first five days.

All these adaptations take time, so you must be patient. If your plants have been grown entirely indoors and are weak and spindly, they will require a long, gradual hardening-off period. Hardening off will take from one and one-half to three weeks, depending on the condition of your plants. The following recommendations are based on our own sometimes sad experience. The first day, place weak plants in direct sun for no more than half an hour. Slowly increase the time in the sun over the first week until they are out for about four hours (see the Timetable for Hardening Off). From then on, increase the amount of sunlight by about an hour a day until the plants are outside all day long.

If your plants are sturdy and have been receiving filtered direct sunlight for around four hours a day indoors, you can give them one and one-half hours of full sun or two to two and one half hours of filtered (shaded) sunlight the first day outside. Try to put the plants out during hours when they would not be getting sunlight inside; this will help them adjust faster. For example, if the sun doesn't strike their window until noon, do your hardening off in the morning if possible. If the plants are in a southeast window, harden off in the afternoon if you can. Each day, increase the time outside by an hour until the plants are out all day. The last few days before transplanting you can leave your plants outside overnight if you like. This saves you the trouble of carting them in and out, and some people think it helps them adjust that much better to conditions outdoors.

Keep in mind that the weather can interfere with even the most carefully managed hardening-off schedule. If it is snowing or unseasonably cold when you plan to begin the process, you will have to wait, of course, until conditions improve. If hail or heavy rains descend while your tender young plants are outside, you will have to bundle up and rescue them from the inclement weather and then pick up where you left off when the sun comes back out.

During the early stages of the hardening-off period, water your plants once a day, and always keep an eye out for wilting, especially on hot days. If your plants do wilt, take them inside and water them right away. As hardening off progresses, you want the plants to develop strong roots and to become used to drier conditions, but you don't want to overly stress them. Encourage this acclimatization by gradually decreasing the amount of water you give the plants. The last few days before transplanting, water them as little as possible, short of letting them wilt. If it is windy when you begin hardening off, protect your plants from the wind for the first few days until they begin to get stronger and more accustomed to dryness. You can place your seedlings on the leeward side of a building or tree to shield them from the wind as long as it isn't too shady there. Or, you can place low barriers such as old fruit crates between your plants and the prevailing wind.

If your seedlings are growing together in a flat, there is an important step in addition to hardening off that you must take to prepare them for transplanting. Two or three days before you plan to transplant, cut the soil into blocks about 3 inches square or larger around each plant (just like cutting a sheet cake). In this procedure, known as blocking off, delicate root hairs are cut off along with the root ends as you draw a trowel or other sharp tool through the soil mass. You are actually lessening the actual transplant trauma by inflicting some of the inevitable damage earlier and giving the plants a chance to recover before they are transplanted.

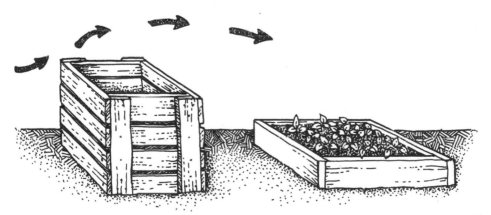

A Windbreak for Seedlings: *To protect seedlings from harmful blasts of wind while they are hardening off, place a crate between the prevailing wind and the flat of seedlings.*

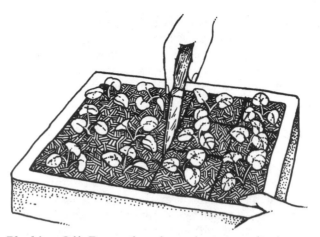

Blocking Off: *Two or three days prior to transplanting, cut the soil into blocks at least 3 inches square around each plant. This process allows the seedlings time to recover from the shock of having their roots torn before they are transplanted.*

Transplanting to the Garden

When your plants have finally become used to being outside for a full day, they are ready to be transplanted. You should, of course, time your hardening off so that the plants are ready when it is safe for them to be in the garden. Hardy crops like broccoli, cabbage, and lettuce can be set out quite early, even before the last expected frost. Tender, more cold-sensitive crops like eggplants, peppers, and tomatoes must not be set out until well after the last frost. Check with your local extension agent for the proper planting time in your particular area.

For final transplanting, pick a calm, cloudy day if possible. If this isn't convenient, transplant in the evening so the plants can start adjusting under the cover of darkness. Transplanting will be less stressful to your seedlings if they are not exposed to the hot sun or drying wind right away. Granted, it's hard to find the "perfect" day, for even on a cloudy day the wind can be very drying and can cause your transplants to lose water faster than their disoriented roots can pull it up. Just as long as you don't transplant under the blazing midday sun and do follow our tips on how to minimize root damage, your seedlings should recover quickly.

It's important to realize that no matter how careful you are, there is likely to be some damage to the roots during the transplanting process. To minimize this damage, have the soil in the pot moist enough so that it will hold together around the roots when the root ball is slipped out. Soil in plastic pots should be thoroughly moist but not soaking wet, while that in fiber pots needs to be a bit drier. If you are using peat pots through which the roots are growing, soak the pots thoroughly and tear the sides in several places before setting them into the garden.

Dig the hole deep enough so that the root mass will sit slightly below the soil surface. Leaving a shallow depression around the base of the plant will allow water to collect there so it can soak slowly down to the root mass. Bury lanky tomatoes on their sides so that most of their long, leafless stem portion is underground. New roots will sprout from the buried stems, making for a sturdy, well-developed root system (see details in chapter 12). If your soil is poor or compacts easily, mix some compost or premoistened peat moss thoroughly with the soil you dug out of the planting hole. Add some of this fortified soil to the bottom of the hole and use the rest to cushion the sides and top of the rootball once the plant is in place. The roots need loose and fertile soil that they can penetrate easily and from which they can absorb nutrients for the growing plant. Soggy soil tends to compact around plant roots and hampers their nutrient and water uptake. If your garden soil is very wet, you'd be smart to delay planting until the soil dries out and loosens up a bit. On the other hand, it's never a good idea to set your plant into a bone-dry hole. If your garden is dry, or if the day is very hot or windy, be sure to water the hole thoroughly before you set the plant in.

To get the plant out of its pot easily, rap the sides soundly with the blade edge or handle of a trowel, or run a knife around the inside edge of the pot. Once you've loosened the rootball, cup one hand over the soil surface with your fingers cradling the stem, tip the pot upside down, and gently shake or tap the pot until the plant is released. Set it into the hole at once, fill in the gap between the hole and the rootball with soil, and tamp down firmly, remembering to leave a depression around the base. Water generously right away. At this point, water stress is the worst enemy your young plants will face. If the wind comes up or the sun comes out or if the transplants wilt, turn on a soaker hose or sprinkler so that the plants receive constant moisture for a couple of hours. Or, cover them with a temporary canopy made of cheesecloth suspended from wooden stakes to block out some of the sun's rays. You can also prop shingles, boards, house screens, or lengths of snow fencing alongside your transplants to create a sheltered, shady haven. Keep a close eye on your transplants for the first few days and water them when they show any sign of wilting.

If you have done a careful job of hardening off, your new garden should begin to grow well soon after transplanting. But if for some reason you were not able to do a complete job of acclimating your plants to garden conditions and some leaves turn white and fall off, don't despair. Even when Diane's tomatoes lost every single leaf in her misguided attempt to speed up hardening off, they grew new ones and eventually gave her tomatoes. But her crop would surely have been earlier and more abundant if she had heeded the voice of experience and hardened them off gradually. Careful hardening off and transplanting may seem like a lot of trouble, but in the long run your plants will thank you by giving you generous yields of high-quality produce.

How to Water Effectively

Once you've gotten all your plants in the ground and they're actively growing, there's an art to making sure they get enough water when they need it throughout the season. Too many gardeners still go by the hit-or-miss method, turning on the spigot when they think of it—oblivious to the fact that the garden needed water several days ago or that perhaps it doesn't really need any for another couple of days. In the first case, the plants will be water stressed, and that condition could adversely affect the ultimate yield. In the second case, water is being squandered needlessly and may even saturate the soil to the point where it interferes with plant growth. Since no one can afford to waste water or stress plants by underwatering, we've gathered together some pointers to help you undertake an effective watering regimen in your garden.

Knowing your soil type is very important, for it will determine how you water. You should never overwater clay soil because it will hold far too much water next to the plant roots and, in essence, "drown" them. On the other hand, if you have a sandy soil, you don't have to worry about waterlogging, for the excess water will just drain through the ground. What you want to do, of course, is water just until your soil has absorbed the right amount of water so that it is thoroughly moist, not soggy. Besides wasting precious water, overwatering will leach minerals into the subsoil, out of reach of most roots. The other extreme, underwatering, is no better situation. When too little water percolates down through the root zone, the result is slow growth or the outright demise of your plants. Frequent light watering that only moistens the top soil layer encourages the roots to grow near the surface. There, they are more subject to drying between waterings, are more vulnerable to perishing under drought conditions, and will not probe deeply enough to extract minerals from the entire depth of the topsoil.

In general, the best way to determine if your garden needs watering is to dig down about 4 inches. (But there are important exceptions—you'll read about these in the individual crop chapters.) If the soil at this depth is dry and won't stick together, it is time to water. Watch your plants, too, for signs that they need water. On hot summer days, some wilting is normal in the afternoon. If, for example, you go out and see your cucumbers positively drooping—don't panic. Their leaves have been giving off water faster than the roots can pull it up from the soil. There may be plenty of water available in the soil, but the plant just isn't getting it quickly enough. Your plants usually muster their forces overnight and regain their perky appearance by morning. However, if you notice that your plants look wilted in the morning, get water to them right away! That's a sure sign that there's not enough water in the soil for the plants to take up. If your soil is a medium loam, you should water for at least an hour so that the soil is deeply soaked. A sandy soil needs to be watered for less time but at more frequent intervals, and a clay soil will only need infrequent watering.

Things Nobody Tells You about Mulches

By now, most gardeners are familiar with the often touted benefits of mulching, especially when organic materials are used. Almost every gardening book carries the common refrain: an organic mulch will conserve soil moisture; deter soil erosion; supply nutrients and humus as it breaks down; thwart weed growth; regulate temperature extremes; and keep the harvest clean and free of mildew, mold, and rot. But what they don't bother to tell you are the hidden character traits of each kind of mulch that will only appear with time and can spell trouble for the gardener who is caught unaware. Here's a rundown of the more commonly used mulches and some well-kept secrets we thought you'd like to know.

A number of mulches fall under the category of "nitrogen robbers"; these are organic materials rich in carbon. Bacteria then rob nitrogen from the soil to fuel decomposition of the mulch—leaving less nitrogen for the plants and even leading to a serious deficiency. Alfalfa hay, shredded corncobs and cornstalks, sawdust, and straw are all guilty of this subversive activity. To avoid a potential deficiency, apply substances high in nitrogen like compost, manure, blood meal, or soybean or cottonseed meal to the soil before mulching. Or, you can compost the carbonaceous nitrogen robbers with the nitrogen-rich materials and apply the resulting mixture as a mulch.

Grass clippings are usually available in abundance, but they can bring along an abundance of problems to plague the garden if not used correctly. Clippings that have started to go to seed will introduce a new crop of unwanted plants—so avoid them at all costs. Too thick a layer of fresh clippings will compact down, blocking soil aeration and causing water to run off instead of soak in. Besides giving off an objectionable odor, they also have the nasty habit of providing a breeding haven for flies and gnats. To avoid this unpleasantness, compost the clippings briefly, or combine them with fluffier materials like wood chips and compost. You must also be careful of your source, and make sure the lawn that yielded the clippings wasn't treated with herbicides. If you're not sure of their status, play it safe and compost the clippings before applying them to the garden.

Unshredded leaves soon compact into an unappealing sodden mass in the garden. Shred them before applying, or mix whole leaves with straw or wood chips to lighten up their texture.

Manure in its fresh state should never be used as a mulch, for it will burn your plants. Use only well-composted manure and be aware that with prolonged use, excess salts can build up and hordes of weed seeds will be introduced to the garden.

Newspaper is another readily available mulching material. Just be sure to always use the black and white pages, never the comics section, or the coated glossy paper that is used in magazines and newspaper supplements. As they break down, these papers will release substances harmful to soil microorganisms. Newspaper is one of the band of nitrogen robbers, so you should add an extra dose of nitrogen to your garden before you mulch.

Peat moss makes a very agreeable mulch—that is, until you let it dry out. In its dry state it is easily carried off by the wind and is almost impossible to remoisten, for the water just runs off the surface without being absorbed. Before spreading peat moss, give it a good soaking in its bag and let it sit overnight. During the growing season, keep the garden well watered so the mulch never gets a chance to dry out.

You may have a bountiful supply of sunflower seed hulls, but it would be a big mistake to use them in your garden. These hulls contain a chemical that will leach out into the soil and stunt or even kill growing plants.

To wrap up this discussion of mulching, here are a few general caveats. Don't jump the gun and mulch too early, or the soil will stay cool long into the season, delaying the planting of heat-loving crops such as peppers and eggplants. Wait until the soil temperature reaches 78°F when you measure it 3 to 4 inches below the surface. Never mulch dry soil, for water will have a hard time penetrating the layer of mulch to reach the soil. Wait for a rainfall or give the garden a good, thorough soaking before you apply the mulch. Also, if you use a dense mulch, keep it pulled a few inches away from the bases of your plants to avoid fungus problems.

Dealing with Persistent Nuisances

There's nothing worse than watching your gardening efforts undermined by the silent, dark forces of nature, namely encroaching lawns, tree roots, and rhizomatous weeds. Here are some tips on how to do battle with the perpetrators and emerge victorious.

When you carve a garden out of an area that was formerly lawn, you're setting the stage for fierce competition between the roots of your crops and the grass roots that remain on the periphery of the garden. Grasses are among the most sapping of plants, and you may notice that the garden plants close to the grassy border are smaller and more feeble than plants growing toward the interior of the garden plot. Even if on the surface there are several inches of bare dirt between the edge of the lawn and the first garden row, underground the grass roots are wending their way towards your crops. You can accept this state of affairs and resign yourself to the fact that the plants on

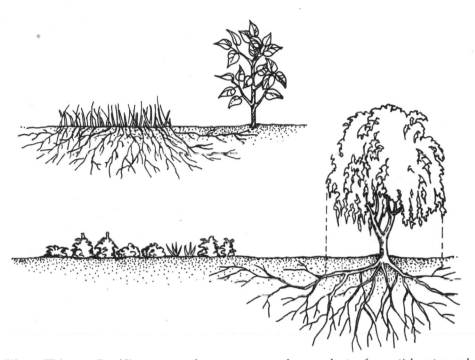

Water Thieves: *Rambling grass and tree roots can rob your plants of essential water and nutrients. Grass (top) spreads by means of horizontal rhizomes that can extend well beyond the edge of the lawn. Most tree roots are found within the tree's drip line, but some trees, such as the willow (bottom), can send roots as far as 20 feet beyond their drip line.*

the outskirts of your garden won't be as vigorous. Or, you can dig up a sort of "no-man's-land," a 12-inch band from which you lift up the sod and replace it with a mulch. This area can serve as a neat-looking pathway that runs around the garden and will allow the grass roots to encroach but without harming your garden plants.

Tree roots are another garden nemesis that can wreak havoc with growing plants. These tenacious subterranean venturers ramble far and wide to pull in enough nutrients and water to fuel the tree's growth. Most gardening guides recommend that you locate your garden outside the drip line (the circular area on the ground that corresponds to the area encompassed by the farthest reaching branches, where most of the tree roots are concentrated). That way you can avoid most of the interference from the roots and your garden won't be drained of water and nutrients. But trees that sprout from the roots, such as aspen, poplar, and willow, will send their roots 15 to 20 feet beyond the drip line, where they will lie very close to the surface. If you must share your gardening area with such trees, you must realize that you will be supporting two crops throughout the season—your food plants and your trees! With this in mind, you will have to water more often, make midseason supplementary feedings, and increase the level of organic material in the soil.

Rhizomatous weeds such as quack grass, Canadian thistle, and morning glory are the bane of many a gardener's existence. It often seems that no matter how hard you try to get rid of them, they just regroup their forces and come back twice as strong and twice as many! Your best plan of action is hand-to-hand combat. You must pull them up by the roots and try to extricate all of the underground rhizome system by which they multiply. If you leave just a tiny piece of one in the ground, it will grow again with renewed vigor. A friend of Diane's learned this the hard way when she had her garden rotary tilled. She did not remove the quack grass prior to tilling and was appalled afterwards by the almost overwhelming increase in the weed population. The tiller had just chopped up the rhizomes and distributed them all over her garden, making the problem much worse than it had been before. Heed this lesson well: in order to eliminate these weeds completely, you must take the time to dig them up and be sure you have gotten out the entire root system!

Chapter 5

Spinach and Lettuce: Rabbit Food for People

Vital Statistics

Family:
Chenopodiaceae—Spinach
Compositae—Lettuce

Species:
Spinacia oleracea—Spinach
Lactuca sativa—Lettuce

Soil:
Very rich organic soil;
heavy or light texture

pH:
Spinach—6.0–6.5
Lettuce 5.8 7.0; optimum
6.0–7.0

Soil Temperature for Germination:
Spinach—35°–75°F
Lettuce—35°–80°F
For both crops, germination rates
decrease at higher temperatures
(see text)

Air Temperature for Best Growth:
Spinach—60°–65°F, daytime;
40°–45°F, nighttime
Lettuce—73°F, daytime; 45°F,
nighttime; can tolerate daytime
temperatures up to 83°F, nighttime temperatures down to 37°F

Seed Viability:
Spinach—3 years
Lettuce—1–6 years; generally 2–3
years

Seed Germination:
Spinach—6–12 days
Lettuce—3–7 days

Seed Planting Depth:
Spinach—½"
Lettuce—from ¼" to top
of soil (see text)

Lettuce and spinach are especially satisfying crops to grow, for they can supply that eagerly awaited, first taste of fresh greens in the springtime. Both grow rapidly and readily in the home garden, and the quality of homegrown produce is far superior to what you can buy in the supermarket (with the surprising exception of head lettuce, as we'll explain later). Spinach, and to a slightly lesser degree, lettuce, can even be overwintered in many areas for an extra-early spring crop, long before most other vegetables are even in the **69** ground. A good stand of spinach or lettuce can put the gardener in the enviable position of having to scour the neighborhood enlisting friends and neighbors to help eat up the harvest. Not everyone faces a glut of greens, however, for some gardeners have a hard time growing these tasty crops. All that's needed is an understanding of their biological clocks for anyone to succeed with these leafy greens—even in problem areas.

Lettuce is an ancient crop, having been grown by the Egyptians some 6,500 years ago. The reason we know this is because drawings of romaine-type lettuce have been found on the walls of Egyptian tombs. Spinach can't claim such early roots as a cultivated crop. It originated in southwestern Asia and wasn't familiar to Europeans until after Roman times. While spinach and lettuce belong to two different plant families, they are alike in so many ways that they must have lived under very similar circumstances in their wild state.

Lettuce (*Lactuca sativa*) belongs to the Sunflower family (Compositae). This is one of the largest plant families and includes other familiar plants like chrysanthemums, dandelions, goldenrod, and salsify. The genus name, *Lactuca*, means "latex " in Latin and refers to the milky, bitter white sap produced by special cells in lettuce plants. This is the liquid you see oozing from the stem when you cut or pick large leaves of leaf lettuce. Some species of *Lactuca* are always bitter, but cultivated lettuce only produces the bitter chemical when it becomes overmature or bolts.

Spinach (*Spinacia oleracea*) belongs to the Goosefoot family (Chenopodiaceae). Several other familiar edible plants are also members of this family;

Lettuce Nutrition

Just because they're all green doesn't mean that different types of lettuce all contain the same amounts of vitamins and minerals. To highlight their differences and show you how they compare nutritionally, here is a breakdown of the four major nutrients per 100-gram serving of the four main lettuce types.

Type	Vitamin A	Vitamin C	Calcium	Iron
Butterhead	970 IU*	8 mg†	35 mg	2.0 mg
Crisphead	330 IU	6 mg	20 mg	0.5 mg
Looseleaf	1,900 IU	18 mg	68 mg	1.4 mg
Romaine	1,900 IU	18 mg	68 mg	1.4 mg

*International Units
†Milligrams

they include beets, chard, and that tasty, wild spinachlike plant, lamb's-quarters.

Both these greens have earned well-deserved reputations as lightweights among dieters. But just because they're short on calories doesn't mean that they shortchange you nutritionally. A one-cup serving of raw spinach, a mere 40 calories, has 100 percent of our daily vitamin A requirement, 62 percent of the vitamin C, 60 percent of the thiamine, and 40 percent of the iron (although there is some controversy about how available the iron actually is to the human body). Lettuce is not as rich in vitamins as spinach and different types of lettuce vary considerably in vitamin content (see the chart on Lettuce Nutrition).

Nutrition aside, once you've grown these crops yourself, you'll see that homegrown leafy greens taste much better and have a crisper texture than storebought ones. If your kids ever balked at eating their spinach, or if they refused to have anything to do with salads, just feed them some sweet and tender homegrown greens and you'll probably have some converts to lettuce and spinach on your hands. Our kids love them so much that they go out in the garden and pick fresh leaves for a snack. Kids aren't the only ones who appreciate homegrown greens; during the early spring and late fall, Diane's family must compete with the deer for these crops. If they decide to be selfish and not share with the local wildlife, they erect a tent of chicken wire over the greens patch to keep the deer away.

The Best Soil for Growing Greens

The title of an article in the February 1978 issue of *Organic Gardening* magazine summarized the key to successful spinach (and lettuce) growing. The article is called, "And Now a Word From the Spinach King: Manure!" It tells of a gardener, Glenn Munson, who ordered manure to spread on his garden. A problem developed when the mucky ground in his garden kept entrapping first the manure spreader and then the rotary tiller. Munson finally gave up trying to spread out the manure and just scattered spinach seed over the area, even though it had a higher concentration of fresh manure in the top soil layer than he would have liked. He didn't expect much of a harvest, but as the season progressed, he started to feel like the accidental hero of "Jack and the Beanstalk"—he ended up with his best spinach crop ever! The plants grew quickly and produced lots of tender leaves which he was able to keep picking over a period of time.

While we don't recommend purposefully preparing a half-manure, half-soil bed for growing lettuce and spinach, these plants can tolerate salt and need the copious amounts of nitrogen supplied by adding lots of manure, either fresh or composted, to the soil. Spinach needs plenty of nitrogen to prompt the rapid growth that gives the tastiest leaves, while lettuce needs a

The Lowdown on Salty Soil

Soil is salty when it contains an excess of sodium, magnesium, or calcium ions. In general, the salty soil an organic gardener may have to contend with will suffer from too much sodium. Salty soil is mainly a problem in dry areas, especially in the arid West. Rain tends to wash salt deep into the soil, beyond the root zone, but where there isn't enough regular rainfall the salts stay near the surface where plants grow. Salty irrigation water can compound the problem by adding still more salt to the upper soil layers.

Manures are a chief culprit in building salt to harmful levels. Poultry manure is notorious for containing more salt than other types because the excretory wastes from the birds' kidneys are mixed in with the digestive wastes from the intestines, creating an especially salty blend. Steer manure from feedlots where cattle are confined in a small area can also be very salty because it contains urine as well as manure. Apply these salty manures in moderation, and keep your eyes open for signs that your plants are languishing; too much sodium could be the problem. If you're gardening in a plot that wasn't always treated organically, be aware that chemical fertilizers also contain lots of sodium, so the soil may be a little heavy on the salt.

Scientists can accurately measure sodium content by passing an electric current through the soil to see how well it is conducted; the more salt in the soil, the better the current passes through it. Unfortunately, the equipment used in this test is so expensive that it's virtually inaccessible to home gardeners. But don't despair; if you suspect that your soil has too much salt, there are affordable ways to check it out. Contact your local agricultural extension service or a soil testing laboratory about having a soil sample analyzed; they will be able to tell you if there's a harmful salt buildup in your garden.

nitrogen-rich soil to compensate for its weak root system. Lettuce isn't quite as salt-tolerant as spinach and won't germinate well in very salty soil. If you consistently have trouble germinating lettuce seeds in your garden, even under the proper temperature, moisture, and light conditions, too much salt may be the reason. Gardeners in regions that tend to have salty soil should try transplanting lettuce seedlings into the garden instead of sowing seeds. Under moderately salty conditions they will do just fine. This makes spinach and transplanted lettuce ideal crops to try in an area which you might have inadvertently overmanured. In any event, if your garden is low in nitrogen, you'd better work manure into your lettuce and spinach beds before planting to avoid a disappointing yield. If you use well-rotted manure or the dehydrated kind you can buy in bags, be sure to add plenty to the soil (1½ pounds per square foot).

Potassium is also a very important nutrient for spinach and lettuce since it speeds their growth, enabling them to mature while the weather is still cool and the daylengths short. On a cellular level, potassium regulates the opening

Now that you know what causes salty soil and how you can be on guard against it, you may be wondering how this particular soil condition affects your plants. Quite simply, it hampers their growth in several ways and can ultimately lead to an untimely demise. Plants have a hard time coping with excess salt because an overabundance in the soil interferes with their ability to take up water. In addition, since the sodium ions are water soluble, they eventually end up inside the plant, carried along with the water the plant absorbs. If massive amounts of sodium build up in the plant's tissues, they can kill it, but the plant does have ways of coping with this influx of sodium so that it can survive.

Plant cells contain systems called sodium pumps which do just what their name suggests—they remove sodium from the cells. One kind of sodium pump deposits sodium ions outside the cell while the other type pumps it into the large central vacuole (which functions as a sort of garbage dump) inside the cell. These sodium pumps require energy to do their job, so they deprive the plant of energy it could use for growth and production of an edible crop. And there is a limit to how much sodium the cells can get rid of, depending on the salt tolerance of the species.

Some plants have very efficient sodium pumps and are, therefore, equipped to tolerate a fair amount of sodium in the soil. Garden crops in this category include beets, broccoli, lettuce, spinach, and tomatoes. Other plants are quite sensitive to sodium and will grow poorly in even weakly salty soils; beans, carrots, onions, and radishes have a low tolerance to salt. With this in mind, if you've accidentally overmanured your soil or in some other way the salt level has risen, your best bet is to try growing the more tolerant vegetables and wait until the salt level has subsided before trying any of the more sensitive ones.

and closing of stomata as well as the rate of water retention. In this way, potassium regulates how rapidly photosynthesis takes place. When you make sure there's lots of potassium available to these leafy crops, you're ensuring that they grow quickly and that they retain enough water to fill out the crisp, fleshy leaves. Two good sources of potassium are wood ashes and granite dust. Just remember that wood ashes are faster-acting than granite dust, so they are effective when applied close to planting time; granite dust should be applied the fall before spring planting, to give the nutrients time to break down. If your soil is acid, the wood ashes will sweeten it, but you should be careful not to let the soil become too alkaline; lettuce likes soil between pH 6.0 and 7.0, while spinach prefers pH 6.0 to 6.5. Pine needles or peat moss will lower the pH again if it has crept too high.

Both lettuce and spinach have fibrous root systems that are not especially deep; most of their roots grow in the first foot of soil. Thus, both plants need plenty of water throughout their growing season. Lettuce roots are not as efficient at nutrient uptake as those of some other crops, and this is one reason why lettuce requires rich soil to grow well. New young lettuce rootlets are the most efficient part of the root system at calcium uptake. However, head lettuces stop producing these rootlets about two weeks before the plants mature, so many varieties of head lettuce are susceptible to calcium deficiency. This deficiency shows up as burnt-looking leaf tips. Nighttime temperatures above 65°F and high humidity also encourage tipburn, for heading lettuce can have the same problems of mineral transport to the inner leaves as cabbage (see page 98). Some varieties, like Imperial and New York types, are more susceptible to tipburn. A good resistant variety is Great Lakes. Of course, the very best preventive measure you can take is to see that your soil has enough calcium to begin with; bone meal is a reliable source of this mineral. Succulent, young growth is most susceptible to tipburn, so don't give your plants an extra shot of nitrogen fertilizer late in the season—you may end up harming them more than helping them. Also, try to keep the soil uniformly moist. If it's too late for preventive measures and you see your plant's leaves starting to brown at the tips, you can slip a paper bag over the whole plant, as described for cabbage, and with luck halt the browning process. While tipburn is a concern with lettuce, you won't have to worry about your spinach plants, for this crop is trouble-free in that department.

The Best Conditions for Seed Germination

Spinach and lettuce may be among the easiest and quickest crops to grow in the garden, but if you don't provide them with the proper conditions from the moment you set the seeds in the ground, you're setting yourself up for a disappointing harvest. Both spinach and lettuce seed will germinate over a wide temperature range (35° to 75°F for spinach; 35° to 80°F for lettuce), but the germination rate falls off dramatically at the higher temperatures. At 70°F only 50 percent of the spinach seeds will germinate; for lettuce the 50 percent mark is 80°F. High temperatures like these induce dormancy in many of the seeds, which makes sense if you look at it from the plant's point of view. Both crops require cool temperatures for good growth (see the Vital Statistics box). If the seeds did germinate when it was warm, the growing season which followed would very likely also be warm. So the plants have a built-in detector which allows them to germinate only when conditions for their survival will be hospitable.

The age of the lettuce seed is another influence on germination. Seed taken from plants which have just flowered will often not germinate under *any* conditions for a couple of months or more. This is another natural protective measure; it assures that the growing season after germination is long enough so that the new plant will have time to flower and produce seeds of its own. If seeds produced by spring-grown lettuce were to germinate, the new plants would probably not have time to flower and set seed during the few weeks remaining in summer, before frost sets in and kills the plants.

If you want to grow a fall crop of lettuce or spinach, there are ways that clever gardeners can fool the seeds into germinating. You can plant them outside under a mulch, watering with cold water every afternoon. The purpose of these cool baths is to keep the soil temperature down; in hot weather there's little chance that you'll oversaturate the soil, since it tends to dry out quickly. This method will work if your area has hot days but cool (50° to 65°F) nights that will help to keep the soil temperature low. Of course, if it rains one day, you can forego the watering.

If you have warm nights or don't want to be bothered with watering the seeds every afternoon to keep them cool, you might try pregerminating the seeds on moist paper towels. Slip the moistened, seed-laden towels into plastic bags and set them in the refrigerator for three to five days before planting. After five days, germination will have begun inside the seed coat, causing the seeds to swell a little, but the roots won't yet have broken out. You can even plant these seeds in 90°F soil, and they will complete germination with no trouble at all because the cool, moist, pretreatment released the seeds from their dormancy.

You can plant spinach seeds ½ inch deep, but sow lettuce seed no deeper than ¼ inch. Some lettuce varieties require light to germinate. If the seeds are planted too deep, light won't be able to filter down to them, and they won't germinate. While other lettuce types will germinate in darkness, they will come up quicker if given light. So, just to be on the safe side, it is always best to cover lettuce seed lightly. We have found that an easy way to keep lettuce seeds moist and yet exposed to some light is to sow them right on the soil surface and then cover them with a mulch of grass clippings. A thin scattering of mulch is best, but if the weather is really sunny and dry, you can make the layer as deep as 1 inch and enough light will still get through.

Starting Seeds Indoors

Both spinach and lettuce can be started indoors to get a jump on the growing season. Since they can be planted directly in the garden so early, it is usually easiest just to sow them outdoors, right in their allotted space. But if you are determined to get a head start, plant two to three seeds in each small pot, following the recommendations for planting depth given above. When the plants are up and have developed two true leaves, thin to one seedling per pot.

As you're caring for your seedlings, remember that spinach and lettuce require cool daytime temperatures for good growth (see the Vital Statistics box). They also need strong light, and we have found that a cold frame is the best place to provide that combination of conditions. If kept under warm temperatures or low light, the plants slow down their growth. When that happens, lettuce will turn bitter, and spinach won't produce large leaves when planted out in the garden. However, if you do have a cold frame or protected area outside where you can put the young plants during the day, once they're moved to their final site in the garden you will be able to harvest lettuce and spinach two to four weeks before you could if you planted directly outdoors. This lead time could make all the difference to gardeners who have hot summers that come on early or who want to harvest a good crop of spinach before long days make the plants bolt. Just remember, when you finally do transplant them into the garden, you should place them at the same depth as they grew in the pots but no deeper, or else they will rot.

Some Tips on Growing Greens

In a very rich soil, spinach plants can be set 4 to 6 inches apart in the row. An overcrowded spinach patch will result in small plants that produce only a few large leaves. Leaf lettuce needs to be at least 8 inches apart for a full complement of leaves to develop. Head lettuce plants should be spaced about 12 inches apart, to allow plenty of room for proper heading. The inefficient roots of crowded head lettuce plants won't be able to absorb enough nutrients while competing with one another, with the result that your crop will be stunted. Extremely crowded plants won't head up at all (although you can still harvest the leaves). When red-leaved lettuce plants are crowded, they won't attain a nice, rich color, for their energy will go into growing, with little left over for production of their attractive red pigment. Spinach and compact lettuce varieties such as Deer Tongue and Tom Thumb can be grown in rows as close as 1 foot apart, while head lettuce and large leaf lettuce varieties require 2 feet between the rows.

Because both of these crops depend on fast growth for success, it is imperative to keep lettuce and spinach well thinned and to keep the weeds down. Lettuce seed is so tiny it's all too easy to plant it too thickly. And if you do, you must be sure to thin the plants right after they come up. Mixing sand in with the lettuce seed will help you sow it more thinly. Spinach seed is larger and easier to handle, so you have more control over the spacing. Even so, you may want to plant more closely than the final 4- to 6-inch spacing, and then thin the spinach rows as soon as the plants have developed two true leaves. This way, you'll get a bonus crop of tender and delicate thinnings. We think these thinnings are a special treat to eat, barely steamed and served with a little butter, or blended in with chicken broth and canned tomatoes for a delicately flavored soup.

The Effects of Daylength and Temperature

Many gardeners have been disappointed by tiny spinach plants that bolt or lettuce leaves that turn bitter before the plants reach their mature size. Both of these problems are a result of the way the plants respond to daylength, temperature, or a combination of the two. Both spinach and lettuce will bolt to seed in response to days that are fourteen to sixteen hours long. In the past, as breeders worked to develop new varieties of these crops, early-flowering plants were destroyed in an effort to select for plants that would hold in good condition longer. However, lettuce seed is now produced in a rather contrived way that doesn't allow for selection against early flowering. Young lettuce plants that are grown commercially for seed are treated with giberellic acid, a plant hormone which makes them flower while still small. This early blooming allows seed growers to control carefully for such diseases as lettuce mosaic virus (which is seed-borne) and to harvest the seeds under controlled conditions (if a large lettuce seed stalk is hit by heavy rain or high wind, most of the seeds can be lost). But it means that the plants' natural tendency to bolt quickly or to hold their leaves in good condition is not apparent, and home growers have no way of knowing how likely their plants are to go to seed early.

Spinach and lettuce that are grown in warm weather will respond faster to long days. Many gardeners think it is the hot weather itself which makes the crops bolt, but actually the heat only accelerates the long-day response. The difference between spinach and lettuce is that spinach requires long days to bolt, while lettuce will flower with or without long days; they just make it bloom earlier than it otherwise would. In other words, if long days never arrived, spinach would never bloom. However, with lettuce, blooming is inevitable. Once a lettuce plant has reached a certain size, it won't be long before it blooms, no matter what the environmental conditions are. But if that plant is exposed to long days in tandem with hot weather before it reaches the critical stage of maturity, the whole flowering process will be speeded up, and your lettuce will be doomed to a short, bitter life.

Lettuce and spinach are both so sensitive to long daylengths that they should not be grown near yard lights or street lights. Even though the light is weak, these artificial sources of light will fool these plants into responding as they would to long days. The plants will bolt early, cutting short your harvest of leaves. If you raise spinach or lettuce under artificial lights indoors for later planting outdoors, you must also keep this fact in mind and see that they don't get more than twelve hours of light per day. Don't make the mistake of thinking that you can compensate for weak light by giving them a longer daylength, or all you will harvest are small, bolted plants.

It's fascinating to learn how plants are equipped to monitor daylength. Spinach and lettuce perceive light by way of a chemical, phytochrome, in their leaves. Phytochrome is activated by light and causes the hormone florigen to travel from the leaf to the apical tip of the plant, where it collects. When enough florigen has been received in the apical tip, it starts to produce flower stalks and buds instead of just leaves. If you carefully pick the largest and oldest leaves of your spinach and leaf lettuce as the plants grow, you can actually delay bolting by cutting down on the amount of hormone going to the apical tip.

Before we learned about this phenomenon, Diane always kept the older leaves on her spinach picked, while Dorothy left the biggest, dirtiest, toughest leaves in place, thinking that they would help the plants grow more quickly with their photosynthesis. Besides, why pick them when they weren't good to eat? Despite leaving those big leaves there to help the plant grow, Dorothy always had spinach that bolted disappointingly early. Diane, by keeping all the older leaves carefully picked, was unwittingly removing a source of the flowering hormone and preventing its buildup in the apical tip. This probably helps account for the fact that she has had great success with spinach, even here in Montana where long days come on fast and hot spells often hit erratically during the springtime. Using this method, she has been able to keep harvesting tender and tasty spinach until the end of June or the beginning of July. In contrast to Diane's thriving plants, Dorothy's spinach plants, with old leaves intact, usually bolted by June tenth at the latest! If you want to follow Diane's example and extend your spinach harvest, be sure to pick the older leaves faithfully every few days, gathering all those leaves which are large and fully expanded.

If you apply this method to lettuce, you can only extend your harvest for about a week, since the plants will bolt when mature under any conditions. And the older lettuce gets, the more bitter latex there is in the leaves, making it unpalatable even before it bolts. The exception to this is the looseleaf lettuce variety Green Ice, which doesn't get bitter until the flower stalk actually starts to elongate. As long as you keep its leaves picked you can enjoy this variety for a few extra days.

Preparing to Bolt: *A telltale sign that lettuce and spinach are preparing to bolt is the shape of their leaves. Spinach leaves (left) change from their usual rounded shape to a more pointed, arrowlike shape and become spaced farther apart as the length between their nodes increases. The leaves of leaf lettuce (center) become more narrow and smaller prior to bolting. Head lettuce (right) exhibits a bulge at the top of the head as the seed stalk prepares to emerge from the head.*

You can tell when your spinach and leaf lettuce are about to bolt by watching the shape of their leaves. As the spinach plant prepares to bolt, its leaves change from a rounded to a pointed, arrowlike shape, and the internodes grow longer, making the leaves appear farther and farther apart. Lettuce leaves become narrower and smaller as the plant gets ready to bolt. When head lettuce is about to bolt, it develops a telltale bulge at the top, signalling that the seed stalk is just about ready to break through the head.

Overwintering for Early Spring Greens

Both spinach and lettuce can be started four to six weeks before the first expected fall frost and overwintered in the garden in most areas for an especially early spring harvest. You have the choice of starting them right in the garden or starting them indoors and transplanting outside when they have developed their true leaves. If the autumn is mild, you may even get a significant harvest of leaves before cold weather shuts down plant growth. While spinach can survive winter in most parts of the country (we successfully overwinter it here in Montana, where temperatures sometimes fall to $-30°F$ on the coldest nights), lettuce is less hardy and won't survive freezing if it is a large plant with lots of succulent growth.

To overwinter spinach, mulch your plants with leaves, straw, or hay so that they are completely covered as soon as the ground has frozen. Dorothy favors unshredded leaves as a loose mulch material that doesn't pack down around the plants. For overwintering, pick varieties such as Bloomsdale Long Standing, Cold Resistant Savoy, and Winter Bloomsdale, which are specifically designed to be grown this way.

While older, succulent lettuce plants are prone to frost damage, young lettuce can easily survive some frost. If you live where the climate is mild, you can overwinter lettuce by providing it with a ventilated plastic covering or by growing it in a cold frame. Mulch is the old stand-by for overwintering plants in the garden. The most effective way to mulch your lettuce is to completely cover the plants as soon as the average temperature drops to 40°F, using the same materials recommended for spinach. Bitterness can be a problem with overwintered lettuce, so you should choose your varieties carefully. Two reliable varieties for overwintering are Oakleaf and Prizehead.

If you live in a part of the country with hot summers and mild winters, you'll have the most success with spinach and lettuce if you grow them during the winter months. Where there's a chance of occasional winter frosts, be prepared to protect large lettuce plants with plastic or blankets to prevent frost damage. Once lettuce has been nipped by frost the leaves rot very easily, and you will have a hard time keeping the plants from succumbing to disease and dying.

Spinach Leaves: *The leaf margins of savoyed spinach varieties (left) grow more quickly than the leaf veins, giving the leaves a crinkled appearance. Most spinach varieties have savoyed leaves, although some varieties have smooth leaves like the spinach on the right.*

Spinach Varieties

Spinach varieties differ significantly in how quickly they respond to hot weather and long days, how cold-tolerant they are, and how long it takes them to reach maturity, so it is important to read catalog descriptions carefully to match your crop to your climate. Varieties that are slow to bolt are best for spring or early summer harvests, while cold-tolerant kinds are best for overwintering. While some spinach varieties have smooth leaves, most have deeply crinkled, savoyed leaves. The leaves of these varieties are crinkly because the leaf veins grow more slowly than the rest of the leaf. A deeply savoyed leaf has more surface area than a leaf that isn't savoyed, if the two leaves are the same size. This means that savoyed varieties produce more food per unit of space in the garden. A disadvantage of savoyed leaves (from the cook's point of view) is that they tend to hold dirt in the leaf crevices and take more effort to clean. If you grow savoyed spinach, mulch it carefully from the time the plants are small to help keep the leaves free of grit and mud splatters.

Hybrid No. 7 is a popular, fast-growing variety for early spring planting; this variety is also good for fall planting in mild climates. Since it bolts easily under warm temperatures, be sure to plant it early in spring or after the hot weather is over in the fall. Melody Hybrid is another good, fast-growing spinach that's suited to the same conditions as Hybrid No. 7 but is slower to bolt. Hybrid No. 7 holds its leaves higher off the ground than does Melody, so it stays cleaner. When Diane grew these two side-by-side, she thought that Hybrid No. 7 was producing better, because she could see more leaves. But when she harvested a test patch, she found that both varieties produced equally well. America is a good variety to plant in the spring in areas where the temperature rises rapidly right around harvesttime because it's more tolerant of warm temperatures at maturity.

Spinach in Bloom: *Spinach flowers are small and inconspicuous, since they are wind-pollinated and don't have to rely on attracting insects to transfer the pollen from flower to flower.*

Saving Your Own Spinach Seed

Unlike lettuce, spinach has separate male and female plants. Commercially produced spinach seed will give you mostly female plants; seed companies select for female plants because they bolt a few days later than male ones. If you want to save your own spinach seed, you will have to let a whole patch bloom and go to seed in order to ensure that some pollen-bearing male plants are included. The wind will carry pollen from the males to the females. Since they are wind-pollinated and need not attract insects, spinach flowers are quite inconspicuous. The petals are greenish-brown, and the flowers are borne on long stems that grow up from the center of the plant. It is difficult to tell the sexes apart until seed is set; only female plants will provide you with seeds. Once your plants have bolted and the flowers have dried and turned brown, just gather the seeds from the elongated stalks, clean away the debris, and store the seeds in a cool, dry place.

It is interesting to note that despite their other similarities, lettuce and spinach plants are different in their pollination habits. While lettuce is almost completely self-pollinating, spinach is almost always cross-pollinated. We say almost always, for occasionally a spinach plant will grow which has both male and female flowers; such a plant can self-pollinate.

Lettuce Varieties

As anyone who's browsed through a seed catalog knows, lettuce comes in a multitude of varieties, each of which belongs to one of four basic types.

Lettuce Types: *Three types of lettuce are, from left: looseleaf, butterhead, and crisphead. A fourth type of lettuce, romaine, has an elongated, loose head of overlapping leaves.*

Looseleaf lettuce is probably the most popular type for home gardens, for the leaves are especially tender and can be harvested at any time. This type of lettuce doesn't form a real head, but in its place a rosette of leaves unfolds with new ones constantly developing in the middle. Looseleaf lettuce matures more rapidly than other types, producing big plants within 40 to 50 days of planting. Looseleaf varieties are among the hardiest and most heat-tolerant lettuces, so they should be your first choice for overwintering or growing where high temperatures are likely to interfere with the lettuce crop.

Butterhead lettuce (often called Boston lettuce in supermarkets) matures into a loose head of very tender, buttery smooth, pale green leaves. Butterhead types take from 60 to 75 days to form their heads, but you don't have to wait that long to harvest; you can always steal a few individual outer leaves from the plants as they grow.

Romaine or Cos lettuce has a loose head of crisp, upright leaves with a thick, juicy mid-rib. It takes about 70 days for most Romaine varieties to mature. This lettuce is the type traditionally used for a Caesar salad. It has a slightly denser texture than the looseleaf and butterhead types, so it serves as a nice foil to their delicate, papery thin texture in a tossed salad.

Crisphead lettuce (also known simply as head lettuce), the ubiquitous lettuce of supermarkets, is noted for its tightly packed head of light green leaves. On the average, it takes 80 to 90 days for a dense, full, mature head to develop. Whatever sort of lettuce you choose, read catalog descriptions carefully, for there are varieties of all types of lettuce designed to resist heat or cold. Some are resistant to tipburn, while a few carry resistance to anthracnose and mildew.

Unfortunately, we have some bad news for those of you who want to grow your own head lettuce. First of all, there's a challenge involved in growing nice big, crunchy heads. And second, for all your effort, you're raising the lettuce that is the least nutritious of all the types (see the chart on Lettuce Nutrition, earlier in this chapter). Despite its nutritional shortcomings, however, there are times when the special, succulent crunchiness of crisphead lettuce is necessary in a recipe.

Dorothy has tried to grow good head lettuce for several years now, because she has a son who prefers it over any other type. However, he is always disappointed when she succeeds, and he claims that her homegrown head lettuce just isn't as good as that in the stores. She used to think he was just being difficult, but she recently found out that he is right! According to Dr. Edward J. Ryder, a plant geneticist with the USDA in California, the crisphead variety Great Lakes, which is the one most often sold to home gardeners, is especially prone to bitterness. Great Lakes and other crisphead varieties available in seed catalogs were developed some years ago (the earliest varieties date back to the 1940s and 1950s). While commercial growers have had access over the years to newer improved varieties, they have never become available to home gardeners. Salinas, Vanguard, and Winterhaven are among the newer head lettuces that are very crisp and resistant to bitterness. But just try to find these varieties in a seed catalog or in the seed packet display at your local garden store! Perhaps if gardeners requested that their favorite seed companies carried such improved head lettuce varieties they might become available to us . . . and we would all have better luck growing a good-tasting head of lettuce!

Saving Your Own Lettuce Seed

Saving seed from lettuce plants is a snap. Before we tell you how to do it, we'll fill you in on a little lettuce flower biology. If you let your lettuce plant go to seed, you will watch it send up a very long stem with many flowering branches. The flowers resemble dandelions, only smaller. Each "flower" on a lettuce plant is actually made up of many tiny flowers, and what look like the petals are actually bracts, which are more akin to leaves. The petallike bracts surround a cluster of true flowers, called florets. Every group of bracts encircles about ten to twenty florets, each with a single, tiny, thin petal. The anthers of each floret are fused into a tube through which the stigma must grow when the floret opens. Since the pollen is released from the anthers as the stigma grows through, most lettuce is self-pollinated. For this reason, if you want to save seed from a non-hybrid variety of lettuce, you don't need to isolate it from other varieties.

To save seed from looseleaf, butterhead, or romaine-type lettuces, just let a plant or two go to seed and keep an eye on the stalk as the flowers fade. You'll know the seed is almost ready to harvest when the yellow flowers have changed to a downy white seed head. When the seed head begins to dry,

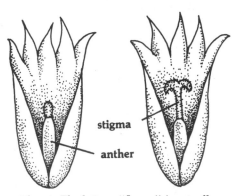

stigma

anther

Lettuce Floret: *The lettuce "flower" is actually composed of many tiny flowers called florets. Lettuce flowers are self-pollinated, since pollen is released from the anthers as the stigma grows through the anther tube. When the pollen is ripe, it will germinate and form a pollen tube which will grow down the style to the ovary.*

bend it over a paper bag and shake it so that the seeds fall into the bag. All the seeds do not ripen at the same time, so you should shake off the ripe seeds every other day or so over a seven- to ten-day period. Separate the good seed from the debris by pouring the contents of the bag from one container to another in a slight breeze or in front of a fan. The air current will whisk away the light debris, leaving you with the seed.

Store the seeds in a cool, dry place. Remember that if you want to use seeds that are less than two to three months old, you will have to put them in the refrigerator for several days to break their dormancy. If you fail to do this, they might not germinate.

If you want to collect seed from head lettuce, let the head mature and then incise a cross design about 3 inches deep in the top of the head. This will allow the seed stalk to break through the wrapper leaves and emerge from the top of the head. If you don't make these cross-cuts, the seed stalk will probably not be able to get out and will just grow around in circles inside the head, never to emerge and set seed.

Problems with Spinach and Lettuce

Spinach is a relatively trouble-free crop, bothered by few pests and diseases. Like other cool-weather crops, however, it can suffer from downy mildew. If this is a problem in your garden, choose resistant varieties such as Dixie Savoy, Hybrid No. 7, or Melody Hybrid.

Collecting Seeds from Lettuce: *To collect seeds from looseleaf, butterhead, and romaine-type lettuces, bend the mature seed head over a paper bag and shake gently to release the seeds into the bag. For head types, make a cross-shaped cut in the top of the head, so the developing seed stalk can make an easy exit from the head.*

In addition to tipburn, which we've already discussed, there are a few other diseases and pests that may attack your lettuce. Lettuce rot first appears as a rotting of the lowest leaves before spreading through the rest of the plant. Moist conditions foster this disease so one good preventive measure is to hill up the rows to encourage good drainage. Downy mildew and mosaic virus plague lettuce but can be avoided by controlling the aphids and leafhoppers which help spread the disease by planting varieties resistant to these pests. If these diseases are a problem year after year, try to rotate your lettuce crop, never planting it in the same spot two years in a row.

Cutworms and slugs will enjoy nibbling on the succulent shoots of your young plants if you let them. Place loose cardboard collars around each plant as it germinates or as it's set out to deter cutworm attacks. Make a thick ring of wood ashes, coarse sand, or sawdust around each plant to keep slugs at bay; the coarse materials will damage their soft underbellies.

Spinach and Lettuce Frontiers

Breeders of both spinach and lettuce are continuing to search for varieties that are more resistant to bolting. They are also working to develop more hybrids which give a uniform crop. Since both of these leafy green crops can suffer from various fungus and virus diseases, resistant varieties are another research goal.

Wild lettuce species have been used to improve cultivated lettuces in a number of ways. Calmar and Valverde contain genes for resistance to downy mildew that were introduced from a species of wild lettuce, and Vanguard is actually a cross between *Lactuca sativa* and a wild lettuce. The wild lettuce genes help give Vanguard its dark green color and crisp texture. Unfortunately, Vanguard is one of those head lettuce varieties that is only available to commercial lettuce growers. We suspect that this is the sort we've been able to buy recently in the supermarket, which has greener leaves, nice heads, and a wonderfully crisp, tender texture. We also believe that, with its greener color, this variety may be more nutritious than other head lettuce types. Since head lettuce is big business for agriculture, undoubtedly more improved varieties are on the way.

Chapter 6

The Cabbage Family: Many Crops in One

Vital Statistics

Family:
Cruciferae
Species:
Brassica oleracea
Soil:
Slightly heavy loam that retains moisture
pH:
6.0–7.5 for all crops except cauliflower, which prefers 6.5–7.0
Soil Temperature for Germination:
45°–85°F for all crops except cauliflower, which needs a minimum of 55°F

Air Temperature for Best Growth:
60°–65°F, optimum
Seed Viability:
3–4 years
Seed Germination:
4–20 days
Seed Planting Depth:
½"

All of the crops assembled under the name *Brassica oleracea* provide perhaps the best example in the plant kingdom of how people can influence the genetics of living things to fit their own needs. There are already examples of this in the animal kingdom. The dachshund, with its short legs and long body perfectly adapted to pursuing badgers down holes, and the greyhound, sleek, racy, and fast as the wind, are descendants of the same wild ancestors. Man simply stepped in and started selecting traits that he wanted, and directed the breeding to arrive at two different dogs.

In the same fashion we have influenced the genes of one plant species, *Brassica oleracea,* to provide us with a great variety of crops. Over the course of hundreds of years we have selected brassicas for leaves growing tightly

Cole Crops: *Although these cole crops are closely related, each one has developed its own special characteristics that set it apart from the others. Shown clockwise from the top right are kohlrabi, broccoli, savoy cabbage, red cabbage, green cabbage, Brussels sprouts, kale, collards, and cauliflower in the center.*

together to form a head, until we arrived at the vegetable we know as cabbage (variety capitata, which means "head"). We have encouraged certain plants to form a tasty, vitamin-rich, loose crown of leaves, resulting in the present-day crops of kale and collards (variety acephala, meaning "without a head"). We have induced the stems of other brassicas to swell into delicious crunchy bulbs, which became known as kohlrabi (variety gongylodes). We have persuaded the flower buds to grow into tender and tasty clumps in the variety botrytis, otherwise known as broccoli (subvariety cymosa) and cauliflower (subvariety cauliflora). And finally, when we managed to coerce the axillary buds into forming tiny, tender heads of their own, Brussels sprouts (variety gemmifera, or "bud-bearer") arrived on the scene.

The fact that all these tasty crops belong to the same botanical species means that they are able to cross-pollinate. (As a matter of convenience, very often all of these variations of *Brassica oleracea* are lumped together and called the "Cabbage family," although they are not a family in the true botanical sense of the term; they are also known collectively as cole crops or cabbage crops, names we will use interchangeably throughout this chapter.) They are less closely related to other familiar garden crops in the same plant family, Cruciferae, such as mustard, turnips, and radishes. All crucifers contain bitter chemicals called glucosinolates, but these have been tamed down to a palatable level in the cultivated varieties. They are still present, however, and give radishes their tang and mustard its zing. Certain types of cabbages contain varying amounts of these substances, which accounts for the subtle differences in flavor. Mild spring varieties possess less than the more robust-flavored fall storage types. The strongly flavored savoy cabbages contain the most glucosinolate, while red cabbages with their mellow taste have the least.

Cole crops originated in the Mediterranean area, with kale probably the first type to be tamed, some 2,000 years ago. Next in line as a cultivated crop was heading cabbage. By the fifteenth century, Europeans were already growing kohlrabi and cauliflower. Broccoli came along later and was raised almost exclusively in Italy, while Brussels sprouts were developed in Belgium in the mid-eighteenth century. Today, these assorted varieties are very popular in the western world and occupy up to 30 percent of the agricultural lands in European countries. Broccoli is still a favorite in Italy as well as in the United States, while cabbage itself is especially favored in eastern Europe.

As a group, the cole crops are a dieter's dream. They tend to be high in vitamins and very low in calories. For example, one stalk of cooked broccoli will give you more than your daily vitamin A requirement, nearly four times your vitamin C allotment, 33 percent of your required riboflavin, and 15 percent of your necessary vitamin B_6, all for a bargain 47 calories! Kale does an even better job than broccoli in providing you with certain vitamins; one cup cooked gives you a little more than twice your daily required amounts of both vitamins A and C. Of course, all these vegetables have an even higher vitamin count when eaten raw. All cole crops are packed with vitamin C, but as we'll learn later, *when* you harvest them and *how* you store them can have a considerable effect on their vitamin C content.

How Cole Crops Grow

If you've ever bought plants labeled "broccoli" at a nursery and ended up with cabbages, it's probably because all cole crops start out with a pair of heart-shaped seed leaves, and at this early stage they look identical. As their true leaves begin appearing, you can start to detect some differences. Young cabbages have rounder leaves than baby broccoli, and kale seedlings tend to be a darker green than the others. With all of them, however, the first few leaves have longer petioles than later ones. With cabbage in particular, the progressively shorter petioles lead eventually to the formation of the head. These cole crops have four distinct stages of growth, some of which you can observe and others you can't. First comes the initial growth stage, when the plant sends stem and leaves aboveground. Next, the outer leaves expand. During the third stage, the outer leaves develop into nutrient storage areas for the fourth and final stage, the development of the edible crop.

What goes on during the third stage has a direct effect on the abundance of the harvest. Scientists have studied this stage extensively in cabbage, and their findings can almost certainly be extended to at least some other cole crops as well, since removal of the outer leaves will lead to small broccoli heads and buttoning cauliflower. During the third stage of growth, nitrogen, phosphorus, and potassium from the soil are stored within the outer leaves. As the cabbage head forms, these nutrients are quickly shuttled from the outer leaves to the developing head. The stored nutrients are transferred from the older, outer leaves into the phloem, which carries them to the newly forming leaves inside the head. Because the head forms so rapidly, the roots are unable to pump minerals fast enough to keep up with the expansion going on aboveground. When scientists deprived cabbage plants of nitrogen during the second and third stages of growth, small heads resulted even though plenty of nitrogen was given during the actual heading stage. There's a lesson in this for home gardeners; it is important to grow cole crops in a rich soil from the very beginning, or the crops will be very puny. Even a dose of fast-acting fish emulsion given at the time the final crop is developing won't help— it will be too late.

Cole Crop Basics

While each one of the cole crops has its own peculiarities, some important generalities can be made about them. Whether it's a full head of cauliflower or a fat bulb of kohlrabi you're after, you need to master a few fundamentals before you can expect your best crop. In most of North America, many cole crop varieties can be grown from seed sown directly in the garden. Yet, most gardeners are in the habit of starting their plants indoors and transplanting them out later, which involves tending them carefully and hardening them off in the interim. Why go to all this trouble? The main reason is that cole crop seedlings offer an attractive feast for a great variety of insects, with hungry flea beetles being especially abundant early in the season at a time that coincides with peak seeding activity. We have both tried direct-seeding some cole crops in the spring, only to see the lovely, heart-shaped seed leaves transformed into fine green lace by flea beetles. Rarely do such chewed-up plants even get beyond the seed-leaf stage; they just gradually disappear. Four- to six-week-old transplants, however, can take a little chewing and still grow into healthy, productive plants.

A good way to grow your own cole seedlings is to use the compact plastic six-packs popular with commercial nurseries. They take up little space but still give your plants enough room to get off to a good start. Fill the depressions with a potting soil that's not overly rich in nitrogen. Too much nitrogen in the soil will prompt spindly, top-heavy growth, which makes the seedlings hard to transplant properly. Plants raised on a high-nitrogen diet also turn out to be less hardy. Put two seeds into each compartment (or other individual containers), thinning to the strongest seedling after they begin to grow. For speedy germination, place the containers in a warm place, up to 85°F. But as soon as the seeds have germinated, move them to a cooler place; cole crops germinate quickly in warm soil but do not grow very well in it. If possible, keep the air temperature no warmer than 68°F and no cooler than 45°F.

If you've ever tried direct seeding and have been discouraged by an onslaught of flea beetles, try mixing some turnip seed in with your cole crop seeds to act as a decoy crop. Flea beetles seem to prefer turnip leaves to those of cabbages. To compensate for losses due to hungry insects, plant three or four cole crop seeds in a group at the final spacing recommended for adult plants. Then, when the seedlings have grown, thin out each clump to leave the strongest plant.

If you take the safe route and start your plants indoors, when it comes time to transplant the seedlings don't be disturbed if their long, thin taproots are slightly damaged. While most tap-rooted plants are set back considerably if the root is injured during transplanting, this is not true for members of the cabbage family; their taproot eventually becomes a fibrous root system. Although their root system is fairly shallow, few roots grow in the first 2 inches of soil, so it is safe to cultivate cole crops lightly at any stage. While cabbage roots can extend as far as 78 inches deep, 70 to 80 percent of them are concentrated in the top 8 to 12 inches of the soil. The roots of cole crops seem to be less efficient than the roots of tomatoes or squash and need evenly moist soil to function at their best. Even though potatoes also have a fibrous root system, theirs is more efficient at water uptake, so they need less moisture than the cole crops. In the same garden, the tomatoes, squash, and potatoes may be thriving, while the cole crops are dying of thirst. Remember this, and keep an eye on them so they never get the chance to become water stressed.

Some Seed-Saving Pointers

If you want to save seed from your cole crops, you must be careful. As we mentioned before, all of them can cross-pollinate. As a further compli-

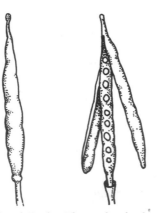

Cole Crop Seed Pods: *The seeds of cole crops develop
inside long, slender pods. The pod reaches its maximum
length three to four weeks after the flower has opened. When
mature, the pod's outer covering, which consists of two
valves, breaks away and opens upward to release the seeds.
Each pod contains from 10 to 30 seeds.*

cating factor, each flower on a plant must be pollinated by pollen from a
different plant. So, in order to get reliable seed that will produce plants of
the same type as the parents, you must have more than one plant of, say,
broccoli in bloom at one time but *no* other cole crops flowering at that time.
Any cole crops blooming within a quarter of a mile of yours are potential
pollinators, so even pollen from your neighbors' gardens can spoil your seed.
When one cole crop pollinates another, their offspring can be weird indeed.
When some friends of ours went on vacation a few years ago, some purple
cabbage which hadn't headed properly went to seed at the same time as the
overwintered kale in their garden. The cabbage seed heads shattered before
their return, so the next year, some tall, leafy red monsters cropped up
unexpectedly, looking like nothing they had ever seen before!

   If you do save your own seeds, wait until they turn brown inside the
yellowed pods before collecting them. Don't wait too long, though, or the
pods may shatter and scatter the seeds on the ground. If you can't pay close
attention, tie a square of cheesecloth over the seed head to catch the seeds
in case the pods shatter. If the seeds are at all wet when harvested, dry them
in a warm place. Cole crop seeds are especially sensitive to storage conditions.
All these crops have such small seeds that their stored food is easily broken
down under poor storage conditions. If they are kept in a warm, humid place,
they may not even last until the next spring. Stored at temperatures well
below freezing, however, these seeds may last more than ten years. The best

way to store them is to put them into a waterproof container with powdered milk or silica gel and set them in the freezer. *Do not* store kohlrabi this way, however; cold temperatures will vernalize the seed, and you will get bunches of yellow flowers instead of succulent stems!

General Problems with Cole Crops

While each cole crop has its own particular brand of problems, most pests and diseases are shared by the whole group. Perhaps the most annoying problem you'll have to deal with is the array of hungry green caterpillars such as the cabbage looper which may descend on your garden. While they will attack any and all cole crops, the caterpillars are more likely to bother some more than others. For some unknown reason, red cabbage is less popular with voracious caterpillars than green varieties. Broccoli is a favorite of caterpillars, but fortunately, it can thrive and provide you with an abundant harvest even while it's serving as a feeding ground for caterpillars. Luckily there are some very effective organic controls that can eliminate the caterpillar problem. You can handpick them, of course, if you're so inclined. Or, you can get the *Trichogramma* wasp to do the dirty work for you. These parasites lay their eggs on the caterpillar, and the wasp larvae kill the caterpillar by feeding on it until it dies. You can buy these wasps through your local organic nursery or through the mail from advertisements in gardening magazines.

One of the best, if not *the* best means of caterpillar control is a preparation made from the naturally occurring bacterium, *Bacillus thuringiensis* (BT for short). BT quite effectively turns the caterpillars into mushy dark brown blobs. It is sold under several different names; Biotrol, Dipel, and Thuricide are just some of the names you can ask for. You can also try the bug juice approach. Collect some caterpillars, grind them up in a blender (you probably would want to retire the blender from kitchen use after a session like this), and dilute the strained concoction to spray on your plants. Even with attempts at control, you'll probably end up with a few caterpillars hidden in the nooks and crannies of your broccoli and cauliflower. A twenty-minute soak in cold, salty water after harvesting should drive them out without affecting the flavor of your produce.

Clubroot is a fungal disease that attacks roots of all cole crops, rendering them unable to take up nutrients and water. It deforms the roots so that they take on an enlarged and club-shaped appearance. If your soil becomes infected with clubroot, keep the pH above 7.2 to help control it, and don't plant any cole crops in the affected area for at least two years. Any disease that affects one of these closely related plants can attack the others, so always consider them as a group when planning any crop rotation scheme.

After this brief introduction to the ABC's of cole crop culture, it's time to turn our attention to the particular needs of each of the individual crops.

Our Cabbage family profile will cover cabbage, kale, collards, Brussels sprouts, kohlrabi, cauliflower, and broccoli.

Cabbage

Cabbage is a very popular home garden crop and rightly so. It grows well during various seasons in different parts of the country and stores in good condition for a considerable time after harvest. But cabbage has a few quirks, and knowing something about them will help you grow the biggest, healthiest heads in your neighborhood.

We have already stated that all cole crops need a fertile, balanced soil right from the beginning. Because cabbage is a mass of leaves, you might be inclined to grow this crop in extremely nitrogen-rich soil. That would be a mistake. As we pointed out earlier, too little nitrogen can make for small, inferior heads. But the other extreme, too much, will cause its own problems. An excess of nitrogen will encourage rapid growth of the inner leaves. They will grow faster than the outer ones, resulting in a split head. Most gardens with plenty of organic matter in the soil will provide the correct amount of nitrogen. Just be careful not to tip the balance by making a massive infusion of nitrogen in the form of fresh poultry or rabbit manure right before planting your cabbage. One final word on good soil for cabbage; don't overlook the importance of potassium. An ample supply of this nutrient will encourage rigid, well-folded, and dense heads to form.

Early-maturing cabbages do better in light soils than do later varieties, which prefer heavy soils. Light-textured soil warms up more quickly than heavy soil, providing the conditions for rapid growth under cool spring conditions. You can even grow a successful crop in soil that is on the salty side, especially if you plant green varieties rather than red ones. Since saline soil tends to hinder the root growth of transplanted seedlings, plan to start your crop by direct seeding. (For more on salty soil, see the box, The Lowdown on Salty Soil, in chapter 5.)

One of the keys to successful cabbage growing is maintaining the proper soil moisture. Cabbage grown under water stress will have a strong, unpleasant flavor, and crops produced in soil which is always on the dry side will be significantly smaller than those grown in moist soils. But while cabbage roots need moist soil to function efficiently, sopping wet soil is just as bad as dry soil. Not only will a fully saturated soil discourage root growth into the deeper portions of the soil (there's no need to probe down deep for water), but it will also limit the nutrient uptake of the cabbage. In addition, soggy soil encourages bacterial and fungal diseases. As the final blow, if your soil is saturated with water, the size of the cabbage heads will be slightly reduced, and they will be late in maturing. The ideal to strive for in growing cabbage is to keep the soil moist but not wet.

Cabbage Varieties

Don't let the cabbages you usually see in the supermarket fool you into thinking that this vegetable comes in only two types: round and red or round and green. Once you start studying the seed catalogs, you'll discover that there are any number of colors, leaf types, shapes, sizes, and times to maturity available.

In terms of color, red varieties can range anywhere from nearly black (Black Diamond) to ruby red (Meteor). Green cabbages come in shades of blue-green to deep-green and almost white. With leaf types, you have your choice between the smooth-leaved varieties (either red or green) and the savoyed, or crinkly leaved varieties (green only). The leaves of savoy cabbages take on their distinctive puckery appearance because the veins grow much slower than the rest of the leaf. You can even select among various shapes; cabbages come in round, flat, or pointed heads. In general, the round and flat varieties tend to be bigger and denser, while the pointed varieties are on the small side. There's actually quite a range of sizes available; for example, in the category of round, green cabbages, you can grow the 2- to 3-pound Morden Dwarf or the 16-pound Jumbo!

Time to maturity is another factor you should consider in your selection. Cabbages are classified as being early, midseason, or late. Early varieties mature roughly between 60 to 80 days, midseason between 80 to 90 days, and late between 90 to 110 days. (All these dates to maturity are figured from the time seedlings are set out in the garden.) In general, late varieties are more subject to bolting.

If you plan on storing your cabbage harvest, it pays to check each variety's reputation in storage. Most smooth green cabbages store better than savoy or red cabbages. Storage varieties of green cabbage can be kept for months under the proper conditions (see Storing Cabbages later in this chapter). Red varieties tend to have the least storage potential.

The cold hardiness of cabbage depends a great deal on variety. For example, Meteor Red can take 15°F, while other red varieties are not very hardy at all. Some good overwintering varieties, such as April Monarch, are hardy only to 20°F, while others, like January King, can take 10°F. Late cabbages such as Late Flat Dutch and Danish Ballhead can be stored in the garden without harvesting as long as the temperature doesn't fall below 20°F. You usually can't go wrong with savoy cabbages, since they're the most cold resistant of all. If you plan to leave your cabbages in the garden rather than bringing them in as soon as the head is firm, you should note what your seed catalogs say about the varieties you plant. Look for phrases such as "stands well without bursting at maturity" or simply, "stands well." The inner leaves of such varieties are less likely to put enough pressure on the outer head to crack it.

Starting and Caring for Cabbage

Get your cabbage off to a good start by planting the seed only ¼ to ½ inch deep. It will germinate over the surprisingly wide range of 40° to 95°F, but germination takes a long time at the lower end of the range. At 50°F, germination takes around fourteen days, while at 68°F it takes only a week. Diane has had cabbage seeds emerge in four days at about 80°F in a very warm cold frame. Of course, she didn't keep them at that temperature once they were up. As soon as they germinated, she moved them to a cooler spot so that the roots would develop into a strong system and the tops would grow sturdy, not spindly.

When you transplant your seedlings, space them carefully. The closer you put them, the smaller the heads will be. The small-headed varieties can be placed as close as 15 inches, but larger types require 20 to 30 inches between plants, with 24 inches between rows. Cabbage spaced too closely will have a stronger flavor than plants that have enough room to spread out. And remember to keep your cabbages weeded or well mulched. You must be the most vigilant about weeding three to four weeks after germination when the plants are still very small. If you keep the weeds at bay while the plants are at this young, formative stage, they can outcompete weeds later when they are larger and sturdier. Since cabbages prefer cool, moist soil, mulching around the plants is the best way to meet their moisture and temperature needs and keep down weeds at the same time.

Winter Cabbage Cropping

Cabbage is a biennial plant, taking two years to set seed. The trigger for flowering is cold temperatures, generally below 40°F. But cabbages need to have reached a certain size before they will respond to cold temperatures; this is why cabbage can be grown during the winter in the South and produce an edible harvest. But to grow a winter crop of cabbage successfully, you must plant at the right time, not too early and not too late, to sidestep the plant's natural tendency to flower in response to cold temperatures. Cabbages whose stems are thicker than a pencil when exposed to low temperatures over a period of two to four weeks will bolt once the temperature warms up, and you'll end up with a harvest of seeds rather than an edible head. To avoid this disappointment, time your planting so that your cabbages won't be large enough to respond when cold weather hits. But you can't delay your planting too late either, for small plants won't be able to take the cold. Young cabbage plants can tolerate light frost, but the plants are much more cold-tolerant when they are half-grown and the temperature drops gradually. As we mentioned in our discussion of cabbage varieties earlier in this chapter, some varieties are more sensitive to cold than others.

Taking all these factors into consideration, you must carefully pick the variety for winter growing that will stand up best to the cooler temperatures, and then plant it at the right time. To help you in your selection, here are some hints on how certain varieties respond to fall planting. Pointed-head varieties generally bolt less readily than round-headed types. Late varieties such as Copenhagen Market are likely to bolt if planted in fall, while an early type such as Jersey Wakefield will produce a good crop as long as the planting is timed just right. For example, in California, Jersey Wakefield planted between mid August and mid September is likely to be big enough to respond when low winter temperatures hit and will bolt in the spring. But if you plant it in October, Jersey Wakefield is not likely to respond to winter weather by flowering, and you will get a nice crop of cabbage in the spring. Since each area of the country has its own set of conditions, you should contact your local extension agent to find out what cabbage varieties can be fall-planted in your area and when to plant them. In any area, the best months to grow cabbages are those in which the average temperature ranges from 59° to 68°F.

Bringing in the Cabbage Harvest

Cabbages can be harvested any time after they have headed. You can test the heads by lightly pushing on them to see if they are solid. A cabbage can look like a head from the outside but still be quite loose-leafed inside. If the head doesn't give when you push on it, that's the sign that it's ready for harvest. If you leave your mature cabbages in the garden, check them frequently for signs of cracking. If a head does break open, cut it and bring it inside right away. You should eat it or make it into sauerkraut as soon as possible, for it won't keep well, even in the refrigerator.

Sometimes your efforts to control cabbage worms fail, and the outside of your cabbages look pretty unappetizing. Don't just assume that the entire head is a loss, however. Cut off the head and keep cutting the outer leaves away; you are likely to end up with a tight central head which the caterpillars haven't penetrated.

If you're harvesting late in the season and are removing garden debris as you go, pull the entire cabbage plant, cut off the head, then discard the roots or add them to the compost pile. If you're harvesting an early spring-planted variety, you have the chance to grow a second crop of little cabbages before the fall frost arrives. To do this, simply cut off the head without pulling up the plant, and leave two or three large outer leaves attached to the stump. The axillary buds of those remaining leaves will grow, forming several small sprouts. Cut off all but one of these, and watch it develop a small second head. In order to coax a second crop to appear, you must maintain a fertile, balanced soil.

Storing Cabbages

For the longest-lasting cabbages that retain their color and nice firm texture, find a place to stash them that's as close as possible to the ideal conditions of 32°F and 90 to 95 percent humidity. Under these conditions, late cabbage can keep for as long as three or four months. Early varieties, however, will only last for three to six weeks. If you only have a few heads, you can clean and trim them and then store them in the refrigerator in plastic bags. If you've got a root cellar, you can wrap the individual heads in newspaper and store them there. Just be forewarned that cabbages have a strong odor which can easily taint your other foods.

Problems with Cabbages

Have you ever cut into a nice firm head of cabbage and found some brown leaves near the center? This problem is called internal tipburn and is due to insufficient calcium. However, the lack of calcium may not necessarily be due to deficiency in your soil but may result from the peculiar way a cabbage head grows. While many nutrients are stored in the outer cabbage leaves, not everything they need can be kept there. As we discussed in chapter 2, minerals from the soil are transferred from plants' roots to the leaves by way of the xylem. Water evaporating from the leaves produces the suction which pulls the sap from the roots into the rest of the plants. But in a cabbage head, the internal leaves are protected within the outer leaves. Water cannot evaporate from their surface, so they don't always get their share of minerals from the roots. If the cabbage is growing in moist soil where the humidity is high, the roots themselves produce enough pressure to force water and nutrients up into the head. But if the soil is dry, or the humidity, especially at night, is low, the root pressure is just not strong enough to move the minerals into the inner part of the head—setting the stage for internal tipburn.

There is a very simple way you can prevent internal tipburn or stop it if it's already started; just place a paper bag over the cabbage head at night to keep up the humidity. Of course, you should remove the bag during daylight hours. This paper bag trick, combined with an application of bone meal to correct any calcium deficiency in the soil, should solve your problem.

Growing Cabbage Seed

You can grow your own cabbage seed if your winters aren't too harsh. Plant your spring or summer crop a little later than you would for fresh use. Plant your winter crop earlier than you normally would, then let the plants overwinter in cool but not killing temperatures (lower than 40°F but above 11°F). Cabbages that are forming small heads at the time winter hits will be the most likely candidates to bolt the next spring. Half-grown plants with loose heads are much hardier than either young or old plants and can even tolerate temperatures close to 0°F, especially when they're mulched or covered with snow. If your climate provides you with several freeze-thaw cycles during the winter or if your plants are exposed to freezing temperatures without snow cover, be sure to mulch your seed cabbages well after the ground has frozen. Otherwise, their apical tips may be killed by the cold, and when this happens, they won't be able to bloom when spring arrives. In addition, alternate freezing and thawing of the ground can damage the roots and even kill your plants if they're not protected with a layer of mulch.

If you notice that the heads are tight in the spring, you might want to borrow a trick from commercial seed growers who make a cross-hatch about 2 inches deep in the top of the head with a knife to help the flower stalk emerge. Remember that in order to produce seed you will need at least two plants in bloom at the same time and that other cole crops in the vicinity should not be flowering at the same time. Harvest cabbage seeds while the pods are still yellow but the seeds have turned brown. If the pods are getting brittle, hold a paper bag under them as you break them off. This way, you're ready to catch any seeds from pods that pop open.

Cabbage Frontiers

Producing improved cabbages is a frustrating business, for very often a desirable trait is linked to a trait breeders would like to eliminate. This linkage of the good with the bad occurs to a greater degree in cabbages than in other crops. For example, size is linked to lateness; it is hard to get a cabbage which will grow quickly to a large size. Increasing the yield of storage cabbages per acre is also difficult, for varieties which produce heavily in a small area do not store well. A dark red color can't be produced in a very early cabbage, and firm heads of savoy cabbage can't be bred because the firmer the head, the smoother the leaves.

But breeders have met the challenges of working with cabbage. A number of varietal improvements have been made, and more are possible. Breeders are always working to get earlier varieties, more resistance to cracking, and very solid heads. Resistance to clubroot has been bred into some varieties of green and savoy cabbages, and resistance to fungal diseases such as downy mildew is also being developed.

Kale and Collards

Most people think of collards as a southern crop, fit for making a good "mess of greens." Kale, on the other hand, has reached some degree of popularity on both sides of the Mason-Dixon line. Both of these nutritious cole crops, however, deserve to be more widely grown throughout the country. They provide hefty amounts of vitamins A and C, calcium, iron, and even supply some protein.

Kale and collards are so closely related that they are botanically the same variety; the difference in appearance comes from the way they grow. While collards have fairly flat leaves, the leaf margins of kale grow faster than the rest of the leaf, giving a distinctive ruffle-edged look to the leaves. Collards start out looking like young cabbage plants, but instead of heading up, they just continue to produce more leaves as the stem elongates, rather like leaf lettuce. A collard plant can get to be 4 feet tall during a long growing season if the lower leaves are harvested as the plant grows. Because both these crops are so closely related, the growth requirements, cold hardiness, and other traits of these two crops are essentially the same. They also share a similar flavor, although there's just enough difference between the two that you can tell them apart.

Kale and Collards Varieties

There are quite a few varieties of kale, and kale connoisseurs argue about which ones have the best flavor. Because there is so much disagreement, we suspect that the taste of kale may depend quite a bit on the type of soil it is grown in. We'll avoid stepping into the fray by simply describing the growth habits of several popular varieties. Harvester is a short-stemmed plant very well suited to overwintering because its low, spreading growth makes it easy to mulch. Dwarf Siberian is an especially hardy variety which only grows 12 to 16 inches tall, but one plant can spread out to 36 inches in diameter! Other widely grown kale varieties include Dwarf Curled, Dwarf Blue Curled, and Dwarf Curled Scotch.

In contrast to kale, your selection of collards is limited because only a few varieties have been developed. Vates is especially tasty, vigorous, and winter-hardy. It grows to about 3 feet tall. Georgia has attractive blue-green leaves with white veins and can tolerate poor soil and extreme heat.

Growing Kale and Collards

Kale is often thought of exclusively as a cool-weather crop, but actually it will do well in any season. Since there are so many other crops which can only be grown in the summer, most gardeners restrict their kale-growing to the more marginal times of fall and early spring. Collards, too, will tolerate a wide range of temperatures. In Texas, collards can be planted in early spring along with turnips and again in the beginning of August for a fall crop. If kept well picked, the spring-planted collards will still be producing in fall.

Both of these cole crops can be grown on lighter soils than winter cabbages and will deliver a harvest even when grown on poor, nutrient-deficient soils that would spell the ruin of many plants. Too meager a soil, however, will show up as poorly flavored greens. For the best quality crop, you want to promote quick growth. This calls for a fertile soil, so you should work in plenty of well-rotted manure or compost before planting. Kale and collards are slightly more drought-resistant than cabbage but have the same inefficient, fibrous root system.

You can sow kale and collard seeds directly into the garden any time from early spring to early fall. The tender young thinnings are very tasty, either sauteed or raw, so you can sow your spring planting thickly and enjoy an early treat. Thick seeding will also help foil the hungry leaf-eating insects that are always hunting for greens early in the spring. Thin the rows so you end up with plants 12 to 18 inches apart in rows set 24 inches apart. If you aren't interested in thinnings, plant your seeds in clumps of three or four at intervals that correspond with the final spacing. Once the seedlings have emerged, thin each clump, leaving the sturdiest one standing.

Cultivate very lightly around your kale and collard plants, no deeper than an inch or two. Keep your patch of greens weed-free, so there's no chance that the weeds will gain the upper hand.

Tips on Harvesting
and Overwintering Kale and Collards

While tender spring thinnings of kale and collards are delicious and the fine greens are always welcome no matter what the season, the best-tasting harvest comes from plants that have been touched by frost. This fact probably accounts for their popularity primarily as fall crops. As the growing season draws to a close, you can ignore these plants while you are busy harvesting your tomatoes, peppers, and other frost-sensitive crops. Then, when these less hardy vegetables have been processed or stored, you can turn to your fresh kale and collards. At this point, you have several options. You can harvest the whole plants, clearing your garden for the winter. If you store them both just above freezing, they'll last for a few weeks. Or, you can leave the kale and collards in the garden, picking the leaves as you want them, effectively stretching the harvest out over a longer period. Both crops can withstand temperatures all the way down to 0°F. Just be sure to apply a mulch after the ground freezes as insurance against any freeze-thaw cycles; the mulch will keep the soil temperature from fluctuating wildly, thereby protecting the roots from damage. If the temperatures in your area go much below 0°F, bury the plants completely with loose leaves or hay to insulate them from the frigid air. When you want some fresh greens, even in the dead of winter, all you have to do is brush aside the protective covering and harvest what you want. Even if the leaves are frozen solid and stiff as a board, gather them anyway and just let them thaw out at room temperature before cooking.

Gardeners in the north can try overwintering a patch of relatively young plants for an extra-early harvest in the spring. To give them enough time to reach a winter hardy stage, be sure to plant kale or collards at least six weeks before the first hard frost is expected. Cover the young plants with a thick layer of mulch as soon as the ground freezes, just to be sure they'll survive the winter. When springtime temperatures are inching up enough to start thawing the ground, uncover the greens, so they can warm up and resume growing. Like cabbage, collards and kale will flower if exposed to temperatures below 40°F. However, before they flower, they will produce a much-appreciated harvest of fresh greens far ahead of any spring-planted crops.

Brussels Sprouts

Young Brussels sprouts plants look a lot like young cabbage plants, mainly because their first leaves have long petioles. As both plants grow, the new leaves develop with shorter and shorter petioles. But the Brussels sprouts plants never get around to heading like cabbage does. Instead, the internodes get a bit longer, and the axillary buds swell, forming the tasty "little cabbages." Like the axillary buds on other plants, those on Brussels sprouts are under the hormonal control of the apical bud at the top of the plant. The sprouts won't form until the top of the stem has stopped growing. How you can use this to your advantage will be discussed later in this chapter in the section, To Top or Not to Top? Like cabbage, Brussels sprouts are a biennial crop sensitive to cold temperatures. After making it through a cold winter, the plant will blossom with the main flower stalk coming out of the top of the stem.

Brussels Sprouts Varieties

In this country, seed catalogs rarely carry more than one or two varieties of Brussels sprouts, namely, Jade Cross Hybrid and Long Island Improved. Jade Cross is a medium-sized plant which does well wherever Brussels sprouts can be grown in the United States and Canada. If you plan to harvest your sprouts into late fall or winter, this is the variety to grow, for it is extremely cold-hardy. Long Island Improved matures later than Jade Cross and is not nearly as hardy. Despite the poor showing in most seed catalogs, there are actually many varieties of Brussels sprouts. These have been developed for different sorts of growing conditions in western Europe and are available to gardeners in North America through seed companies such as William Dam

Seeds, Limited (P.O. Box 8400, Dundas, Ontario, Canada L9H 6M1). The European varieties tend to be taller and require a long, cool growing season. This makes them best suited to mild coastal regions. Some of the European strains have been developed for growing on a specific type of soil, so be careful that whatever variety you buy is adapted to your soil. A variety developed for light soil will produce a short stem on heavy soil, while a variety intended for heavy soil will grow too fast on light soil, producing loose sprouts.

You might think that a tall plant would produce more sprouts than a short one, but this is not always true. The shorter-growing varieties often have shorter internodes, so the sprouts are packed tightly on the stem. This can lead to difficulties in harvesting, especially if you want to pick your sprouts bit by bit from the bottom up. Dorothy had particular trouble with one variety, Early Dwarf Danish. On her plants, the sprouts were wedged so close together that they were flattened in shape rather than round. Once she got them off the plants, though, they were delicious! The original Jade Cross strain also had sprouts that were close together. Breeders developed a new version, Jade Cross E, with longer internodes, making it easier to harvest. If you live in a short-season area, you are better off growing one of the shorter varieties, for the tall ones take longer to mature. But if you live in a mild climate and want to harvest gradually over a long period, then the taller varieties are the ones for you.

Growing and Harvesting Brussels Sprouts

The most important thing to remember about Brussels sprouts is that they grow best when the weather stays cool. If your summer daytime temperatures average 65°F or less, then you should be able to grow an outstanding crop. Gardeners in Florida, along the Gulf Coast, and throughout much of the Midwest are out of luck; these areas get too hot for Brussels sprouts to do well. Their outstanding cold-hardiness makes Brussels sprouts a good crop for northern gardeners, for they can harvest fresh vegetables from the garden well into the deep, dark days of winter.

Culture for this crop is much like that for cabbage, since Brussels sprouts have the same sort of root system. One thing you must watch out for, however, is a very rich or very peaty soil. Under these conditions, the plants may grow too quickly, forming loose bunches of leaves rather than nice tight sprouts. Your best bet is to start Brussels sprouts indoors as you would cabbage, for direct-seeded plants face the usual problems with flea beetles. When you set out your plants, place them about 2 feet apart in rows 2½ to 3 feet apart. If you leave more space than necessary between the plants, they will grow too fast and the sprouts will be too loose. In the case where you want to harvest all your sprouts at once, plant them a little closer together than we recommended above. This will delay lower sprout growth so that all the sprouts mature at the same time, and you can harvest them in one session.

When you actually plant your Brussels sprouts depends on the fall and winter conditions in your area. The best quality sprouts mature during cool fall weather, and a touch of frost enhances their sweet flavor. Sprouts that mature during warm weather are likely to be loose and not very sweet. One year Diane eagerly set out her Brussels sprouts seedlings in mid-April and had sprouts forming by mid-August. Unfortunately, August that year was exceptionally warm, and the loose sprouts were invaded by a discouraging assortment of insect pests which burrowed all the way inside, making the crop a total loss. She learned her lesson the hard way and now transplants her Brussels sprouts in late May or early June so that the sprouts form no earlier than late September or early October. Her garden usually gets hit by frost then, which makes the sprouts nice and sweet.

Brussels sprouts are said to be hardy down to 10°F. But from our experience, Jade Cross Hybrid and Dwarf Danish will actually survive much colder temperatures. Instead of harvesting our sprouts in the late fall, we mulch the plants with about a foot of leaves after the ground has frozen. The tops of the Jade Cross plants protrude above the mulch, but it doesn't seem to matter. One year, when winter temperatures here in Montana stayed above −15°F most of the time, Dorothy harvested overwintered Brussels sprouts for Easter dinner! Other years her family has eaten them fresh from the garden on Christmas Day. The only time winter weather completely ruined her sprout crop was when it dropped down to a very chilly −30°F. The plants were still green, but the sprouts were flabby once they thawed out and had an off flavor. The only other problem Dorothy has had with winter sprouts was directly attributable to a hungry wild rabbit who lived in the vicinity. When he began to graze across the tops of her sprouts, nibbling just a little bit off of each one, she had to venture out in the cold with saw in hand and cut down her frozen plants. Dorothy took them into the kitchen, let them thaw out, and then harvested her tender crop of sprouts. She chose to use her sprouts right away, but if she hadn't been able to, they would have kept in the refrigerator in fine shape for a few days.

If you don't trust your weather or don't like to blaze your way through the snow and cold to pick your Brussels sprouts, you can dig up the plants and transfer them (with plenty of soil around their roots) to a box in an unheated garage or deep cold frame. Water them lightly to keep the roots from drying out, and the sprouts will continue to mature.

In areas with mild winters, where frost arrives in late December or January, if at all, you can plant Brussels sprouts in the fall. With this timing, there will be sprouts forming when frosts begin. Brussels sprouts, like cabbages, will bolt after 40°F temperatures, so you can't expect them to form sprouts in the spring.

When you harvest your sprouts will dramatically affect their vitamin C content. If temperatures hover around freezing (31° to 33°F) right before harvesting, the vitamin C level will be at its peak. If temperatures have been below 31°F for two or three weeks prior to harvest, the vitamin C content will be lower. Temperatures above 33°F also can decrease vitamin C.

To Top or Not to Top?

Many garden books recommend cutting off the top rosette of leaves to encourage sprout formation, while others tell you only to remove the yellowing leaves between the lower sprouts. Once you understand what results you get from topping your plants, you can decide if it's the thing to do or not. As we pointed out in chapter 2, the apical tip of a plant produces a hormone which inhibits growth of the axillary buds found at the leaf bases. Brussels sprouts are no exception. The hormone, however, has its greatest effect closest to where it is produced. This is why the first sprouts to form are those near the bottom of the plant, since they're farthest from the apical tip. Plants that are not topped (meaning the apical tip is left intact) will produce a crop of sprouts gradually, starting at the bottom and working their way up the stem. These plants need picking several times as the sprouts mature. (If the lower sprouts are not picked, they can become overmature and loosen.) So, if you want to harvest your sprouts gradually over a long period of time, don't top your plants.

On the other hand, if you want to pick all your sprouts at once, cut off the very top rosette, including the apical tip, four to eight weeks before you want to harvest. This will stop hormone production, allowing all the axillary buds to grow into sprouts at the same rate. Topped plants that are left outside and not picked for a while will hold their crop better than untopped ones.

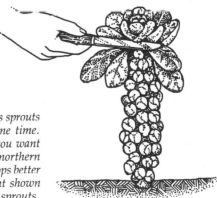

Topping Brussels Sprouts: *Topping your Brussels sprouts plants will allow you to harvest the crop all at one time. Cut off the top rosette four to eight weeks before you want to pick the sprouts. This is a good practice for northern gardeners, since topped plants usually hold their crops better than untopped ones. The middle leaves of the plant shown here have all been removed to expose the maturing sprouts.*

Northern gardeners who want to leave their sprouts outside, should pay heed to this and top their plants. In regions that have early frosts, topping will also increase the yield by allowing the top sprouts to fill out when they might not mature otherwise.

Topping can be done too early or too late, however, with bad results in both cases. If you top too early, you will decrease your final yield because the plants won't have enough leaves to feed the developing crop through photosynthesis. The other extreme, topping too late, can cause the lower sprouts to grow too big. The best time to top is right after the lower sprouts have begun to form.

On both topped and untopped plants, feel free to remove the older yellowed leaves from the lower parts of the plants. This will give the sprouts more room to grow and will make it easier to pick them when the time comes.

Kohlrabi

Kohlrabi certainly doesn't rank among the ten most popular home garden crops, and many gardeners aren't even quite sure what it looks like. This is a shame, for kohlrabi is ideal for gardens too small to accommodate cabbage. It is a very versatile vegetable that can be used as a substitute for expensive water chestnuts in Chinese dishes, as a crunchy salad addition, or as a steamed or sautéed side dish. The flavor of kohlrabi is milder than that of cabbage, so even if you are not a cabbage fan, you may become a kohlrabi lover.

The mature kohlrabi plant does look rather strange at first glance. The edible portion, the swollen, bulblike stem, sits squat on the soil, with a few rather spindly leaves radiating out from it. For all its homeliness, it is a delicious, easy-to-grow cole crop that really deserves a bigger fan club.

Kohlrabi Varieties

Until recently there were only two types of kohlrabi commonly offered to gardeners in North America: Early Purple Vienna and Early White Vienna. While these varieties are good, a newer and more reliable type called Grand Duke Hybrid is now available. In Europe, gardeners have a wider selection of varieties, some of which produce small early bulbs and others which form larger, later ones. (Note: European vegetable varieties are available from a number of companies, including Epicure Seeds, P.O. Box 23568, Rochester, NY 14692; Grace's Garden, 10 Bay St., Westport, CT 06880; J. A. Demonchaux Co., Inc., P.O. Box 8330, Topeka, KS 66608; Le Jardin du Gourmet, Box 248, West Danville, VT 05873; Nichols Garden Nursery, 1190 North Pacific Highway, Albany, OR 97321; Thompson and Morgan, Inc., P.O. Box 100, Farmingdale, NJ 07727; and William Dam Seeds, Ltd., address on page 103.)

Growing and Harvesting Kohlrabi

You should never plant kohlrabi seed outdoors if there's a chance that temperatures may dip below 40°F, for the seed will probably be vernalized, giving you little flowering plants instead of fat bulbing ones. You are better off waiting until average outdoor nighttime temperatures rise above 40°F. If that's not possible, then plant indoors at room temperature. Direct seeding of kohlrabi generally works better than transplanting, for the secret of success with this crop is steady, rapid growth. Transplanting can be enough of a shock to the plant's system that all it will manage to produce is a small, tough bulb. If you do start seeds indoors, follow these guidelines to lessen the shock: make sure that you use good potting soil which has no nutritional deficiencies; give each plant its own little pot or compartment; and do not let the seedlings become root bound before transplanting. Begin hardening off as early as possible and set out the plants in the garden while they are still small.

Whether you're sowing seed or transplanting, space your kohlrabi 4 inches apart in rows 15 to 18 inches apart. Never plant kohlrabi in a shady spot, for shade-grown plants produce long narrow bulbs instead of plump ones. Also, their flesh will not be as crisp as that of sun-grown plants.

You should be aware that early and late varieties of kohlrabi have different reactions to cold temperatures. Some early varieties will bolt whenever they are grown at low temperatures (even when they are young seedlings) without forming a bulb at all. However, these same plants usually won't bolt if the cold nights are offset by warm days. Late kohlrabi, on the other hand, is very similar to cabbage—only older plants are affected by cold temperatures (below 40°F). If late varieties are grown at low temperatures in their early stages of development, they won't bolt. Late kohlrabi plants that are ready to go to seed give a clue to their intentions by producing long, oval bulbs instead of round ones.

You can see that when you plant your kohlrabi depends a great deal on whether it is a late or an early variety. But most American seed catalogs just do not give this important information. From the names, it seems that the common Vienna varieties would both fit into the early category. Aside from guessing, about all you can do is write to the companies for information, ask other gardeners nearby what varieties they have grown successfully at which season, and just plain experiment. If you try one variety of kohlrabi and it doesn't work for you, don't give up! Another type might be just fine for your area.

If only one or two varieties are available to you and both of them bolt when planted in early spring, try planting them a bit later when nighttime temperatures are warmer. Although it is less heat-sensitive than some cole crops, kohlrabi does grow best when average daytime temperatures are no higher than 70°F. If the temperature soars above the 70-degree mark for a few hours each day, don't worry. But if the weather is consistently hot, be prepared for woody kohlrabi. Remember, the part you eat is the stem. The hotter the temperature, the more water the stem must transport from the roots to the leaves to keep them from wilting. During prolonged hot weather, the plant will develop more xylem tissue to transport water, and it is the transport tissues that form the woody part of any plant.

To avoid woody bulbs, harvest your kohlrabi while it is still young and tender, about 1½ to 2 inches in diameter. We have seen blue-ribbon kohlrabi at the county fair that was 4 to 5 inches across and still crisp and tender inside, but that is truly unusual.

Fortunately, kohlrabi keeps well in storage so you don't have to worry about it perishing before you can eat it all. The bulbs will keep for several weeks in a plastic bag in the refrigerator, or they can be stored alongside the cabbage in your root cellar. If you live where winters are cold, you can bury your kohlrabi bulbs in the ground and cover them with a thick layer of mulch to keep the ground from freezing. The coolness and moisture of the soil will keep them in good condition well into winter.

Cauliflower

Cauliflower is the prima donna of the Cabbage family. This crop is so sensitive to temperature, both hot and cold, that you can do everything right and still end up with little or no harvest. But if you are a persevering gardener who loves a challenge, the lure of those fat, tight, creamy white heads is worth the risk of frustration and disappointment.

Cauliflower grows like cabbage with the first leaves having long petioles. As the plant gets older, the leaves that form have shorter and shorter petioles until they attach directly to the thickening stem. When this happens, the plant is ready to form a head. The head is actually a giant cluster of fleshy flower buds. These are quite different from flowers as we think of them on other plants, and most of them would not actually develop into real flowers if the head went to seed. Often, only the buds on the edge of the head will ever bloom.

Cauliflower Varieties

Seed companies have perhaps shirked their duty to their customers more with cauliflower than with any other crop. Their catalogs should tell you honestly what conditions the varieties are suited to and what conditions might lead to problems. In the long run, these companies would benefit from such honesty. But it seems that they feel compelled to make each and every variety they sell sound like *the* perfect type for every garden. This attitude makes it very hard for you to pick a variety of cauliflower that will succeed in your area. Some varieties are very sensitive to hot weather and won't produce a head at all in the heat. Others react to cold weather by premature heading, giving you nothing but a tiny head, or button. Still other varieties are very susceptible to the condition known as riceyness, where the curd appears fuzzy and separated. The cause of riceyness is uneven growth of the tiny flower buds that make up the head. A whole gamut of environmental conditions can bring on riceyness in cauliflower, but again, different varieties rice under different conditions.

About all you can do to pick the right cauliflower varieties for your area is to look for the hints which sometimes appear in catalogs, such as "Relatively free of 'riceyness' in hot weather" (Johnny's Selected Seeds, Albion, ME 04910, 1982 catalog, Stovepipe variety); or "Avoid early spring planting which will result in bolting" (Johnny's Selected Seeds, 1982 catalog, Mini Snow variety). You can also ask your local extension agent and other experienced gardeners what their recommendations are. And finally, you can keep your own detailed record of what happens to the cauliflower you plant. Try to figure out why a particular type didn't work. Was the temperature high (or low) when the plant was ready to head? Did you have some cold nights while the plants were young? Some of the conditions you note may be normal ones for your area, but others may be unusual exceptions that do not occur in a "normal" year. (We must add here that we live in a place where there has not been a "normal" year for the past ten, at least, which makes picking cauliflower varieties rather interesting and challenging!)

Growing Cauliflower

Cauliflower is a bit touchy about germination. If you plant outside in soil that is 50°F, you may have to wait twenty days before the seedlings appear. On the other hand, at 68°F germination, little green nubbins should pop up in only six days. Seeding while the weather is still cold can also lead to another problem, called "blindness"; temperatures just above freezing can destroy the apical tip of some varieties, effectively stopping short any further growth of the plant. Once a young plant has more than seven leaves, it is resistant to blindness. If you have a short spring with frequent frosts, you can avoid any problems with germination or blindness by starting your cauliflower indoors or in a protected cold frame. If your area has a long, fairly frost-free spring, you can safely direct-seed cauliflower. In the South, where cauliflower is planted in the fall, it is important to start the plants early enough so that they will be past the seven-leaf stage by the time frosts may strike.

Like kohlrabi, cauliflower is very susceptible to checks in growth. The process of growing transplants, unless it's done very carefully, can shock the plant's system to the point where a nice, full, white head will never develop.

For this reason, you should give indoor-grown plants their own growing compartments and carefully tend them. Provide them with a cool room or unheated sun porch. When they're exposed to warm indoor temperatures they grow quickly, and then when they're greeted by cool outdoor temperatures after transplanting, they will most likely button. You can sidestep the buttoning response by growing your cauliflower seedlings in 57° to 68°F temperatures. Time your indoor seed sowing so that the seedlings can be planted out in the garden when they are four to six weeks old. Plants this young are still susceptible to blindness, so don't set them out when nighttime temperatures can still get close to freezing.

If you are buying plants at a nursery, pick those with long petioles on their leaves. Plants that have thick stems and short petioles are more likely to button when you plant them in your garden. They have probably been grown under cold temperatures (below 57°F) or crowded conditions. They may have gotten too little nitrogen, or they may just be too old. Also beware of cauliflower plants grown in an undivided flat rather than in individual compartments. When you cut the soil to separate these plants, their roots will be damaged. All it takes is a setback like that upon transplanting to shock your plants into buttoning.

If you decide to go ahead and seed your cauliflower directly into the garden, plant two to four seeds about ¼ inch deep in clusters 1½ to 2 feet apart. When the seedlings are up and growing, thin each cluster to leave the sturdiest one. You should thin by the time the seedlings have their fourth true leaves so that the roots of the plants you leave behind aren't disturbed.

Because cauliflower must grow evenly and rapidly for successful heading, plant it only after the weather has settled down (when there's little chance of frosts, rain, or cold, cloudy weather) and nights are not cold. Rapid, even growth also depends on rich, organic soil with lots of nitrogen, for cauliflower grown in soil with too little nitrogen will button. But an overdose of nitrogen can be a problem, too, since it can cause the plants to grow too fast and develop heads too slowly. These heads often have a loose curd that falls apart when cooked, and they may develop leaves inside the head. Cauliflower is also susceptible to soil deficiencies of the micronutrient molybdenum. The leaves will have narrow lower blades, and there won't be enough leaf to adequately cover the developing head. Plants with these symptoms are also likely to produce small heads. Ground limestone will add the necessary molybdenum and will correct an overly acid soil at the same time.

There are a few other soil conditions that can adversely affect your cauliflower crop. Young cauliflower is very sensitive to salty soil, so you must make sure that the potting soil you use to start your seeds as well as the soil in the garden doesn't have an excess of salt. Avoid using high-salt manures like poultry and steer manure as ingredients in your potting soil mix, and don't work them into the garden right before you plan to plant. Since manure teas can also be high in salt, you should use an alternative fertilizer like fish emulsion to avoid any problems. (For more information on salty soil, see the box in chapter 5, The Lowdown on Salty Soil.) Young cauliflower also has an aversion to acidic soil (pH lower than 6.5). Steer clear of using peat moss in potting mixes and as a soil enhancer in the garden, since it may create an unfavorably low pH level. In terms of texture, your garden soil should be on the heavy side for the best cauliflower heads to form. A light soil can dry out too easily, leading to buttoning. Cauliflower grown on light soils may also form a loose head after a sudden rise in temperature, something that doesn't happen as often on heavier soils. The time to check for excess salt, a low pH, and too heavy a soil are *before* you plant; once you expose your cauliflower plants to these conditions, you are undermining your chances of a successful crop.

Temperature and Heading

Cauliflower heads best when the daily temperature averages 57° to 68°F. Some varieties will form heads at temperatures above 77°F, but most do not. (If you are lucky, you may find a hint in a catalog such as: "Heads well in warm weather.") If temperatures have been right for heading and the process has begun, a shift to hot weather can inhibit head development, perhaps causing leaves to grow up between the curds. High temperatures can also cause the curd to loosen. If the weather is consistently hot, you may end up with no heads at all.

What Went Wrong?

Here's a checklist to help you figure out why the giant white cauliflower heads of your dreams failed to materialize in your garden.

Buttoning: A premature flowering of the plant. Buttoned plants have fewer and smaller leaves than normal and form small heads which soon flower.
   Conditions causing buttoning:
   - Growing temperature is too cold (generally below 40°F)
   - Soil is poor or low in nitrogen
   - Soil has excessive salt concentration which slows growth
   - Strong weed competition slows growth
   - Drought
Riceyness: The result of uneven growth of the flower buds in the head. The curd looks fuzzy and may separate.
   Conditions favoring riceyness:
   - Temperature is too high
   - Soil has too much nitrogen
   - Humidity is too high

Your climate will determine whether you'll have better luck growing a full, firm head of cauliflower in spring or fall. If you live in the South and are raising cauliflower during the fall or early winter, bear in mind that the temperature must be at least 42° to 44°F for the head to form. Most cauliflower can stand an occasional dip down to 28°F, but won't head after a 25°F night. The exception to this is the variety Snow Crown, which will survive a temperature of 20°F.

How to Harvest Snowy White Heads

Direct sunlight is the worst enemy a developing cauliflower head can have. If it's not protected from the sunlight, the sensitive head will turn brown and develop a strong flavor. Even varieties that are advertised as self-blanching quite frequently have to be covered up, although not as carefully as the standard varieties. There are several ways you can protect your developing cauliflowers from the sun. As soon as the curd is walnut-sized, you can pull up the leaves and tie a string around them near the top or hold them together with a clothespin. If you prefer, you can break the petioles of some of the larger leaves and just bend them over the top of the head to protect it.

Be sure to check the cauliflower every few days at first and then every day as it approaches maturity. As long as the head is still small and very compact, leave it be. But once the curd begins to loosen, you must cut the cauliflower no matter how big (or small!) it is, for the curd will only get looser. Ideally, you should be able to harvest your cauliflowers when they are about 6 to 8 inches across the top and still fairly compact. If you must transport the head for any distance, it is wise to cut some wrapper leaves along with it to protect the curd.

Storing Cauliflower

You can hold your harvested cauliflower heads in good condition for two to four weeks, as long as you keep them at 32°F and 95 percent humidity. A root cellar is the most likely spot to have this set of conditions. If you leave the heads in a plastic bag in your refrigerator, the keeping time is cut down to two weeks, and there's a good chance that the curds may turn brown. If this happens, don't throw the head away. Just lightly scrape away the brown portion leaving white curds. After scraping the head, you should cook it right away, or it will turn brown again.

Growing Cauliflower Seed

As you might suspect, growing cauliflower seed is a tricky business. Many of the buds never develop flowers, and the flowers that do form often are not fertile. Firm heads, the kind you would want to save seed from, bolt much more slowly than the undesirable loose heads. To get the best seed set, you should have dry and warm weather. If the head bolts unevenly and the part that's not flowering starts to rot, cut out the rotting portion. Because cauliflower is subject to uneven flower development, the seeds that form quite often do not ripen at the same time. When this happens, you must collect the seeds a few at a time, as you would cabbage seed.

Cauliflower Frontiers

From what you've just read in this section on cauliflower, you can see that there is lots of room for improvement! Breeders are trying to develop varieties that are not so sensitive to temperature fluctuations. Also, work is underway to perfect the self-blanching of heads by increasing the number of wrapper leaves; the self-blanching varieties available now don't really have enough leaves to completely cover the head and keep it from turning brown.

Broccoli

Broccoli is the second most popular cole crop in the United States after cabbage, but even so, little research has been done on its culture. However, now that it's becoming a more important commercial crop, more work is being done to understand its needs and to develop new varieties. Broccoli's popularity is well deserved; it is one of the most nutritious of all cole crops and other than cabbage, no cole crop can compete with broccoli in terms of ease of culture and amount of edible matter per plant. Broccoli leaves as well as heads make tasty eating, and you can harvest up to five leaves per plant without reducing your total yield of spears. The spears we eat are the undeveloped flower heads. After you cut the main head, broccoli plants will continue to give you a harvest of smaller, but equally delicious sideshoots. And when your plants are finished at the end of the season, you can eat the remaining leaves.

Broccoli Varieties

Broccoli varieties differ in how they head and in how long they will hold the head before flowering. Some types form very large initial heads followed by small sideshoots. Others form a small head and then larger sideshoots. It is up to you to decide whether you want a large initial harvest with less later on in the season or if you want a steadier yield of smaller pickings all along. We like to plant enough of the large heading type, such as Premium Crop, so we can harvest the large heads for freezing and then use the sideshoots for fresh eating during the rest of the season. Broccoli does have a premature heading stage similar to buttoning in cauliflower, but fortunately most varieties are not especially susceptible to it.

For a change of pace, you might want to consider growing purple broccoli. There are several varieties on the market, and their rich purple hue adds a nice touch of color to the garden. King Robert Purple produces a giant central head, while Christmas Purple Sprouting and Early Purple Sprouting produce a long succession of sideshoots with no central head ever forming. Purple broccoli tends to be both hardier and more heat-tolerant than the standard green type. Many gardeners contend that it is easier to grow because pests seem to leave it alone more so than green broccoli. While the color's different, the flavor is unmistakably that of broccoli. When you cook the purple heads or stalks, the purple color changes to emerald green, as if by magic.

Growing and Harvesting Broccoli

Like other cole crops, broccoli will germinate over a wide temperature range but comes up most quickly when the temperature is between 75° to 80°F. If your climate doesn't get extremely hot and if there is little variation between daytime and nighttime temperatures, you can sometimes get both a spring and fall broccoli crop. Start your spring crop in the house or greenhouse so the young plants aren't exposed to temperatures below 40°F. You can seed the fall crop directly in the garden in late spring. Set out your spring plants when the weather has warmed up and all chance of frost is past. The seedlings should be four to six weeks old when transplanted, and temperatures should for the most part stay above 40°F. At this time, a constant temperature below 40°F may cause the young plants to bolt. You must be especially careful with the varieties Waltham 29, Green Mountain, and Spartan Early; plants four weeks or older will head prematurely when exposed to 40°F. Three-week-old plants, however, are too young to respond to the cold. Like cabbage, very young broccoli plants of these particular varieties appear not to be cold sensitive.

Space broccoli plants about 2 feet apart in rows 2½ to 3 feet apart. If you crowd broccoli, the main head will be smaller, the stem may be hollow, and the crop will mature later. Broccoli needs a rich soil but not nearly as rich as cauliflower requires. Unlike cauliflower, broccoli is rather salt tolerant and can be grown on salty soils such as those found in the southwestern part of the country. Soil that is extremely high in nitrogen will give you broccoli with hollow stems. For the tenderest, most succulent spears, be sure your broccoli gets an even and adequate supply of water; water stress in the garden shows up as fibrous spears on the dinner table.

Broccoli heads best in cool weather. If it is very hot, the flower buds will open prematurely, creating a loose head. Once that happens, the head will be tougher and stronger in flavor than a nice tight one. Another drawback

More Broccoli to Come: *After the central stalk of the broccoli plant is cut off, the small side shoots waiting patiently in the axils of the leaves will develop as a second crop.*

is that these spears will not keep well in storage. The best temperature for heading is about 68°F. When you see your broccoli beginning to form a head in the middle of the plant, check it every day or two so you can harvest it at its peak. If the head begins to look loose, cut it right away even if it is small. A common complaint heard from beginning gardeners is that their broccoli plants never formed a head but flowered instead! Don't expect your broccoli heads to look just like the kind you see in the supermarket. With many garden varieties, the heads will be much smaller and will have shorter stems than the type you're accustomed to buying. Even if you harvest a small central head from your plant, don't be discouraged. You will still get many sideshoots as a secondary crop. If you forget about your broccoli and some flowers do develop, cut off the shoots right away so that more shoots will form later. Once you let the flowers go to seed, your plants are finished as far as an edible crop is concerned. But if you keep your broccoli picked, it will continue to produce well into the fall after other crops have been killed by frost. Several broccoli varieties are reliable producers once the cold temperatures settle in; Premium Crop can tolerate temperatures down to 15°F, while Italian Sprouting is hardy to a low of 10°F.

Unfortunately, broccoli has a short storage life. Even under the best conditions (just above freezing at 90 to 95 percent humidity) it will only retain its quality for two weeks. It isn't likely to last more than a week in the refrigerator.

If you're interested in saving seed and you've never done it before, broccoli is a good crop to start with. Since it's an annual, it will flower at the end of one season and needs no special treatment. Just let some sideshoots go to seed after you have harvested enough broccoli for the table and collect the seeds as you would those of cabbage.

Broccoli Frontiers

The unfortunate trend in broccoli breeding is toward varieties that form a huge central head so that commercial growers can get the most out of their single harvest. We hope that varieties which have a more modest-sized head followed by a good secondary crop of sideshoots will continue to be available to home gardeners. Breeders are also trying to develop varieties that will not bolt prematurely and that will hold a head for a longer time in the garden. The variety Northwest Waltham was developed from Waltham 29 in an effort to reduce premature bolting, and with luck, in the years to come, more varieties with this trait will be appearing on the market.

Chapter 7

Onions and Their Allies

Vital Statistics

Family:
  Amaryllidaceae
Species:
  Allium cepa (and other species)
Soil:
  Fertile, with plenty of organic
  matter; able to retain moisture well
pH:
  6.0–6.8
Soil Temperature for Germination:
  50°–85°F; 75°F, optimum

Air Temperature for Best Growth:
  70°–80°F
Seed Viability:
  2 years
Seed Germination:
  4–13 days
Seed Planting Depth:
  ¼–½"

Onions and their allies have been among our most valuable crops for over 5,000 years. The members of this interesting group have long been valued for a variety of purposes besides the obvious culinary one. People once wore garlic and onions around their necks to ward off vampires and evil spirits. Even today, many people swear by the medicinal properties of some Onion family members. For instance, there are those who claim that nothing cures the common cold quite like munching on a garlic clove. Others make a point to eat plenty of onions, in the belief that these vegetables can lower cholesterol levels and blood pressure. While onions are among the least expensive vegetables in the supermarket, they are also among the easiest and most interesting crops to grow. There is something very satisfying about watching those slim stalks fatten up almost right before your eyes! Some people, however, have had frustrating experiences trying to grow onions; their difficulties can almost always be traced to a lack of understanding of how this environmentally sensitive plant functions. The reasons behind what causes onions to   **117** bulb, why they sometimes rebel and send up a flower stalk instead of forming a fat bulb, and how proper curing and storing can extend your supply well into the winter all have to do with onion biology.

Besides the familiar bulbing onion, the Onion family includes such diverse members as chives, Egyptian onions, garlic, the Japanese bunching or Welsh onion, leeks, and shallots, to name a few. Most of these related plants (collectively known as "alliums" after their generic name) originated in the Orient. There are records of onions being cultivated in central Asia more than 5,000 years ago. As ancient people wandered the globe and moved into areas with different climates, they took their onions with them and selected types that would thrive in the new environments. This centuries-long process of selection is fortunate for us, because it resulted in such a wealth of onion varieties. Today's gardeners can be sure to find an onion that meets their needs, no matter what sort of growing conditions they have.

In order to grow these garden staples successfully, then, it is important to understand how different types of onions respond to environmental conditions so that you can choose varieties wisely. This chapter will give you all the basics you need to know to grow a successful crop of bulbing onions. It will also introduce you to some of the other alliums with which you might not be so familiar but which are equally delightful to grow (and to use!). These off-beat alliums include Egyptian onions, potato onions, ever-ready onions, shallots, garlic, elephant garlic, leeks, Japanese bunching onions, and regular and garlic chives.

How Onions Get Their Flavor

All onions derive their special flavor from organic sulfur compounds within their cells. These chemicals are released only when the cells are damaged, such as when the cook slices or chops the onion. Enzymes within the onion tissues are responsible for releasing the sulfur compounds. If you cook onions before cutting them, the heat destroys most of the enzymes, with the end result that the onion flavor is greatly reduced. For this reason, if you're planning on drying some onions, don't blanch them first, or the final product will have little flavor.

Those same sulfur compounds bring tears to your eyes as you cut up onions. They are set free by the knife as you slice into the onion. They drift through the air, coming in contact with the water in your eyes. There they dissolve to produce a weak, eye-irritating sulfuric acid solution. Your tear ducts automatically release tears to wash the acid away and there you are, crying over your onions. You can minimize this problem by using a very sharp knife which will disturb fewer onion cells as you slice than would a dull one. You can also peel and begin to cut up the onions in the sink under a trickle of cold water. When the onion is cold, less of the irritating chemicals are released, and the water carries much of the irritant away. A variation on this technique is to put the onions in the refrigerator long enough before you plan to use them so that they become thoroughly chilled—this method also cuts down on the amount of sulfur compounds they'll let loose.

The sole function of these sulfur compounds is not to annoy the chef but to act as antibacterial agents. Strong-flavored onions, which contain more sulfur compounds than mild ones, keep longer partially because they can fend off decay better. Breeders who have tried to develop sweet onions which store well have had little success, for as storage life increases, sweetness declines.

Bulb Onions

Bulb onions come in a wonderful variety of flavors and colors. There are red, white, and yellow onions that range in flavor from sweet and spicy to pungent and downright hot. Some onions keep for months in storage, while others must be savored within a few weeks of harvesting; otherwise they're likely to sprout or rot before you get to use them.

The pigments in the skin (properly called the scale) that give red and yellow onions their attractive colors also help to lengthen storage life, for they can prevent some of the fungal diseases that are common to onions. Smudge and neck rot disease occur mainly in white onions, for their skin lacks the protective pigments. If you happen to be growing white onions and notice that they are falling prey to one of these diseases, you might try mixing some yellow or red onion skins with water in a blender, straining the liquid, and spraying it on your white onion plants to see if it will check the fungus infection.

When you add diced, sautéed onions to your omelets or blend them into your favorite meat loaf, you probably don't realize that you're incorporating a reliable source of iron, calcium, potassium, and vitamin A into your meal. When you use bulbing onions in their immature form as green onions (or scallions), you're providing your family with almost twice as much iron, close to sixteen times more calcium, and one-third more potassium than an equal portion of corn supplies.

What Makes Onions Form Bulbs?

Depending on light and temperature, onions can do one of three things—bulb up, remain bulbless and stay scallions all season, or bolt and produce flowers. Most of the time you will want them to bulb up, so it is important to understand how light and temperature affect the plants. Daylength influences bulb formation, while temperature chiefly affects flowering.

Each onion variety will bulb only after it has been exposed to days of a particular critical length. One day of the critical length isn't enough to trigger bulbing in most varieties; an onion plant needs to be exposed to several weeks with days of the critical length before the bulb will start to develop. Some onions need short days to form bulbs while others need long days. If you live in the Deep South and plant a long-day variety such as Autumn Spice, chances are your onions will never bulb up, for such varieties, developed for northern growing, may require sixteen-hour days for bulbing. Southern day-lengths are never that long, and in fact, the longest day a southern gardener in, say, South Carolina could expect would be under fourteen hours. (Refer to the daylength map on page 41 to see how many hours of daylight there are in your particular area.) A northern gardener, on the other hand, would end up with tiny onions if he tried to grow a short-day variety such as Red Creole. The reason is that the plants would still be very small when they were triggered to bulb by the daylength signal. As a matter of fact, Red Creole can bulb up after producing only one tiny leaf if the daylength reaches the critical point! Because daylength plays such an important role in the success of the crop, southern gardeners should plant varieties that require only twelve- to fourteen-hour days for bulbing, while northerners should choose the longest-day varieties.

Temperature also plays a minor role in bulbing, for if it is especially cool, bulb formation may be delayed, even after the proper daylength is reached. Thanks to this phenomenon, high-altitude gardeners and those living in cool northern regions may find that they can grow short-day varieties after all. Cool temperatures delay bulbing, and the plants will be able to pour all their energy into developing good top growth before actually forming bulbs. High-altitude and cool-climate gardeners might have problems with long-day varieties, for bulbing could be delayed until it is too late for mature onions to develop before heavy frosts set in.

Scientists working in Ithaca, New York, have experimented with growing onions at different temperatures, with some interesting results. They planted the same variety under different growing temperatures; some grew at 70° to 80°F, others at 60° to 70°F, and still others at 50° to 60°F. The onions grown at the warmest temperatures had mature bulbs with dead tops at the end of the growing season, while those grown at the coolest temperatures had no mature bulbs at all. The plants grown at the intermediate temperature range had mature bulbs, but their tops were still green at the end of the season, which can lead to problems in storage. Although you certainly have no control over the temperature during the course of the growing season, at least you'll know what to expect at the end of a particularly warm or cool season.

A few other factors can also come into play to affect bulbing. Larger plants bulb up faster than smaller ones, which is why planting large onion sets will give you an earlier crop than will small sets. In general, plants grown from sets mature first, those from transplants second, and those from seeds last. Spacing also affects bulbing time—onions planted close together will mature earlier than those planted farther apart (but the onions will be smaller).

While different onion varieties vary greatly in their tendency to bolt, in general, once an onion plant has reached a critical size (which again depends on the particular variety), temperatures of 40° to 50°F will cause it to bolt and send up a flower stalk instead of form a bulb. This fact has important consequences for gardeners in both northern and southern areas. If you live in the North, you will want to plant your onions as early as possible so that the plants will be large when they reach the critical daylength for bulbing. But on the other hand, you won't want to plant too early, or a late spring cold snap could turn your onion patch into a flower garden! One year Dorothy confidently planted a northern variety, Autumn Spice, looking forward to fat storage onions in only 98 days. But instead of bulbing up nicely, almost all her plants went to seed instead. With the wisdom of hindsight, she realizes now that this variety is probably especially sensitive to cold temperatures and is not suitable for growing in Montana, where cold spring weather is unfortunately all too common.

Southern gardeners who overwinter their onions must plant late enough in the fall that the plants do not get bigger than about ¼ inch in diameter before the onset of cool winter temperatures, or their crop may bolt come spring.

Bulb Onion Varieties

Unfortunately, few seed catalogs give the information you need to know to choose the right onion varieties for your region. If you buy from a small regional supplier such as Johnny's Selected Seeds (who specializes in vegetable varieties for the North), you can be fairly confident that the onions you select are adapted to your area. But if you buy from a national supplier, you will need more to go on to make a wise choice. Unfortunately, much of the information given in catalogs is just about useless. For example, one catalog says that a particular variety is "slow to bolt in unfavorable weather," a phrase that leaves you wondering what "unfavorable" means. You could guess that it meant too cold, but it would be just a guess. On the other hand, George W. Park Seed Co., Inc., and Herbst Brothers Seedsmen, Inc., identify their onions as long-day or short-day (called "tropical" in the Herbst catalog) varieties. Consult the table, A Sampling of Bulb Onion Varieties, to find some varieties which are suitable to your climate. If you need more information, you might try writing to your favorite seed company requesting information on the daylength requirement for bulbing, bolting temperature, and days to maturity for the varieties that interest you. Maybe if enough customers ask for such data, more seed companies will include them in their catalogs.

As with so many other crops, your own records can be your best guide to choosing onion varieties. If you plant a variety that never gets around to
(Continued on page 124)

A Sampling of Bulb Onion Varieties

Variety Name	Average Days to Maturity	Characteristics
Northern (long-day) Onions		
Autumn Spice	92	Medium-sized bulb with hard flesh and strong flavor; excellent for northern areas; a good keeper.
Downing Yellow Globe	105	Most widely grown northern onion for storage; large, chunky bulbs; good in short-season areas.
Early Yellow Globe	100	Popular in the Northeast; nice medium-sized cooking onion with strong flavor; stores well.
Ebenezer	105	Widely grown for sets by commercial growers and home gardeners because it resists bolting and stores well; white and yellow varieties available.
Elite	110	Tall, globe-shaped bulb; pungent flavor; stores well.
Southport Red Globe	105	Round bulbs with purple-red skin and pinkish flesh; pungent flavor; stores well.
Southport Yellow Globe	115	Medium-sized bulbs with excellent flavor.
Sweet Spanish (also known as Yellow Utah)	120	Mild, sweet onion with large bulbs; good for fresh eating; does not store well.
Southern (short-day) Onions		
Creole C-5	110	Large red onion that performs well under hot, humid conditions; excellent keeping qualities.

A Sampling of Bulb Onion Varieties—*Continued*

Variety Name	Average Days to Maturity	Characteristics
Southern (short-day) Onions (*continued*)		
Crystal Wax	95	Mild-flavored onion that seldom bolts; does not store well; makes good pickling onions when closely planted.
Excel 986	180	Sweet, mild-tasting Bermuda type; excellent keeper.
Granex	162	Popular in the Deep South; large, round onion with mild, sweet flavor; stores well if hung to dry in an area with good air circulation.
Red Bermuda	93	Crisp texture with mild flavor; large, flat bulbs have red skins; outstanding quality when used fresh.
Red Creole	170	Small- to medium-sized, pungent bulbs are resistant to thrips; susceptible to bolting; stores moderately well.
Texas Early Grano 502	168	Excellent for fall planting; exhibits some resistance to thrips; mild flavored but doesn't store well; not susceptible to bolting.
Japanese Winter Onions		
Late Sprouting Yellow	—	Smooth, round, yellow bulbs keep well in storage; suited for mild winter areas.
Winter Onion OWY 171	270	Large, flat, round, yellow onions; very hardy; has produced a crop after exposure to −16°F without snow cover.

forming bulbs, you can surmise that either your climate is too cool for it or the daylength wasn't long enough to trigger it to bulb. A variety that bolts when planted from seed is probably too sensitive to cold spring weather for your area, unless you planted especially early or had an abnormally cool spring. If your plants bulb up prematurely and you end up with too many small onions that can only be used for stew, you will know that you must either scrap that variety in favor of another or plant it earlier so that the plants have a chance to grow larger before bulbing.

You must also take storage life into consideration when choosing onion varieties. While the Spanish types are wonderfully mild and sweet, they generally do not keep very well, so you will probably want to plant some better keepers along with them to get you through the winter. Storage onions generally have firmer bulbs, with more protective skin around them, than do the milder, more quick-to-perish types. Most seed catalogs are better about describing eating and keeping qualities of onions than they are at giving daylength and temperature requirements, so you'll have an easier time selecting varieties based on how you want to use the final crop.

Several varieties of a new type of bulbing onion have recently become available in North America—these are the Japanese winter onions, popular in Europe and Asia. Seeds of these onions are planted in mid-August and the plants are mulched during the winter for harvest the following June. Mainly suited for northern gardeners, Japanese winter onions fill the gap between crops of standard bulbing onions, and they keep well for several weeks in storage. At this time, only Johnny's Selected Seeds and William Dam Seeds offer them.

Bulb Onions: *Bulb onions come in a vast array of sizes and shapes, from elongated cylinders for slicing to fat, round globes for a variety of uses.*

Planting the Onion Crop

Onions are a versatile crop, for they offer you the choice of starting them from sets, transplants, or seeds. While all these methods work well, there are various advantages and disadvantages associated with each that we'll examine in detail.

Onions from Sets

Onion sets are really just miniature onions which were grown under crowded conditions so that they formed bulbs while the plants were still small. Growing your onions from sets will give you quicker results than growing them from seed, and sets are a lot easier to plant and care for than seeds. You have the option of placing them in the ground at their final growing distance if you like, or you can plant them closer together and use the thinnings as scallions.

Unfortunately, there is one rather serious problem with growing onions from sets. If the sets are larger than ½ inch in diameter and have been stored at temperatures of 40° or 50°F, most of the resulting plants will bolt instead of producing the big, firm bulbs you're after. In our own gardens, some years we've gotten beautiful onions from sets, but other years we've ended up with nothing but flowers. Diane especially remembers the time she carefully picked out all of the biggest sets from the bins in the gardening store, congratulating herself all the while on how big her onions would be since they started out as such large sets. What a disappointment it was when almost the entire crop bolted!

Onion sets should be stored either at just above freezing (33°F) or above 65°F, but never in between (which is probably the treatment Diane's eager-to-bolt sets received). There is no way of knowing if sets you purchase have been stored properly or not. All you can do is buy from a reputable dealer and store the sets at the correct temperature after you bring them home. If you can pick out sets individually, choose small ones if you don't know how the sets were stored. It is true though, that the bigger the set the bigger the resulting onion will be, so if you *are* absolutely certain that the sets were properly stored, pick out large ones instead to harvest the fattest, fastest-maturing bulbs.

Onion sets present another problem as well, in that they are often sold simply as "white," "yellow," or "red" onions with no mention of the variety, much less of daylength requirements or bolting temperatures. These caveats aside, however, onion sets generally produce good storage onions—after all, the sets themselves had to survive the winter without rotting or sprouting. Most of the onion sets sold in the United States are grown in the Chicago area and, by necessity, are long-day varieties. Those of you in the South will have trouble getting harvestable bulbs from these plants. If you can find sets that were grown in your own area, you will have better luck.

To sum up, while growing onions from sets is a good idea and is certainly the easiest way to go, be mindful of all their problems and pitfalls. Until you can find a reliable source of sets, don't count on them to provide your entire onion supply. Once you know which varieties will grow well in your own area, you can grow your own sets and store them properly to guarantee an abundant harvest.

There's no trick to growing your own onion sets. Some varieties (Stuttgarter, Ebenezer White, and Ebenezer Yellow, for example) are available to home gardeners as seeds and are especially well adapted for growing sets. You might want to try one of these the first time around. You can sow the seeds at the same time you plant the bulk of your onion crop intended for eating. Plant the seeds in a small area, spaced ¼ inch apart so that the resulting bulbs will be small. Make sure they get plenty of water, for the crowded plants will use up water faster than plants that are more widely spaced. Once the plants have bulbed and the tops start to fall down, push over the remaining tops. When the greens have withered, dig up the little bulbs and let them dry outdoors in a warm, shady spot. If you have a spare window screen handy, elevate it on a couple bricks, and you've got yourself a handy rack for drying sets that allows air to circulate freely around all their surfaces. Let the sets dry until their skins are crackly, and the roots have completely dried and withered. Then gather them up and store them either above 65°F with some humidity (not over 65 percent, however) or at just above 32°F. Be aware that the higher temperature can result in excessive loss of moisture from the sets, rendering them useless in the garden.

When planting time rolls around, remember which end is up. Orient the sets with the root end down and the top up, and position them so that the top is close to the surface of the soil, between ½ to 1 inch deep, depending on the size of each set.

Onions from Transplants

Onion seedlings for transplanting can be bought through the mail and are sometimes available in gardening stores. They are generally quite expensive, and often are not identified by variety. As is frequently the case with sets, you won't know if you are buying onions which have the proper day-length requirements for your area. Dorothy once bought through the mail some plants called "Texas Sweeties" and wondered whether the name was any indication that they were a short-day variety. Apparently the appellation "Texas" only meant that the plants were grown in that state, for they flourished and bulbed just fine here in Montana. If a gardener living further south had bought the same plants, they might never have bulbed up! This episode points out that when onion plants don't carry a varietal name, you are taking a chance when you buy them.

There are also other drawbacks to purchasing seedlings. Plants that you buy have been out of the light and soil for at least several days by the time you get them. And you don't know what sort of conditions they were grown under, either. For these reasons, such plants are bound to be handicapped considerably no matter how carefully you plant them.

Actually, there's no need to rely on commercial sources since growing your own onion plants for transplanting is easy. And when you grow them yourself, you know for sure that the variety is appropriate, you know what growing conditions they experienced, and you can avoid the worst shocks to the transplants when you set them out. Start your onions about six weeks before you plan to plant them outside. Sow the seeds thickly in rows or clumps, or scatter them all over the flat or other planting container. We have found that a milk carton laid on its side and cut in half provides plenty of space for a sizeable crop of transplants. Plant the seeds ¼ to ½ inch deep. Be sure to keep the soil damp until the seedlings emerge, which should take about five to ten days at room temperature. At the optimum temperature, 75°F, germination may take as little as four days

Once the seeds have sprouted, the best place to grow your seedlings is outside in a cold frame or on an unheated sunporch (where they are protected from frost), if possible. Just be careful about exposing your plants to cold temperatures if you are growing a variety like Red Creole, which tends to bolt after a bout with low temperatures. The advantage of growing onions in a cold frame or other bright, cool location is that they will need no hardening off beyond the usual decrease in watering. Also, they will grow slowly into sturdy plants that are well equipped to take up life outdoors in the garden. Onions raised inside at higher temperatures will grow more quickly, but into skinny, weak plants that will need an extensive period of hardening off in order to adjust gradually to the cooler outdoor temperatures. If you have no other choice but to grow onion seedlings indoors, be sure they get lots of light. In the absence of sunny south-facing windows, be sure to supplement the sunlight they do get with fluorescent light. You must remember, however, to turn off the fluorescent fixture when the sun goes down; if you give your baby onion plants (particularly if they happen to be long-day types) too many hours of light, they will be triggered to form bulbs even though they are very tiny. And once an onion plant begins to bulb up, it stops producing new leaves, the number of roots actually declines, and you are stuck with baby onions in June.

Many gardening books recommend trimming the roots and/or tops of onion plants just before transplanting. This is often necessary with purchased transplants, for the ends of their roots have been damaged, and their tops must be cut back to compensate for the lack of adequate roots. With home-grown plants, however you're better off just separating them carefully and placing them 4 to 6 inches apart in shallow furrows about 2 inches deep. Finish the transplanting by quickly pushing dirt around their roots and watering them immediately. This procedure will minimize transplant shock so that your plants' growth is checked as little as possible. Don't forget that because onions run on an inner clock that is set to daylength, you want them to grow as fast as possible in order to produce the plumpest bulbs.

Onions from Seeds

Onion seeds are especially perishable; if they are kept in warm, moist air they can lose their ability to germinate in less than a year. For this reason, most authorities recommend against saving leftover onion seed. But if you take the special precautions for storing seeds described in chapter 1, you may be able to keep onion seeds viable for two years or even longer. Scientists have kept onion seeds viable under very dry conditions (around 6 percent humidity) for as long as nine years. As with any seeds you store, you should run a germination test before planting to see if it is safe to rely on your stored onion seeds. When using old seeds, you also run the risk of planting seeds whose food reserves are less than adequate, and the result will be weakened plants that can produce only small bulbs.

Since onion seeds are so small, you should plant them no deeper than ½ inch in the garden. Keep the soil moist, so the seeds won't dry out and so the soil won't crust over; once a hard layer forms, the delicate seedlings have a hard time breaking through. This may require some inventiveness and special care if you live in an area where wind tends to dry out the soil. One method that buffers the effects of the wind is to prepare a seedbed that is depressed about an inch from the level of the surrounding soil. Sprinkle the seeds on top and cover them with ¼ inch of a fine-textured mulch such as premoistened peat moss, grass clippings, or some of your own compost pressed through a sieve. The final spacing of your plants should be 4 to 6 inches apart; but you may want to seed quite a bit more thickly to provide yourself with some fresh green onions during the growing season.

Onion seed will germinate over a wide range of temperatures, from 50° to 85°F, with best results obtained at 75°F. If your garden soil is cool, it may take as long as two weeks for the seeds to germinate; try not to grow too impatient and remember to keep the soil uniformly moist until those tiny plants appear.

How an Onion Grows

Whether you start your onions from seeds, transplants, or sets, it will help you a great deal to understand something about the process by which onions grow and mature.

When onions germinate, they look very different from plants like cabbage, peppers or tomatoes. That's because onions are monocots and have

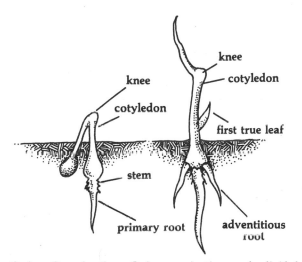

Onion Germination: *Onion germination can be divided into two main stages, the knee stage and the flag stage. In the knee stage (left), the cotyledon grows toward the surface of the soil in the shape of a loop. A knee formed at the bend of the loop is the first part to break through the soil. In the flag stage (right), the loop has straightened out, and the first true leaf can be seen next to the cotyledon.*

only one cotyledon, while the others are dicots, with two cotyledons. When the onion root pushes out of the seed coat, the cotyledon starts to grow through the soil toward the surface. It forms a loop that onion growers have dubbed the "knee." This is the part that breaks through the soil, so the first sign that your onions are on their way is a row of tiny green loops. The loops continue to grow until they are 2 to 3 inches tall. By that point, the old seed coat, which is still attached to the tip of the cotyledon, has been pulled out of the ground. Growth between the old seed and the knee has stopped, while the area from the knee to the stem continues to grow. At this stage the loop begins to straighten out so the little plant looks like a flag. During the flag stage you can see the first true leaf growing alongside the cotyledon.

The onion plant is put together very differently from a dicot. While most familiar garden crops have a recognizable stem that supports the plant and holds the leaves up into the sunlight, the onion plant has hardly any stem at all. The onion stem is the thick woody area just above the roots which you cut away when you are chopping or slicing an onion in the kitchen. Even in a full-grown onion, the stem is no more than ¾ inch wide and ½ inch tall.

The onion leaves arise from this stem area and grow straight up. When compared to other common plants, onion leaves also have a rather peculiar shape. Each leaf is like a hollow tube at its base; the new leaves grow up

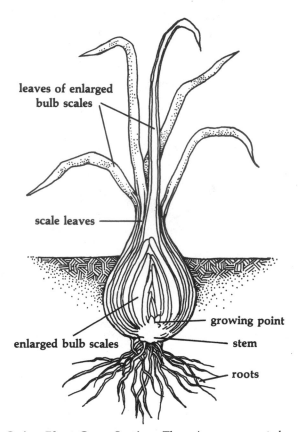

leaves of enlarged
bulb scales

scale leaves

growing point

enlarged bulb scales

stem

roots

Onion Plant Cross Section: *The onion, a monocot, has a very small stem located just above the roots from which all the leaves arise. The mature bulb is simply a collection of fattened leaves.*

through the tube formed by the overlapping bases of the older leaves. Only one side of each leaf actually grows upward to form the hollow, green spike we recognize as a leaf. The rest of the leaf stays put, firmly encircling the newer leaves that emerge from inside its hollow core. As the plant grows, these leaf bases become longer and longer, creating a structure that looks like a stem but is properly called the "neck" of the plant. The neck is not a stem at all but is merely a conglomerate of all the leaf bases and growing leaves inside them.

The process of bulb formation gets underway when some of the leaf bases start to thicken. The first thickened bases send up fresh, green leaves, but soon the thickening bases put all their energy into becoming part of the bulb and do not send up blades at all. The end result is that these thick, tubular leaf bases become the rings of the mature onion. This may be the first time you've realized that the onion bulb is not a tuber or a root at all but is actually a collection of fattened leaves!

If you take one of your onions out of storage and cut it in half down the middle from top to root, you'll be able to see that the rings are really short, fat leaves growing up from the small stem. The dry scales covering the outside of the onion are the oldest three or four leaf bases which never thickened and have dried into a protective covering for the bulb. The next three to five leaves have thick bases and also leaf blades which form the neck of the onion. Nestled inside these are leaves which consist only of thickened bases. At the very center are the youngest and smallest leaves, which can sprout and grow through the top of the bulb during storage.

When an onion is mature, the inner leaves are no longer producing blades. The resulting hollow center in the neck weakens it, and the top begins to bend over, signalling that the onion is reaching maturity. When an onion bolts and forms a flower stalk, the stem grows right up through the neck, forming a tough, fibrous tube that pierces the center of the bulb. The plant channels all its energy into this flower stalk, so no more fleshy leaf bases are being formed. This means that the bulb does not increase in size, and in fact, it may actually shrink a bit, for the stored food in the bulb may be used to build the flower stalk. There's no need to write off onions which are going to seed as a total loss. If you don't want to save the seed for next year's crop, you can still make use of these onions in the kitchen. There'll be no decline in flavor; the bulbs just won't be very big, and you must cut the tough stalk out of the center before using them.

Occasionally, onions form double bulbs. One explanation for this growth abnormality is that the center of the bulb may have been damaged in some way, causing it to split and form two lateral buds instead of one central stem. For some reason, double bulbs also often result from larger onion sets. Dorothy inadvertently raised a crop of double bulbs a few years ago when she planted some red onion sets. As a further twist in their curious development, one of the buds resulted in a flower stalk while the other produced a nice (if small) red onion.

Onion Roots and the Soil

You'll get the best crop of onions when you provide the conditions they need to grow well, and in order to do that, you must first understand how onion roots grow. The onion seedling produces only one primary root; all the other roots are secondary ones which grow directly from the stem. Each secondary root has a short life span, and new ones are constantly growing to replace those that die. For the new roots to form, the soil must be moist.

Onion roots do not branch much and are generally confined to a 6-inch area around the bulb. In addition, they rarely descend deeper than 10 inches into the soil, so keeping the ground moist enough for onions can be a challenge during hot, dry weather. Onions grown under water stress are generally stronger in flavor and smaller in size than those which have received enough water, so it's important to be sure your onions get enough moisture.

Onions do best in a fertile soil with lots of organic matter. A heavy clay soil that becomes waterlogged is not conducive to healthy growth, and a sandy soil will require such frequent watering that you will probably leach out the nutrients necessary to fuel the fast, even growth that leads to large bulbs.

To provide the moist, rich soil onions need, dig some compost or well-rotted manure right into the rows where you will be planting. Since onion roots do not extend very far, this localized treatment will be very effective. Because onions do very poorly in salty soil, avoid using large quantities of poultry manure. Onions grow best in soil that is not too acid (pH 6.0 to 6.8 is the ideal range). If you must sweeten your soil to bring it within the proper range, use wood ashes; they will also add valuable potassium. Sprinkle some of the ashes around the bases of your onion plants, too, where they will discourage the onion maggot fly from laying its eggs.

Although onions need rich soil, too much nitrogen can delay bulbing. So, if you plan to enrich your soil with fresh manure, do it in the fall if you plant your onions in the spring or in spring if you plant in fall. Be sure your soil has adequate phosphorus, for a deficiency can result in onions that have thick necks and a short storage life. Sometimes a potassium deficiency also produces thick necks. If the oldest leaves are yellowing and their tips are turning brown, dig some wood ashes in around your onions to give them a potassium boost. Although nutrient deficiencies are a distinct threat to the health and well-being of your onion crop, these plants do have something of a built-in support system. As we mentioned in chapter 2, the roots of some plants form beneficial associations with fungi. Onions are among these plants; their roots can afford to be on the skimpy side for they cooperate with fungi which help them extract phosphorus and sulfur more efficiently from the soil.

Beware of Weed Competition

You really have to watch out for weeds in the onion patch. Your tiny onion plants are in very rich soil, yet they grow slowly at first. Because their leaves grow straight upward, they produce practically no weed-inhibiting shade. These two particular growth habits account for the fact that weeds can quickly engulf your young onion plants. You must fend off the onslaught by keeping them well weeded, especially while they are tiny. Seedlings at the flag stage are especially susceptible to weed competition, for it is at this time that the first true leaf is unfolding. If weeds run rampant and crowd your onion seedlings, their growth will be slowed and you will end up with small bulbs. In an experiment designed to gauge just how much growth is slowed, a scientist at the University of Philippines, College of Agriculture let the weeds in an onion patch grow unchecked during the first seven and one-half weeks of seedling growth. All he got were very tiny bulblets. Not only did the weeds crowd and shade the onions, but they took up so many of the nutrients from the soil that the weak onion roots were nutrient-stressed. The moral of the story is, if you want big onion bulbs, keep your patch weeded for at least the first two months of growth.

The best plan of attack is to pay frequent visits to the garden so that you can get to the weeds before their roots have spread very far. If you wait too long and the weeds are fairly well established, the shallow onion roots are more likely to be disturbed when you finally get around to weeding. You'll also disturb them less if you weed your onion patch only when the soil is moist. One of Dorothy's tricks when she finds weeds growing close to her small onion plants is to use a screwdriver to take out the weeds. She gently presses the end of the screwdriver into the soil next to the weed on the side farthest from any onion plants, then gingerly pulls out the weed. Mulch is a good ally to call upon to help keep down weeds, but you should wait until the soil is warm before applying it. Remember also to keep thinning the onions regularly and use the fresh green scallions in your kitchen; an overcrowded onion patch will have the same problems as a weedy one.

Harvesting Bulb Onions

When the tops of your onions begin to fall over, that's your cue that they have finished growing and are into the very last stages of bulbing up. At this time you should stop watering them. There's a very good reason for this; as the bulbs reach the final phase of the maturation process, nutrients from the leaves are being transferred into them. If the leaves are wet while they are dying down, fungi or bacteria can invade and be transferred into the bulbs, infecting them. As if that weren't bad enough, wet bulbs just won't cure properly.

When at least 25 percent of the tops have fallen over, you can speed up the drying process by pushing the rest over. After the tops fall, nutrients from the leaves move into the bulb and increase its weight. This process stops when the leaves die and turn brown. If you push down the tops too early, while the leaves are still growing, you will be interfering with the natural sequence of events leading to the dormant dry bulb, and your onions will sprout sooner in storage than properly matured ones. Onions which haven't matured properly will also have thick, moist necks instead of narrow, dry ones. The damp necks are a perfect breeding ground for fungi and bacteria, and the onions will be very likely to rot in storage.

You must not let your onions sit in the field too long or they can become overmature. Another danger after the tops fall over is that the upper portion of the bulbs may be exposed to too much sun. They can become sunburned and lose their protective outer scales, and thus be more susceptible to disease and early sprouting. You have probably seen sunburned onions at one time or another; they're easy to spot with shrivelled-up circular areas on the outermost thickened leaf bases. Diane, unfortunately, has seen all too many onions with this affliction. One summer she was so busy harvesting other crops that she left her white onions in the rows too long. By the time she got to them, they were already sunburned, and they began to spoil soon after harvesting.

Once the onions have started to dry and their tops have withered, you can lift the bulbs. The time that lapses between pushing the tops over and digging up the bulbs really depends on environmental conditions; with a spell of warm, dry weather, the bulbs can be ready to dig within two days. The next step is to cure them. Curing is simply the process of drying the onions evenly so that no moist sites remain which would be susceptible to decay. The longest-lasting storage onions are those with hard, dry bulbs completely surrounded by scales. You must be sure to cure your onions out of direct sunlight so that they don't sunscald. If you're careless and leave them where the sun can reach them, their skin will be bleached and softened, providing an easy route for disease organisms to enter and spoil the bulb. It may seem strange, but onions cure best at a high humidity of 60 to 70 percent. When they're dried at a lower humidity, most of the scales are often lost, cutting short their storage life. You can give them too much of a good thing, though. If the humidity is extremely high, above 80 percent, the bulbs are more likely to rot and will be very slow to cure.

You can cure your onions in the garden if you arrange them so that the leaves fan out on top of the bulbs and shade them from the sun. Lay the onions down in bunches, with the leaves of one bunch lying over the bulbs of the previous bunch. This open-air method is only practical in areas having sunny, warm weather at curing time. At this stage, onions can't be left out in the rain, and cool temperatures inhibit proper curing. Dorothy knows all about the effects of cool temperatures from first-hand experience. Several years ago a very cool summer kept her onions from bulbing up quite as fast as they should have. When fall came, their tops began to topple over as they were supposed to. But cool fall weather arrived ahead of schedule and the tops refused to turn completely brown and dry. Dorothy dug up the crop anyway, but even then the tops never turned brown and the onions just wouldn't cure properly. Needless to say, Dorothy was buying onions at the store that winter.

During damp or extremely hot weather, bring your onions into a sheltered area such as a shed, carport, attic, or garage for curing. Under warm and dry conditions the curing process usually takes at least two weeks, so if you're faced with less-than-ideal curing conditions, be prepared for it to take longer. During this time it is very important to make sure that the air circulates freely around your onions. If you are curing them indoors, try to find a very airy location (such as a screened porch) where you can spread them out in a single layer. A window screen propped up on bricks (as described earlier under Onions from Sets) is another good place to cure onions.

Once the curing is done, you can cut or break off the tops to within 1 inch of the neck. Leave the scales on; they help protect the bulbs from storage diseases and inhibit early sprouting. Don't remove the tops when the neck is still wet or you will create a site for fungi and bacteria to enter. Diane learned this the hard way. A couple years ago she planted Sweet Spanish (also known as Yellow Utah) onions, which aren't meant for long storage. She ignored this fact and tried to cure the bulbs anyway. After three weeks of patient curing the necks were still thick and hadn't dried out. After two more weeks she gave up and realized that the reason this variety wasn't recommended for storage was because it had such thick necks. So she cut off the tops and began an onion-eating marathon! Her family ate onions at every possible opportunity, but they just couldn't finish them off before spoilage set in, only four weeks after she had cut off the tops. Most of the spoilage occurred at the neck; looking back, Diane realizes she probably would have had better luck just leaving those green leaves on instead of cutting them and opening the bulbs up to infection. Remember, if you should find yourself in a similar situation, you can always chop your onions and freeze or dry them rather than just let them spoil.

Storing to Avoid Sprouting

For best results, you should store your onions as close to 32°F as possible without freezing them, and at 60 to 70 percent humidity. If you can provide these conditions, your efforts will be rewarded by little, if any, sprout growth and your onions (if they're a good-keeping variety) should remain usable for six to eight months. Sprouting generally indicates overly warm storage temperatures, improper curing, or premature harvesting. A spare refrigerator set at a low temperature, with a pan of water in it to keep up the humidity level, makes an excellent place to store onions. An unheated basement or storeroom where temperatures stay above freezing or a corner of a garage attached to the house also make good places to stash your onions. Be sure to allow for plenty of air circulation by storing them in mesh bags or setting them in shallow layers in slatted wooden fruit crates raised off the floor on bricks.

Growing Onions for Seed

You may want to try your hand at growing your own onion seed. If so, choose an open-pollinated variety rather than a hybrid variety (see chapter

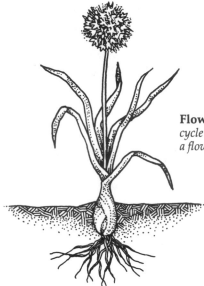

Flowering Onion: *Onions complete their two-year life cycle by sending up a long flower stalk on which is borne a flower head made up of a cluster of tiny individual flowers.*

1 for a discussion of hybrids). Onions grown for seed must be encouraged to bolt; this is easily done by storing them at 40° to 50°F for at least two weeks. For most gardeners, this will mean picking out the nicest bulbs from the crop you've grown for eating and then storing the select few for the winter before planting them again in the spring. After this cool rest period, most of the replanted bulbs should flower.

Onion flowers take a long time to mature into dry seed heads, but it is important that you be patient and wait until the seeds are thoroughly dry before harvesting them. This drying period can take up to two weeks, and you'll know the seeds are ready when you can rub them easily from the flower heads. There are anywhere from 6 to 120 seeds per flower head, and they tend to ripen at an uneven rate, so some will be ready before others. Visit your onion flowers regularly to harvest the seeds as they dry. When you've collected them all, store the seeds under cool and very dry conditions.

Insect visitation is critical for good pollination of onion flowers. In Idaho, the onion fields are pollinated by hives of bees that must be brought in to make up for the natural insect population which has been killed by insecticides. Onion breeders who grow hybrid seed for sale have found that flies can pollinate onion flowers better than bees. If you don't find bees visiting your onion flowers, you might try to attract flies by putting some spoiled meat or other smelly food near the onions as they are flowering (but watch out for neighborhood dogs and cats!).

Problems with Onions

Onions aren't subject to many devastating diseases while they're in the garden. However, quite a few bacteria and fungi can attack onions, especially while in storage. For this reason, you should carefully go through your stored onions every few days and remove any that are spoiling or sprouting. These onions may have some good parts you can use in the kitchen right away, but the diseased portions should be discarded. Only add them to the compost pile if you are sure it will become hot enough (at least 160°F) to destroy the bacteria or fungi.

Onion thrips: These minute insects ($\frac{1}{25}$ of an inch or less long) are serious pests not only to bulbing onions but to other kinds of onions as well. Thrips cause damage at both the adult and larval stage by piercing plant cells and sucking out the contents. If you notice on your plants small, whitish patches that may run together to form silvery areas, they probably have been visited by thrips. You can help control these nasty insects by keeping the area around the onion patch free of weeds which can shelter the thrips during the winter. If these pests are a serious problem in your garden, try growing Spanish onions; they are often quite resistant.

Onion Frontiers

Breeders keep trying to develop new onion varieties that will keep well but still have a mild taste. This is difficult, but there are a few mild varieties that keep moderately well (Fiesta 61 and Granex Yellow F-1, for example). The breeders are also looking for ways to stop plants from bolting using natural plant hormones. Much recent breeding work has been aimed at developing plants which produce no functional male parts. Such varieties are useful in producing hybrids, for the male parts need not be painstakingly removed from the flower clusters by hand to avoid self-pollination.

Other Types of Onions

Besides the well-known and widely grown bulbing onion, the genus *Allium* includes many other cultivated crops, all of which contain similar organic sulfur compounds giving them that distinctive oniony or garlicky flavor. Although they all taste somewhat different, the resemblance is clearly there. With many plants and animals, confusion exists as to their identity because common names are often unrelated to scientific ones. For example, the name "robin" in England, North America, and Australia refers to three completely different, basically unrelated birds. With alliums, not only is there confusion over common names, but there is also disagreement among sci-

---

Onions—Many Kinds, Many Names

To help you keep track of the various alliums, we've organized a family tree of sorts to introduce you to some of the less familiar members and show you which ones are related to which.

Allium cepa
  Common Onion Group:
    Bulb onion
  Aggregatum Group:
    Potato onion (also multiplier
    onion, potato hill onion,
    underground onion; rarely,
    Egyptian onion)
    Ever-ready onion
    Shallot (Spanish garlic)
  Proliferum Group:
    Egyptian onion (also top, tree,
    nest, evergreen, or winter
    onion)
Allium sativum
  Garlic
  Rocambole (a form of *Allium
  sativum;* also called sand leek,

Allium sativum (continued)
    serpent garlic, Spanish garlic,
    Spanish shallot)
Allium ampeloprasum
  Great-headed Garlic Group:
    Elephant garlic
  Leek Group:
    Leek
Allium fistulosum
    Japanese bunching onion (also
    Welsh onion, evergreen onion,
    ciboules)
Allium schoenoprasum
  Chives
Allium tuberosum
  Garlic chives (also Chinese or
  Oriental chives)

---

entists over scientific names. There are six species of commonly cultivated alliums. Two of these are further divided into groups. An assortment of names has been suggested for these groups, but scientists cannot agree on which names are the correct ones. In this chapter, we will try to sidestep the controversy by only using common names which are widely accepted.

Unfortunately, in using common names, we run into the same sort of problem as with robins: The same name may be used in various regions to refer to completely different species. For example, the name "multiplier onion" may be applied to Egyptian onions, potato onions, or the perennial Japanese bunching onion. To add to the confusion, the same crop may go by a different name in different areas of the country. The chart, Onions—Many Kinds, Many Names, lists the names most widely used for all the commonly cultivated onions. In all cases, the first name in the list is the one we use here when discussing each type of onion.

The most confusing part of scientific onion classification is how to divide up the members of the species, *Allium cepa*. Three groups are generally accepted, with the division made on the basis of how the plants grow. The Common Onion group includes all bulbing onion varieties that form a single large bulb in the ground. The Aggregatum group is the most confusing, for it includes three different types: the potato onion; the ever-ready onion, which is cultivated in England but is rarely grown in North America; and the familiar garden shallot, which has several varieties of its own. All of these onions produce a cluster of bulbs at the base of the plant. The third category, the Proliferum group, contains the Egyptian onion which forms a cluster of tiny bulblets at the top of the plant. Now let's take a closer look at all these onions, for each has its own unique qualities which make it a valuable addition to the home garden.

The Egyptian Onion

The Egyptian onion is very popular with home gardeners, and with good reason. It is a very hardy perennial that sends up its welcome green shoots early in the spring, signalling to the winter-weary gardener that his garden has revived. The Egyptian onion also provides fresh green onions long before any other perennial crops have awakened. And this interesting plant with its crown of aerial bulblets seems to be trouble-free, a relief from fussier plants that have to be carefully monitored for signs of invading pests and diseases.

You can start Egyptian onions in your garden from clump divisions or from bulblets. As the plants grow, they send up several shoots, and a clump develops. These clumps can be carefully broken apart and each shoot planted separately to start a new bed. As summer progresses, each plant sends up a tough, hollow green stem at the top of which a bunch of bulblets develops. The bulblets look like miniature onion bulbs, even as far as having a papery brown outer covering. These bulblets provide the plant with a built-in, sure-fire way of propagating itself. If you leave the bulblet cluster alone, the stalk will bend down as the maturing cluster gets heavier. Each bulblet, which has already started to sprout while the stalk was still erect, will very conveniently root itself where it comes in contact with the ground. You can direct this reproductive process by gathering the bulblets before they begin to sprout and then plant them yourself. Plant the bulblets about an inch deep, and space them closely if you want to use the harvest as green onions. The final spacing to allow full-sized plants to mature is 4 inches between plants in the row and 15 inches between the rows.

If you don't want to plant the bulblets, you can eat them instead. Cure them in the shade until hard and store them in a cool place. During the winter you can peel the bulblets and use them to add an oniony flavor to soups or to your favorite meat, fish, and vegetable dishes.

Since Egyptian onions are perennials, you can harvest indefinitely from the same plants. Although they are very hardy, there are a few steps you should take to make sure they carry over from year to year in the best possible shape. As winter approaches, mulch your Egyptian onion bed with fluffy

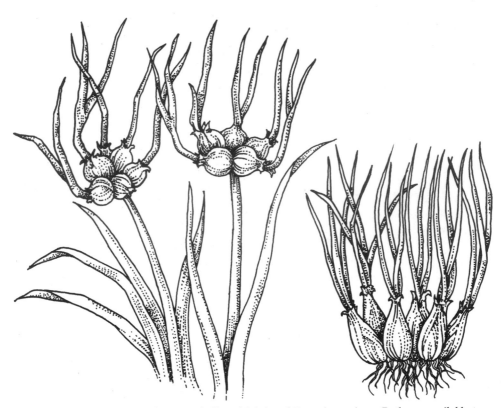

Onion Relatives: *Shown here are shallots (right) and Egyptian onions. Both are available to gardeners ready to try something a little different from the familiar bulb onions.*

material such as straw until the plants are covered by about a foot of mulch. You should be sure to do this before the ground freezes. Come early spring, around February or March, you will see lovely green leaves poking their way up through the mulch, just asking to be eaten.

The Potato Onion

This old-fashioned onion with the curious name has been a subject of conjecture among gardeners, although not much is actually known about it. Some people say it is called the potato onion because of the brown color of its papery outer scales. But others insist that the proper name for this crop is "potato hill onion." These folks say that it was brought west by the pioneers in covered wagons who planted it as a companion to their potatoes. During the westward journey, so it is said, these onions were perhaps the only fresh vegetable available and protected the pioneers from scurvy. Potato onions are hard to come by without a cooperative neighbor to give you a start. One seed supplier you can try is S & H Organic Acres (P.O. Box 27, Montgomery Creek, CA 96065).

Potato onions should be planted in midwinter in mild climates and in early spring in colder areas. Culture is basically the same as for bulb onion sets, except the bulblets should be planted 10 inches apart. Potato onions come up quite early. Later on in the season, as the bulb cluster forms, brush the surrounding soil gently away so that the bulbs are exposed to the sun to assist their ripening. As you do this, you'll notice that the entire bulb cluster is surrounded by a protective covering of papery scales. In this respect, potato onions differ from their cousins, shallots, which grow as a cluster of bulbs each with its own covering.

The tops of potato onions die down in midsummer, long before shallots are ready. Don't leave them in the ground and forget about them or they will sprout again in late summer and not be of much use for cooking. Cure and store them as you would bulb onions. Potato onions have a mild flavor and can be used to help tide the cook over between crops of bulbing onions.

The Ever-Ready Onion

Little is known about this interesting version of a multiplier onion, except that it helped sustain the British during World War II when commercial bulb onions were in short supply. The ever-ready onion forms a cluster of ten to twelve bulbs with reddish-brown coats. The bulbs are narrower than those of potato onions, and the leaves are especially narrow. The sets are planted in March, and the bulbs are harvested in the fall. The name "ever-ready" apparently refers to the fact that the tops of these plants do not die down after the bulbs have formed.

Shallots

Shallots are considered the gourmet member of the Onion family, for their delicate flavor can enhance and enrich almost any meat, fish, or vegetable dish. In the supermarket, shallots command a gourmet price, too, which is ridiculous considering how easy they are to grow. As a matter of fact, about the only regular tending shallots need is conscientious weeding. They grow well in poorer and drier soil than bulbing onions, and their midsummer harvest coincides conveniently with the proper planting time for fall and overwintering crops, setting the stage for succession cropping. This early harvest, combined with the fact that they take up little space in the garden, makes shallots a fine crop for the gardener with limited space.

Shallot Varieties

Luckily for gardeners, there are several varieties of shallots to choose from. The most familiar is the French shallot, which has a pinkish-brown skin and slightly tear-shaped bulbs. Another European variety, the Frog-legged shallot, has longer and thinner bulbs than the French shallot. While many cooks claim that Frog-legged shallots have the finest flavor, these bulbs don't store well. Any bulbs that aren't used by early winter simply shrivel and dry up in storage. Frog-legged shallots also are not very prolific, so you may have trouble amassing enough bulbs to use for cooking in addition to some extras to start next season's crop. Dutch shallots, with their yellow skin, are the largest and most strongly flavored shallot variety.

Growing Shallots

If you choose to grow the rather temperamental Frog-legged shallots, try planting them in the fall and mulching heavily before the ground freezes. Other shallots can also be grown this way, but they don't seem to produce any earlier or more abundantly then when spring-planted, and you run the risk of losing them to the harsh winter weather. In most cases, you'll get better results when you delay planting until the ground is no longer frozen in the spring. Dorothy always plants her shallots in a bed rather than in straight, equidistant rows. She does this by placing each starter bulb 6 inches from its neighbors and staggering the rows to keep the 6-inch distance between bulbs. Using this method, she harvests an abundant crop of shallots for a family of four avowed shallot-lovers from about 9 square feet of ground. Admittedly, this harvest is more than a lot of gardeners would want, but the important thing to remember when gauging how much to grow is that you need enough to be able to set aside part of the harvest to start next season's crop.

Over the course of the same season, both Diane and Dorothy discovered the importance of keeping shallots weeded. Dorothy planted her shallots near the edge of the garden and was just too busy to keep up with the weeds. Diane gave her shallots a prominent place in her garden where they couldn't be forgotten and worked some wood ashes around them at planting time. What a difference there was in the crops! Diane's conscientious care was rewarded with a huge harvest of big fat bulbs, while Dorothy brought in only meager clumps of tiny bulbs. The lesson here is plain to see: weeding may be tedious work, but it sure pays off at harvesttime.

As shallots grow, the bulbs first send up clumps of healthy green leaves. You can cut a few of these early summer leaves to use as seasoning if you like. As more bulbs form, the plants work their way up through the soil until the clusters are almost completely aboveground. Eventually the tops die down, telling you it's time to harvest. Gently dig up each cluster of bulbs and cure them in the garden for anywhere from several days to two weeks, bringing them in if rain threatens. Basically, you are treating them the same way you would normal bulb onions. Do not separate the bulbs but keep them in clusters for storage; just break off the bulbs as needed. French and Dutch shallots store very well in a paper or net bag set in a cool, dark part of the house. Shallots are more likely to dry out than sprout in storage.

Garlic

Garlic is known in folklore as well as in gardens and kitchens. The assignment of magical properties to this special allium is probably due to its genuine antibacterial and antifungal properties, but whether or not garlic plays a legitimate role in improving human health is hotly debated. Its usefulness in the garden and kitchen, however, cannot be disputed. Garlic planted among brassicas helps keep down the population of cabbage worms, and garlic solutions sprayed on plant leaves repel a variety of sucking and chewing bugs. Proof of the germicidal activity of garlic can be found by reviewing the number of plant diseases that garlic sprays have been judged effective against. Garlic sprays have been found to affect angular leaf-spot, cucumber scab, and downy mildew in cucumbers; anthracnose and a bacterial disease in beans; and brown rot disease in peaches, almonds, and apricots.

The chemical that works these wonders, and also gives garlic its special flavor, is called allicin. Allicin is formed by enzymes in the garlic bulb from the odorless, water-soluble amino acid, alliin, when garlic is injured or chopped up. Because allicin is only produced upon trauma to the bulb, recipes calling for garlic instruct the cook to chop or mash the clove before adding it to a dish. As in onions, the enzymes which perform the flavor-inducing conversion are inactivated by heat or freezing, resulting in very subdued garlic flavor. A fine French recipe for mashed potatoes is based on this principle—two entire heads of garlic are used for only 2½ pounds of potatoes! The cloves are peeled but not mashed or chopped. Then they are simmered in butter before being incorporated into the potatoes. The resulting dish has a wonderful, rich flavor which diners don't ascribe to garlic at all. Some people enjoy eating whole, roasted garlic heads for the same reason. After roasting the heads for an hour at 325°F, these garlic lovers peel the cloves and squeeze the soft, buttery contents onto crackers, vegetables, or meats. You should be aware that once it is formed, uncooked allicin is quite unstable and will break down into other less-pleasing chemicals. This is the reason why salads or other dishes using uncooked chopped garlic should be eaten the first day after mixing; otherwise, they will develop a strong, disagreeable flavor.

The garlic head is formed in quite a different fashion from the onion bulb. Each individual garlic clove is actually a swollen axillary bud, the papery covering of which is the remains of the leaf that gave rise to the bud. Because

Off-Beat Alliums: *You can obtain variations of the pungent flavor of garlic from (left to right), elephant garlic, rocambole, and garlic.*

the garlic clove is not made up of individual swollen leaf bases like an onion, it lacks the rings of an onion. But onions and garlic do share one thing in common: as in onions, the true garlic stem is a small area inside the bulb. This means that the visible portion we usually call the stem is nothing more than a collection of leaf bases.

While long days help induce garlic to form bulbs, temperature is a much more important factor. Garlic sets must be exposed to cool temperatures (below 68°F) during the winter or they will not form compound bulbs even under long days. Although they're both alliums, you should never store your onion and garlic sets in the same place; onions need warmth and garlic needs coolness. Extended periods (meaning anything longer than two months) of temperatures below 50°F, however, can harm your garlic sets. The central cloves will form higher on the false stem than normal, giving the head a rough appearance.

Garlic Varieties

Garlic is one of those rare crops that do not produce flowers. All reproduction is vegetative—that is, the cloves which form the bulb can produce new plants, but seeds are never made. Because there is no sexual reproduction, the genetic makeup of each new garlic plant is just like that of its parent. This makes breeding for improved garlic impossible, for two strains cannot be crossed to get a new type of garlic. Each garlic variety is referred to as a clone, meaning that all individuals are genetically identical (just as each strawberry plant which develops from a runner is genetically identical to the parent plant). Some garlic clones do tend to bolt, but instead of forming flowers, they produce clusters of tiny bulblets. These bulblets can be planted to yield compound bulbs, but they are likely to be small.

The mysterious thing about garlic is that, even though it cannot reproduce sexually, it has many clones which differ greatly from one another. Did all the clones develop long ago, at a time when garlic could reproduce sexually? If that were so, then all the clones would have had to lose independently the ability to reproduce sexually—a very unlikely event. But it is also difficult to imagine that the variability of garlic results from mutations in cells that aren't involved in sexual reproduction, for such "vegetative mutations" are generally quite rare. This diversity among garlic clones may be a mystery, but it is fortunate for home gardeners for it allows each of us to try different sorts of garlic and find clones from the supermarket or from seed companies that will produce reliably in our gardens. Once you come across clones that thrive in your garden, be sure to save some of each year's harvest for planting the following year; if you use up all your garlic in the kitchen and have to turn to an outside source for planting stock, you may have trouble finding that particular clone again.

At least one type of garlic is different enough from the others that it has often been mistakenly thought of as a different species. This is rocambole, a mild garlic that is widely grown in Europe. Rocambole (also called serpent garlic) regularly produces a central stalk topped by a head of tiny bulblets. For this reason, some gardeners confuse it with the Egyptian onion. But rocambole is definitely a garlic both in flavor and aroma, although gentler than the standard varieties. The cloves of rocambole are easy to separate and peel, for their dry covering is very loose.

Growing Garlic

In the North, garlic planted in October will establish its roots before winter sets in and will really take off in the spring to form nice, big, healthy bulbs. Some northern gardeners choose to plant their garlic in July, right after harvesting that year's crop. Either way, the bed should be mulched after cold weather sets in. Southern gardeners can plant garlic in the late fall or early winter (late November or December) if they are relatively confident that the soil temperature will drop below 68°F during the winter. Remember not to plant garlic where other onion family plants grew the year before, since they share pests such as thrips. Garlic will thrive in rich soil but can also produce well in poorer soils than bulb onions.

Just before planting, you must break up your garlic bulbs into individual cloves. Stop short of peeling the cloves, however. Once the cloves are separated, they don't keep well, so you should get them into the garden right away. Some gardeners feel that only the outer cloves should be used for planting, since they're generally the larger ones. Larger cloves produce larger bulbs, for the extra store of nutrients results in a faster-growing young plant. Space your garlic cloves about 5 inches apart, either in rows 15 to 18 inches apart or in a bed, as described for shallots. Plant them about 2 inches deep. Overwintered garlic will begin to peek out over the mulch quite early in the spring. Leave the mulch in place to discourage the weeds, and treat your garlic patch as you would your bulb onions.

Garlic is ready for harvest when the tops turn yellow, usually early enough in the summer to allow the bed to be used for a late planting of a fall crop. Cure garlic just like you would bulb onions. Garlic intended for kitchen use stores best at 32°F and 65 percent humidity. Garlic sprouts most quickly at 40°F, so avoid this temperature for a long-lasting storage crop.

Garlic Problems

While garlic is usually a trouble-free crop, it can become infested with the stem and bulb nematode. This tiny worm is too small to spot easily with the naked eye, but you will know your garlic has it if the bottom of the plant is swollen and spongy and the skin has lengthwise splits. Sometimes nematode-infected plants have twisted leaves and stems as well. If you pull up your garlic and find that the roots and stem stay behind in the ground, that's another sign that you may have nematodes. Infected cloves are the usual cause of nematode infestation. It takes many years for the worms to die out completely, and you should not plant host crops such as celery, garlic, onions, parsley, peas, or salsify in the area for four years. If your garden soil does have a bad case of nematodes, you can help it recuperate by always cleaning up your garden debris and placing it in the garbage rather than in the compost pile. Also, do not use any garlic from an infected patch for planting.

Elephant Garlic

The "elephant" portion of this plant's common name no doubt refers to the hefty size of the heads it produces. On the average, each clove weighs 1 ounce, and before you can even hope to fit it into your garlic press, you must chop it up into many smaller pieces. Garlic aficionados love it because a single clove yields 2 to 3 tablespoons of minced garlic with relatively little work. Even people with a lukewarm affection for garlic will enjoy this particular plant, since the cloves are much milder in flavor than standard garlic, and can even be sliced raw into salads and eaten without recrimination.

Actually, the second portion of elephant garlic's name is misleading, for it is more closely related to leeks than to regular garlic. While cloves of garlic and elephant garlic do look similar, the resemblance is only skin-deep; when you examine them closely, you realize they are really very different. The elephant garlic clove is a single thick storage leaf, as compared to the enlarged axillary bud which is the garlic clove.

Tiny bulblets appear around the outside of the elephant garlic head; you can save these and plant them in the spring for a fall harvest of small bulbs. Although these bulbs aren't large enough to be of use in the kitchen, you should store them carefully and plant them the next spring to yield a harvestable compound bulb. Space the starter bulbs 10 inches apart to allow plenty of room for the plant to grow. While they're growing, elephant garlic plants look just like giant, vigorous garlic plants and should be treated in much the same way. If you garden in a region where cool, damp summers make growing a good crop of regular garlic a rather iffy proposition, give elephant garlic a try, since it tolerates cool and damp conditions well.

As it matures, elephant garlic produces a cluster of several cloves and a gigantic, impressive flower stalk; the flowers, however, rarely produce seeds. For best bulb production, you should remove the stalk before it develops into the flowering head to help channel the plant's energy into bulb development. Sometimes, an elephant garlic plant will fail to send up a flower stalk. When that happens, there's a corresponding change in what goes on underground. Instead of making a clove cluster, it forms a single, massive clove referred to as a round. There's no difference in flavor, and you can use rounds in the kitchen or save them for planting the following spring, just like you would cloves.

Leeks

Like shallots, leeks are considered a gourmet member of the Onion family. Their mild, sweet flavor and creamy texture are delightful, and when combined with potatoes, leeks make one of the most delicious soups imaginable. It is strange to think that leeks are more closely related to elephant garlic than to Japanese bunching onions, which they resemble superficially. But if you have ever left some leeks in the ground long enough for them to flower and then pulled them up, you will have seen the tiny bulblets which form around the base of the plant like miniature versions of elephant garlic cloves. While leeks do require quite a bit of attention, you don't need to worry about providing the proper conditions for bulbing; leeks never bulb up, and you eat the elongated leaf bases of the plants. Leeks make tasty vegetables at any stage of growth, but most gardeners wait until they are about an inch in diameter before harvesting them.

Leek Varieties

Fortunately for gardeners everywhere, there are many varieties of leeks which are adapted to different growing conditions. Most varieties require a long growing season. In mild areas, leeks are generally planted very early in the spring, directly outdoors. Northern gardeners generally get their plants started at the same time indoors, for later transplanting to the garden. Many leek varieties are very cold hardy and can be left in the garden, covered with

More and More Alliums: *Japanese bunching onions (top) and leeks (bottom) are two more onion-related crops for the adventuresome gardener.*

mulch, well into the winter even in northern areas. If you want leeks that overwinter well, choose varieties like Catalina which have dark blue-green leaves; as in other crops, such as kale, the blue-green color appears to be related in some way to hardiness. If you live in a cold-season area and do not want to start your leeks indoors, try one of the relatively quick-growing summer leeks such as King Richard. This variety is ready in only 75 days and produces a pleasing, long white stem. Be forewarned that summer leeks do not keep well in storage, nor do they overwinter well in the garden, so you should dig them up before heavy frost hits and use them in short order.

Growing Leeks

Leek seeds keep better than onion seeds; under favorable conditions, two-year-old seeds will produce a vigorous crop. Leek seeds do appear to be very sensitive to high humidity, however, so if you live in a damp area you should buy fresh seeds each year.

Leeks are usually the first crop that northern gardeners get started in anticipation of spring, for the earlier the seed is planted, the bigger the final stalks will be. February is not too early to get those seeds underway indoors, germinating them at room temperature and using the same methods we recommend for onion seed and seedlings. In frost-free areas, leeks are grown as a winter crop and are planted in late summer when maximum daytime temperatures no longer exceed 80°F.

When you plant your leeks in the garden, whether as seeds or as transplants, place them in a trench 6 inches deep and 6 inches wide. Cover seeds with ⅛ inch of soil, and place transplants a little deeper than they were growing in the flat or pot. One friend of ours claims that the secret of growing fine leeks is to clip away both the tops of the leaves and the bottom half or so of the roots before transplanting, and in fact, this treatment may well reduce transplant shock. The final spacing for leeks should be 4 to 8 inches, depending on how big you want the final stalks to be. As the leeks grow, gradually fill in the trench an inch or so at a time so that the fattening stems are covered. Be careful never to bury the point where the leaves branch out from the stems. When they grow in darkness, the stems won't turn green, and your harvested leeks will be nice and white and succulent.

If you plant leeks from seed, be sure to enjoy the thinnings in your kitchen, unless you want to transplant them to increase your final crop. Young leeks can be substituted for green onions in any dish, although they impart a different but equally enjoyable flavor.

Japanese Bunching Onions

Although these plants are most commonly called Japanese bunching onions, they are also referred to at times as Welsh onions. This name has nothing to do with Wales, for apparently these onions have never been grown commonly there. The name seems rather to be a corruption of the German word *welsche*, meaning foreign, which was probably used to describe the plant when it was introduced into Germany near the end of the Middle Ages. The confusion over the name matches the confusion about the plant, only some of which we can clear up. Japanese bunching onions are the typical Oriental onion and are featured extensively in Oriental cuisine. Chinese and Japanese recipes in English-language cookbooks often call for "scallions," but the plants we know as scallions are not the same as the Japanese onions. The scallions that Occidental cooks normally use are just immature bulb onion plants, usually of a white variety. But this isn't a fair substitution, for the flavor of Japanese bunching onions is not the same as that of our scallions. If you are a fan of Oriental cuisine, you should grow the real thing in your garden and find out what you've been missing.

Japanese Bunching Onion Varieties

There seem to be two different classes of Japanese bunching onions. Some types, such as Kujo Green Multistalk, He-Shi-Ko, and Sakata's Evergreen White Bunching Onion, can definitely be grown here as perennials. The tops may die down over the course of a harsh winter, but in spring a cluster of shoots will form where each original plant grew. For a continuous harvest, break off a few shoots from the cluster as they are needed. Later in the season you can divide the clumps and replant them to propagate the crop.

Other Japanese onions, such as Ishikura Long, are described as single-stalked plants, which implies that they never form a cluster. You can stretch out the harvest with some of these varieties by overwintering them under a protective mulch.

To further confuse the issue, hybrids have been developed between Japanese bunching onions and other species. The hybrid variety Beltsville Bunching is the result of a cross between a bunching and a bulbing onion and displays its heritage by producing scallions with a slightly swollen bulb. Louisiana Evergreen and Delta Giant are the offspring of a cross with shallots, which explains why they produce a shallotlike crop.

Growing Japanese Bunching Onions

To get a good crop of Japanese bunching onions, just follow the cultural guidelines for bulbing onions. In the North, you can plant them in the fall and apply a deep cover of mulch to get a head start, or just wait for spring to roll around before planting. In the South, plant these onions in the fall for a continuous crop over the coming year. For a change of pace, you can try blanching bunching onions like leeks to produce long white stalks.

Chives

Chives are an elegant addition to the herb garden and can be cultivated quite easily from seeds or clump divisions. They are not widely grown commercially, so little is known of their biology. They do die down in the winter, and it takes a long, cold season to break their dormancy. However, that isn't the only way they can be roused from their dormant slumber. One scientist discovered that if dormant plants were heated to 110°F for 36 to 48 hours, dormancy was broken and the plants grew vigorously when potted. If you wish to grow chives indoors during the winter, you might try this trick to get them going.

The easiest way to grow chives is to get a clump from a friend or buy one in a garden store. If you start them off from seed, they'll take a little longer to mature, meaning that you won't be able to cut any leaves for the first two to three months. Chives will grow well in any good garden soil, but rich, loose soil prompts the fastest growth. Plant seeds just like onion seed. Space your seeds or clumps in small areas (about 2 inches square) about a foot apart; the chives will soon fill in to make a solid row.

To harvest, cut the individual leaves ½ to 1 inch above the soil. When the plants start to flower, harvest as usual but throw out the flowering stalks, since they're tough and strong-tasting. We've found the best tool for cutting chives is a pair of scissors.

Chives: *Garlic chives and chives look very similar but can be differentiated from one another by the shape of their leaves. Chives (left) are round and hollow, whereas garlic chives (right) are flat sided and triangular in cross section.*

In cold areas, chives should be mulched in the winter just to be on the safe side. They are quite hardy, but extreme cold can kill them. The one time Diane lost her chives was the year she didn't get around to mulching them. The unprotected plants succumbed to winter weather of temperatures between 0° and −10°F and little snow cover.

Garlic Chives

Garlic chives are another Oriental specialty that is gaining popularity in North America. It's easy to understand why when you've savored their mild garlicky flavor. Overall, they resemble ordinary chives except that their leaves are triangular in cross section instead of round and hollow. Garlic chives are not quite as hardy as ordinary ones and require a rich soil for good growth. Other than that, you can grow them exactly like regular chives.

Chapter 8

Radishes, Beets, and Carrots: Pungent and Sweet Roots to Eat

Vital Statistics

Family:
Cruciferae—Radishes
Chenopodiaceae—Beets
Umbelliferae—Carrots

Species:
Raphanus sativus—Radishes
Beta vulgaris—Beets
Daucus carota—Carrots

Soil:
Loose, well-drained, sandy loam

pH:
Radishes—6.0–6.5
Beets—6.5–8.0
Carrots—6.0–6.5

Soil Temperature for Germination:
Radishes—45°–95°F; 85°F, optimum
Beets—50°–85°F; 85°F, optimum
Carrots—45°–85°F; 80°F, optimum

Air Temperature for Best Growth:
45°–75°F; 60°–65°F, optimum
for all three crops

Seed Viability:
Radishes—5 years
Beets—4 years
Carrots—3 years

Seed Germination:
Radishes—3–10 days
Beets—1–2 weeks
Carrots—1–2 weeks

Seed Planting Depth:
Radishes—½–1½"
Beets—½–1"
Carrots—¼"

There is something almost magical about pulling on a cluster of leaves and watching a colorful, fat root slide out of its hiding place in the soil. Radishes, beets, and carrots provide the gardener with a symphony of color from cherry red and gleaming white through deep violet-red to sunny orange. While these popular garden vegetables belong to unrelated plant families and produce their succulent roots in different ways, there are many similarities in their growth patterns and in their reactions to the conditions under which they grow, so it makes sense to discuss them all together.

Radishes, as members of the Mustard family (Cruciferae), are related to cabbage, horseradish, turnips, and watercress. Like other family members, radishes contain pungent chemicals called glycosides which impart the characteristically sharp flavor. Beets are in the Goosefoot family (Chenopodiaceae), which also contains spinach, Swiss chard, and that invasive weed, shepherd's purse. Carrots belong to the Parsley family (Umbelliferae), which gives gardeners and cooks so many wonderful herbs and spices—fennel, parsley, dill, caraway, coriander, and anise are all umbelifers. Unfortunately for seed-saving country gardeners, the wildflower Queen Anne's lace is also in this family and, in fact, is a variation of the same species as the cultivated carrot—meaning that these two plants can interbreed.

Radishes have been cultivated for thousands of years, as evidenced by writings in Egyptian pyramids dating from 2000 B.C. that mention eating radishes. Speculation has it that these roots probably originated in that same area. Beets were originally grown for their tasty leaves, but by the time of the ancient Greeks, the roots were also being enjoyed. In contrast to the venerable heritage of table beets, sugar beets, a commercial crop from which table sugar is refined, were not developed until the late 1700s.

While not too many details are known about the early stages of radish and beet cultivation, we do know more about the long and interesting history of carrot cultivation. The first carrots were not orange at all—they were purple or violet colored and were grown in the remote mountainous country of Afghanistan in the tenth and eleventh centuries. Like beets, these old-time carrots leaked their purple pigments into the cooking water and were used to color sauces a rich brownish-purple. Some time later, yellow carrots started to appear; these had lost the genes directing the manufacture of the purple pigments (anthocyanins).

The cultivated carrot slowly spread from Afghanistan to other countries, and around 1600, plant breeders in the Netherlands carefully worked with the yellow carrots to produce an orange one. During this selection for orange carrots, only four major varieties were developed (Late Half Long, Early Half Long, Early Scarlet Horn, and Long Orange). To this day, every carrot variety in cultivation is descended from one of those four original Dutch types. This explains why present-day carrots, despite their ostensible diversity, are all quite similar genetically.

Nutritional Profiles of Root Crops

When compared to the nutritional merits of beets and carrots, radishes seem to make a poor showing. But before you write them off completely, note that a cup of radishes does contain 26 percent of the vitamin C you should consume in a day. Many people don't realize that all kinds of radishes, from the scarlet globes to the long brown or white roots, make delicious fresh pickles and are delightful when cooked, adding a nice crunchy texture to stir-fried dishes. Young radish leaves are often overlooked as tasty greens, but they are also good to eat, especially when steamed or sautéed with an equal quantity of spinach. We like to add some sautéed shallots and stir in some yogurt for a delicious creamed vegetable dish.

Beets are an especially versatile crop, for it's a toss-up whether the leaves or the roots are better tasting. Nutritionally speaking, beet greens are hard to beat for they're rich in vitamin A—185 percent of the daily requirement is found in just a cup, along with 20 percent of the riboflavin and 28 percent of the iron you need. The naturally sweet roots also contribute to good nutrition. A cup of cooked, ruby-red beet roots provides 20 percent of your daily vitamin C requirement.

With carrots, you can almost *see* their abundant vitamin content. The orange color is due to the pigment carotene, which the body converts to vitamin A. Just one cup of grated raw carrots gives you three times your daily vitamin A requirement. Carrots are also a good source of other nutrients. That same cup of grated carrots will also give you 70 percent of your daily thiamine requirement and 65 percent of your riboflavin requirement. When you eat carrots, just wash and scrub them. Don't peel them, for many of the carrot's nutrients are concentrated in and immediately under the skin. While store-bought carrots often have a tough skin, probably from being stored for so long and shipped such long distances, you'll find that the skin on your homegrown carrots is very tender.

The Importance of Good Soil for Good Roots

Loose soil is vital for producing fat, tender roots; this rule applies to any root crop you may care to raise. If you ignore this rule and grow your root crops in heavy clay or in rocky soil, any roots that develop will be forked or otherwise abnormally shaped. Carrots grown in compacted ground or heavy clay will often be short and stubby, even if the variety you planted was supposed to be long and slender; long-rooted beets such as Cylindra can have the same problem. In a very graphic display of how poor soil can hamper root crop growth, scientists have found that carrots grown in loose soil can be *twice* as large as those raised in compacted soil. Even though the common, round, red radishes are usually small and grow near the surface, the tiny, young radish taproots can have trouble working their way through heavy or compacted soil. If you get any radishes at all from such a plot, they will be misshapen and tough. Dorothy's first venture into gardening included putting in a modest row of radishes. Since her house was rented, she didn't dare disturb the flower beds too much, so she chose a spot where little was growing

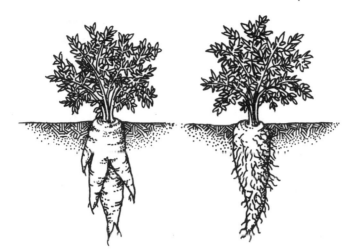

Forked and Hairy Carrots: *Heavy, compacted soils cause carrot roots to fork and become abnormally shaped (left). Excessive nitrogen in the soil from green manure crops or the application of fresh manure can lead to an abundance of feeder roots that result in hairy, undesirable carrots (right).*

(her first mistake). She'd heard that radishes were easy to grow, so she planted them in that little patch and waited. When rain came, it all pooled up in the radish bed, for the soil there was compacted clay (her second mistake). At least she didn't have to water them! But she waited in vain for nice round radishes; not even one plant formed a plump root, and eventually all she had was a bunch of puny flower stalks.

If your soil is at all heavy, it will pay off in the end if you take the time to lighten it before putting in any root crops. Work the soil deeply, loosen it well, and then leave it alone. Never step on the part of the garden where your root crops will grow, or you'll undo all your hard work. A rotary tiller is ideal for loosening the bed; if you don't have one, dig and loosen it with a spade or shovel to a depth of 8 to 10 inches, breaking up any clods and removing any stones you unearth.

When you're faced with heavy clay soil, you can lighten it along the intended root-crop rows by digging a trench 3 to 4 inches wide and 8 inches deep. Fill the trench with any one of the following mixtures, using the proportions of 2 parts to 1 part to 1 part: soil, well-rotted manure, and sand; peat moss, wood ashes, and sand; shredded leaves, wood ashes, and sand. Check the pH of your mixture—it should be 6.0 to 6.5 for radishes and carrots and 6.5 to 8.0 for beets. If the pH needs adjusting, add peat moss to make it more acid or wood ashes to increase its alkalinity.

After you've planted the crops, water gently with a fine spray from a soaker hose rather than from an overhead sprinkler that will beat and compact the earth with large droplets of water. Do not flood-irrigate these crops until they are two to three weeks old, and then only if you have no other choice.

Although root crops like a rich soil, that soil should not be too high in nitrogen. Never use large amounts of fresh manure in the carrot bed, for too much nitrogen encourages the growth of feeder roots, resulting in hairy carrots that won't be very appealing. Fresh manure can also cause the carrot roots to fork and become misshapen. (Scientists still aren't sure why this is so.) If you grow soybeans or other legumes as a nitrogen-rich green manure crop, don't plant carrots in this area right after the green manure crop has been tilled in. Instead, wait at least six months before planting a carrot crop. Scientists who compared carrots raised in soybean stubble with those grown in rye stubble (a grass, as opposed to a nitrogen-fixing legume) found that the rye-stubble carrots were fine, while those grown in soybean stubble had more top growth and small and very hairy roots. Beets and radishes can be grown without problems in soil that is richer in nitrogen than the ideal soil for carrots, but it is wise to avoid fresh manure in these areas, too.

All three of these crops are more likely to be limited by the potassium or phosphorus content of the soil rather than by the nitrogen content. Enrich

How Food Is Stored in Roots

While radishes, carrots, and beets all store food in their roots, those roots grow in different ways. All roots have xylem tissue to bring water and minerals up from the soil to the rest of the plant and phloem to carry nutrients into the root (see chapter 1). The tissue from which the xylem and phloem develop is called the cambium. The cambium produces xylem cells toward the inside and phloem cells toward the outside of the root. In addition to the transport cells, xylem and phloem tissue may have an abundance of storage cells which contain nutrients.

The core of a carrot is the xylem, which contains some storage cells, while the outer portion of the carrot is the phloem, which contains more nutrient-storing cells than the xylem. That explains why the core is the smallest portion of the carrot root. The core separates easily from the outer portion, because the cambium separates easily between the xylem and phloem.

The radish root, on the other hand, has many more storage cells in its xylem. The cambium, which doesn't separate easily, is near the outside of the root and the outermost part of the radish root is a thin layer of phloem, with only a few storage cells mixed in. Radishes also differ from carrots in that the swollen, crisp part we eat is more than just the root. The very top part of the radish is actually the embryonic stem, which develops storage cells right along with the root.

Beets differ from both carrots and radishes in that several cambia form rings. Each cambium ring produces xylem toward the inside and phloem toward the outside, with storage cells mixed in with both. The rings we see in a sliced beet are those rings produced by the cambia.

your soil with wood ashes and bone meal to provide plenty of these two key minerals; work them thoroughly into the row before you plant your seeds. (It's very important to disperse wood ashes well throughout the soil since a concentration of wood ashes will harm any seeds with which they come in contact.)

Carrots and beets are both susceptible to a deficiency of the trace element boron. If you've been adding compost or other organic matter to your soil, it's unlikely that you will have this problem. However, if you should start finding black cores in your carrots or black, corky tissue inside your beet roots, the prime suspect is a boron deficiency. If you have any doubts about your soil's boron content, call your county extension agent and ask if soils in your area tend to be boron-deficient. Granite dust or a compost rich in sweet clover or vetch will provide adequate boron for your garden.

Why Storage Roots Are a Luxury for Plants

When we grow radishes, beets, and carrots, we want to harvest good-sized, tender roots. But in order to reap a satisfying harvest, we must first

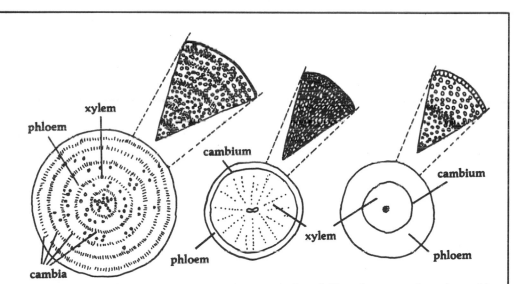

Cross Section of Root Crops: *The cambium in the beet (left) produces secondary rings with each ring producing xylem to the inside and phloem to the outside, both with the same amount of parenchyma cells. The xylem tissue in the radish (center) has more parenchyma cells than the phloem and, therefore, makes up most of the root. The cambium separating the xylem and phloem is located near the outside of the root. In carrots (right), the phloem tissue has the most parenchyma storage cells, so it constitutes most of the root. A small core of xylem is located in the middle of the root, with the vascular cambium surrounding it.*

realize that growing these roots is a luxury for the plants. Plants need leaves in order to carry on photosynthesis and grow. They have to produce flowers and then seeds in order to continue the species. Development of big, fat roots that store excess carbohydrates can happen only after these two basic functions are taken care of. If environmental factors are in any way unfavorable, a carrot plant can survive and probably even reproduce—but without forming the big storage root which we treasure. Under adverse conditions such as insufficient light, inadequate nutrients, limited water, or too much weed competition, these plants will devote whatever energy they have to meeting their basic survival needs and will not produce the plump, succulent roots we want.

Scientists studying sugar beets have observed this tendency to put storage root development last. They found that if the soil is limited in nutrients, sugar beets will devote their energies first to respiration to stay alive, then to top growth to increase photosynthetic area. Only after these two requirements are met will the plant develop storage roots and accumulate sucrose in those roots.

The same has been found to be true for radishes. If radishes are grown under low light intensities, such as the levels present in a greenhouse during the winter, the familiar swollen roots never develop. The low level of sunlight limits the amount of food that the plant's leaves can produce, so there is not enough food for the radish to channel into a storage root—in fact, there is nothing to store! Dorothy found this out the hard way last spring, when she tried to grow radishes very early in the season in her small greenhouse. She wasted valuable space on them and ended up with plants that looked just like those ill-fated radishes she grew in the wet clay—puny plants with a few small flowers and no sign of swollen roots! Carrots are no different from beets and radishes, for under conditions of nutrient stress, enlarged roots just won't develop.

So remember, big, fat storage roots aren't the number one priority as far as your plants are concerned. You must encourage them in that direction by providing close-to-ideal conditions so the plants can turn their energy away from merely surviving to building up a store of carbohydrates in a swollen root. A good place to start to make sure your root crops have the best conditions is to offer them a rich soil that contains plenty of organic matter.

The Best Growing Conditions for Radishes, Beets, and Carrots

Root crops need to grow rapidly and evenly in order to produce a nice-sized, tender crop. While they are still young, they all send down a long, slender taproot. Although this deep root is able to draw water up from the deeper soil levels, you can't let your plants depend on that for all their moisture. It's essential to give these crops abundant water. If you don't, they will become tough as extra xylem cells develop to help bring more water up from the deep soil layers. These extra cells are visible as white rings in beets grown under water stress. If you are growing your root crops in a concentrated block or otherwise closely spaced, be extra careful to give them enough water, since there will be more roots competing for the water in that area.

A layer of mulch will help hold in moisture around your crops, as well as keeping down competition from weeds. Mulching will also protect the tops of the enlarged roots to prevent rough shoulders on beets and green shoulders on carrots. Exposure to dry air makes beet shoulders rough and can crack the roots as well. When the top of a carrot is exposed to light, it forms green chlorophyll, along with other, bitter-tasting chemicals which make the top of the root inedible.

Your root crops won't grow well if they have to compete with weeds or with one another. Since carrot and radish seeds are small and beet seeds are actually fruits containing several seeds, all these crops must be carefully thinned while the plants are small. Weeding is also vital. If you give the weeds a chance to establish themselves, the competition for nutrients will leave your crops with no extra energy to put into storage roots. Sure, weeding is tedious, but taking that extra time to thin and weed will really pay off come harvest-time. The size of the harvested roots will be twice that of unweeded plants, and the roots will be tender instead of tough. Keep radishes, beets, and carrots well weeded until they are about half-grown; from then on they should be able to outcompete any weeds that might spring up if you can't find the time to weed them. Be careful when weeding not to disturb the plants. They have tiny feeder roots that will be damaged if you chop the soil with a hoe, so carefully pull by hand all the weeds that are growing within a foot of the plants. Do your weeding when the soil around the plants is moist. And get those weeds out before they become too big; if you disturb the roots of your root crops, you can end up with stunted plants or misshapen roots.

In 1973, scientists were able to show just how much weeding can help beets. In the experimental plots, when beets had to compete with weeds, they formed fewer, smaller leaves with less chlorophyll in them than did the plants grown in weed-free plots. When the beet patch was allowed to get really weedy (from 15 to 240 weeds in each square meter), the beet roots were reduced in size by 45 to 98 percent! The researchers also found that once the beets were well underway—two to four weeks after coming up—they could outgrow any weeds which tried to invade their patch of ground.

Why Root Crops Bolt

Radishes, beets, and carrots are all sensitive to daylength, but not in exactly the same way. Beets and carrots are biennial crops and usually do not bolt until their second year. Since we eat them during their first year of growth,

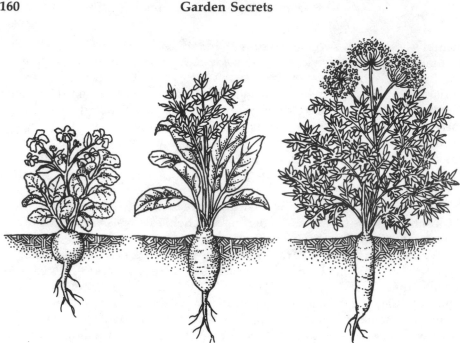

Flowers of Root Crops: *Since radishes (left), beets (center), and carrots are harvested long before they bloom, many gardeners never see these plants in flower. But for those who save their own seed or are unfortunate enough to have problems with early bolting, the flowers are quite familiar.*

most gardeners never see these plants flower. However, there are conditions that can bring on flowering the first year, much to the gardener's frustration. And once beets or carrots have bolted, the roots turn bitter and tough and become inedible.

Any time beets or carrots are grown in temperatures below 45°F and then exposed to long days, there is the chance that they will bolt. Some varieties are more susceptible to early bolting than others. For instance, with carrots, Scarlet Nantes bolts more readily than Royal Chantenay and Danvers Half Long. This is why most gardening books tell you to plant these crops around the last expected frost date or only a couple of weeks earlier, despite the fact that they are quite frost-hardy. The larger the plants are when exposed to the cold, the greater the chance that they will bolt when days get long.

Diane has always planted her Royal Chantenay carrots early, about six weeks before the last expected frost date. But one year she was especially conscientious. She enriched the soil with wood ashes and bone meal before planting her seeds, and she weeded and thinned the carrots just when she was supposed to. The carrots responded to this treatment and grew quickly and by June, she was already harvesting young carrots. But in July she got a nasty surprise—some of the carrots bolted! She had never had trouble with this variety bolting before, but then she'd also never had such big carrots so early in the season. The carrots had grown so fast that they were large enough to respond to the cold spring days and long June days by bolting. Even so, she only lost about 50 carrots out of two 50-foot rows, not too high a price to pay for learning a gardening lesson.

Beets are more susceptible to early bolting than carrots, and in areas that experience the twin forces of cold springtime temperatures and long June days, beets shouldn't be planted any earlier than three weeks before the last expected frost date. To be on the safe side, gardeners in those areas may wish to grow the slow-to-bolt varieties Vermilion and Spring Red, both carried by Stokes Seeds, Inc.

Spring radishes—the kind most gardeners grow—are annuals and will bolt when days get long, regardless of the temperatures they've been exposed to. But, the less-familiar winter radishes are biennials and react to temperature and daylength much like carrots and beets do.

If you want to save seeds from any of the biennials (beets, carrots, or winter radishes), you must step in at the end of the first growing season and see to it that these plants get a cool (below 45°F) rest period over the winter. Start by picking out a few of the plumpest, healthiest, most vigorous roots from the garden. If you are in a mild-winter area, your best bet is to place the roots in a plastic bag and set them in the refrigerator. If you garden in an area with cold winter temperatures, you can leave the chosen roots in the ground, well mulched, of course. When spring rolls around, take the refrigerated roots and replant them in the garden or pull back the mulch from the inground roots. Either way, the plants should bolt and produce elongated flower stems from which you can harvest the seeds after they are mature.

Radishes

Most gardeners find that radishes are a very satisfying crop to grow, for they mature so quickly into such pretty, tasty globes. One of the joys of springtime is a tender salad of lettuce thinnings and tiny radish slices served with a light lemon juice and oil dressing. If you are a real radish fan, you can grow mid- to late-season varieties to accompany the more familiar early-season ones. That way you can eat these crunchy roots throughout most of the growing season, instead of facing a springtime feast followed by famine.

Radishes Great and Small: *Radishes come in a wide variety of colors, shapes, and sizes such as the small red or white globe types (upper right), the large Daikon (bottom), long, white, tapered Icicle (left), and the winter radish Black Spanish (top center) with its white flesh and contrasting black skin.*

Radish Varieties

The most familiar radishes are the very early, round, red ones. Some of these varieties are ready to eat in 20 days or less (there's a variety called "18 Days," which is ready that quickly even here in Montana), while others take as long as 35 days. But spring radishes don't have to be round and red. There are round, white radishes and long, taper-rooted white or red radishes. Our favorites are the white-tipped red varieties, such as Sparkler, and the long white ones, like Icicle. You can use these to make crispy pickles, add them to stir-fried dishes, or simply savor them raw.

If you have adventuresome tastes and loose, sandy soil, you may want to try growing the large Japanese Daikon-type radishes. Daikon radishes are especially mild and flavorful and one root—which can be a foot or more long—can feed the entire family! They are very tasty whether used raw, for cooking, or for pickling. Daikons are more resistant to heat than conventional radishes; different varieties are suited to spring, early summer, and late summer sowing and mature within 45 to 70 days. Any roots harvested in the fall can be stored the same way you'd store winter radishes or carrots.

Biennial winter radishes, such as China Rose and Black Spanish, are very attractive with their creamy, white flesh, and deep rose and black skins, respectively. They take from 55 to 60 days to mature and can be stored all winter in barely moist sand or in plastic bags in the refrigerator. Black Spanish is heat-resistant and can be planted in mid-July, while China Rose likes cool weather and should be planted in late summer.

Secrets of Radish Success

While radishes are considered easy to grow, they can often be disappointing. That's because they are quite finicky about growing conditions. If it is too cool (below 60°F) they will develop slowly and have a biting hot flavor. If the temperature is too high (above 70°F), radishes will grow too fast and become pithy and hot. Radishes that are pithy have grown so fast that the cell walls separate from one another. Pithy radishes are fit only for the compost pile, for if you've ever bitten into one, you know it's like eating a sponge.

The ideal conditions for raising a successful crop of radishes are a temperature range from 60° to 65°F and a fairly rich soil with an abundant, even supply of water. Uneven watering, where dry spells alternate with wet spells, will check the roots' growth, making them hot, pithy, and tough. Rapid, even growth is the secret to crisp, pleasantly piquant radishes. Prompt harvesting is important, too, for most radishes do not hold their quality long in the garden. Many times we've pulled just enough for a tasty salad one day and come back a couple of days later to find that the rest of our radishes were already getting pithy, tough, and unpalatable.

You can grow radishes in the spring or fall, depending on local conditions, as long as the weather is cool. If your summers are hot, plant your radishes as soon as the air and soil temperatures average 45°F in the spring. Don't worry if a late frost strikes; radishes can tolerate some frost. Radishes for fall eating should go in after the heat of summer is past. Plant your radish seeds from ½ to 1½ inches deep. If you save your own seed, plant the largest seeds to get the largest radishes. Radish seed you buy will look pretty much the same size, for commercial seed companies discard all the smaller seeds which would make smaller radishes.

In 1962, the Proceedings of the American Society for Horticultural Science reported the work done by scientists studying Cherry Belle and Comet radishes. These researchers found that deeper planting leads to larger radishes. If you like large radishes, plant the seeds 1½ inches deep and space them 1½ inches apart in the rows; the rows themselves can be as close as 2 inches. If you prefer average-sized radishes, plant the seeds ½ inch deep and space them 1 inch apart.

The researchers also found that radishes grew best when the temperature was between 60° to 65°F, although they did fairly well between 50° and 55°F. Temperatures in the 70° to 75°F range led to pithy roots. The study also revealed that the best daylength for these two particular varieties was twelve hours; many plants bolted under sixteen-hour days. Comet bolted after only

30 days, while Cherry Belle held for 45 days. Since Cherry Belle is ready to eat in 22 days, bolting should be no problem with this variety, making it a good one for northern gardeners.

Radishes will germinate in soils ranging from 45° to 95°F and will come up most quickly when the soil is 85°F. This doesn't help the gardener, however, since soils that hot are produced by days that are much too warm for good radish development. But as long as the soil temperature is between 45° and 95°F, your radishes should germinate in three to ten days. As soon as they are up, thin them to stand 1 to 2 inches apart, depending on the variety and on how big you want them to be.

A good way to enjoy radishes without devoting any extra garden space to them is to plant them among other crops that germinate slowly, such as carrots. Some gardeners plant the radish seeds right in the row with the carrots with good results. Dorothy worries that pulling the radishes may hurt the delicate carrot seedlings nearby, so she plants the radishes in their own row just an inch to the side of the carrots. Either way you interplant, when the radishes are ready to pull, the carrots are ready to thin, so you might as well do both jobs at once; it will keep you from forgetting that tedious but important task of thinning the carrots. If you do plant your radishes right with the carrots, be sure as you go along to gently cover with soil any carrot roots that are exposed when you pull the radishes.

In general, radishes are untouched by pests and diseases, the flea beetle and root maggot being the notable exceptions. For serious flea beetle infestations, your best defense is a dusting of diatomaceous earth or rotenone. If you have a history of problems with root maggots in your garden, the best preventive measure you can take is to dig hardwood ashes into the soil and spread them on the top after planting to repel the flies that lay the eggs that produce the maggots.

Harvesting and Storing Radishes

It takes a little practice to learn when radishes are ready to pull. Some varieties send up only a few short leaves before the root swells; it's amazing that those few leaves can produce enough extra food to allow the radish to form. If the seeds were not deeply planted, the radishes may begin to peek out of the ground as they round up. If you aren't sure whether your radishes are ready to pull, probe gently around the base of the leaves with your index finger, and you will be able to tell if the root has swelled yet. And remember that all the radishes of one variety will mature over a period of just a few days; don't expect them to hold for long in the garden. (You may want to stagger your plantings to extend your radish crop.)

If you have more radishes than you can eat, cut off the tops and store the roots in a plastic bag in the refrigerator. If you leave the tops on, they will begin to rot after a week or two, turning the entire contents of the bag into a slimy and unpleasant mess. But if you remove the tops, you can store the roots for up to four weeks.

Radish Frontiers

Plant breeders are working on developing radishes that will grow well in the heat and that are slow to bolt. They are also working on decreasing pithiness and pungency. Most radish research is being done in Europe and Japan, because there's a greater consumer demand for them there. European and Japanese breeders are working on hybrid radishes, and one of these days, more hybrid varieties will be available to home gardeners.

Beets

Many gardeners just don't realize how delicious beet greens are to eat. Dorothy was shocked by this oversight one year when she bought some beets from a truck gardener. After pulling the roots, he twisted off all the leaves and added them to the big pile of beet greens he had already made. When she asked about the greens, he said she could have them all for free if she wanted. That year her family ended up with a freezer full of wonderful greens for the winter—thanks to the seemingly widespread ignorance of the tasty value of beet greens.

Beets get their lovely rich color from pigments called anthocyanins. The particular anthocyanin of beets is called betacyanine. This pigment is water soluble and is not destroyed by heat, so when beets are cooked, the beta-cyanine leaks into the water and stains it red. Betacyanine can be used to dye Easter eggs, and as any beet-lover knows, it should be wiped up immediately from kitchen counters or they will have long-lasting red splotches on them. Golden beets lack betacyanine but do display another pigment present in all beets—betaxanthine—which gives the roots a beautiful golden color. Beta-xanthine breaks down when heated, so yellow beets do not stain the cooking water the way red ones do.

Beet Varieties

To the uninitiated, a beet is a beet is a beet, but to gardeners in the know, there are different beet varieties suited to different purposes. If you're new to beet growing, study the seed catalogs carefully to see just what your selection is. If you want to store your beets fresh to have them on hand for winter use, try Detroit Dark Red, Lutz Green Leaf, Long Season, or Winter Keeper. If you'd rather can your beets, small varieties like Little Ball or Gladiator are very easy to work with. Several varieties have especially delicious greens as well as fine roots. Dorothy's personal favorite for greens is Burpee's Golden Beet, but Early Wonder, Formanova, and Lutz Green Leaf also have abundant, tasty tops. Formanova and Cylindra are good for small gardens and for slicing because of their long, slender, cylindrical shape.

Beet Shapes: *From left to right are shown a long slicing variety, a variety that is grown for both its roots and tops, and round beets that are ideal for canning.*

Growing and Harvesting Beets

Beet seeds are actually fruits containing several seeds. When you plant these little star-shaped fruits, several seedlings will come up where each was planted, and you must thin this tight clump if you want a crop that's uniform in size. If you don't thin, the more vigorous seedlings will take over and although you will get a harvestable crop, the roots will be uneven in size. Some newer varieties of beets, such as Mono King Explorer, have only one seed per fruit. When you plant them far enough apart to begin with, there's no need to thin them later.

If you've ever had trouble getting beet seeds to sprout in the garden, that's because they contain a germination inhibitor. In order for them to sprout, this inhibitor must be leached out. You can help the process along by soaking the seeds in water the night before you plant them.

Sow beet seeds ½ to 1 inch deep, 2 inches apart, in rows 1 to 2 feet away from each other. When the plants are anywhere from 2 to 4 inches tall, thin them to stand 3 to 4 inches apart. (Use the larger spacing if you want big, chunky beets, and the smaller one if you want beets for pickling.) Be sure to take the thinnings to the kitchen and steam them lightly, roots and all, for a special springtime treat. Beets will germinate in soil temperatures between 50° and 85°F; however, optimum germination occurs at 85°F. Beets take one to two weeks to come up, depending on the temperature (the warmer, the faster).

As far as pests and diseases go, aphids, leaf miners, nematodes, and webworms may visit your beet patch from time to time, but they don't usually pose a serious threat. Check the undersides of the leaves for the small white egg clusters left by the leaf miner and just pinch off any infested leaves. Ladybugs will keep any advancing aphids at bay, and if you see any web-worms, just pick them off by hand. Crop rotation is a must for controlling nematodes. If you have a nematode problem in the soil, try not to plant beets or any other susceptible crops for four or five years, to give the worms a chance to die off.

There's no hard and fast rule about when you should harvest your beets. Let your own preference as to size be the judge of when it's time to pull them up. Just remember that they're more tender when they're on the small side; large beets tend to be tough and woody. You can scrape some soil away from around the stem and feel to find out how big the roots are. Don't leave your beets out in the garden for too long after they are mature or they'll pass their sweet, tender, juicy prime. Some varieties (such as Hybrid Pacemaker) keep better in the row than do others.

After you pull up the beets, cut off most of the greens, leaving about a 2-inch stubble attached to the root. This simple step will help the beets keep longer in good condition. If you were to leave the greens on, they would quickly start to deteriorate and serve as a source of infection for the roots. Besides, when you trim away the greens, you're getting what amounts to a second harvest from the same plant. Just be sure to eat or process your beet greens as soon as possible; they will keep in the refrigerator for a maximum of two weeks. The roots will keep much longer, depending on the variety. Those bred for long storage can be kept in good condition for as long as five months, in temperatures close to 32°F, at 95 percent relative humidity.

Beet Frontiers

The great commercial importance of sugar beets has had some pleasant repercussions for home gardeners. The new monogerm (single-seed) beets were originally developed for commercial sugar beet growers who wanted easy, even spacing of their crops. (It's not very efficient to have to go back over a huge field to thin the clusters.) After being developed for sugar beets, the monogerm trait was bred into table beets as well. Plant breeders are also working on pest and disease resistance for sugar beets which should trickle down and influence varieties bred for home gardeners, too. The problem with relying on sugar beet developments for improvements in table beets is that sugar beet growers are only concerned with the roots, and not at all with the more nutritious tops of the plants.

Commercial growers of table beets don't concern themselves with the tops either, for beet greens are not an especially popular commercial crop. What large-scale growers and home gardeners look for in a crop are often at opposite ends of the spectrum. Commercial growers want uniform, small beets which can be harvested all at once. The home gardener isn't in such a rush to harvest, and even favors a more dispersed harvest rather than a sudden glut. Commercial growers don't care about the ability of the roots to hold in the garden and to stay tender, for they can get more money for small canning beets than for large ones. In the eyes of a home gardener, a long-standing beet that stays tender means that good quality, fresh produce can be harvested as needed, over a rather extended period. Only when plant breeders start to consider directly the needs of the home gardener will we see more rapid advances made in the area of beet varieties.

Carrots

If you're looking for an especially high-yielding crop that stores well in its fresh state to carry you through the winter, look no further than carrots. Their contained growth habit allows you to space them closely together, increasing the yield per square foot of garden space. Under the proper storage conditions, carrots stay in edible shape for up to six months, providing your family with the welcome taste of a homegrown fresh vegetable during the winter months. The lovely, sunny carrot color comes from the pigment carotene, which the human body converts to vitamin A. The darker the orange color, the more nutritious the carrot is for you. If you are looking for the most nutritious carrots to grow, zero in on those described in seed catalogs as having a good golden color.

Carrot Varieties

Despite the limited genetic base of carrots (which we discussed at the beginning of the chapter), there are still several types suited to different uses and garden conditions from which you can choose. If an early harvest of carrots is what you're after, try one of the small, sweet kinds such as Little Finger (65 days), Planet (55 days), or Tiny Sweet (62 days). When selecting main-crop carrots, you must take your soil into consideration. Not all of us can grow those long, straight, 8-inch beauties that the supermarket carries. Long carrots such as Imperator will only grow well in loose, sandy, rockless soil. If your soil is at all heavy or rocky, try the shorter (about 6 inches long), stump-rooted varieties like Danvers Half Long or Royal Chantenay. Even in very difficult soil you can have a successful crop of carrots when you grow a short, fat variety such as Oxheart, or the round varieties such as Gold Nugget or Konfrix. For winter storage in the garden, Royal Chantenay or Oxheart is good, or you can try any variety which is described as holding well in the garden.

Choosing Carrots: *There are so many carrot varieties, you can easily find a carrot that is tailored to your needs. You can choose stump-rooted carrots (bottom left) or round-rooted types (top left) for difficult soils; short varieties (top center) for heavy, rocky soils; and long, straight carrots (bottom) if you're one of those fortunate gardeners with loose, rockless soil. Early baby types (top right) are perfect for container-growing or for anxious gardeners who want a crop in less than 65 days.*

Tips on Growing Carrots

For a good crop of carrots, you should lavish attention on them before they have even come up. The early stages of a carrot's life are the most critical, and this is the time it demands the most regular attention. Once they've germinated and gotten off to a good start, you can stand back and let them grow. Because their seeds are very small and slow to germinate, carrots are sometimes tricky to get started, particularly if the weather is especially sunny or windy after planting.

Conventional gardening practice is to plant carrots in single rows, but we've found that we get better results when we plant in blocks. Block-planting gives us a much higher yield for our garden area and the slightly depressed planting area creates a moist haven for germinating seeds that tends to counteract the drying effects of sun and wind. We've also found that it's easier to space the seeds evenly in a block than it is in a narrow row. If we drop a cluster of seeds in one spot (which is all too easy to do with tiny carrot seeds), we can just lightly brush them out over the wide area of the block. Another advantage to this method is that when you set aside a block of soil for the carrots, the area in which they grow won't be stepped on and compacted. The conventional arrangement of narrow rows with paths running between them leads to compacted soil perilously close to where the carrot roots are growing. Despite all these pluses, there is one minus to block-planting; early weeding and thinning can be a bit trickier than in single rows.

If you'd like to follow our lead and try block planting, here are a few guidelines. To make a narrow block (4 to 6 inches wide), drag the flat surface of a garden hoe along the ground. For a wider block (12 to 14 inches wide), use the head (teeth-side up) of a garden rake. Don't make the block too wide, though, for all the plants inside should be within comfortable reach so that you can weed and thin easily. The act of pulling the tool across the ground will displace some soil and, in addition to marking the boundaries of the planting area, will create a slight depression. This sunken planting area (which should be no deeper than 1 inch) will collect and hold water around the germinating seeds and shelter them from any drying winds which may be swirling through your garden.

Once you've marked off the block, scatter the seeds as thinly as possible (mixing them with sand can help here) and cover with ¼ to ½ inch of sieved compost, fine soil, or dampened peat moss. Water thoroughly with a gentle mist of fine droplets.

Carrots germinate over a wide temperature range (45° to 85°F) and come up most quickly at 80°F. They should be up within a week or two, but if the soil is especially cool (that is, below 50°F) they may take three weeks to show their feathery heads. While you're waiting for them to emerge, be sure to keep the top half-inch of soil (or compost or peat moss) moist. Never let it dry out, or you'll be waiting in vain for a carrot crop to come up. If the sun is hot or the wind is blowing pretty steadily, you may have to mist your carrot patch faithfully every day until the seedlings emerge.

When the plants are 3 to 4 inches tall, thin them to stand 2 to 3 inches apart. It's always hard to get in there and pull up so many promising young plants, but it really is necessary for a good crop. Thinning thick clumps of young seedlings can be a little touchy, for you don't want to disturb the roots of the seedlings you leave behind, for fear of prompting misshapen roots to form. We find that patience and a steady hand are two of the best tools you can bring out to the garden. Just zero in on the one seedling in a cluster you want to leave in place, and very gingerly pull away the rest from that area, one by one. If the seedlings are almost on top of one another, be sure to grasp them close to the soil line—that way you only get one at a time and don't dislodge the remaining seedlings too much. As the carrots grow, thin them again so that their final spacing is about 3 to 4 inches apart. This second thinning can be done as the roots are fattening up and turning orange, so you will be able to add those thinnings to a salad. Just how much space you leave between plants will depend on how wide the carrots are. If you're growing a slim variety such as Burpee's Gold Pak or Imperator, you can space them 2 to 3 inches apart, but with fat varieties like Royal Chantenay or Oxheart, you really need the 4-inch spacing.

Well-drained soil is a must for carrots. If the soil surrounding the roots retains water, they will absorb too much and will split. Even in well-drained soils there is the danger of splitting if you overwater. Underwatering is no better, for it will encourage the carrots to develop many feeder roots to soak up what moisture is available, and your carrots will be hairy. They may also be tough because of the extra xylem they develop to carry what water is available. To avoid either extreme, water only when the top 4 inches of soil have dried out, and then water thoroughly.

There aren't many pest and disease problems you should encounter when growing carrots. Root maggots are the most common pest, but they can be lured away from your carrots by a trap crop of radishes. Once the maggots have infested the radishes, pull them up and discard them, leaving your carrots to grow unmolested. Carrot rust flies, carrot weevils, bacterial soft rot, and nematodes can all be controlled with a simple three-year rotation pattern alternating peas, carrots, and lettuce. If wireworms become a particular nuisance, sprinkle wood ashes along the carrot rows. If leaf blight is a recurrent problem, control it by soaking the seed for ten minutes in 126°F water before planting.

Harvesting and Storing Carrots

Many people are surprised the first time they bite into a homegrown carrot to find just how sweet and crispy this vegetable can be. Once you've tasted the homegrown product, supermarket carrots will pale in comparison. The sweetness of your carrots will depend in part on their genetic composition, so you should pay particular attention to those varieties noted for their fine flavor. But the growing environment also influences how sweet your harvested carrots will be. When carrots are allowed to remain in the soil through the cool fall and into winter, the starch in the roots is slowly converted to sugar. The longer you leave those storage carrots in the ground, the sweeter they will be. That explains why commercially grown carrots don't taste as good—they are harvested as soon as they reach mature size and are never given the chance to develop that delectable sweetness.

Actually, you can harvest your carrots any time after they've reached a usable size. When you want to pull them up, first water the carrots so that the roots will slide out of the ground easily. Some varieties, such as Little Finger, have weak tops that break off as you pull on them. To avoid this frustration, loosen the soil next to the row or block with a garden fork and then pull gently on the leaves right at the top of the root. If you constantly have problems harvesting your carrots, try the variety Royal Chantenay which has strong tops.

Once you've unearthed your carrots, trim off their green tops right away (leaving about an inch of stubble at the top of the root). Otherwise, the topgrowth will draw moisture out of the roots, leaving them flabby instead of crunchy. Carrots store very well in plastic bags in the refrigerator, layered in moist sand in a container stashed in a cool place, or anywhere with a temperature of 32°F and a relative humidity of 95 percent.

Our favorite way to store carrots, however, is right in the garden. If you leave your carrots in the ground after they have grown, the cool autumn temperatures will encourage them to build up their sugar content. Just be sure that carrots you intend to store in the garden are planted in well-drained soil. If not, fall and winter moisture will waterlog the soil and the carrots will rot. Also, be sure to leave a buffer zone of bare soil around the storage area to discourage rodents from settling in for a long winter's nap (they don't like to move across bare ground). This year Dorothy's inground carrot cache was right next to a stand of weeds, and when she went out to dig carrots for Christmas dinner they had all disappeared. The only thing that some satisfied, tunnelling rodent had left behind were a few orange crumbs.

If the winters get cold enough so that the ground freezes in your area, bury your carrots under a thick mulch, such as a foot of unshredded leaves. Lay down the mulch while the ground is moist but before it freezes. Cover it all with a sheet of heavy plastic and anchor the plastic around the edges with heavy rocks or a few shovels full of soil. Extend the mulch at least 6 inches around the row in all directions to make sure the carrots are well insulated from the cold.

When you need carrots, lift up the plastic from one end and carefully dig up a portion of the row or block, loosening the carrots and then pulling them out. Remove all carrots which have become loosened from the soil; if there are more than you need right away, they will keep just fine in the refrigerator. Dorothy likes to dig enough at one time for about a week's use, which is two pounds for her family of four. As springtime nears, be sure to eat up the last of the carrots, for when the soil warms, any that are left in the rows will bolt and turn very bitter and woody.

Carrot Frontiers

An exciting area of carrot breeding is the reintroduction of genetic material from wild Eastern carrots into the cultivated Western varieties. These wild species, descendants of the first carrots grown in Afghanistan, will help in the development of disease resistance and will broaden the genetic base of carrots. This is very important work, for it will remove the threat of a single disease wiping out our familiar Western carrot varieties, which currently have such a narrow genetic base.

Chapter 9

Potatoes: Those Tasty Tubers

Vital Statistics

Family:
Solanaceae

Species:
Solanum tuberosum

Soil:
Sandy loam; good drainage
and looseness important

pH:
5.0–6.0; 5.5 or lower
if scab is a problem

**Soil Temperature
for Sprouting of Sets:**
50°–60°F

**Air Temperature
for Best Vine Growth:**
60°–70°F, daytime; 45°–50°F,
nighttime; lower than 30°F
kills vines

**Soil Temperature
for Tuber Formation:**
50°F optimum

Seed Potato Viability:
6–7 months

Seed Potato Planting Depth:
8"

Growing potatoes in your garden can be very rewarding, for the yield from even a small area can be surprisingly high. Once underway, potato plants require little attention except for watering because their foliage is so vigorous. But cultivating these fine tubers can also be frustrating. You may end up with a bunch of tiny potatoes that are too small for baking, or your crop may be scabby, requiring extensive peeling before you can use it and curtailing its storage life. And the actual act of storing potatoes through the winter in good eating condition is rather tricky. But a little advance understanding of the biology of potatoes will give you the edge you need to grow them successfully and store them properly.

Potatoes belong to the same botanical family as tomatoes, peppers, and eggplants. Underscoring these family ties, some seed catalogs sell "pomatoes," which consist of potato root stock grafted onto a tomato top. This novel "halfbreed" plant will produce a small crop of both potatoes and tomatoes. **173**

Potato breeders sometimes do the reverse combination—tomato roots with potato tops—so the potato part will be able to invest all its energy into making seeds instead of tubers.

Potatoes have an especially colorful history. They are native to the Andes Mountains of Peru and Bolivia and are still grown there in greater variety than anywhere else in the world. Andean potatoes are much more colorful than the tubers we are familiar with; depending on the variety, the skin may be red, blue, purple or brown. Different types tolerate a great range of climatic conditions, and some can even produce a crop at an elevation of 6,000 feet.

The *conquistadores* introduced potatoes to Spain in the early 1500s. One explorer's journal quaintly described this new vegetable as "a kind of earth-nut, which, after it has been boiled, is as tender as a cooked chestnut, but it has no more skin than a truffle, and it grows under the earth in the same way." The *conquistadores* recognized the high nutritive value of potatoes and included them in their sea-going larders, thereby warding off the scurvy that plagued so many early seamen.

Potatoes were quickly accepted in Spain, for the people were already growing and enjoying sweet potatoes. The superficial similarity between the two (sweet potatoes are in an entirely different plant family—the Morning Glory family—and are actually tuberous roots, whereas potato tubers are modified underground stems) led to the name for the new vegetable. Sweet potatoes in Spanish are called *batata*, and potatoes soon became *patatas*. Both translated into English as "potatoes" so a gardener of yore talking about a "potato" could have meant either vegetable.

Potatoes soon became popular throughout the rest of Europe, and in the mid-1700s, royal edicts in both Sweden and Germany required that everyone grow this crop. If you were a German and didn't comply, you could have had your nose and ears cut off! Potatoes became one of the staple foods in many European countries, and the Irish, unfortunately, were forced by economics to rely too heavily on them. This dependence had tragic consequences when the late blight disease hit and caused one of the worst famines in history.

The Potato's Nutritional Profile

Before the potato famine, many Irish people lived on a diet of boiled potatoes and milk. This might sound like a pretty boring diet to you, but surprisingly enough, seven pounds of potatoes plus one pint of milk would meet all your daily nutritional needs, even if it didn't scintillate your taste buds. Potatoes are one of the most nutritious foods around, but unfortunately, their association with the junk food industry has given them the undeserved reputation of being an all-starch, no-nutrition food.

Despite the fact that most people eat potatoes as a source of starch, potatoes are high in protein. Many commonly grown varieties contain 6 to 8 percent usable protein on a dry weight basis, and some varieties even contain as much as 10 percent. In terms of amount of protein produced per acre, potatoes rank second only to soybeans! The fact that the quality of this protein is high only enhances their nutritional stature. A standard measure of protein quality is net protein utilization (NPU). The following NPU ratings of several important foods should give you an idea of how well potatoes measure up as a protein source: eggs—100 (an ideal protein), beef—80, potatoes—71, soy flour—56, wheat flour—52, and peas—44. If you ate nothing but potatoes, you would satisfy your protein needs before fulfilling your caloric requirements! The high NPU of potatoes also means that they can satisfy the protein requirement of more people per acre than any other major crop.

Another noteworthy nutritional feature is that potatoes are high in vitamin C. The average amount of potatoes consumed each year per person in the United States—about 120 pounds—provides enough vitamin C to meet the recommended daily allowance. These unassuming tubers also contain substantial amounts of copper, folic acid, iron, vitamin B_6, and vitamin B_{12}.

Potato Varieties

In light of the nutritional bonanza they offer, it is hard to understand why potatoes are one of the least commonly grown vegetables in home gardens. While potatoes are grown commercially all throughout North America and are planted or harvested during every month of the year, they rank among the ten *least* favorite home-garden crops. Many gardeners don't bother with potatoes because they take up quite a bit of garden space and are readily available in the supermarket at relatively low prices. Plus, fresh-from-the-garden doesn't seem to be as critical a factor in their flavor as it is for other crops like corn, peas, and tomatoes. But, as any gardener who has ever grown potatoes will tell you, nothing you can buy tastes quite like the tiny, creamy new potatoes dug straight from the garden. Some especially delectable varieties, such as the nutritious baking potato, Butte, and the special salad potato, German Fingerling, are only available to gardeners and will never be found in your local grocery store. If you don't grow your own, you miss out on these special treats.

When you do decide to devote a corner of the garden to potatoes, you may have trouble finding a good selection of varieties to choose from. While there are many different kinds of potatoes in existence, relatively few varieties are readily available to home gardeners. Often, seed potatoes will be sold simply as red or white, with no indication of which type of red or white is in the bag. And considering the vast differences among potatoes, how satisfied you are with the results of your gardening efforts will depend heavily on which variety you grow.

Potatoes come in three basic types, based on their time to maturity—early, intermediate, and late. If you want to store your potatoes for several months into the winter, you should pick a late variety that will come out of the garden at the end of the season. Early varieties will not store into the winter as long as the late ones do simply because they have been out of the ground longer. But early types will give you a harvest of delectable new potatoes sooner than late varieties. Here is a rundown of the characteristics of some of the more common potato varieties.

Russet Burbank is probably the most commonly grown potato variety in the United States and is close to 100 years old. It is late maturing and stores better for a longer period of time than almost all other varieties. You can keep Russet Burbank without sprouting for five months at 45°F. It is used primarily as a baking potato, although it is also wonderful for frying.

Butte was introduced in 1977 as a new baking variety from Idaho. Its excellent all-around quality makes it equally useful for frying. Butte has 25 percent more protein and 50 percent more vitamin C than Russet Burbank.

Potato Picks: *Growing your own potatoes gives you the opportunity to try different varieties not available in the supermarket and, most of all, lets you enjoy freshly dug new potatoes. Clockwise from upper right are Red Pontiac, Kennebec, Butte, Norland, Norgold Russet, and Russet Burbank in the center.*

Although it is late maturing, it will sprout after only three months of storage at 45°F. Butte needs more water to grow well than does Russet Burbank.

Centennial Russet potatoes are well suited as spring or early summer crops in California. They do not do well in short-season areas. They mature medium-late and are good for baking. This variety will keep in storage for five months, like Russet Burbank, but tends to accumulate sugar which can cause an unpleasant flavor.

Kennebec is another medium-late variety used for baking, boiling, and frying. Kennebec is a cook's delight because it doesn't get watery or soggy. With its thin skin, it makes delectable new potatoes. It doesn't store for very long and while it is in storage, sugar builds up. Kennebec also tends to set tubers close to the soil surface where they can easily push out of the ground and turn green. With this popular variety, it's a good idea to plant in a thick mulch pocket which can be hilled up as the potatoes mature. (This technique is described later in the chapter.)

Nampa has the desirable characteristic of growing and bearing well in high daytime temperatures. It is a medium-late variety used for baking.

Nooksack was developed in 1973 by the Washington State University–USDA Cooperative Potato Breeding Program. Its outstanding characteristic is a long storage life. As a matter of fact, it stores so well that it may also be slow to sprout when planted! This late baking variety yields less than Russet Burbank but produces a high proportion of large potatoes.

Norgold Russet is an early variety used mainly for boiling that also lends itself to baking and frying. The tuber flesh keeps its white color and develops a pleasant mealy texture when cooked. It has a short storage life and accumulates sugar at a rapid rate. This is a good, all purpose russet-type potato.

Norland is a very early boiling potato not suitable for long storage.

Red Pontiac is a medium-late boiling variety. It yields better than Norland but is very susceptible to scab. This potato has an attractive color combination of white flesh and red skin.

In general, small, waxy, new potatoes are recommended for boiling and for use in salads because they hold their shape when cooked. Most white potatoes, when mature, are best used for baking, mashing, or frying to take advantage of their dry, mealy texture. Mature red potatoes, however, are excellent for boiling and steaming.

As a final note on potato varieties, we'd like to mention that the terms "Idaho" and "Maine" refer to the geographic region where the potatoes were grown, and not to two distinct varieties. Actually, many varieties fall under these two groups, but the basic differences seem to be in mineral content and texture. Idaho potatoes contain higher levels of calcium than Maine potatoes for the simple reason that Western soils contain more of this mineral than do Eastern soils. Idaho potatoes are also thought to have a mealier texture than their Maine counterparts.

If you live in the West, you should grow red and white varieties if you want both boiling and baking potatoes for winter storage. Or, you can grow a white variety such as German Fingerling for boiling and steaming. Eastern gardeners may be able to get away with planting an "all-purpose" white variety only, but it won't produce dry, fluffy baking potatoes. Eastern gardeners who enjoy the flavor and mealiness of an Idaho potato should try BelRus, a new russet baking potato developed by the USDA together with researchers from Maine and Florida.

What Is a Potato?

We already mentioned that a potato is an underground stem. But what does that really mean? If you have ever disturbed your potato plants to rummage for new potatoes, you have probably noticed that each tuber forms from a small swelling on the end of a long, white stolon which grows from

Potato Plants: *A potato develops from a small swelling at the end of a modified underground stem known as a stolon. The stolon grows from the underground part of the potato stem and even has tiny purple or dark brown bracts (rudimentary leaves) spaced along its length.*

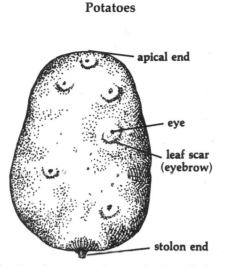

Potato Tuber: *Try to visualize the potato tuber as what it really is—a stem. At one end is a scar where the tuber was broken off from the stolon. At the opposite end is the apical tip from which the first sprouts will grow if the entire tuber is planted. The potato also sports numerous tiny "eyes," each of which has an "eyebrow" below it. The eyes are axillary buds, and the eyebrows represent leaf scars.*

the underground portion of the potato stem. If you look closely at a stolon, you will see that it is a modified stem with small purple or dark brown bracts along its length; these are rudimentary leaves. The tuber that you ultimately harvest is merely the swollen end of this underground stem.

Now let's look at a potato more carefully. One end has a cluster of eyes close together, while the other end has a scar where the stolon that connected it to the plant was broken off. If you stand the potato on end, with the stolon scar against the table, you can picture it as a swollen stem. You may recall from our discussion of plant structures in chapter 2 that all stems have a series of nodes and leaves, with internodes stretching in between. The potato is no exception. Each potato eye has what you could call an "eyebrow," except that it is found below the eye instead of above it. These eyebrows are actually the traces of what would have been leaves on an aboveground stem.

You may remember, also, that all stems have axillary buds above the leaves which can grow into stem branches. On the potato tuber, the eyes are the axillary buds, and they are right where they should be, just above the leaf scar on the swollen stem, the tuber. The top end of the tuber with its cluster of eyes represents the apical tip. If you plant an entire potato, the first sprouts will come from that end because in the potato tuber, just as in the aboveground stem, the apical tip inhibits growth of the axillary buds. But when you cut a seed potato into separate pieces for planting, you break the apical dominance, and all the eyes are free to sprout.

Choosing Seed Potatoes

What you use for seed is very important with potatoes. Many people are content to take a chance and plant sprouting store-bought potatoes or home-grown ones. This may work out in many cases, but these gardeners are taking a big risk. There are over a hundred diseases that can affect potatoes, and they do not always manifest themselves before the seed potatoes are planted. Your tubers may look perfectly fine but still carry one of these diseases—and you won't know it until your growing plants or maturing tubers start to look sickly. Some potato varieties are more susceptible to certain viruses than are others. Unfortunately, a resistant potato can act as a carrier, showing no signs of disease itself but infecting other varieties. Once your soil has been contaminated by a potato disease, you can't grow potatoes in that part of the garden for at least three or four years without risking reinfection.

You can greatly reduce the risk of losing your crop to disease by starting out with certified disease-free seed potatoes. These potatoes are generally grown in northern areas where plants affected by virus diseases will show detectable symptoms and where aphids are usually not a factor in spreading diseases. You may be tempted by the prospect of saving a little money and by the easy access to store-bought potatoes, but using sets that are not certified as disease-free can end up costing you a bundle in terms of a significantly reduced yield or a crop that is completely ruined. Store-bought potatoes, in addition, are often chemically treated to inhibit sprouting and may be reluctant or even refuse to sprout in the garden. Two types of chemical sprays are used, maleic hydrozide and chloropropham, the latter of which is very volatile. An acquaintance who works in a potato research station planted some potato tubers for seed that he knew had not been treated with chloropropham. He was confident that they would sprout when he planted them, but he was disappointed when the tubers didn't start to sprout until July, and even then only a portion of the ones he had planted finally came to life. The mystery was solved when he found that another person had stored a sack of chloropropham-treated potatoes in the same room with his seed potatoes. Apparently, enough of the chemical got into the air to inhibit all the potatoes in the room.

If you have your heart set on growing a particular potato variety, you may have no alternative but to order sets from a mail order catalog. But if you do have a choice, buy whole seed potatoes by weight at a local nursery rather than buying precut sets by mail. Potato sets are tiny pieces cut out of potatoes which contain one or two eyes each. The cut surfaces are treated with fungus-killing chemicals to forestall any damage. There are several drawbacks to using mail-order sets that you should be aware of. For one thing, mail-order companies often send their sets too early for safe planting, and the sets do not store well in the refrigerator for more than a few days. Some of them may shrivel up and die anyway because the single eye was damaged during processing or shipping. And even if they do arrive in good shape at the right time for planting, commercial potato sets are much smaller than the optimum size that promotes good, vigorous, early growth of potato plants.

The size of the potato set is a critical factor in the eventual development of the plant and its production of tubers. The sprouting potato stems draw all of their early nourishment from the starch stored in the seed potato. They must grow up through several inches of soil before they can reach the sun and begin to make their own food. Researchers have spent a great deal of time determining just what is the best size for a potato set. They've found that a set weighing 3 to 4 ounces and having two or three eyes will give the best results. Sets weighing 1½ ounces or less, a typical weight for a purchased set, will result in a weaker plant which yields far less than a plant grown from a larger set.

It's interesting to note that despite the research that has been done, commercial potato growers continue to plant sets which weigh only 2 to 2½ ounces. This is not due to ignorance or perversity on their part, but rather to the fact that the seed-potato planting machines were designed and built before anyone knew that larger sets were better. A commercial grower cannot plant 3- to 4-ounce sets because they will get caught in his seeder!

One final guideline to remember when choosing your sets is that you're better off buying ones that have not already begun to sprout. Sometimes, however, sprouted sets may be all that are available. Then you must be very careful not to break off any of the stems which have sprouted. In addition to being fragile, such sets will contain less stored food because the leaves which have been forming in the dark have not been able to photosynthesize any food for the growing stems. Instead, they have been draining the reserves of starch in the tuber that are needed to fuel vigorous growth in the garden. When you finally put these sets in the garden, you will probably find that they get off to a lackluster start.

Preparing Your Seed Potatoes for Planting

If you've been fortunate enough to buy whole seed potatoes of the variety you want, you're in good shape. Before you can begin planting, there's one important step you must take and that's cutting your whole tubers into sets. When you cut your tubers, leave a good amount of starchy food for each piece. Make sure that each set has at least two but not more than four eyes. This guideline is significant because a plant that develops two or three stems will produce the most tubers. Any more than four eyes will result in too many stems, and the competition between them will lead to smaller potatoes. If you have really small seed potatoes (less than 2 to 3 inches in diameter), leave them whole. Because of the apical dominance of the eyes clustered at the end, only one or two stems will form from each seed tuber. Whether small uncut sets or cut sets from larger potatoes produce a better yield is still a controversial point in the potato business. However, either method appears to be fine for the home gardener.

Once you've cut your sets, you've pierced their protective armor (i.e., their skin), and if you were to plant them right away, you would be leaving them wide open to invasion by fungi or bacteria in the soil. To avoid potential disease problems with cut sets, schedule their planting so that you can place them out in the open air for one to 1½ weeks before you intend to plant. Of course, if you're using small, whole sets, the skin is still intact, so you have no worries about fungi or bacteria and you can plant anytime.

To dry cut sets choose a place with diffuse light where the temperature ranges between 55° and 65°F, with about 85 percent humidity. An indoor site is best, for the wind can dry out the cut surfaces too much, and a cold spring night can freeze the sets and ruin them completely. It doesn't matter what you place your sets on to air-dry. We use cardboard boxes because they're convenient, but any dry surface will do.

Soon your sets will start to sprout, and their cut surfaces will heal over. The new leaves will begin to produce food for the developing plant, and poisons called alkaloids will also form in the set and shoots. Exposure to light encourages the formation of these alkaloids. Maturing potatoes that stick out of the ground and are exposed to light will also develop alkaloids, and you can tell this has happened whenever you see a potato with distinctly green parts. You should never eat green potatoes because the alkaloids they contain can make you sick; just how sick depends on how many you eat, how sensitive you are, and your body weight. The alkaloids do, however, serve a purpose for they protect the set from insects and some fungal disease.

When you see that the sprouts on your sets have reached 1 to 2 inches in length, and the cut surfaces have developed a corky layer, you know that it's time to plant.

The Deep-Planting Method

There are several good ways to plant potatoes, and which method works best for you will depend on the climate in your area. If you have warm days and nights in the spring, you can plant your sets 6 to 8 inches deep right from the start. But if your soil is cold and your spring weather tends towards the cool side, you will be better off planting them only an inch or two deep at the outset and mounding up the soil around the sprouts as they grow until they are buried 6 to 8 inches deep (a process known as hilling-up). Since the stolons form on the underground stem portions, the more of the stem that is underground, the more stolons you are likely to end up with and, hence, more potatoes. Also, by having the sets deep in the soil, all of your potatoes will develop well below the surface, and you will not have to discard any green potatoes.

Potato plants need plenty of space if they are going to produce lots of big tubers. To give them enough room, place the seed potatoes at least 9 inches apart (12 inches is even better) in rows 30 inches apart. The closer you plant the sets, the smaller your tubers will be because the plants will be competing with one another for nutrients and available sunlight, and in the process, will be hindering each other's growth. For years, we both planted our potatoes 6 inches apart in rows 24 inches apart and always ended up with meager yields of dinky potatoes. Now we plant at the proper spacing and get much better crops.

If you have heavy clay soil, you might want to try Diane's grandmother's potato-planting method. First she digs individual holes for her sets and then lightens the soil in the holes by mixing in peat moss. She plants the sets 4 to 6 inches deep and, as the potatoes sprout, she hills them up with more of the peat moss/soil mixture. Besides lightening up a hopelessly heavy soil, the peat moss is acidic and helps inhibit formation of scab. (Pine needles are also acidic and have the same propensity for discouraging scab.)

Those of you who are new potato fans will cause considerable disturbance to your deeply planted or hilled-up plants as you poke around looking for those lovely little gems. Whenever we have planted deeply, we've noticed that the disturbed plants wilt after we dig around them, but they do recover when watered and go on to produce more new potatoes. When we go on these early forays, we know we are sacrificing the late-season harvest, for these plants will not give us a very good yield of large storage tubers. To guarantee that we can enjoy new potatoes and still harvest enough large storage tubers to tide us through the winter, we plant some sets just for new potatoes and do not expect them to give us many potatoes for storage. We plant a different bunch of sets for our winter potatoes and do not disturb them at all in our hunt for new potatoes. One other tip we can pass along if you do plant deeply and want to harvest some new potatoes, is to do your digging in the evening when the soil is damp to minimize the disturbance to your plants.

The Surface-Planting Method

If you live in a humid climate, you can use a different method that calls for planting your potatoes right on the surface of the ground and covering them with a deep layer of fluffy organic material. This method often does not work in hot, dry areas, because the loose mulch dries out too readily. For surface planting to work, the soil under the potatoes must be loose so the roots can grow down into it.

If you decide to use this technique, an easy way to provide for the roots is to lay down a layer of leaves about a foot deep in the fall on the spot where you plan to put your potatoes the following spring. Anchor the leaves with

a sheet of plastic. By planting time the leaves will have compacted and composted into a spongy layer of soft, rich leaf mold through which the potato
roots can grow. Place your sets in rows (following the spacing given earlier
under The Deep-Planting Method) and cover them with a foot or more of
hay, straw, or pine needles. If you've got a good supply of well-aged sawdust
or peat moss on hand, you can use a 6- to 8-inch layer of these instead.

Potatoes planted on the surface require a bit more attention than those
planted deeply, but when harvesttime comes, you will have less work to do.
You may have to keep adding more mulch as the season progresses to make
sure the layer is deep enough to prevent green potatoes from forming. It's
also a good idea to add on an extra few inches of mulch when the plants start
to flower. One year, when Dorothy planted her crop on the surface, she ran
out of straw before the plants flowered. Her potatoes were easy to get at, but
almost all of them were green.

If you do care for your potato patch properly, however, all you need to
do to harvest those new potatoes is to gently lift the mulch and pick them

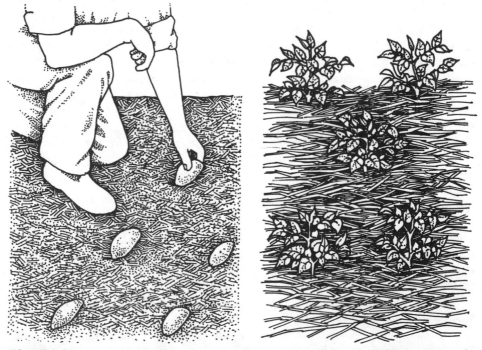

Planting Potatoes: *A good planting method for humid areas is to plant the potatoes on the
surface of the ground, and cover them with a thick, loose layer of organic mulch. The roots find
their way into the soil, and the plants grow up through the mulch.*

carefully off the stolons without disturbing the plant's roots. The mulching method has yet another advantage; in hot areas it helps keep the soil cool. This is important since potatoes grow better in cool soil (50°F) than in warm soil (80°F). In addition to lowering the yield, warm soil can encourage the growth of a rough, scaly skin on your tubers.

Those of you who garden in the cool North and have lots of clay in your soil should make sure, however, that the ground is warm enough (at least 50°F) before you cover your sets with mulch. Otherwise, the mulch keeps the soil too cool and your plants won't grow well. A friend of ours here in Montana gives the soil time to warm up by waiting until the stems are 6 to 8 inches long before she covers her sets.

Out of fairness to those gardeners who are contemplating using a hay mulch, we should mention that it has one serious disadvantage—it leaves lots of weed seeds behind. The year the potatoes are grown in it, weeds are held down and you don't need to worry much about them. But the next year, when you plant a different crop in that same spot, you will be plagued by a veritable carpet of grass seedlings. One year you put off work and the next year you make up for it!

Blooming and Tuber Formation

Potato plants start to form tubers even before they bloom, so the old saying that you can dig for new potatoes when the plants start flowering is usually correct. Oddly enough, potatoes can form tubers without blooming at all, for the two processes do not depend on each other in any way. However, the conditions that favor one also tend to favor the other, so they usually occur at about the same time. Russet Burbank potatoes start to develop small tubers when the plant is only 8 to 10 inches high and small flower buds begin to show at the top of the plant. By the time the plant is 50 percent in bloom, there may already be many small tubers present and even a few sizable ones weighing 4 to 5 ounces!

A few varieties, such as Kennebec, need to be exposed to daylengths of ten hours or less before they produce tubers. Daylengths greater than ten hours inhibit tuber formation; the plants grow beautifully, but they won't give you a crop. These short-day varieties are not for you if you garden in the north. Fortunately, most modern varieties have had their daylength dependency bred out of them, so they can be grown successfully in any part of the country.

Some Guidelines on Potato Culture

It's very important that you pay attention to the amount of nitrogen that is available to your plants. This nutrient is a very critical element in plant growth and tuber development, and either too much or too little of it will adversely affect your eventual harvest. Too much nitrogen will encourage lush foliage growth at the expense of tuber production. If the soil where you plan to grow your potatoes needs nitrogen, it is best to apply any fresh manures or other high-nitrogen fertilizers like cottonseed meal or dried blood in the fall rather than in the spring. This interval between fertilizing and planting will neatly sidestep the problem of having too much nitrogen present by allowing some to leach away. Fresh manure can also encourage scab, another reason to avoid it in spring. If your soil lacks nitrogen but you didn't do anything about it in the fall, go ahead and plant, and when your plants are about a foot high, give them a shot of compost or manure tea. You can keep feeding them while they are blooming, too.

Don't wait too long to give your potato plants the nitrogen they need, however. If they are in the throes of a nitrogen deficiency they will respond by forming tubers prematurely. Once this process has begun, nothing will reverse it. You can pour on nitrogen to your heart's content and still end up with a poor yield of insignificant potatoes. These measly little potatoes are also likely to sprout in storage much earlier than healthy potatoes. The correct amount of nitrogen is such a critical factor in proper tuber development that commercial growers snip off bits of their plants and send them to laboratories to be tested for nitrogen content. These growers can't afford to have an inferior crop, so they leave nothing to guesswork.

A deficiency or excess of potassium can also cause problems that won't be evident until it's time to prepare and serve your potatoes. Tubers grown with too little potassium may become soggy and unappealing when cooked, while those grown with too much can be overly dry and mealy.

Picturing your potatoes growing under the ground makes it easier to understand why a loose, well-drained soil is so important for this crop. The stolons which eventually give rise to tubers push out through the soil away from the base of the plant. Once the tubers begin to swell on the ends of the stolons, they grow rapidly, and to accommodate this expansion, you should provide them with loose soil. If the tubers have to expand in heavy soil that is hard to move, they will be misshapen and have deformed eyes. As a tuber forms, it needs oxygen to fuel its rapid metabolism. In a soggy or dense soil that is low in oxygen, the pores through which air enters the developing potato will become very large, resulting in a rough skin.

Like other plant parts, the potato tuber increases in cell number first, then expands rapidly as the cells enlarge. First the number of cells multiplies by about 500 times. Then each cell increases its volume to 10 times the original by filling with starch and water. While the tubers are growing, they command nearly all the plant's resources. In the first two weeks of their development alone, the tubers claim almost all the nitrogen, phosphorus, and potassium that the plant is absorbing. To give you an even more graphic idea of just how much the tubers draw from the plant, scientists have determined that plant sap flows into them at a rate of 20 inches per hour! If potato plants do not get enough water during this period of tuber development, the tubers will grow much more slowly. Then, when enough water is provided, the normal growth rate will resume, resulting in knobby, misshapen tubers. Because it disrupts the normal growth process, irregular watering can also cause hollow heart (a cavity in the middle of the potato) and other problems such as growth cracks.

The upper part of the potato plant also reacts to water stress, with important consequences for tuber growth. If the plant isn't getting enough water it will wilt and the stomata will close, slowing photosynthesis. Even if you water right away, the stomata will only reopen very slowly. Since the leaves at this time are sending 75 to 85 percent of the food they produce to the tubers, such a slowdown will ultimately decrease your harvest. This same wilting and decline in tuber production will occur at prolonged high temperatures (above 90°F), even if you conscientiously keep the soil moist. Because potatoes have such an aversion to extended heat waves, if your area has regular periods of prolonged high temperatures, it would be best to try planting your crop in a cooler part of the season for better yields.

One final word on caring for your potato crop: If the plants are not mulched, you should spend the time to weed them carefully, for weeds can reduce a potato crop by anywhere from 16 percent to as much as 76 percent.

Digging and Storing the Crop

Steamed new potatoes tossed with butter and parsley are a special home-grown treat; so are peas and new potatoes. Not only do new potatoes have their own special flavor and texture, but they also offer some nutritional bonuses. For starters, new potatoes have more protein than mature ones. This accounts for their firmer texture. In addition, the combination of new potatoes and peas is a "perfect food"; the amino acids in the one complement the amino acids in the other to make complete protein, just as nourishing as that found in meat. While we usually eat peas and potatoes as a side dish, this nutritious combination can really serve as a main dish.

While you can conveniently dig for new potatoes at any time, you should leave the crop of mature potatoes for storage in the ground for at least two weeks after the plant tops have died down. If you don't let the tubers age in the ground, they won't develop the tough skin that's necessary for long-term storage. A friend of ours was told by someone who didn't know any better to wash his newly dug tubers, which had not been properly hardened, before storing them. He went ahead and turned the hose on them and their fragile skins promptly peeled right off! Besides giving the skins a chance to toughen, the underground rest period also allows the potatoes to convert sugars into starch, making them better for baking and frying.

Commercial potato growers have machines called vine beaters which literally thrash the vines to death at the end of the season, thereby making sure all the vines die off at the same time. Then, after the tubers have aged in the ground, they can all be harvested together. If you want to even out the uneven rate at which the vines die down so you can harvest all of your crop at once, follow the commercial growers' example and beat your vines with a stick. If you live in the north, an early frost may do the job for you. But in any case, be sure to leave your tubers in the ground for two weeks after the vines have died, no matter how they met their end. Another gardening friend of ours, who was a bit wiser than the one who ended up with the naked potatoes, grew a midseason variety that ended up giving her a late crop. In order to ensure that she could harvest mature potatoes before the ground froze, she cut off the vines before they died a natural death and was able to dig her properly matured potatoes before a hard frost hit.

A garden fork makes the best potato-digging tool. Plunge the fork into the soil about 10 to 12 inches away from the dead plant, and lift up. This technique should give you the least possible number of speared potatoes. Eat any potatoes which do end up impaled on the fork as soon as possible. The tines can carry disease organisms into the vulnerable insides of the tubers, with the result that these wounded potatoes won't last long in storage.

Leave the tubers you've unearthed outdoors for several hours in a spot shielded from direct sun. Let them dry until any remaining dirt crumbles off. You can wash the potatoes if you insist, but you must be careful not to break the skins in the process, and you should be sure that they are dry when you put them into storage.

As you arrange your potatoes for storage, remember these pointers. Put the healthiest tubers of the longest-storing varieties at the back or bottom of your box or bin, and keep the shorter-storing potatoes within easy reach so they will be eaten first. Keep in mind that potatoes which were stressed by lack of water, high temperature, or rough handling in harvesting, or those that were attacked by a disease, may sprout earlier than those grown under better conditions. Make sure that air can circulate throughout your stored potatoes. Air movement keeps condensation from building up and encouraging spoilage.

Unfortunately, most home gardeners have trouble providing the ideal storage conditions for potatoes. Potatoes demand high humidity (95 percent) and cool temperatures (40° to 50°F) in order to store for the maximum time and remain in edible condition. Also, they must absolutely be stored out of the light to prevent greening and sprouting. The storage area itself doesn't have to be dark; you can just cover your potatoes to shield them from the light. The best storage location is one that has a cool, moist atmosphere and isn't likely to experience freezing temperatures. In many homes, the basement fills the bill. One friend of ours stores his potatoes in well-covered wooden boxes on the cement floor of his cool basement. Before setting his boxes down he wets the floor to boost the humidity in the immediate area.

Wherever you finally settle on stashing your potatoes, you must be sure to keep the temperature as close to 40°F as possible without letting it get any colder. Lower temperatures encourage the starch in the tubers to turn to sugars, which can give them an off taste. Have you ever made french fries from homegrown potatoes and noticed that the fries were unusually dark in color? This is a visible clue that the potatoes were kept too cool so the starches were turning to sugars, and the heat of the oil actually carmelized the sugars! If the temperature ever dips so low that the potatoes freeze in storage, you'll be in the unenviable position of having a whole cache of tubers that are no longer fit to eat.

Problems with Potatoes

Potatoes, like all plants, have their share of diseases and pests. But fortunately for the home gardener, most of these won't totally devastate your crop. And by following the cultural advice given earlier in this chapter, you can avoid many of the more common problems, such as knobby or undersized tubers. Here's a rundown of some problems that you may encounter.

Colorado potato beetle: This is the most common insect pest that plagues potatoes. Surprisingly enough, this native insect was not originally a potato-eater. Its host was a wild relative of potatoes, but when Americans began cultivating potatoes in the late 1860s, this enterprising beetle switched over to the new crop. Colorado potato beetles will also attack eggplants, so if you're growing both of these solanaceous crops in your garden, you may find that it fast becomes a mecca for these hungry pests.

Overall, potatoes have few insect pests because the poisons found in their leaves are effective deterrents. But the Colorado potato beetle "tunes in" on these chemicals and locates potato plants by their telltale aroma. Because they feed on the poisonous leaves, the beetles themselves are also poisonous. They carry a distinctive, bright pattern of black and yellow stripes on their backs so that birds and other predators will be able to recognize and avoid them. This color scheme also makes them easy for the gardener to find.

If you see just a few beetles on your plants, you should be able to pick them all off. Don't forget to turn the leaves over, too, and look for small clusters of bright orange eggs on the undersides. Both the adult beetles and the larvae (which have plump reddish-orange bodies and dark heads) feed on potato leaves, and it doesn't take them long to nearly denude your plants. If there are just too many beetles or larvae to pick off by hand, shake powdered rotenone over your plants, and the beetles will disappear. One rotenone treatment should do the trick, but keep an eye out in case some beetles escape and reproduce.

Internal blackspot bruises: You may have at one time or another cut open a potato, found a black bruise inside, and wondered how it got there. Sometimes, when potatoes are handled roughly during harvesting, the injury to the outside stimulates cells inside the tuber to produce a black pigment, even though the outside looks perfectly normal. The way to avoid this problem is to gently set, not drop, your potatoes into containers or onto the ground when you're harvesting them.

Early dying or verticillium wilt: This unpleasant potato affliction is caused by a fungus. If the leaves of some of your plants begin to turn yellow and die earlier than they normally should, pull the vines and dig out the tubers right away. Although your crop will be small and you'll have to eat them quickly since they haven't had the chance to age in the ground, you may be able to prevent the fungus from spreading any further among the plants. Keeping the soil moist will help delay the spread of the fungus to the rest of your crop. You should destroy the vines instead of adding them to the compost pile, for you don't want to contaminate the rest of your garden. The very best preventive measure you can take is to use certified seed potatoes.

Spores of early dying fungus have been known to persist for as long as seven years after an infection, successfully overwintering in the soil and feeding off of dead organic material. Once your soil has been infected, you must wait at least three or four years before you can safely plant in the contaminated spot any other crops that are susceptible to this disease. This can really put a crimp in your gardening style, for besides potatoes, susceptible crops include eggplants, mint, muskmelons, peppers, strawberries, tomatoes, and watermelons.

Common scab: This holds the dubious distinction of being one of the most common potato diseases. A soilborne bacterium begins the infection which weakens the tuber, and other organisms often join in. Dry soil, especially early in the plant's life, favors the development of scab. So do high calcium levels in the soil, a neutral pH, and the use of uncomposted manures. Scab also afflicts beets, carrots, rutabagas, and turnips, so if you have a bout with this disease in your garden, you will have to avoid growing all these crops in the infected area for at least three years.

Scab begins to form as small rough spots on growing tubers. If you see any telltale signs that it is developing when you are harvesting new potatoes, be sure to keep your soil moist; this may be enough to control a light scab infestation. By "moist" we mean keeping the soil wet throughout the top 9 inches, which can call for watering every five days for five to seven hours at a stretch!

If scab is a continuing problem in your garden, try growing resistant varieties such as Early Gem, Norgold, and Targhee. Avoid susceptible varieties like Bliss Triumph, Kennebec, Norchip, Pontiac, or Russet Burbank. Crop rotation can also lessen a recurrent scab problem. Rye and soybeans are both good rotation crops that may help reduce the severity of scab. These plants naturally increase the acidity of the soil, and some scientists believe they may also encourage the growth of beneficial microorganisms that produce antibiotics which inhibit scab.

Potato Frontiers

Scientists are trying to breed new and better potato varieties, but they must first overcome several obstacles that stand in their way. In order to produce new strains, flowers of one variety must be pollinated with pollen from another. With potatoes this isn't as easy as it sounds. In many cases the potato flower is sterile and can't be fertilized. Even when the flower is pollinated, it can fall off before fertilization occurs. Since potato plants channel most of their energy into tuber formation, flower production is almost an afterthought. To shift this balance, scientists prevent tuber formation by grafting the top of a potato plant onto tomato roots so that the potato can devote most of its energy to flowering.

Despite the difficulties of getting potato plants to flower and produce seed, it's now possible for you to purchase true potato seed to start your crop instead of using hunks of tuber. Seed for the variety Explorer is available to home gardeners from a number of seed suppliers, and although it is rather expensive, it does offer you a certain degree of convenience over commercial sets. If bad weather or other complications delay planting, the seed or seedlings will hold over in better shape than the sets will. Explorer is the first variety to be offered this way, but as research continues, a greater selection of varieties will probably be made available. You can start these seeds indoors the same way you start pepper or tomato seeds, and then transplant the seedlings outside after all danger of frost is past. Once they're in the ground, you treat these plants the same as plants sprouted from tubers.

Potato breeders, in their quest for the "perfect" potato, are trying to incorporate such characteristics as: disease resistance, more dry matter and less sugar, less discoloration of raw potato flesh, higher yields, increased protein content, and higher vitamin content.

Breeders (who gear most of their work to the needs of commercial growers) have not been trying to develop resistance to the Colorado potato beetle because commercial growers simply spray to eliminate this pest. Besides, varieties which are naturally resistant contain too many poisonous and bad-tasting alkaloids to be the least bit palatable. Breeding virus-resistant strains has also been difficult. A plant that is naturally tolerant to a virus can carry it but not show any signs. Although they are disease-resistant, they could have the virus and pass it on to more susceptible varieties. Therefore, they cannot be certified as disease-free. Breeders have had success developing some potatoes resistant to cyst nematodes. These plants can be infected by the worms, but their roots produce a substance which stops the development of female nematodes. These resistant varieties can actually reduce the number of nematodes in your soil.

It's also interesting to note that breeders are looking outside the genetic pool of cultivated potatoes and are turning to wild potato species. Some of these untamed relatives have very sticky hairs that entrap aphids. Needless to say, this trait would be very helpful in organic pest management in the garden. However, breeders are still a long way from introducing a hirsute, aphid-fighting potato since they are having trouble incorporating this beneficial trait without also introducing some undesirable ones.

Chapter 10

Beans and Peas: Those Luscious Legumes

Vital Statistics

Family:
Leguminosae

Species:
Phaseolus vulgaris—Snap, green, and kidney beans
Phaseolus limensis—Lima beans
Pisum sativum—Peas

Soil:
Well-drained sandy loam preferred, but any well-drained soil will do

pH:
Snap and Shell Beans—6.4, optimum
Lima Beans—6.2, optimum
Peas—5.5–6.8

Soil Temperature for Germination:
Snap and Shell Beans—60°–85°F; 80°F, optimum

Soil Temperature (*continued*)
Lima Beans—70°–85°F; 85°F, optimum
Peas—40–75°F; 75°F, optimum

Air Temperature for Best Growth:
Snap and Shell Beans—80°F, maximum; 60°–70°F, optimum; 50°F, minimum
Lima Beans 80°F, maximum; 60°–70°F, optimum; 50°F, minimum
Peas—55°–70°F

Seed Viability:
3 years for all these legumes

Seed Germination:
6–17 days

Seed Planting Depth:
2–3" for peas and common beans; 2" for lima beans

If you've never tasted tiny peas shelled, cooked, and served fresh from the vines in the backyard, you don't know what you're missing. Peas and green beans are among those peerless homegrown crops whose quality can never be equalled by any supermarket produce. What the supermarket bills as "fresh" are peas and beans that were actually harvested weeks before they reached the produce counter, and they are usually overmature even before they leave the farm. During the long interval between farm and table, the natural sugars in the food start turning to starch, the crispy crunchy texture turns flaccid and tough, and the nutrient content begins to decline. What you end up with are too-old vegetables that are bland and stringy instead of sweet and crunchy. No wonder so many kids hate these vegetables! But when you grow your own, you can pick them when they are still young, fresh, and delicious.

Raw beans and peas are just about the tastiest and most nutritious snacks around for children. The only problem is that once your kids get hooked on munching these sweet, juicy, and crunchy vegetables, they can turn out to be worse pests in the pea patch than any insect you can imagine! Ours love to take a colander full of fresh-picked peas into the TV room to shell and eat while watching their favorite show. Kids aren't the only ones to go for raw legumes; even more "sophisticated" adult palates are turning to snap peas and young green beans as nutritious substitutes for potato chips to serve with dips. Beans and peas are not only fun for kids to eat but also to plant. The seeds are large and easy to work with, and a beanpole teepee makes a fun summer hideout which comes complete with built-in snacks.

Mankind's affinity for legumes is nothing new. People have been eating peas, in particular, for a long, long time. Archaeologists have uncovered carbonized pea seeds in Middle Eastern and European neolithic settlements that are at least 9,000 years old. Since these oldest known pea seeds probably represent a crop already under cultivation, the wild ancestors of cultivated peas still remain shrouded in mystery.

Lima and snap beans both originated in the same geographical area—from Mexico southward to Brazil and Argentina. Snap beans are the older of the two; they've been cultivated in these regions for over 7,500 years, while limas have been cultivated for 4,500 years. Although they share what can roughly be described as a common geographical birthplace, they did evolve under different conditions. Limas learned to thrive in the lower, more tropical regions, while snap and shell beans became adapted to cooler, higher altitudes. Their different origins help explain their different cultural requirements. While there are varieties of limas that can tolerate cool weather (Cowey Red and Winfield, for example), most require warmer weather than do snap beans.

The Nutritional Profile of Legumes

Besides tasting downright delicious, peas and beans pack a nutritional wallop that's hard to beat. A cup of fresh peas contains about 9 grams of protein and 122 calories. In terms of satisfying your daily vitamin requirements, that same cupful will supply you with 70 percent of the vitamin C, 45 percent of the thiamine, 40 percent of the niacin, and 20 percent of the vitamin A you should receive in a day. Edible-pod peas have less protein and fewer calories but are also high in vitamins. Snap peas, which have edible pods and seeds, are probably comparable in nutritional content to regular peas. Green snap beans have only 2 grams of protein and 35 calories per cup, but surprisingly, this same cupful supplies 60 percent of the vitamin C as well as a portion of the vitamin A you need each day. Yellow snap beans contain less vitamin C than green ones. Cooked dried beans are a more concentrated food, with as many as 300 calories in a cup. Along with their stick-to-the-ribs heartiness they supply large amounts of thiamine, niacin, and riboflavin, plus some calcium and iron. They're high in potassium but low in sodium, good news for people on a low-salt diet.

While peas, lima beans, and cooked dried beans contain a hefty dose of protein, that protein is not complete. It is deficient in three essential amino acids: tryptophan and two sulfur-containing amino acids, methionine and cysteine. Peas growing in a soil with adequate sulfur have more of the last two amino acids, and hence, the quality of their available protein is higher. You really don't have to worry about the level of sulfur in your soil since plenty of organic matter naturally provides an adequate supply.

Savvy cooks know that beans can be eaten with other protein sources, such as grains and dairy products, to provide complete protein. Dishes like succotash and bean enchiladas give you protein that is comparable to the protein available in meat, for corn has enough amino acids to make up for what beans lack.

Beans and Peas Are Unique

Besides being tasty, nutritious, and easy to grow, beans and peas are good for your garden. As members of the very large Legume family, they have the ability to form special associations with bacteria in the soil which enables them to fix nitrogen—that is, to take the nitrogen from the air trapped

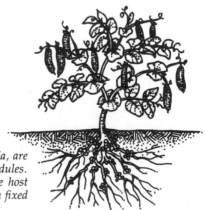

Root Nodules: *Rhizobia, the nitrogen-fixing bacteria, are housed in legume roots in knoblike structures called nodules. In the nodules, the bacteria receive carbon from the host plant and, in return, provide the plant with nitrogen fixed from the air.*

in the soil pores and convert it chemically into a form that they, as plants, can use. To understand just how significant this special talent of legumes is, you need a little background on how soil nitrogen and plants interact.

Nitrogen is only available to plants when it is combined into compounds such as ammonia, urea, or nitrates; when thus combined, the nitrogen is considered to be in a "fixed" form. Fixed nitrogen in the soil occurs through any of these four means: the application of chemical fertilizers, the breakdown of organic matter into its component parts, the activities of certain free-living bacteria and blue-green algae in the soil, or the activities of plants like legumes which cooperate with soil bacteria in fixing nitrogen.

Since nitrogen is usually the limiting factor in soil productivity, the ability to use the limitless supply of atmospheric nitrogen enables legumes to thrive where most other plants can barely grow. There are 13,000 species of legumes in the world, living in every kind of environment from tropical forests to arctic tundra. These plants account for about 40 percent of the nitrogen fixed world-wide, so they are extremely important to the ecological balance on Earth. While many legumes such as alfalfa, beans, clover, and lupine are small plants, there are others that come in considerably larger sizes. Some legumes are bushes; others, like acacias, are small trees, and still others are large forest trees like the Kentucky coffee tree and the honey locust tree.

The bacteria that live in legume roots are called rhizobia; their scientific name is *Rhizobium*. Each legume species has its own special *Rhizobium* species living in lumps on the roots, called "nodules." The nodules create a special environment for the bacteria so that they can efficiently fix nitrogen. The enzyme nitrogenase, which enables the bacteria to perform their task, is ineffective when oxygen is present. Another chemical found in the nodules, called leghemoglobin, binds any free oxygen so the nitrogenase can do its work. Leghemoglobin is very similar to the hemoglobin in your red blood cells, and performs the indispensable task of latching onto oxygen molecules so they don't come in contact with the rhizobia. If you pull up a healthy clover plant and examine the roots, you'll notice that the nodules are actually pink; the color comes from the leghemoglobin.

The bacteria which infect peas, snap beans, and limas are all different. (Despite the fact that nodulation is something that helps the plant, the process by which the bacteria enter the plants is a sort of infection.) Although you may have grown beans in a particular part of your garden, you can't count on that population of bacteria to help out a new crop of peas you want to grow there. In this situation, you should probably inoculate the pea seeds with a dried preparation of bacteria before planting them in the former bean patch. The reverse is also true. Inoculant powders are readily available through seed catalogs and usually contain the various bacteria appropriate for peas, limas, and snap beans. These preparations, however, do not contain the bacteria which infect clovers, cowpeas, scarlet runner beans, or soybeans. If

How Rhizobia Enter Legume Roots

Just how do the nitrogen-fixing bacteria get inside bean or pea roots? As the young legume root grows, it secretes into the soil an attractant chemical which lures the proper species of *Rhizobium* to the roots. (The bacteria have tiny flagella which enable them to move through the water held in the soil pores.) When the bacteria reach a small root hair and touch it, they stick to the root because a protein on the surface of the root hair bonds chemically with a sugar molecule on the surface of the bacteria. Each legume/*Rhizobium* species pair has its own specific protein/sugar combination, so only the correct species of *Rhizobium* will bind to the root hair of a particular legume.

In at least one species of *Rhizobium* (associated with a clover), the next step is especially interesting. The clover root releases the amino acid tryptophan into the soil; the bacteria respond by converting the tryptophan into auxin, a potent plant-growth hormone. The auxin makes the root hair curl around and through the mass of attracted bacteria, increasing the chances of further bacteria/root hair contact.

The bacteria gain entry into the root hair through an infection thread, a tunnellike ingrowth of the root hair. (Imagine the root hair as a long balloon; if you pushed your finger into the balloon, you would produce a cavity like the infection thread.) The infection thread keeps growing further inward into the root hair and is filled with multiplying bacteria. Eventually it grows all the way back to the base of the hair and enters the main part of the root. Then its tip ruptures and bacteria spew forth into the main root cells. The cells containing the multiplying bacteria enlarge to the point where they form a root nodule.

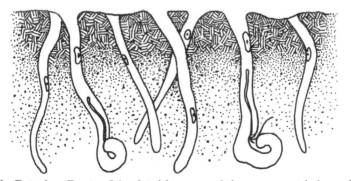

Rhizobia Entering Roots: *Stimulated by a growth hormone, root hairs curl around and envelop bacteria in the soil. The bacteria enter the root through an infection thread, a tunnellike ingrowth in the root hair. The infection thread filled with multiplying bacteria grows inward until it reaches the main part of the root. In the root the thread will burst, spewing forth its content of bacteria which then multiply to form the nodules.*

you're planning to grow one of these crops, you will have to buy a separate inoculant.

Once nodulated beans or peas have grown in a particular spot in the garden, the soil in that area will contain the proper bacteria, and they will be capable of inoculating plants for several years. But if you have any doubt about whether your soil has the right bacteria for the legume crops you want to grow, you should buy some inoculant, for it can dramatically increase your yield. Trials conducted by Herbst Brothers Seedsmen revealed that inoculated beans gave 65 percent more beans than uninoculated plants, while inoculated peas yielded 77 percent more than uninoculated ones.

The results are so impressive, and the inoculant is so easy to apply, that there's no reason for any of your beans or peas to go uninoculated. The "shake and plant" technique is a simple and effective way to apply the bacterial powder to your seeds. Dampen the seeds, pour them into a paper bag, and sprinkle them with the powder. Close the bag, shake them up, and plant right away before they dry. Once the inoculant powder has been wetted, the bacteria are activated; by allowing the powder to dry out again, you would be killing off these beneficial bacteria.

The Long and Short of Growing Legumes

Peas, limas, and snap beans all come in both bush and pole varieties. A bush variety seed produces a bushy plant. A pole variety seed produces a single vine. Which type of growth habit you choose will affect the duration of the harvest as well as the kind of care you give the plants throughout the season. In general, bush types will produce an earlier crop, and the harvest will be concentrated over a shorter period. The short internodes that make these plants bushy also account for this accelerated maturation. The rate of growth is the same for pole and bush types, but since the bush varieties spend less time growing stem between nodes, they mature faster, and their flowers are produced in quicker succession. It's easy to see that bush beans and short-vined or dwarf peas (the pea version of bush beans) are best if you want an early crop and want your harvest concentrated into a few pickings. On the other hand, if you want a sustained harvest and are willing to wait a few more days before it comes in, grow pole beans and tall peas. Although bush beans have the shortest time to maturity, pole beans and tall peas mature early enough for northern gardeners to get a good harvest from them. Pole limas, unfortunately, take too long to mature to be very reliable in the North, so gardeners in short-season areas should plant bush limas.

When it comes to growing bush bean varieties, there's no need to provide something for them to grow on. Short-vined peas are often billed as not needing support, but they really do grow better if they have something to hold them up off the ground. Not only do they grow better, they yield better, too; unsupported dwarf peas may yield 17 percent less than those which have something to rest on. Tall peas and all varieties of pole beans should have something to cling to as they grow. But that doesn't necessarily mean that you can expect them to cling to the same kind of support.

Peas and beans climb in different ways and need different surfaces when it comes to supports. Peas have thin tendrils, which are actually highly specialized leaves, that twine around a trellis or other nearby objects to help hold the vine up. A tendril rotates slowly through the air as it grows until it touches something. As soon as the tendril makes contact with a support, it begins to wrap around it. These slender, green appendages move quickly—a tendril can completely encircle a string or wire with one turn in less than an hour, and you can see the beginning of the curling action within two minutes of contact. The colder the temperature is, the slower the coiling goes, and if it dips much below 50°F, the tendrils won't coil at all. If one of your pea vines isn't making good contact with its support, gently push the vine up against the wire fence or strings, and it will grab hold quickly. You shouldn't make the mistake of expecting your peas to grow well on poles; their tendrils are too small to completely surround the pole and won't be able to cling securely.

Pole beans climb in a very different way. They have no tendrils, but their stems react to contact with surfaces. If the stem is growing without the aid of poles or a trellis, it grows in wide circles along the ground, spiraling around other stems it may meet. But when you plant your beans with the proper support, as soon as the stem touches a pole, it immediately begins to grow along the surface. When it comes to an edge, it turns along the edge, always maintaining contact with the surface as it climbs upward in a spiraling manner. This serpentine growth habit means that beans can be trained along strings, poles, or chicken wire supports. The vines will make smaller spirals around a string than up a pole, but either sort of support will work.

Providing support for long vines is important for several reasons aside from saving garden space. Climbing takes the leaves up into the sunlight and gives each leaf its share of sun for more effective photosynthesis. Also, if vines are allowed to trail on the ground, air can't circulate freely around them, and the damp vines can quite easily become infected with diseases. The beans or pea pods themselves can become mud splattered if the vines are on the ground, and can develop rust or rot from lying on damp soil.

Peas and beans are also very sensitive to winds that carry abrasive sand or dust particles. In a windy area, the yield from these crops can be significantly reduced. If you have strong prevailing winds, plant a row of sunflowers on the windward side of your peas and beans to protect them.

Surefire Supports for Beans and Peas

One of the best ways to grow climbing vines is on a chicken wire fence—both pea tendrils and bean vines can cling to it. While it takes some work to put a tall fence together, once it is made it can easily be taken down at the end of the season and stored in a shed or basement to be reused year after year. For tall varieties such as Sugar Snap and Alderman peas and all pole beans, begin with stout, 8-foot-long supporting poles. Two-by-fours cut lengthwise to make two-by-twos work well. Lay your poles down on the ground parallel to one another, about 5 feet apart. Make 10-foot-long sections of fencing, locating one pole at each end and one in the middle. You can make as long a row as you like with these fence sections, tying or wiring the end poles of two adjoining sections together to give stability.

Leaving the bottom 18 inches of the poles free for burying in the ground, use heavy staples or U-shaped nails to attach chicken wire to the rest of the pole lengths. Catch every wire that crosses a pole with a nail or staple. Since chicken wire is generally only 6 feet tall, you will have to secure smaller widths of wire along the top to fill the space between the poles. If you prefer, you can string twine along the top part. When your fence is made, you can take it to your garden and set it up (carrying and setting up takes two people). With one person supporting the fence, the other one can stand on a chair or ladder and use a sledge hammer (carefully!) to pound the poles into the ground. If your ground is very rocky, dig holes for the fence poles instead, making sure to firm the ground around the posts by pressing with your foot. Put the fence in place before planting your seeds so that you don't disturb them. Then the fence can mark your rows as you plant. As the season progresses, you may have to use guy wires tied to nearby trees or anchored in the ground with pegs to help support any sagging fence sections.

Most pea varieties do not grow taller than 3 feet, and supporting them is much easier. Cut 6-foot-tall chicken wire in half to make 3-foot-tall lengths. Cut a length of wire to match the length of your pea row and take it to the garden along with some sturdy, pointed 4-foot-long stakes. Weave the stakes through

The Distinctive Legume Flowers and How They Grow

Legumes are unique aboveground as well as belowground. The structure of a legume flower is very different from that of the flowers of other plants. The distinctive appearance of the flowers of peas, beans, lupines, acacias, and vetch makes these very dissimilar-looking plants instantly recognizable as legumes. Even the puffy flower heads of clover reveal on close inspection clusters of tiny, typical legume flowers. The characteristic form of legume flowers is easy to see in a pea blossom. The graceful pea flower resembles a delicate white butterfly with outspread wings. The flower has one large petal the wire at about 3-foot intervals, and pound them into the ground, keeping the wire taut between stakes, until their tops are at the top of the wire. This makes a quickly assembled and stable support for peas that is easy to remove and store for use next year.

The simplest way to support dwarf peas is to buy 18-inch-tall folding border fencing at a hardware store, anchor it into the ground, and plant your peas along both sides. Some dwarf peas will grow a bit taller than the fencing, but it still will support them sufficiently until the end of the harvest.

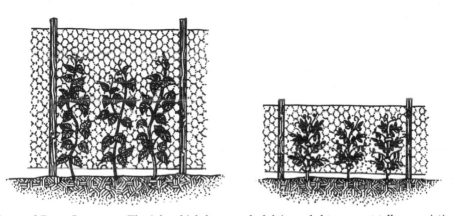

Pea and Bean Supports: *The 6-foot-high fence on the left is needed to support tall pea varieties, as well as all pole beans. Place 8-foot-long 2 by 2s 5 feet apart, and secure chicken wire to the posts with staples or nails. The shorter pea varieties can be supported with a 3-foot-high fence like the one on the right. Weave 4-foot-long stakes through the wire at 3-foot intervals the length of the row, and pound them into the ground. Although the support on the left is harder to assemble initially, both are easy to take down and store for use the following year.*

which stands up vertically, two side petals which form wings to the side, and a pair of bottom petals which have fused in the shape of an upside-down V with extensions on each side. You cannot see any pistil or stamens, for these are hidden inside the flower.

Peas and beans are largely self-pollinated. In some varieties, such as Blue Lake bush beans, the stamens open and shed their pollen on the pistil before the flower even opens, so cross-pollination is virtually impossible. Lima beans, on the other hand, do achieve up to 18 percent cross-pollination with the help of bees.

After the flower is pollinated, the pod begins to grow. If you look carefully, you'll see the miniature pod appear, just as the petals are withering. You

Pea Flower: *You would be wise to plant peas in clear view so you can enjoy their beautiful, delicate flowers. The flower consists of one large petal positioned vertically, two side petals that spread out like wings, and a bottom pair of petals fused together in the shape of an upside-down V with extensions on both sides (detail). With all parts put together, the graceful blossom resembles a butterfly in flight.*

may never have thought of them this way before, but pea and bean pods are actually modified leaves. A little investigative work in the pea patch bears this out. If you open a pea pod carefully, you can see that half the peas are attached to one edge of the pod seam and half to the other edge. These two edges represent the margins of a leaf which have fused to form a closed pod. The opposite seam on the pod (along the flatter edge) is actually equivalent to the vascular midrib of a leaf. When you string a bean or pea, what you're removing is the tough midrib vein of xylem and phloem.

To develop stringless beans or peas, breeders look for plants whose vascular tissue contains few tough fibers. It is impossible, though, to breed a completely stringless bean or pea, for such a plant would have no xylem or phloem to transport nourishment to the pod and developing seeds. Once you realize that the pod is actually a modified leaf, it should come as no surprise to learn that as much as 66 percent of the food needed by developing peas during their peak growth period inside the pod is supplied by photosynthesis of the pod itself. This insight into how peas grow should help you see why it's important to grow your peas on supports: that way, the pods can be out in the sun making food.

Legumes and the Soil

Beans and peas have shallow, fibrous roots, so you must be careful when weeding around the plant bases. Your safest bet is to hand-pull any weeds within a one-foot radius of legume plants. Keep the pea and bean rows thoroughly weeded until the plants are about half grown; from then on, they can outcompete the weeds. These crops are very sensitive to overwatering and will languish in water-logged ground, so make sure they are planted in light, well-drained soil. Gardeners growing peas during a cool, damp time of year must be especially on guard against overly wet soil. If you don't garden in raised beds, you can dig in sand to help with drainage or build up a ridge of soil and plant your peas on top of it to make sure excess water can drain off. Legume roots only extend about 1½ feet down, so they are also susceptible to drought. What legumes need, then, is evenly moist soil that is neither dried out nor waterlogged. A high content of organic material will help hold the water in the top soil layer.

Because beans and peas fix their own nitrogen, your soil doesn't need to be rich for them to grow well. As a matter of fact, if there is a lot of nitrogen in the soil, the rhizobia will just shut down operations, and your garden won't benefit from the presence of legumes at all. All the plants need is enough nitrogen to support their early growth, before the rhizobia get down to business. If you plan to work in a little manure to fuel their early growth stages, you must take measures to be sure that the soil isn't too salty, for peas and snap beans are sensitive to salt. Add the manure the fall prior to spring planting so that rain and melting snow can leach excess salts from the soil by planting time.

Potassium and phosphorus are important nutrients for legumes because they assist in blooming and pod formation. Don't skimp on these nutrients; work generous amounts of bone meal and wood ashes into the ground before you plant your beans and peas. Just remember that wood ashes can raise the soil pH, so you may have to add pine needles or peat moss to bring it back down to a suitable range for your plants. Peas and beans can tolerate acid soils better than many garden crops, but if the pH falls below 5.2, manganese in the soil can become toxic to the plants.

Snap and Shell Beans

Beans are one of the most rewarding crops you can grow in the garden, for the plants are vigorous, thrive over a wide temperature range, and provide an abundant harvest of tender pods within a relatively short span of time. As is the case with peas, there are numerous names tossed about in reference to the different sorts of garden beans that are classified in the species *Phaseolus vulgaris*. The terms "snap bean," "string bean," and "green bean" all refer to any of the popular varieties of green beans grown for their crisp pods, even though most modern varieties do not require stringing. "French beans" are somewhat more finicky varieties (they don't do well in cool, wet weather) which are harvested when the pods are very slim and sweet.

"Wax bean" refers to yellow garden beans, which generally have a milder flavor than the green ones. Most wax bean pods start out green but turn yellow as they lengthen and mature. Drying beans, such as kidney, navy, and pinto beans are simply varieties of green beans grown for their mature dry seeds rather than for their immature pods. Now that we've given you a rundown of the basic categories of beans, we'll give you some pointers to help you with your variety selections.

Bean Varieties

When you're flipping through the glossy pages of a seed catalog or perusing a rack full of seed packets, there are several criteria you can use to guide your selection of bean varieties. The first thing you must decide is whether to grow pole beans or bush beans. As we pointed out earlier, pole beans take more work (you must provide them with support) but less space and give you a somewhat later but more prolonged harvest. Bush beans don't require support, and they give you an earlier, concentrated harvest.

Some gardeners insist that pole beans have a better flavor than bush varieties and always grow the climbers. Certain varieties of pole beans are classics; Kentucky Wonder is the standard by which others are judged. If you want to gain a certain notoriety among your gardening acquaintances, the pole bean variety to grow is Oregon Giant, which climbs up to 10 feet tall

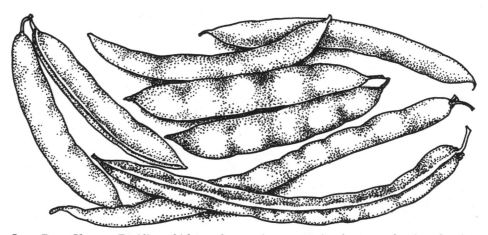

Snap Bean Shapes: *Deciding which snap bean variety to grow involves more than just choosing between green and yellow. A broad range of sizes and shapes is available, from the flat, wide pods of Romano (center) to the lanky pods of Kentucky Wonder (front).*

New Discoveries: *Remus and Daisy bush beans produce all their pods high on the plant so they are easy to pick. They also set their crop all at once, which makes harvesting a pleasure if you want to pick all your beans at one time.*

and produces long, flat, speckled pods. Romano pole beans are popular with many bean lovers. The flat pods of this Italian bean have a distinctive flavor which true bean connoisseurs claim can't be matched by any other bean, not even Bush Romano (also known as Roma).

The number of green bush bean varieties is seemingly endless, so it is difficult to recommend particular ones. A quick glance at any seed catalog will reveal that bush beans come in a number of pod shapes and lengths. Some have flat pods and others, round ones; some have lanky, 8-inch pods while others have short, 2-inch pods. The only guideline to follow here is your own preference. Flavor also differs among varieties, so your best bet is to experiment with several kinds to see which you like best. To our mind, Blue Lake bush beans have an especially fine flavor, but their short pods make them more work to prepare for freezing or canning than longer-podded varieties.

Some bush beans produce more heavily than others, too. Several especially prolific varieties are Green Crop, Tendercrop, and Topcrop Stringless. In general, the more branched the plant, the more beans it will set because a branching plant has more nodes, and flower clusters are produced at the nodes. Another factor that affects plant size and yield is the degree to which the plant's growth pattern is determinate. Certain varieties, such as Remus and Daisy, are advertised as being superior because they set all their beans high on the plant. As you might guess, these varieties were developed with the commercial grower in mind; plants with all the beans at the top are easier to harvest. These determinate types also set their crop all at once, for the plant grows to a certain size and then blooms.

In marked contrast to determinate-type bush beans are other varieties that keep on growing after the first flowers have set and provide a more continuous harvest. If you live in an area where the climate is unpredictable and heat waves can hit the garden at the same time the beans are likely to be flowering, you are better off growing varieties which bloom over a longer period. Temperatures above 86°F can cause bean blossoms to fall off, and seeds won't set at temperatures over 95°F. If a hot spell settles in while a determinate bean variety is blooming, you'll lose your whole harvest.

There's another way to hedge your bets if your area is prone to early hot spells. Some bean varieties, such as the popular Contender, set flowers twice. If heat ruins the first crop, the second one still has a chance. And if you are spared from the heat altogether, so much the better; you'll get two bountiful harvests from the same plants.

Wax beans can be incredibly prolific. Dorothy's personal favorite is Beurre de Rocquencourt (available from Johnny's Selected Seeds), which begins to produce within 48 days of planting and goes on and on, providing pods continuously for a couple of weeks. This variety is recommended for areas like ours, where nights are cool. Sunglow is a popular wax bean with fatter pods than Beurre de Rocquencourt, and its pods hold longer on the plant before the seeds develop. Cherokee Wax is a well-known variety with oval pods, while Top Notch Golden has distinctive flat pods. Wax beans make wonderful pickled beans but, in our experience, do not usually freeze as well as green beans.

Purple-podded beans are a delightfully colorful addition to the garden and have a delicious, mild flavor to boot. The foliage is a darker green than that of most beans, and the stems as well as the pods are purple. The pale purple flowers look like they belong in a delicate watercolor painting, making the plants something to behold when they're in full bloom. Since purple vegetables in general seem to be bothered less by insect pests than green ones, you might want to try these if your bean plants keep getting chewed up by the local wildlife. Royalty was the first purple bush bean developed and is the one still offered in many catalogs. However, Royalty has some shortcomings, namely short, weak plants which let the long pods droop on the ground where they tend to curl and get mud spattered. Breeders went back to the drawing board and came up with an improved purple bush bean, Royal Burgundy. This newer variety has sturdy, upright growth that holds the long, straight pods well off the ground. Both of these purple bush beans tolerate cool, wet soil better than green varieties and can be planted earlier in the spring. In the kitchen, these obliging beans signal the chef when they're cooked to perfection—the purple pods turn green when just crisp but ready to eat.

More and more varieties of drying beans are being offered by seed companies every year. This expanding selection comes at a time when people are becoming more concerned about being as self-sufficient as possible; jars of fat, pretty, dried beans on the pantry shelf are reassurance that there will be food to eat no matter what happens in the world-at-large. Which varieties you choose depends on your personal taste (flavors and cooking characteristics vary a great deal from one variety to the next) and on the length of your growing season. In short-season areas, your choices are rather limited, but you can still grow several tasty kinds. Jacob's Cattle (also called Trout) beans are about the earliest type, producing a harvest within 88 days of planting. These are also one of the prettiest beans, with deep red speckles covering the white seeds. They can be substituted in recipes where you'd normally use red kidney beans and white beans. Maine Yellow Eye is popular for baked beans and is ready to harvest in 92 days. There are other varieties as well, like Mexican Pinto beans, that have strains which will mature in short seasons. Short-season gardeners shouldn't despair of ever growing a good crop of dry beans; they should just be diligent in seeking out early maturing varieties from such sources as Vermont Bean Seed Company and Johnny's Selected Seeds. Those of you who have the luxury of a long season can choose to grow any one of a wide variety of drying beans, including the old standbys like navy beans, red kidney beans, and black turtle soup beans.

A good all-purpose bean to consider is Dwarf Horticultural. When the red-streaked pods are small, you can cook and eat them like green beans and savor their especially nutty flavor. Within 65 days of planting, you can harvest these beans as green shell beans and use them in the same recipes as lima beans (this is especially important if you live in areas where limas don't do well). Finally, the mature, large, red-streaked, tan beans themselves can be dried for winter use in your favorite bean recipes.

Tips on Planting and Raising Beans

For a good crop of beans, plant them when both the soil and air have warmed up. Planting early during cold weather won't give you an early harvest, for in the cold, the phloem of bean plants just clogs up, and carbohydrates and nutrients can't be transported within the plant. You can sow bean seeds a week or two before the last expected frost if the weather and soil are warm enough; purple-podded beans can go in even if the soil is still on the wet side. Beans will germinate when the soil temperature is between 60° and 85°F. At 68°F, germination takes about eleven days, while at warmer temperatures your beans may poke through the soil in just six days. Plant the seeds 2 to 4 inches apart and 2 to 3 inches deep in rows spaced 20 inches or more apart.

If you're a space-conscious gardener, you can plant your bush beans in a solid block instead of in rows to make better use of available garden space. That way you avoid the idle space between rows, and the plants don't seem to interfere with one another the way corn, onions, and some other crops do. Block planting is especially good for shell beans you intend to dry since they need no care other than watering once the plants are up. Their abundant foliage shades out weeds very effectively when planted this way. We also block-plant purple-podded and wax beans, mainly because the pods are easy to distinguish from the stems and it's no problem to spot all the ripe beans. With green beans, it's all too easy to miss the pods when they are block-planted, since pods and foliage blend into a mini-jungle.

To block plant, first excavate the bean bed to a depth of 3 inches. If you'll be harvesting the crop as snap beans, make the bed no more than 2 feet wide so that all the pods are easy to reach from one side or the other. After you've dug out the 3 inches of soil, scatter the bean seeds at random over the bed, trying to keep them about 4 inches away from their neighbors in all directions. Gently step on the seeds to firm them into the ground, then replace most of the soil you removed, leaving the final smoothed surface of the bed about ½ inch below the surrounding ground. This slight depression ensures that the seeds will get plenty of water.

Plant pole beans on either one or both sides of their supports with the seeds spaced 2 to 4 inches apart. Keep the rows 36 to 48 inches apart, depending on how tall the beans will get. If they will climb higher than 5 feet, use the wider spacing.

Your beans will really take off when temperatures are between 60° and 70°F. The lowest they can tolerate and still keep growing is 50°F. If it is too hot, you can lose your crop since, as we explained earlier, the blossoms will drop off and the seeds won't set. If your summers are usually scorchers, plant your beans as early as possible so that they will mature before the temperatures really start to soar. If it's hot while your plants are flowering, you may be able to save your crop by spraying the plants with cold water during the afternoons to cool them down. Be careful not to disturb the plants or work around them while they are wet, however, as this can spread disease. Also, remember to keep your plants well watered once the blossoms appear and the pods start forming; water stress leads to tough, stringy pods.

Bringing in the Bean Harvest

Snap bean pods are ready for harvest a week or two after flowering, which translates to roughly six to eight weeks after planting. Once the harvest begins, you should pick your beans every two or three days. It's especially important to keep up with pole beans and bush beans that don't set their crop all at once to prolong the harvest. If you let these beans go until the seeds reach their full size, the plants will stop producing. If you get tired of picking them green, go ahead and let the pods fatten and develop seeds. Although the beans won't be as pretty to look at as those varieties developed specifically for drying, your dried snap beans will make delicious winter eating.

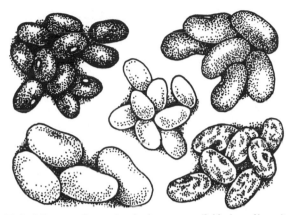

Dried Beans: *Beans for drying are available in a diversity of shapes and colors. Choices include, clockwise from the upper right, red kidney, pinto, Great Northern, Black Turtle, and navy beans in the middle.*

We think snap beans are best when the pods are thin, before the seeds get very big, but many people prefer them when the seeds have begun to swell. Experiment with picking at different stages to see which one you prefer. Fresh snap beans can be stored at 40° to 45°F with a relative humidity of 90 to 95 percent for a week or slightly longer.

If you want dried beans, the usual procedure is to let the pods stay on the plants until the beans are large and hard and the pods are dry and papery. The weather is a very important factor if you're planning to dry your bean crop, for the pods cannot dry properly when the air is damp. If you have a spell of wet weather after the beans have filled the pods but haven't yet dried, pull the plants and set them in a protected place such as the garage. Don't let these drying beans freeze. When the pods are dry and crackly, you can shell them. An easy way to do this is to put the pods in an old pillow case and tie it shut with string. Put the pillow case in your clothes dryer, turn it on low, and tumble the beans for about a half hour. The dry heat and bouncing action should be enough to break open the pods and release the beans. When you pour the contents out of the pillowcase, the heavy beans will be easy to separate from the lighter pod material, especially if you do it out in the garage in front of a small fan. The current of air will blow away the light, papery debris, and the heavy beans will fall straight down into a waiting bowl. The dryer method ensures that the beans are thoroughly and evenly dried, so they can be stored immediately. If you don't opt for this method, your beans may not be dry enough to store when they're shelled. Let them sit out in a single layer in a warm, airy place until they're hard enough that you can't dent them with a fingernail.

If you live in an area where bean weevils are a problem, spread the shelled beans in a single layer in a baking pan and pasteurize them for 15 minutes in a 175°F oven. This heat treatment will kill any weevil eggs that may have been laid inside the beans.

Saving Bean Seed

To save bean seed for planting, let the seeds dry on the plants just as you would for dry beans. Don't let them get too dry before you pick them or the pods may split and drop their cargo onto the ground. And don't use the dryer technique or the oven method of pasteurization on seeds intended for planting—the heat can kill them. One year Dorothy planted some Jacob's Cattle beans which never came up; she had forgotten to label which seeds had been pasteurized and must have picked up the wrong jar. To make sure the seeds are evenly dry, put them in an open container, a single layer deep, for a couple of weeks, and stir them with your hand every few days. Then store them in an airtight container in a cool, dry place.

Problems with Beans

If you save your own bean seed, be on the alert in your garden for seedborne diseases and pests. Because there is so much stored food in beans, they are a favorite target for many unwelcome invaders. If you have a lot of trouble with insect pests, try planting purple beans instead of green and yellow ones. Insects seem to be less likely to attack purple vegetables than green ones. No one knows for sure why this is so, but there are several theories. One is that insects which are used to zeroing in on green colored plants aren't attracted by the purple color. Another is that the purple pigments are distasteful to insects.

Anthracnose: This fungus is especially devastating to beans and is carried in the seeds. Infected plants develop dark brown, sunken spots on the pods and seeds. In humid weather, the spots may have pink centers. Moist, cool weather favors the onset of anthracnose, which is most common in the northeastern and northwestern parts of the continent. If your beans suffer from this disease, check the source of your seeds. If you have been growing your own, you may have to give up this practice and buy fresh seeds every year. If you bought the seeds, try to find out where they were grown. Most bean seed is now grown in the dry western states where anthracnose is not a problem, and the chance that western-grown seeds carry the disease is slim.

Anthracnose is the reason that gardening books caution you not to work among your beans when the foliage is wet. It can spread like wildfire from plant to plant under those conditions. Fortunately, there are bean varieties resistant to anthracnose, so if it's a recurrent problem in your garden, check for these varieties in seed catalogs.

Rust: This can be a bothersome disease for many gardeners, especially those throughout the East and on the Pacific Coast. The fungus causes many rust-colored lesions to form, usually on the undersides of leaves, although they can also appear on petioles, stems, or pods. The leaves will turn yellowish and drop off in the advanced stages of the disease. If you live in an area with a reputation for rust, your best defense is to grow resistant varieties such as Pencil Pod and Golden Wax. Keeping the garden clean and disposing of any diseased plants are two habits worth cultivating to help discourage the rust-causing fungus (not to mention many other diseases).

Mexican bean beetle: This spotted, brown-colored beetle attacks the leaves of young plants, leaving them with a skeletonized appearance before moving on to the pods and stems. Try to plant as early as possible since these voracious beetles tend to prefer late-season crops over early-season crops. If you spot any of these pesky scavengers on your plants, remove them by hand and be sure to check the undersides of leaves for tiny yellow egg clusters. Try interplanting potato plants as a catch crop between every two rows of beans, or alternate rows of garlic and nasturtium with the beans to help repel these pests. Introducing praying mantises into the garden may also help in reducing the beetle population. Some bush snap varieties such as Regal and Gold Crop exhibit a certain degree of resistance to bean beetles and are worth trying if all else fails.

Nematodes: These tiny, eellike worms form knots on plant roots, preventing the transfer of nutrients to the aboveground parts. Malformed blossoms, leaves and stems, poorly developed plants and yellow foliage are signs that nematodes are sabotaging the roots of your plants. Don't plant beans or any other susceptible crop like lettuce, peppers, squash, and tomatoes in the same spot more than once every five years since it takes at least that much time for the soil to become free of nematodes.

Potato leafhopper: Gardeners in the East and South may have a few bouts with this wedge-shaped, spotted, green insect. If you see your bean leaves turn white and curl up, you can be almost sure that the culprit is the leafhopper. Blue Crop, Eagle, Tendercrop, and Tenderette are good snap bean varieties to grow if you've had problems with this pest.

Bean Frontiers

Worldwide, beans are a very important crop, with 11 million metric tons of dried beans and 2 million metric tons of fresh ones produced each year. Breeders are trying to develop higher-yielding beans, for these plants have a low yield compared to cereal crops. There is some disagreement, however, about the best way to go about improving yield. Some breeders want to select for high yields in specific environments, while others think it is better to look for types which have wide adaptability along with increased yield. When varieties can only do well in limited environments, there is always the risk of crop failure during an off year. While plants with wide adaptability may not produce as much every year, they are not as susceptible to loss over the long haul.

Breeders are also producing more varieties that bear their pods at the top of the plants, making them better suited for mechanical harvesting. Fortunately, some of these varieties (such as Remus) still retain that nutty, fresh bean flavor and are equally suitable for home gardeners who don't want to stoop and hunt among the leaves for their beans.

While beans are a nutritious food, they do contain some chemical substances that can interfere with good nutrition. Two of these are trypsin inhibitors, which affect the body's metabolism of the important digestive enzyme, trypsin, and hemagglutinins, which can cause red blood cells to clump together. As we all know, cooked dried beans can also cause intestinal gas, and two different chemicals are involved in this problem. Breeders have enlisted the aid of biochemists and nutritionists in a coordinated effort to reduce the levels of all these problem chemicals in beans. To date, progress has been slow, and they're still working their way toward a solution.

It stands to reason that because beans have been around for such a long time, there are almost countless variations on the basic bean that have sprung up worldwide and have been handed down, generation to generation. Most of these strains are not available to home gardeners via commerical channels, and in many cases, they have been kept alive only because one individual lovingly and carefully saved seed and replanted year after year. At best, this is a tenuous existence. What happens when that one individual dies or is unable to continue gardening, and no one picks up where he left off? All too often the answer has been that the particular bean strain has died out. Fortunately, many people have become concerned about the accelerating loss of heirloom bean varieties and the imperative need to preserve genetic variety for future breeding efforts.

One foresighted man dedicated to preserving heirloom bean varieties is John Withee, founder of Wanigan Associates, a group of bean aficionados who share his concern. With the help of many home gardeners and farmers, Withee has managed to collect over 1,200 strains of beans and is still seeking to expand his collection. In 1981, he donated samples of his entire collection to the Rodale Research Center in Maxatawny, Pennsylvania, and to Kent Whealy, founder of The Seed Saver's Exchange. Both the Rodale Research Center and Whealy, with the help of concerned gardeners across the country, are working to increase the store of seeds in the collection to ensure the preservation of each bean strain. If you are interested in joining in the effort to maintain the diversity of beans and want to participate in a growers' network to save and propagate heirloom seeds, write to Kent Whealy, RFD 2, Box 92, Princeton, MO 64673. (The Seed Saver's Exchange doesn't deal only in beans; under Whealy's direction, heirloom seeds of many common garden vegetables are traded back and forth among gardeners committed to saving and propagating non-hybrid varieties.)

Lima Beans

Due to their tropical origins, lima beans need warmer conditions than snap beans do. And since you must wait until the beans have developed in the pod before picking them, limas take a longer time to mature to an edible stage than do snap beans. For both of these reasons, limas are a reliable crop only in the warmer, longer-season areas of the continent. But their delicious, unique flavor and their excellent nutritional properties make them worth trying wherever there is hope of getting a crop.

Lima Varieties

With limas, you have your pick between bush and pole varieties. Since the pole kinds can reach up to 8 feet tall, they need a good, sturdy support such as the one described earlier in the box, Surefire Supports for Beans and Peas. In addition to the two sizes of vines, you have two sizes of beans to choose from as well. Baby limas (also known as butter beans) have small seeds, while regular limas have large ones. The ancestors of baby limas were first domesticated in Central America, while the progenitors of large-seeded limas came from South America. There are other edible beans besides limas which belong to this same species—Java beans, Red Rangoon beans, and White Rangoon or Burma beans—but as a rule these aren't grown in North America. All of these contain at least a trace of the poison, hydrogen cyanide, so they must be treated with care in the kitchen. Lima beans themselves are not thought to contain significant amounts of hydrogen cyanide, but no systematic tests have been done on their content of this poison. They certainly can't contain dangerous levels, for people have been eating these beans for years with no harmful side effects.

Among gardeners whose season is long enough for limas, King of the Garden is an especially popular variety. Christmas limas are another fine, large-seeded pole bean with a delicious, buttery flavor. Although catalogs say Christmas limas take 85 days to mature, they will produce a harvestable crop for us here in Montana, so they must be more tolerant of cool weather than some other lima varieties. Fordhook 242 is a reliable bush lima, and Early Giant, maturing within 65 days, is worth a try in short-season areas. For baby lima lovers, Henderson Bush Lima (65 days) and Thorogreen (67 days) are good gambles for short-season areas. Some pole baby limas you might want to try include the prolific Carolina (also called Sieva) and Florida Speckled Butter Bean, which grows well under conditions of drought and heat making it a good choice for southern regions.

Tips on Growing and Harvesting Limas

Plant your heat-loving limas only after the soil has warmed up to at least 70°F, the minimum temperature they need to germinate. It's not worth the effort to plant before the soil temperature has inched up past the 70°F mark; many varieties will just rot in the ground at 68°F. Some gardeners like to germinate their limas indoors before planting. If you'd like to give your limas a head start, sprout them on moistened paper towels in a warm (70°F) place, and when the first root emerges, plant them in a biodegradable pot for later transplanting in the garden. (Be sure to use peat pots or other containers which you can peel away easily without disturbing the roots. See chapter 4 for a discussion of suitable containers.) Plant your lima seeds or seedlings 3 to 6 inches apart in the garden, using the greater distance for large-seeded varieties. Use the same guidelines for between-row spacing that are recommended for snap beans. Pay attention as you plant and place each lima seed with its "eye" down. (This is the small, colored portion of the seed where it is indented, which is the place where it was attached to the pod.) There's a good reason why you must pay attention to this detail. The root emerges from the eye, and because lima seeds are so large, it may be difficult for the embryonic stem to push the cotyledons up through the soil if the seed is upside down. If you are growing large-seeded limas, be sure to plant them in loose soil so that the massive seed can push its way up without a struggle. Limas need well-drained soil for the best growth, but unlike peas, they don't do well when planted in ridges. While limas like warm weather, very hot weather can be bad for them. Temperatures over 90°F can inhibit seed setting. Even a prolonged spell of 70°F weather early on in the season can affect your eventual harvest. These warm temperatures will trigger the plants to flower before they have reached full size; although you'll get an earlier harvest, it won't be as abundant as one from full-sized plants.

Harvest your limas while the beans are still green. If you let them linger on the vines too long and they've turned white, you'll end up with a starchy and unpalatable batch of beans. When Diane is lucky enough to get a crop of limas in her cool mountain valley, she candles the pods against the setting sun before picking to see how large the beans are. This way she knows for sure when the beans are plump and ready for harvest. If you're growing your limas for drying, follow the guidelines given for shell beans under Bringing in the Bean Harvest.

If you store lima pods in a very cold place—close to freezing—they will keep well for about ten days. In a cool basement, they will only keep for a

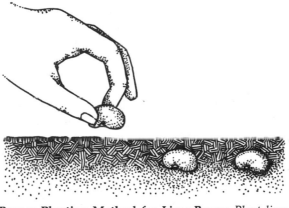

Proper Planting Method for Lima Beans: *Plant lima beans ½ inch deep in the soil, with their eyes downward. The eye is the small colored portion of the seed that is indented and is the place from which the root will appear.*

couple of days. When you shell limas, take a tip from us; we use a pair of old scissors to cut open the pods rather than struggling to shell them by hand.

Problems with Limas

There are only a couple of problems you are likely to encounter with your crop of lima beans.

Downy mildew: Limas and peas are both bothered by this disease. If your lima bean patch constantly falls victim to it, try growing the variety Thaxter, which is resistant to downy mildew.

Lima bean pod borer: This inch-long caterpillar is especially active in southern gardens. It does its dirty work by burrowing into the pod and eating the seeds inside. While it may consume many seeds in a baby lima pod before its appetite is satisfied, one bean may be all it needs from a large-seeded variety. You can hand-pick these pests, but be prepared for the fact that they crawl quite rapidly.

Rust: Lima beans are susceptible to rust. (See the discussion of this fungal disease that appears earlier in the chapter under problems with beans.)

Peas

Even a small garden has room for a few pea plants. A row of dwarf peas with their delicate tendrils and soft white flowers even makes an interesting addition to a flowerbed. The trick to growing a good crop of peas is to be sure to plant them so that they will mature during cool weather. If the temperature gets above 80°F while the peas are blooming, the flowers will not be properly pollinated. And an extended warm spell while the vines are developing will hasten flowering, causing the plants to bloom when they're still small and not ready to support a heavy crop. At the other end of the thermometer, peas can take a lot of cold before they keel over and die. The vines can survive 20°F while growing and 28°F during flowering. The pods themselves can tolerate temperatures as low as 24°F and still deliver undamaged peas. As further testimony to the pea's cold-hardiness, here in Montana we can plant a late pea crop in August and harvest some pods after the first frosts in September.

In areas with a milder climate, peas can be grown as a winter crop, and in many parts of the United States and Canada, the spring planting can go in as early as January or February. Gardening folklore has it that St. Patrick's Day is the day for planting peas, a fitting custom since the green that is associated with that holiday is the color of peas as well as of shamrocks. Wherever you garden, peas should be the first crop you get into the ground, as soon as the soil is dry enough to work.

Pea Varieties

The names given to the three basic types of peas can sometimes be confusing, but we'll try to set them straight for you. Garden pea and English pea refer to the familiar shelling varieties of which you only eat the seeds. Snow pea, Chinese pea, and sugar pea are interchangeable names that all refer to the Oriental edible-pod varieties. These peas produce earlier than garden peas, for you harvest them as soon as the pods reach their full size but before the peas themselves have fully developed. The third type of pea, the snap pea, is also the newest. An innovation in pea breeding produced the thick, juicy, edible pod filled with sweet, fat peas that characterizes these snap peas.

Garden peas come in a great array of varieties of all heights, from rambling 5-foot vines to the more petite dwarf vines that usually measure under 2 feet. Little Marvel is a perennial favorite among dwarf varieties. Maestro is another dwarf variety that has the added feature of resistance to downy mildew. We've had good results when we've grown Maestro for a fall crop. Tastewise, many gardeners claim that Lincoln peas have the best flavor of all, but personally, we go crazy over Green Arrow, a vigorous variety with long pods, each containing ten or eleven peas, with a wonderful, rich flavor. If your climate is unpredictable and hot spells pay frequent visits in the spring, grow Wando, another delicious variety which happens to be more heat-resistant than others.

Pea Types: *The three types of peas are, from left to right: the garden or English pea, of which you eat only the peas; the snow or sugar pea, also known as the edible-pod pea, which is eaten, pod and all, before the peas reach full size; and the snap pea, a newer variety that has an edible pod filled with sweet, fat peas.*

A new development in peas is the almost leafless varieties such as Novella. This rather eccentric growth habit is the result of genes which direct tendrils to form instead of leaves. While Novella is sold with enthusiastic descriptions in seed catalogs geared for home gardeners, it was actually developed for commercial growers who want varieties that can be block-planted and can grow upright without support. The open structure of the plant gives free access to circulating air, thereby discouraging diseases that commonly afflict plants with dense, leafy growth under moist conditions. Another attractive feature (especially for gardeners who want to process the harvest) is that the peas mature almost simultaneously. The only problem is, the peas that Novella produces don't taste very good! They lack that sweet, home-grown flavor, probably because each plant has too little photosynthetic area to produce the amount of sugar it takes to make the peas taste sweet.

If you are really in a hurry for peas, try growing the extra-early variety, Alaska. As you're planting, you'll notice that this particular variety has round, full seeds instead of the wrinkled seeds common to many other peas. That's because these peas contain more starch than sugar, so the seeds hold their shape when dried. Alaska is a lot cold-hardier than regular peas and is ready to harvest in as few as 56 days from planting. While they aren't as sweet as wrinkled-seeded peas, Alaska peas are better than the average fare you can buy at the supermarket which has been shipped in from parts unknown and has lost in transit what flavor it had. If you allow Alaska peas to dry on the vine, you'll find that they are delicious in recipes calling for split peas.

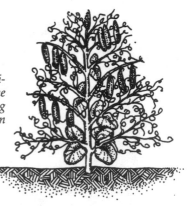

Novella Pea: *The revolutionary Novella pea is a semi-leafless variety that has very few leaves except close to the main stem. Tendrils are formed instead of leaves, allowing lots of sunshine to reach the developing pods. The plant can also stand by itself without support.*

There's a veritable blizzard of snow pea varieties to choose from. Some, such as Mammoth Melting Sugar, are tall and produce very large, flat pods. You must provide these with tall fences for support. Other varieties have dwarf vines, ranging from 15 to 30 inches tall. Several of these short-vined varieties, such as Dwarf Gray Sugar, have lovely, two-tone purple flowers that add a delicate touch of color to the garden. Snow peas are best eaten raw or only lightly cooked (overcooking renders them limp and a drab shade of green), and are especially suited to Chinese stir-fry dishes. Usually you must pull the strings off the pods before cooking or eating.

The interesting development of the snap pea involved a combination of luck, persistence, and know-how. At the Gallatin Valley Seed Company in Twin Falls, Idaho, a new employee named Dr. Calvin Lamborn came to work in 1969. As Dr. M. C. Parker, then Research Director, showed Lamborn around, he explained his frustrations in trying to develop a snow pea with fewer strings and a more tender pod lining. Parker had just about given up on the project, for every time he came up with a more tender pod it was misshapen and, therefore, less desirable. Parker also showed Lamborn a mutant shell pea which had appeared in the fields. This mutant was called a tight pod because the pod hugged the seeds closely. Upon closer examination, Lamborn found that the pod walls of this mutant were very thick, which is why they clung so tightly to the seeds. At that point, something clicked, and he realized that if he could incorporate the thick walls of the tight pod into regular snow peas, maybe he could get a tender pod that wasn't distorted. Since the peas of the tight pod were also of high quality, Lamborn hoped he could come up with a tender pod which contained edible shelling peas as well.

After crossing the tight pod with an edible-pod variety, Lamborn saw his hunch pay off, for the cross yielded better results than he had ever hoped for. From that point on it was a question of breeding and selecting until he had a reliable variety which bred true with predictable traits. In 1980, after ten years of development, snap peas were introduced to home gardeners with rave reviews.

The first variety of snap peas to be introduced was Sugar Snap. Sugar Snap vines grow very tall—around 7 feet—so they absolutely must be grown on a tall trellis or wire fence. Both the peas and the pods of Sugar Snaps stay sweet and tender for a long time on the vines. They are so delicious that many gardeners have trouble harvesting any for use in the kitchen; adults and children alike tend to sneak into the garden, pick a handful of Sugar Snaps, and eat them on the spot. Aside from stringing, Sugar Snaps really need no preparation prior to eating and may help teach many otherwise suspicious people just how delicious raw peas can be. If you do want to cook these tasty vegetables, don't cook the pods longer than three minutes, or they will turn mushy.

In 1982, a full line of short-vined snap peas became available to home gardeners, under the names Sugar Bon, Sugar Mel, and Sugar Rae. These dwarf, compact plants will grow no taller than 2 feet, making them easier to manage and not so space-greedy. The early-maturing Sugar Bon and the late-maturing Sugar Rae will help spread out the delectable harvest over a longer period. Sugar Bon and Sugar Mel have resistance to powdery mildew.

Tips on Growing and Harvesting Peas

Peas can germinate at temperatures as low as 40°F, but it takes them almost 36 days to do so. At 68°F, the peas will be up in only 8 days. So, you can see there is little point to putting in your peas extra early, even though they can take quite a bit of cold. You will risk having them rot in the ground as they slowly come to life.

When planting time rolls around, remember to take the trouble to give your peas something to climb, even if they are dwarf plants, as we described earlier, under The Long and Short of Growing Legumes. Put your support in place first, then plant your peas 2 to 3 inches deep on both sides of it, spacing the seeds 2 to 3 inches apart. Keep a margin of at least 3 feet between each double row and support unit; if you can spare the space, a 4-foot margin makes it easier for you to pick from the vines.

How do you know when the time is right to harvest those plump, green pods from the vine? Garden peas are usually fat enough for picking anywhere from 20 to 30 days after blooming. As the peas swell the pod, you should check them often for they can become overmature very quickly, a condition signalled by the loss of the bright green pod color. Timing the harvest is critical, for if you wait too long, that sweet, fresh garden-grown pea flavor is gone. Young garden peas at their flavorful prime are sweet because they are full of sucrose which has been transported from the leaves or pod to the seeds. As the seeds mature, the sucrose is changed into starch, the storage form of carbohydrate; the seed, as a natural part of its life cycle, is getting ready to nourish a young plant during germination and early growth.

Pod size can sometimes be a deceptive indicator of the size of the peas within. With some varieties, there is lots of space between the walls of the pod and the peas; the pod can seem very fat while the peas are still very tiny. But with other kinds, the pod hugs the peas quite closely and will be ready to pick at a smaller pod size than the other type. You will learn from experience which varieties fit into which category.

You should pick snow pea pods just as they reach full size but before they begin to swell with developing seeds. Ideally, the seeds should only be the size of BB's when you harvest the pods. If you should happen to overlook the pods and they fatten up to full-blown maturity, be sure to pick and discard them when you do find them, otherwise, the vines will stop producing. When snow peas have inched their way past their prime, the pods become tough and stringy and the peas become bitter.

Snap peas can be harvested any time after the pods have developed. The young pods are delightfully sweet, but the longer you leave the pods on the vine (up to a certain point, of course), the sweeter and juicier they become.

You should be aware, however, that all three types of peas become starchy and tough once they've passed their peak of maturity. If you haven't kept up with the harvest and are faced with a lot of overmature peas on your plants, don't just throw them away. You can make pea soup with them without bothering to go through the process of drying and splitting them. Lots of people think that fresh pea soup tastes better than the kind made with dried peas.

If you are growing smooth-seeded peas expressly for drying, let the pods dry on the vine until most of them have turned brown. Pull the vines and stack them in a warm, airy, sheltered place for a final drying session. When the pods are crackly, shell the peas and store them in lidded containers.

Once you've harvested your peas, if you can't shell and eat or freeze them right away, place the pods in a plastic bag and set them in the refrigerator. While peas are at their tastiest when fresh, even those you keep in your refrigerator for two weeks will be better than any you could buy in the supermarket. Don't shell your peas before storing them, for shelled peas convert sucrose into starch more rapidly than unshelled ones. Not too many people know that the pods of garden peas are good to eat, too. They do have a tough, inner, waxy layer that helps prevent the pod from losing moisture which you should carefully peel away. These pods are actually quite tasty as long as they're not too old and tough (the pod walls develop fibers as they age). Because they lack this protective waxy layer, snow peas and snap pea pods tend to shrivel up in storage before garden peas do. Their pods quickly lose their crispness even when stored in plastic bags, and sugar snap pods in particular can develop an off taste after just a week or so in the refrigerator. If this should befall your snap peas, you can still peel away the pods and just eat the peas themselves.

Saving Pea Seeds

If you want to save your pea seeds for next year's garden, just let the pods dry on the vine until you can hear the seeds rattle inside. Watch them carefully so that you can pick them just as they are approaching dryness. If you ignore them, you run the risk of having the pods break open and dump their seeds on the ground. If rainy weather descends while the plants are drying in the garden, rush out, pull up the vines, and stack them in a dry, airy, sheltered place. On the average, it will take one to two weeks for these uprooted vines and pods to dry. When the pods are papery and brown, thresh or hand-crack them to release the seeds. Make sure the seeds are completely dry before you store them in an airtight container in a cool, dry place.

Problems with Peas

In general, peas are bothered less by pests and diseases than most garden crops. Perhaps this is true because they grow and mature during cool weather, before most pests have had a chance to build up their populations. There is one peculiar pest that bothers peas, though; this is a tiny worm which burrows into the root nodules where it feeds on the rhizobia, preventing them from fixing nitrogen for the plant. Peas that suffer from these worms can develop severe symptoms of nitrogen deficiency. If you have this problem, next time plant your peas in another part of the garden.

Powdery mildew: This disease can be a problem with peas, for it thrives during the cool, wet weather that peas also appreciate. When it strikes, the leaves of the vines become covered with grayish patches that grow, even to the point where they cover the pods. In Montana, mildew doesn't usually strike spring-planted peas until the main harvest is just about over, so it is not a serious problem. But when we plant in August for a fall harvest, we are careful to choose a mildew-resistant variety such as Maestro.

Pea Frontiers

Breeders are continuing the work they started with the almost leafless variety, Novella, so home gardeners may see more varieties of this type appearing in seed catalogs. Another area of interest for breeders is increasing the yield of peas by developing varieties that carry more than one pod at each node. There are already a few varieties (such as Recette) which produce three pods at each node. Not only do such varieties give a larger yield, but more of the peas are produced at one time, facilitating mechanical harvesting and making life easier for the home gardener who wants to process the harvest.

Because peas are self-pollinating, each variety is quite inbred. Many people are becoming concerned about the narrow genetic base of our modern pea. Unfortunately, until recently, no one systematically saved old varieties, so much of the genetic variability of peas has been lost forever. If you're concerned about the loss of heirloom pea varieties, contact the Seed Saver's Exchange (the address is given under Bean Frontiers, earlier in this chapter) for more information on how you can participate in stemming this loss.

With the higher cost of grain, interest has been sparked in using peas for livestock feed. Varieties with a higher amino acid content would be needed here, which might also increase the protein quality of peas grown for human use as well. In this instance, the narrow available genetic base of peas makes the search for high-quality protein peas difficult.

Chapter 11

Corn: The Oddball Crop

Vital Statistics

Family:
Gramineae
Species:
Zea mays
Z. mays var. *rugosa*—Sweet corn
Z. mays var. *praecox*—Popcorn
Soil:
Any good, rich soil
pH:
5.5–6.8
Soil Temperature for Germination:
60°–95°F; 95°F, optimum

Air Temperature for Best Growth:
50°F, minimum; 60°–75°F,
optimum; 95°F, maximum
Seed Viability:
1–2 years
Seed Germination:
3–12 days
Seed Planting Depth:
3–4"

It may seem hard to believe, but corn is actually a huge grass that would make a lawn fit for a giant. Imagine what would happen to the family corn plot if all the towns which have laws about mowing grass to a certain height strictly enforced their rules! Despite the fact that it takes up so much space, corn is one of the most popular home garden crops, for no ears you buy in the store can come close to the delectable sweetness of fresh-picked, home-grown corn. Since corn literally begins to lose sweetness the second it is picked, it is not a crop which keeps its quality when mass-produced and shipped. Really dedicated corn-lovers (like Diane's children) can't wait long enough for the corn even to be cooked—they pull the ears right off the plants, peel back the husks, and munch away. Growing corn is fun, too, for adults and children alike enjoy watching the tall stalks shoot up so quickly from the small, shriveled corn seeds.

Corn has been cultivated by people for so long that its origins are lost in time. Scientists have for years carried on a lively debate about where corn

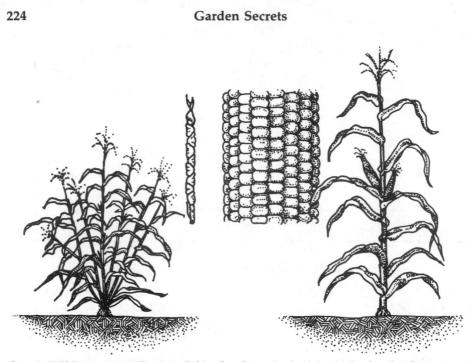

Corn's Wild Ancestor? *Teosinte (left), of undetermined origin, is closely related to corn and looks much like today's sweet corn (right). It is two-thirds the size of a modern corn plant and has numerous small spikes at the nodes. Each teosinte stalk arises from the ground. The kernels of teosinte pop just like popcorn and can even be ground into a crude flour.*

came from. Shedding a glimmer of light on this unsolved mystery, archaeologists made an exciting find in Tehuacan, Mexico in 1960—tiny corn cobs which date back to 5000 B.C. Much of the controversy about the origins of corn hinges upon whether these 7,000-year-old cobs represent an ancient wild corn which the Indians had gathered, or an early variety of domesticated corn. A key trait that distinguishes cultivated corn from its wild relatives is that the husks enclose the kernels tightly and do not open, so the kernels can't drop from the ear when ripe as do the seeds of wild grasses. Unfortunately, no one has been able to determine for certain whether or not the ancient corn found at Tehuacan could shed its seeds.

Today, there are no clearly identifiable species of wild corn to be found growing anywhere in the world. But there is a grass called teosinte which is related to corn closely enough to cross readily with it. As a matter of fact, teosinte grows frequently in Mexican corn fields, and the farmers actually encourage interbreeding of corn and teosinte because they believe it improves their crop. The corn expert George W. Beadle believes that teosinte is the true ancestor of corn because when the two are crossed for several generations, the resulting ears look like a slightly larger version of the ancient cobs and have many of the same botanical differences from corn as are evident in those cobs. Teosinte does make a good candidate as an attractive crop for early humans to have cultivated, for its kernels will pop like popcorn making an acceptable food, and it can be ground into a flour (although the flour is very coarse because the teosinte kernels are hard).

A different opinion is held by another prominent corn scientist, Dr. Paul C. Mangelsdorf. He believes that the wild ancestors of corn have completely died out and that teosinte is a hybrid between those ancestors and an archaic type of popcorn called pod corn.

The fact that we can't determine for sure how the plant we know as corn came to exist in its present form emphasizes just how ancient a crop plant corn actually is. A key change that occurred in corn as it evolved from the wild type to its cultivated form is the development of kernels that adhere to the cob. Wild plants must be able to scatter their own seeds so that the next generation can survive. If a corn cob fell to the ground and the seeds germinated all in one place, the resulting seedlings would all be so close together that none of them could grow to maturity. But for human consumption, kernels which stay in place are a lot easier to gather than those which fall off. So once the modern form of corn had developed, the only way for it to survive was to live in a continuing partnership with people. Instead of having its seeds scattered at random by a natural process, corn became dependent upon human intervention to separate the kernels and plant them season after season to ensure the continuity of the crop.

The great Indian cultures of Mexico and Central and South America, such as the Aztecs, Mayas, and Incas, based their civilizations on corn. One could really say that these ancient people "built" corn by selecting and propagating the best races over the centuries. All the different forms of corn that we know today—dent, flint, popcorn, and sweet corn—had already been cultivated by the time Columbus discovered America. We owe the incredible variety of corn types to the ingenuity and imagination of these people. We are further in their debt when we realize that they have provided us with an incredibly diverse collection of genetic material for the development of even more kinds of corn.

Here in North American gardens, we see only a tiny fraction of the existing sorts of corn. Dr. Mangelsdorf, who has spent his whole life studying the origins and evolution of corn, points this out in his book, *Corn: Its Origin, Evolution, and Development* (see the Bibliography). He describes the seemingly inexhaustible variety of corn plants grown around the world in this way:

> There are early maturing varieties, such as the Gaspe flint from the Gaspe Peninsula in Canada or Cinquantino from the Pyrenees Mountains of Spain which mature in sixty to seventy days, and very late varieties in the American tropics that require ten or eleven months to reach maturity. The number of leaves varies from eight to forty-eight,

the height of stalk from less than two feet to more than twenty, the number of stalks produced by a single seed ranges from one to fifteen. The size of the ear varies from the tiny ears of some of the popcorn varieties which are no larger than a man's thumb to the gigantic corn grown in the Jala Valley of Mexico, which produces ears up to two feet in length borne on stalks so tall that the ears may be conveniently harvested from horseback and so stiff and strong that they are sometimes used for pickets in enclosures for domestic animals.

Reprinted by permission
of Harvard University Press.

Little-Known Corn Facts

When most of us talk about corn, we are referring to the sweet corn that we use as a table vegetable. Corn with sugar-filled kernels is a relatively recent development in the course of this plant's evolution as a cultivated crop. The starch in a corn seed is an important source of nourishment for the corn seedling. From a biological point of view, a seed that stores sugar instead of starch is inferior. The first corn types, struggling to survive, most certainly had kernels with a very high starch content to ensure self-preservation. It was only later, when humans stepped in and assured the crop's perpetuation, that a plant producing sugar-filled kernels could be possible.

The reason why sweet corn is sweet can be found by investigating its genetic makeup. Sweet corn is in a class by itself due to a defect in its genes which inhibits the conversion of sucrose from the leaves into starch in the kernels. The gene for this defect is called "shrunken 1," for the lack of starch in the kernels causes them to shrivel when dried. Field corn leaves also produce sucrose which is transported to the developing kernels. But once inside the endosperm (food storage area) of the seed, the sucrose is converted by enzymes into dextrin and then to starch. Since sweet corn has the shrunken 1 gene to slow down this conversion, the kernels accumulate sucrose and some dextrin rather than starch. While we all enjoy the pleasantly sweet flavor that results, the lack of starch does pose some problems. Because there is little starch to nourish the seedling, sweet corn seeds do not germinate as easily or store as well as starchy types. This calls for special care by the gardener, and an attention to cultural details that other, starchier types of corn don't require. Sweet corn is also more susceptible to disease than field corn.

While most gardeners are acquainted with corn's delectable, succulent eating quality, very few are aware of the fact that this crop is one of the most efficient of all cereal grains in utilizing energy from the sun. Most plants can only use sunlight up to a certain point, regardless of how brightly the sun is shining. At high light intensities, the level of carbon dioxide (CO_2) in the plant leaf drops because the plant is using it up so fast. This low level of CO_2 limits the ability of the plants to photosynthesize. Corn, however, can adapt to low CO_2 levels and can increase its photosynthetic rate very quickly, thus utilizing more of that precious sunlight. This special ability is the reason why people sometimes contend that they can hear the corn grow—they are right in recognizing that corn grows faster than other crops. Crabgrass, a plant unfortunately familiar to every gardener, is able to exploit light the same way corn does. You aren't just imagining that crabgrass grows faster than your crops it really does!

Corn's Nutritional Profile

The diet of early Mexican and South American Indians was based soundly on corn, beans, and squash. This is an especially nutritious trio of vegetables, for they complement each other to create a well-balanced blend of the protein, vitamins, and minerals essential to good health. Corn provides carbohydrates, small amounts of protein, and fat. Beans supply the bulk of the protein and supplement the two essential amino acids that most corn varieties lack (tryptophan and lysine), as well as providing vitamin B_2 and another B vitamin, nicotinic acid. Squash rounds out the menu by supplementing the carbohydrate calories, providing large amounts of vitamin A, and supplying some fat (in the seeds).

How does corn measure up by itself? Compared with the most nutritious vegetable of all, broccoli, corn turns out to give significantly less nutrient value for the number of calories it contains. While corn has more protein than broccoli, it has fewer vitamins, only one-fifth as much iron, and three times as many calories. But if you look at it another way, an average ear of corn, which supplies so much pleasure, only contains 70 calories. Like potatoes, corn is only fattening because of all the butter we insist on eating with it!

Corn Varieties

There are so many different varieties of corn (a typical seed catalog will list from 20 to 40 corn varieties) that it is impossible for us to recommend specific varieties. What we can do is give you some ideas about how to choose the best variety for your own garden. As with most crops, corn is available in open-pollinated and hybrid forms. The descriptions in catalogs will often rave about the vigorous, superior growth of the hybrid varieties over the standard, open-pollinated types. This isn't just an inflated sales-pitch—there actually is a scientific basis for hybrid superiority.

Corn is a plant that grows best when it has a varied genetic makeup; inbreeding leads to a significant loss of vigor. While the genetic variability necessary to keep standard varieties vigorous leads to unevenness in the quality of the crop, each plant of a hybrid variety, as explained in The Making of a Hybrid Variety in chapter 1, is just about genetically identical to others of the same variety. But because each plant has a great variety of individual genes it has great vigor. Thus, hybrid corn grows faster, is more uniform in size, and yields more than do standard varieties.

If you live in the Corn Belt, where growing conditions are excellent for corn, you might be able to grow open-pollinated varieties which give you a satisfactory crop. But if you live in an area which is in any way marginal for corn, you're better off sticking with hybrids. As you might guess, Montana is not exactly prime corn country, and the one year Diane planted two varieties of nonhybrid corn she was very disappointed. She was barely able to harvest an average of one ear per stalk from that ill-fated crop, while the minimum that she usually gets from hybrids is two ears from each stalk. Some of the ears from the standard varieties were nice and big, but others were disappointingly small. These plants also had a high percentage of stalks which produced male and female flowers intermixed. While they may have been interesting to look at, they were a complete bust as far as Diane's harvest went since no edible ears result from such flowers.

With many garden crops, such as tomatoes, you can save seeds each year from the plants that grew best, and in this way continuously improve the yield by selecting the strains that are best adapted to local growing conditions. But if you try the same thing with open-pollinated corn, instead of steadily improving the plant, you will slowly decrease its genetic variability.

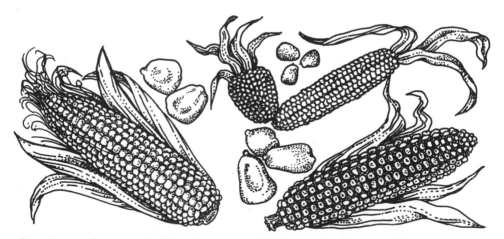

Corn Types: *Sweet corn (left) has large ears with plump, regularly arranged kernels. Popcorn (center) is produced on narrow ears or strawberry-shaped ears and has small, pointy kernels. Field corn (right) has oblong ears with elongated kernels that are less regularly arranged than those of sweet corn.*

Corn which is inbred too long yields poorly and grows weakly. This kind of weakened, inbred corn must be crossed with another race to produce corn that grows vigorously and yields well. As you can see, your ability to improve your own corn is limited, for in order to keep it healthy you must introduce new races every few years to maintain the genetic diversity of your seed.

Perhaps the ultimate example of the perils of genetic uniformity in corn is the epidemic of corn blight that destroyed a large part of the United States' corn crop in 1969. Ironically enough, the problems that year were due to the breeding of hybrids rather than to inbreeding of standard varieties. A few years before, corn breeders had discovered a gene which resulted in male-sterile corn plants, that is, plants which produced no pollen. These plants were very convenient for breeders for it made unnecessary the tedious process of detasseling corn for hybridization. This gene—called the T-type cytoplasm gene—had been incorporated into 70 to 90 percent of all hybrid corn varieties by 1969. Then, in that year, a mutant strain of the fungus causing corn blight arose, and it proved especially devastating to plants with T-type cytoplasm. Since most of the corn being grown in the United States at that time carried the gene for T-type cytoplasm, by 1970 the new blight strain had spread to every state east of the Rockies, and the corn crop was devastated.

That near-disaster alerted corn breeders and other close observers of the nation's food supply that it is imperative to keep corn more diversified, to avoid the perils of inbreeding. The incident focused attention on the need to establish seed banks where breeders can store and propagate hundreds of corn varieties (as well as varieties of other crops). Ideally, when problems with one strain develop, the breeder should be able to turn to the seed bank to find other strains containing genes that will confer disease resistance or other desirable traits to the variety he is working with. Only now is a serious effort being made to collect and preserve all the known existing corn strains, so they will be available if and when the need arises. In some cases, this preservation is a race against time, for once a variety or strain is allowed to die out, that particular combination of genetic material is lost forever.

The mouth-watering descriptions of extra-sweet corn varieties such as Illini Chief, Early Xtra Sweet, and Florida Staysweet that appear in seed catalogs may have whetted your curiosity as to what sets them apart from regular sweet corn. A gene called "shrunken 2" accounts for the phenomenal sweetness of the extra-sweet varieties. Shrunken 2 almost stops the conversion of sucrose to dextrins so that the kernels have even more sucrose in them than conventional sweet corn and are even more shrunken when dried. This lack of dextrin does cause some varieties of extra-sweet corn to have a rather watery texture; in ordinary sweet corn, the dextrin confers a creamy texture.

Many extra-sweet varieties must be isolated from regular sweet corn in the garden (see Corn's Unique Problem) to guarantee their sweetness. This may pose a logistical problem for some home gardeners. Another drawback from the gardener's point of view is the low vigor of these varieties. Since there is so little starch in the kernels, there is even less food for the growing seedlings than in ordinary sweet corn. This means that garden conditions must be close to ideal for these rather finicky extra-sweet varieties to grow well. Fortunately, there is a group of extra-sweet corn varieties that has had most of these temperamental traits bred out of it. Varieties like Mainliner, Kandy Corn, Golden Sweet, and Earliglow belong to the Everlasting Heritage line, meaning they all carry the Everlasting Heritage (abbreviated E.H.) factor. These varieties germinate well and don't have to be isolated like other extra-sweet corn.

Next to their especially delightful flavor, one other attractive quality of these extra-sweet varieties is that they hold their sweetness much longer than regular varieties. This makes them ideal for gardeners who want to sell their corn at a roadside stand. Extra-sweet varieties also last longer on the stalks and do not become overripe as quickly as other types. Small families and those who want to freeze or can in small batches instead of all at once will find this trait to their advantage.

You may have wondered if there was any substantial difference between yellow and white corn, besides the obvious one of color. It turns out there is a big difference, right where it counts, in flavor. White kernels appeared as mutants in yellow corn types and breeders soon realized that the ears with white kernels were much tastier than those ears filled with all yellow kernels. Taste buds don't lie, as laboratory analysis subsequently showed; the white kernels *were* sweeter precisely because they contained more sugar than the yellow ones.

Despite the sweeter flavor of white corn, yellow corn is still the more popular type because many people mistakenly associate the white color with immaturity. To bridge the gap between the two corn types, breeders have developed ears with a mix of both yellow and white kernels. That way, people can enjoy the sweeter tasting white kernels along with the nice yellow color. It's also interesting to note that in terms of nutrition, the yellow corn comes out ahead of the white in vitamin A content.

No matter what color kernel you prefer, remember that your most important concern should be to pick those varieties which will grow well and mature during the season in your area. More than any other crop, corn fails in the home garden because gardeners choose varieties unsuited to the climate and/or season length. In Montana, many people reap an abundant harvest of beautiful corn. But just as many complain that their corn grew great but froze before it bore any ripe ears. Seed racks in gardening and hardware stores tend to sell standard varieties that thrive in the Corn Belt but just can't make it in marginal areas. With this in mind, you'll increase your chances for success with corn if you *under*estimate the number of days in the growing season. As an illustration, where we live, there are usually 90 frost-free days during the summer. But in order to get a decent crop of corn, we have to grow varieties which are rated on the packages as requiring only 68 days to maturity! The reason is that the optimal growing temperature for corn is 75°F, and if the average temperature is below that level, the corn will mature more slowly than the amount of time listed on the seed packet. Because we live in the mountains, our nights are cool, and that slows down corn growth considerably. If you live in a cool area, be sure to pick corn varieties very conservatively, and check with the county agent and local long-time gardeners to find out which varieties can be counted on to give you a crop.

Corn's Unique Problem

There is one more thing you must keep in mind while planning your garden and choosing a variety of corn to grow. You may decide you want to grow popcorn for fun along with your sweet corn, but unless you have a very large garden (or a long enough season to stagger the plantings so the two separate crops won't be tasseling at the same time), you'll have to give up that idea. And popcorn isn't the only problem, for many corn varieties must be separated in order to produce a quality product; extra-sweet varieties, white corn, flint corn (the Indian corn that is ground for meal), and popcorn all require isolation from one another and from other sorts of sweet corn.

In order to understand why this is so, you need to know a little about how corn develops. With crops such as tomatoes and cabbage, we eat the fruit or part of the mother plant. But with corn, the portion we savor is the seeds themselves. The flavor and texture of the corn kernels are affected by the pollen that lands on the stigmas as well as by certain characteristics of the mother corn plant. In all higher plants, including corn, there is a double fertilization which takes place once the pollen tube breaks through to the egg cell. The pollen grain carries two sperm cells. One of these fuses with the egg nucleus to form the embryo, while the other unites with the nucleus of the central cell to form the endosperm.

Remember that most of the corn kernel is endosperm, so it is this endosperm which gives the corn its flavor and texture. Whatever the source of sperm fertilizing the endosperm, the genes of that sperm will influence the characteristics of the endosperm. If the sperm comes from field corn, the field corn genes will trigger the conversion of sucrose from the leaves into dextrin and then to starch, making a starchy kernel instead of the sweet one you'd expect. If popcorn pollen fertilizes sweet corn, the endosperm will be starchy, and the outer skin of the kernel will be tough.

To avoid any unpleasant surprises when you peel back the husks, you should realize that if two different sorts of corn are growing side by side and shedding their pollen at the same time, many of the kernels on each cob of one variety will contain genes from the other sort of corn. If you are growing just two kinds of super-sweet corn or two varieties of regular sweet corn, this cross-fertilization will make no difference. But if one variety is a type requiring isolation, you're in trouble. Regular sweet corn pollen that filters over to the extra-sweet corn patch will cause starchy kernels in the extra-sweet corn. Surprisingly enough, the reverse of this pollen transfer has the same outcome; pollen from extra-sweet corn will meddle with regular sweet corn kernels, turning them starchy. The notable exceptions to this are the E.H. extra-sweet varieties; if cross-pollinated by regular sweet corn, their kernels will retain their sweetness.

Since corn is wind-pollinated, the pollen can be carried long distances through the air. If you plant varieties 250 feet apart, the ears will probably contain some kernels that are affected by cross-fertilization and are not true to type, but most of the ear will be normal. A distance of 700 feet should ensure complete isolation in most gardens. However, much depends on wind conditions in your area, and you may also need to take your neighbors' gardens into consideration. Dr. Mangelsdorf tells the story of a professor who found one blue kernel on an ear of his corn and wanted to know where the pollen had come from. He searched and searched the neighborhood until he found the culprit corn—5 miles away!

There are a few ways to get around this problem of vagabond pollen. If you have a small garden but a long season, you can plant varieties with at least a fourteen-day difference in their time of maturity; then they won't be shedding pollen at the same time. Or, you can time your plantings to provide the fourteen-day differential. At any rate, you should always remember that popcorn and flint corn will harm any sweet corn variety and should be planted conservatively. You don't want to make enemies of your neighbors if you live in a subdivision with small lots but many corn lovers!

How Do the Ears Form?

The process by which corn produces ears is a fascinating testimony to the simple yet complex way nature works. Becoming familiar with this process will help you to better understand why various cultural practices such as block planting and careful watering are important and how they work with, rather than against, the natural process your plants are undergoing.

For starters, you should be aware that the tassels contain the male corn flowers. When your plants are still quite short (3 to 4 feet tall), peek down into the tops of the plants where you can see the tassels starting to emerge from the top leaves. How many leaves the plants have and how long they take to make tassels is significantly influenced by temperature and daylength. Short or hot days will lessen the time to tasseling, while long or cold days will increase it. (Perhaps our long northern days are another reason why our corn matures slowly here in Montana.)

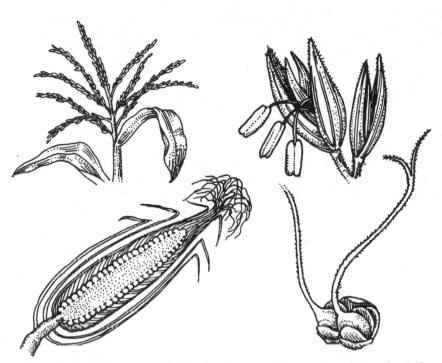

Corn Reproductive Structures: *The tassel in the upper left corner is a cluster of male flowers that are borne in tiny spikelets. The spikelets are grouped in pairs (upper right), and each spikelet contains two flowers with three anthers in each flower. Female flowers are also paired in spikelets (lower right). In many varieties, even though each spikelet has two flowers, only the upper flower will develop into the kernel. The longitudinal section in the lower left corner shows the developing cob with the silks attached to the kernels.*

Once the tassel emerges, all the leaves of the plant have been formed, and all subsequent growth occurs through lengthening of the internodes. Imagine the corn stalk as one of those telescoping fishing poles that are popular with hikers. When all the sections are pushed in, the pole is short, just like a corn stalk with the nodes close together. When you pull the rod out, it lengthens, and the joints are farther apart, just like the nodes on a corn plant after it has grown. When the internodes expand, they carry the developing leaves up into positions where they do not shade one another, and each leaf can photosynthesize freely, maximizing use of the sun's energy. During this period of rapid growth when the internodes are lengthening, your corn needs plenty of water and abundant nutrients. If your plants are looking at all yellow during their early stages of growth, feed them right away with fish emulsion and mulch them with compost. Otherwise, they will use up the limited soil nutrients during this critical growth spurt, leaving nothing behind to nourish the later stages of development.

The tassel itself is a cluster of male flowers. In grasses such as corn, the flowers are borne in tiny spikelets. Corn spikelets are paired, and one spikelet in each pair has a tiny stalk while the other is stalkless. Each spikelet in turn has two flowers, and each flower has three anthers. Thus, there are six anthers per spikelet. The anthers form the pollen grains, just as in other flowers, and as the wind rustles the tassels, these grains sprinkle downward toward the silks or are carried aloft to pollinate the female flowers of other plants.

Corn enhances its own chances of successful pollination by producing incredible amounts of pollen. Each anther is estimated to carry 2,500 pollen grains, and since there are roughly 7,200 anthers on each plant, about 18 million grains are produced by a single corn plant! If you think those figures are staggering, one scientist estimated that 42,500 pollen grains were produced for every square inch of a Nebraska cornfield. Pollen grains are very small, $\frac{1}{250}$ of an inch in diameter, which makes them easily transported by the wind. If the pollen gets wet, either through careless watering or from an untimely rainfall, the water will carry it right down to the ground, and it won't get a chance to pollinate the silks.

Corn plants actually flood the air with this abundance of pollen over a week-long period. Bees are often attracted to the corn patch by the blizzard of pollen that is present at this time. When we see that the bees have taken over our corn field, buzzing from stalk to stalk to load up on pollen, we know that the pollen release is in full swing. Although wind is the main pollen-carrying agent, the bees' work may actually be helpful to some extent in pollination. We have noticed that as they gather pollen they sometimes shake the whole tassel just a little, releasing more pollen in the process.

Many people with a slightly misplaced sense of corn botany assume that the silks alone are the female flowers. In reality, the silks are only one part, and the other parts of the flowers are hidden on the immature cob inside the husks. The base of the cob is actually a compressed stem. Despite its shortness, it has just as many nodes as the stalk that holds up the tassels, but the internodes haven't grown. Instead, it stays like an unexpanded hiker's fishing pole and never elongates. Because the leaves on this rather squat stalk are borne on such short internodes, they overlap one another, forming the husks which wrap around the corn ear.

The female flowers, like the male ones, are carried on paired spikelets, which cover the tiny, young cob. While each female spikelet has two flowers, only one of these (the upper one) develops completely in most kinds of corn. After the flowers are pollinated and the ear has developed, the kernels are arranged in pairs because the spikelets were paired; this is why an ear of corn has an even number of rows of kernels. The variety Country Gentleman, however, is an exception to this phenomenon of even-numbered rows, for the lower flower also develops and eventually becomes a kernel. This over-

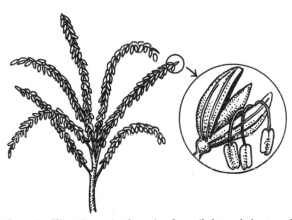

Corn Pollination: *Anthers in the spikelets of the tassel produce pollen grains. When mature, the spikelets droop downward and release their pollen as the wind passes through their flowers. The pollen grains fall down onto the silks where they will form a pollen tube and grow into the ovary. The wind also carries a lot of the pollen off to other plants.*

abundance of kernels creates a rather crowded condition, so that there is no orderly arrangement of kernels on the ear. Instead, they look as if they have been stuck on at random.

Since the husks enclose the flowers, the styles have to be long enough to extend to the outside where they can be pollinated. The familiar corn silks are nothing more than these styles. Each silk is covered with fine hairs and looks feathery when examined under a microscope. These hairs increase the surface area of the silks and better the odds that pollen grains will be captured as they drift through the air. Each immature kernel (which is a potential seed) is attached to its own silk, which must be pollinated in order for the kernel to develop. Since there may be 1,000 kernels on an ear, there are up to 1,000 silks as well (a fact that anyone who's had to clean an ear of corn will hardly find surprising). If a large number of these silks go unpollinated, the ears that result will not be well filled. Poor rates of pollination usually occur under wet, rainy conditions, but hot, dry winds or temperatures above 95°F can also wreak havoc with the corn crop, for pollen dies quickly if it dries out.

When a pollen grain lands on a silk, it produces a very long pollen tube which grows all the way down through the silk to the female flower. As we mentioned earlier, when the tube reaches the flower, one of the sperm nuclei unites with the egg to form the embryo while the other combines with the central nucleus to form the endosperm (the food storage part of the kernel). The kernels require a lot of energy from the plant as they progress through their stages of development. Sucrose is manufactured in the leaves by photosynthesis and is then transported through the phloem to the developing kernels. There it is either retained as sugar (in extra-sweet varieties), partially retained (in standard sweet corn), or converted to starch (in field corn and popcorn).

Getting Started from Seed

You can save unused corn seed for up to two years, but be forewarned that some varieties do not store well, so it is safest to buy fresh seed each year. If you do have some leftover seed, store it in a very dry, cool place, and do a germination test before counting on it to produce a crop.

You must plant corn seed in fairly warm soil or it will just sit there and rot instead of sprouting. Corn will take as long as twelve days to germinate in 59°F soil but only three days in 95°F soil. You can make sure the soil's nice and toasty by using a black plastic mulch to warm it up. Cover the soil a few days before planting time. When you're ready to plant, cut holes for your hills or rows, and sow the seeds as usual. This method is a good one to use if you are babying along a special variety of corn. Aside from providing warm soil, you can speed up germination and increase the number of seedlings that will ultimately emerge in your garden by placing the seeds between moist paper towels the night before planting.

To ensure proper growth, plant your corn seed 3 to 4 inches deep. You'll realize the significance planting depth has on your future crop by taking a look at how the plants develop. As with other seeds, the first part of the corn to break out of the seed is the root, followed by the young stem or stalk. The growing stalk is surrounded by a protective sheath which accompanies it through the ground and keeps it from getting damaged. The area between the old seed and the bottom joint of the corn stalk, called the mesocotyl, is especially important to the plant. It is here that all the elongation of the stem occurs, which brings the shoot to the surface of the soil. The mesocotyl stops growing when exposed to light, so once the shoot reaches the soil surface, the mesocotyl stays where it is, and the shoot keeps pushing upwards.

The permanent root system grows from the buried mesocotyl, so if you were to plant your corn only ½ inch deep, the root system could only develop from a small part of the stem. The result would be a poor root system which wouldn't be able to meet the nutrient and water demands of the plant, nor could it anchor the plant firmly in the soil. Planting too shallow is bad but too deep is no better, for the mesocotyl of the corn varieties sold to home gardeners can't grow any longer than 4 inches; if you planted deeper than that, your corn would never be able to reach the soil surface. It's interesting to note, though, that some varieties of corn grown by the Indians in the southwestern United States have a mesocotyl that can grow 12 to 14 inches and so take advantage of the higher moisture levels that lie deep in the desert

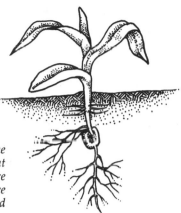

Young Corn Plant: *The mesocotyl, the area between the old seed and the bottom joint of the stalk, plays an important role in the growth of a corn seedling. This is the area where elongation takes place, which brings the shoot to the surface of the soil. The root system also grows from the buried mesocotyl.*

soil. These varieties are highly drought resistant during the germination period (since they are planted so deeply), and later throughout the growing season, their well-developed, permanent root system can gather more moisture than a shallower, less extensive one.

Starting Corn Indoors

The fact that it's possible to start corn early indoors if you give it special care seems to be little known among gardeners. If you'd like to try your hand at getting the corn crop off to an early start, follow Dorothy's example. One year she wanted to try an extra-sweet variety, and she knew her only chance was to give it a head start. Dorothy soaked the seeds between paper towels until they began to germinate, and when the root appeared, she planted them about 2 inches deep in the deepest peat pots she could find, two seeds to a pot. When the shoots began peeking out, she placed the pots in full sun in her attached greenhouse. A south-facing window with no obstructions between it and the sun would also provide enough light, but if you can't give the seedlings full sun, forget about starting them early for you will be giving them no advantage. Don't start your corn indoors more than two weeks before it can be planted outdoors, and when you do set it out, plant the peat pot and all so the roots are not disturbed during transplanting.

Getting a Head Start in the Garden

Most gardening books tell you to plant your corn two to three weeks after the last expected frost. Northern gardeners can take a chance by planting their corn seed outdoors two weeks before the last expected frost or even earlier. For gardeners in these marginal regions, taking such chances is often the only way to get a crop. When you plant early, be prepared to leap into action if the weather turns cold. Cover the patch with plastic or cover the individual plants with clear plastic cups with the bottoms cut out. These impromptu cloches will provide a warm, protected, mini-environment around the growing plants. If frost threatens, you can cover the hole in the bottom of the cup (which is the top of the protector) with foil or plastic wrap. If you have a sudden late frost, however, don't despair—corn is a lot hardier than we give it credit for.

One year Dorothy planted her corn before leaving on a June vacation and made arrangements with a friend to keep an eye on it while she was away. As she drove home through the potato-growing country of Idaho at the end of June, she wondered why the tops of all the potato plants were brown. The reason became clear soon enough—a frost had hit the entire mountainous region of the Northwest on June 26! Dorothy's friend said the corn had completely disappeared, but when Dorothy went to check on it the next day new shoots were already sprouting through the soil. Luckily she had planted her corn deeply enough that the growing tip was not killed by the frost. If she had been home on the frosty night, she probably would have dug up the corn patch in disgust and planted a late crop of beans or carrots in its place. In retrospect, she's glad she didn't have the chance, for she harvested some tasty corn that year despite the setback.

Arranging Corn Rows Strategically

As we mentioned earlier in this chapter, corn is wind-pollinated. For this reason, you must design your corn patch to take advantage of the wind and encourage the best possible transfer of pollen. Too many gardeners learn this the hard way, as did one enthusiastic but inexperienced gardener who shared this tale. He went out to the garden and with the help of his little daughter, planted a nice, long, single row of corn. Visions of a sweet, juicy harvest blossomed in their imaginations—so they were naturally very disappointed when in reality all they got were a few skimpy, poorly filled-out ears.

As this well-intentioned gardener learned, if you plant corn in a long row, the wind just picks up the pollen and carries it away from the corn, leaving it, for the most part, unpollinated. But if you plant several rows close together, the wind will carry the pollen from one plant to another as it blows, ensuring good pollination. If you are only planting a small amount of corn, arrange it in several short rows to form a block rather than in one or two longer rows. If you plant in hills, sow six seeds per hill, arranging the seeds a couple of inches apart and then thinning to three plants per hill. Space the hills 2 feet apart in all directions. If all you have room for is three or four hills, place them in relation to one another so they form the corners of a triangle or square.

How far apart you space your corn plants in a row depends in part on the variety; taller, more vigorous kinds need more space than smaller, early types. Veteran gardener and author Richard V. Clemence studied corn spacing and found that if his Xtra Sweet Hybrid corn plants were 2 feet apart in all directions, he got the highest yield, harvesting up to four ears per stalk. When he planted in 1 by 2-foot spacing, only two ears developed per stalk, while in 1 by 1-foot blocks, only one large and one much smaller ear were produced per plant. Diane spaces her small, early varieties 8 to 12 inches apart in rows 36 inches apart. With this generous spacing most of her corn produces one large ear, with a smaller one maturing four to eight days later.

Interplanting with Corn

Corn takes up so much valuable growing room that many gardeners take a cue from a traditional Indian practice and grow pumpkins, melons, or beans along with their corn. If you live in a warm area with a long season, you can experiment with this technique. But if corn is in any way a marginal or temperamental crop in your area, don't ask it to share its resources with any other plants, or you could end up with little or no corn to harvest. Another space-saving idea is to plant cucumber, melon, or pumpkin hills along the outer edges of the corn patch. The long, wandering vines will meander in and out among the corn stalks, helping to prevent weeds from growing, and precious space elsewhere in the garden can be planted to other crops instead of being covered with the sprawling cucurbit vines. Some gardeners also swear that this viney border around the corn patch keeps marauding raccoons from making nocturnal raids. The vines, so the theory goes, hamper the raccoons' movement, making them edgy and apprehensive about climbing through to get at the corn.

Another effective way to get the most mileage out of your garden space is to plant pole beans along with your corn. There are a few things you should keep in mind, though. First of all, select a tall corn variety such as Country Gentleman or Iochief, which will grow 6 to 7 feet tall and provide sturdy supports for your bean vines. Second, plant the corn a couple of weeks before the beans to give it a head start. Otherwise the rapidly growing beans will overwhelm the corn, and you'll get no corn crop. Sow just one bean seed about an inch from each corn seedling, and plant the beans only along the outside of the south side of the corn patch. Beans planted in the middle or on the north side will be shaded by the cornstalks—they won't get enough sunlight to produce many beans and will just get in the way of your corn.

Corn's Relationship to the Soil

Before the permanent root system forms from the mesocotyl, the tiny corn plant must depend on small secondary roots that branch off the primary root (the root that appeared initially upon germination). Most of these secondary roots are in the top part of the soil, and it is not until the plant starts to shed pollen that the roots penetrate deeply into the ground. At that time they can extend 3 or more feet down and 3 to 4 feet laterally; this is why corn does best when widely spaced, for then the roots of the plants don't compete with one another. But before this extensive root growth can occur, you must be sure the young plants have plenty of water and good, rich soil to fuel this rapid burst of underground activity. Also keep in mind while you are cultivating around your young plants that the lateral roots growing near the surface will be easily damaged if you probe too deeply.

Corn requires abundant nitrogen (remember, it is a grass) and lots of phosphorus. The lower leaves are the first to show nutritional deficiencies, so keep an eye on them. If they show any sign of yellowing, the plants need nitrogen fast, so give them a good dose of fish emulsion, compost tea or manure tea (or any other source of readily available nitrogen), and work rich compost or well-rotted manure into the soil. Corn is also sensitive to soil deficiencies of trace elements such as boron, iron, magnesium, and zinc. Because these deficiencies show up as spots or discolorations of its leaves under relatively low stress, scientists often use corn when they study the effects of nutrient deficiencies on plants. Since you're mainly interested in harvesting a good crop and not in studying deficiencies, work barnyard manure into the corn patch; this all-around fertilizer will provide trace elements as well as increase the nitrogen and phosphorus content of the soil.

Corn provides some dramatic examples of the effects of manure on soil fertility. In a long-term study, scientists monitored nitrogen levels in a Nebraska corn field from 1912 to 1972. For the first ten years, no fertilizer was used, and corn yield declined rapidly from year to year. From 1941 to 1972, the field was manured every year. By 1972, the nitrogen level in the soil was up to 90 percent of its initial 1912 level, even though there had been a crop of field corn growing there every year. Of equal note was the fact that the corn yield was up again as well.

Don't be tempted to use this study as a rationale for growing your corn in the exact same location in the garden year after year. Corn should be rotated because it takes so much from the soil. Also, although the results of this study offer excellent testimony to the virtues of manure, bear in mind that whatever benefits manure in general may bring, some manures in particular require careful use. In another study reported by scientists at the University of Delaware in 1975, large amounts of poultry manure (56, 90, 168, and 224 metric tons per hectare) were applied to various plots of soil, and the corn yield decreased because there was too much salt in the soil.

All fresh manures work best when they are dug into the corn patch during the fall prior to spring planting. Winter rains and melting snow will leach some of the salts deep down into the subsoil, out of the root zone. Soil organisms will get a head start breaking down the manure, thereby releasing some of the nutrients so they'll be available to your plants come springtime.

A Few Words on Weeds and Watering

Corn grows relatively slowly for the first four to six weeks, and during this period it is very important to keep it free from weed competition. As with other crops, you can mulch corn plants once the soil warms up to discourage weeds and retain soil moisture.

Corn requires a total of 12 to 24 inches of water during the season to produce well, so you must be generous with your watering. When you see the corn leaves rolled up lengthwise, that's the signal that the plants are very water-stressed. Actually, you should be watering your patch regularly so that it never gets to that point. Water stress can have dire consequences, for if it occurs while the plants are shedding pollen, the pollen may not be viable and may not be able to pollinate the female flowers.

On the other hand, you don't want to water too heavily during this period of pollen release, or you will wash the pollen down to the ground, keeping it from reaching the silks. If you absolutely must water during pollen shedding time, do it from below by means of flood irrigation. Or, turn a soaker hose upside down so the spurts of water are aimed at the soil where there's no chance that the tassels will get wet.

If you're willing to experiment, try watering your pollinating corn at night. Diane's husband, Dave, uses corn pollen for some of his plant research. He has found that he can't collect any pollen in the morning until the corn has been in direct sunlight for at least an hour. The anther must come out of the spikelet and dry out in order for the pore to form and release the pollen. Since corn pollen is not shed during the night, watering at that time ought to be safe. If you want to completely avoid watering during pollination, water heavily just as the tassels begin to develop and then lay down a thick layer of mulch around the plants. Unless it's a hot, dry summer, you should be able to wait until after the pollen is shed before watering again, with no harm done to your crop.

What to Do about Suckers

Many corn varieties produce small side shoots called suckers. Since suckers generally do not produce ears, many gardeners believe that by cutting off the suckers they will reduce an energy drain on the plant. But a number of scientific studies have shown that where corn is concerned, it is better to leave the suckers on the plant rather than cut them off. Most of these investigations indicated that there was no difference in yield between plants with or without suckers. But a few did show that cutting off the suckers was actually detrimental to the corn plant. It is possible to damage the main stalk or disturb the roots while removing suckers—so why waste your time taking them off and risk damaging your plants too?

The suckers can actually bring along a few unexpected bonuses. Now and then, Diane has actually harvested some very small ears from particularly vigorous suckers. And if you're gardening in a cool area, the extra photosynthesis of the suckers can be important in providing nourishment for the plants.

Harvesting at the Peak of Perfection

You can't just eyeball your corn to see if it's at its ripest, sweetest, most succulent best; you must use your hands and feel the ears along their length to check if the kernels are plump and full. If you think the ear is ready, carefully slit a part of the husk with a sharp knife and peek at the kernels to make sure they are filled out. Press your fingernail into a kernel; a ripe one will be bursting with a milky liquid that will spurt out when you puncture it. A final assurance of ripeness is the color of the silks. Brown to blackish silks signal that the corn has matured to a ripe stage.

Depending on the weather, it can take anywhere from 15 to 30 days for the ears to mature from the time the silks first appear. Once you have developed a feel for ripe ears, you can confidently harvest them without painstakingly checking each one individually. Some varieties ripen all their ears at once, while others provide a gradual harvest with the top ears ripening first and the lower ears later. If it is hot while you are harvesting, with temperatures in the 80s and 90s, corn can become overmature almost overnight, so check the ears carefully every day.

When you pick an ear, hold the main stalk with one hand and grab the ear with the other, then twist it gently but firmly downward. The ear should separate without damaging the rest of the plant. There's a lot of sense to the old maxim that you should have the water boiling on the stove when you go out to pick your corn. A normal ear of sweet corn will start converting its sucrose to starch as soon as you separate it from the plant. (The notable exceptions to this are the extra-sweet varieties which will hold their sweetness for two to fourteen days after harvest.) Every minute that passes between picking and cooking means starchier corn. With standard sweet corn varieties, don't allow more than an hour to go by between picking and eating, or you will surely taste the difference. Hold off husking the ears until just before tossing them into the pot of boiling water, for husking speeds up the conversion of sugar to starch in all varieties, even the sweetest ones. When you are harvesting corn for freezing or canning, pick it in the morning or evening for this is when it is at its sweetest. Then rush like mad to get it processed as soon as you can.

Storing Corn and Saving Seed

The best advice on storing fresh corn is—*don't!* No matter how you store it, corn will lose its quality very quickly. But if you absolutely cannot eat it right away and have to store it for awhile, keep it in a spot as close to 32°F and 90 to 95 percent humidity as possible, and do not remove the husk. Extra-sweet varieties are the kind to grow if you know you will have to store your corn in the fresh state since they deteriorate more slowly than ordinary sweet corn. Do your best to plan so that you will be able to freeze, can, or dry your harvest when it is at its peak of sweetness.

If you're growing popcorn, there are a few steps you need to follow before you can store the crop. Leave popcorn ears on the plant until the husks are completely brown and dry (there should be no trace of green left). Then twist the ears off the stalks and peel away the dry, papery husks. Pile the ears in a basket, and set it in a dry, dark place. During this curing period, the outer shell of the kernel is becoming dry and hard to seal out the air, while the inner portion retains the moisture that causes the whole kernel to explode when heated.

The curing process usually takes three to four weeks. At this point you should test-pop a few kernels to see how they do. If they don't pop well, they may not be dry enough, or conversely, they may be too dry. There's an easy way to gauge whether they're too dry. Put a few sample kernels in a jar, sprinkle some water on them, and let them sit for half an hour. If the kernels are too dry, this water treatment should revive them and they should pop just fine. If they still don't pop, they haven't dried enough, so let the ears air dry for another week or so. Test a few kernels again to see how they pop. When the kernels reach the stage where they pop satisfactorily, strip them from the ears and store them in a lidded container. If, at a later date they don't pop with vigor, just give them the water treatment and that should restore any moisture they might have lost in storage.

If you want to save your own corn seed, grow varieties that are advertised as open-pollinated. Let the ears stay on the plants until the stalks have turned papery and brown. Then pick each ear, peel back the husks, and let it cure until the kernels are very dry. At this point you can loosen the seeds from the cob, place them in an airtight container, and store the stock of next year's garden in a cool, dry place.

Problems with Corn

While corn has relatively few diseases, it is susceptible to a great variety of insect pests. These are covered extensively in *Organic Plant Protection* (see the Bibliography). One special problem which the urban corn grower faces, beyond dealing with the normal pests and diseases, is corn's great sensitivity to smog. Several strains of Golden Cross Bantam (T, AM, NK, and FM cross strains) are especially susceptible to smog damage. This damage shows up first on the leaves as discolored areas that appear water-soaked. The leaves then die, giving the corn a scorched look. If you live in a smoggy area, take note that you should consult with your county agent and gardening neighbors about varieties which fare well in your region. Bonanza and Merit are two smog-tolerant varieties.

Corn Frontiers

As you may suspect, breeders are concentrating their attention on producing extra-sweet varieties which are easily grown, and on varieties that produce corn of reliable quality in a short growing season. They are also trying to produce varieties resistant to various diseases. Because commercial growers rely on pesticides, pest-resistant varieties are low on the priority list of corn breeders.

Chapter 12

Tomatoes:
Love Apples for All

Vital Statistics

Family:
Solanaceae
Species:
Lycopersicon esculentum
Soil:
Sandy loam; good drainage
important
pH:
6.0–6.8 (absolute 5.5–7.5)
Soil Temperature for Germination:
60°–75°F

Air Temperature for Best Growth:
70°–75°F, daytime; 50°–55°F,
nighttime; lower than 32°F
kills the plant
Seed Viability:
5–7 years
Seed Germination:
5–14 days
Seed Planting Depth:
½"

Every summer gardeners all across the country wait eagerly for the first ripe tomato of the season. Somehow the homegrown, vine-ripened tomato has come to symbolize all the satisfactions of home gardening, perhaps because its quality so far surpasses anything you could hope to buy in a store. If you take the time to become familiar with some tomato facts of life, you can hasten the day you pick that first tomato, increase the harvest from your vines, and get the best flavor from the late fruits that you may be forced to ripen indoors at the end of the season.

It's hard to believe that something as nutritious and tasty as a tomato could belong to the dangerous and deadly Nightshade family (the informal name for Solanaceae). A wild-growing member of this family is actually known as deadly nightshade, an apt name indeed, for its unripe berries are poisonous enough to kill people and livestock. While many solanaceous plants are very dangerous, there's no cause for alarm since most family members that are important to us—eggplants, peppers, and potatoes—are benign.

You should be aware though, that all members of the Nightshade family do contain powerful poisons, called alkaloids, to varying degrees. All parts of the tomato plant, except the tomatoes themselves, are toxic if eaten. Even those succulent fruits carry within them a small amount of the tomato's own alkaloid, called tomatine, as they develop. To set your mind at ease, let us add that all traces of this alkaloid disappear by the time the fruits ripen. If you look closely at tomato leaves, you can see that they are covered by many tiny hairs. The chemicals in these hairs may inflict an annoying skin rash on the sensitive gardener who brushes up against them.

It took a long time for the juicy, red tomato to shed its poisonous reputation in Europe and the United States—in fact, tomatoes weren't cultivated as a food crop in these areas until well into the nineteenth century. Prior to that, they were grown strictly as ornamental plants, and no one dared to eat them. This long period of avoidance is certainly unfortunate, for people were forsaking a tasty source of vitamins A and C.

The ancestral wild tomato still thrives in the Andes Mountains of South America. With its scraggly, sparse vines and clusters of hard, marble-sized fruits it is a far cry from its domesticated cousin. Some modern tomato varieties, such as Sweet 100 and Early Cascade Hybrid, recall their humble ancestor with their long trusses and viney growth. But the satisfying juiciness and sweetness of their fruits puts them in a completely different class from the original tomato. In its native habitat the tomato grows year-round, but in temperate regions this cold-sensitive plant behaves as an annual, growing and producing an abundant harvest as long as the weather permits. Because the tomato is actually a perennial, it could live for several years in regions free from heavy frosts.

Tomato Varieties

As befits the most popular of home garden vegetables, there is a practically limitless array of varieties to suit almost any gardener's fancy. As you flip through seed catalogs, it's easy to be overwhelmed and simply opt for the variety with the prettiest photograph. To help you narrow down the field and make an informed choice, here are a few criteria to keep in mind: First, how do you intend to use your harvest? Some tomatoes hold up well under canning, others are best when used fresh, and still others, the paste types, have a low juice/high meat ratio that makes them ideal for sauces and ketchup.

Second, how long is your growing season? There's a wide range of times to maturity. If you're a northern gardener your selection is pretty well limited to early varieties (those that ripen within 55 to 70 days). Gardeners with a longer season can indulge in mid-season (70 to 85 days) and late (85 to 100 days) varieties to disperse the harvest.

Tantalizing Tomatoes: *Many winter nights can be spent browsing through seed catalogs trying to decide what kinds of tomatoes to grow. A few of the seemingly endless types are Beefsteak (bottom right), cherry tomatoes (bottom center), paste types (bottom left), and round types such as Marglobe (upper middle).*

Entering the realm of aesthetics, what size and shape appeal to you? Sizes range all the way from the diminutive cherry tomatoes to the jumbo beefsteaks. In terms of shape, they come in gradations from perfectly round to flattened to pear shaped . . . and someone's even bred a square tomato! The colors vary as well; you can choose among the characteristic red, pink, yellowish-orange, and white.

If you're gardening under special limitations, like a cool, short season or a cramped growing area, never fear—there's a tomato for you. The Sub-Arctic series give an abundant yield of extra-early tomatoes in 53 to 61 days even in cool climates. There are many varieties suited for container growing, and some can even be trained to cascade out of hanging baskets. And last but not least, there are varieties that exhibit disease resistance. The letters V (verticillium wilt), F (fusarium wilt), and N (nematodes) after the variety name indicate that they carry a resistance factor.

Getting Started from Seed

When you wipe up a cutting board after slicing a ripe tomato, you probably have noticed that the escaped seeds were encased within a slippery, jellylike envelope. This sheath has chemicals which keep the seed dormant so that it won't germinate in the damp, warm environment inside the tomato. Commercial seed growers get rid of the sheath by shredding the tomatoes, screening out the big pieces of flesh, and letting the seed-studded liquid ferment. The seeds sink to the bottom of this brew, ready for drying and packaging. You can accomplish the same thing with your homegrown seeds by soaking them overnight in a glass of water to which you have added a squirt of dishwashing detergent (the detergent helps separate the sheath from the seeds). In the morning, rinse and drain the seeds, spread them in a single layer on a blotter of paper towels, and when they are thoroughly dry, store them as described in chapter 1 until you're ready to plant.

When spring planting time arrives, you'll be wise to remember that tomatoes hail from a southern mountainous region. They need warm soil to germinate well, but they also prefer cooler nighttime temperatures. A soil temperature of 70° to 75°F during the day and 60° to 65°F at night is ideal. Give the seeds an overnight soaking before planting to leach out whatever inhibitors may be left. This step also increases uptake of water by the dried and dormant plant embryo that sleeps within the seed, setting the stage for germination. When you plant, cover the seeds well with ¼ inch of soil, for tomatoes germinate better in the dark than in the light.

Nurturing Seedlings from House to Garden

Your final product—the mature, fruit-bearing plant—can be dramatically affected by how you treat its tiny beginnings. Despite the long years of selective breeding, tomatoes will respond best to a day/night schedule like that of the mountains—warm days and cool nights. It's best to give your tomatoes what they prefer right from the start by providing them with cool (50° to 55°F) nights from the time their first slim cotyledons have opened up. During the day, the temperatures should range between 70° and 75°F. By doing this you will encourage your plants to form flowers earlier and to produce more blossoms. You must also be careful to give them the proper daylength of eight to twelve hours. If you keep them in a room that is illuminated late into the evening you'll end up with late-maturing fruits and a reduced harvest overall unless you induce darkness by covering the plants at nightfall.

After the cotyledons have expanded fully, carefully transplant each delicate seedling to a roomier pot, at least 4 inches in diameter, to provide plenty of space for vigorous root growth. Set the seedlings deeply enough so that the surface of the soil comes right up to the lowest set of leaves. Roots will grow out of the sides of the buried stem, strengthening the root system. This new root growth is spurred on by the hormone, auxin, which is present in the stem. Light destroys auxin, but when you bury the stem the auxin is free to go to work stimulating root growth. (Rootone and other products used for rooting cuttings are so effective because they contain auxinlike chemicals.)

After this initial transplanting, water your seedlings well. A cold frame (see chapter 4) provides the best environment for young tomato plants until it's time to transplant them into the garden. There, the natural shift from cool spring nights to sun-warmed days will match the plant's needs. If you don't have a cold frame, you can grow the young plants in a south-facing window. This set-up will be vastly improved if there's another window in the room

Planting Tomato Plants: *Young tomato plants being transplanted into the garden do best when planted on their sides. Set the seedling in the hole on an angle, and bury it up to the bottom leaves. This allows more roots to develop along the buried stem.*

that can be left open at night to provide cool, but not freezing temperatures. Remember to take care not to expose your plants to light after sundown.

When the big day comes and the risk of frost is over, move your thriving, hardened-off young plants out into the garden. Just as you did when transplanting to a bigger pot, set the plants deeply, with the lowest leaves at ground level. If your seedlings grew leggy despite your careful tending, you can remove some of the lower leaves and bury even more of the stem. In gardens where the soil is shallow, you can bury the stem at an angle in the soil.

From now through the end of the season be sure to keep your tomatoes well watered, but don't overdo it. While their fibrous roots can probe down as deep as 12 feet, most of the roots remain in the top 12 to 18 inches of soil and seem to be more efficient at water uptake than cabbage roots. When your plants have reached the stage where they're producing fruits, avoid watering from above because water droplets on the developing tomatoes can cause them to crack.

Limited and Infinite Growth

While you were reading your seed catalogs in eager anticipation of the gardening season, you probably came across some photographs of proud gardeners standing next to giant tomato vines towering 8 to 10 feet in the air. And most likely, the glowing advertisements for compact, bushy tomatoes that grow and yield cheerfully in tubs on the patio caught your eye as well. How can essentially the same plant grow in such dramatically different ways? The original growth habit of tomatoes is the sprawling sort called indeterminate. Throughout the season, indeterminate plants steadily increase in size by recognizable increments. As the tip of each branch grows, it produces a series of three leaves and then a cluster of flowers (called a truss) followed by another three leaves and another truss and so on. The tip itself is never transformed into a flower cluster, with the result that the vine just keeps on growing.

In 1914, a peculiar new sort of tomato plant appeared spontaneously, and fortunately for us it was noticed. This plant grew in a unique way, quite different from indeterminate plants. The stem tips, instead of producing a unit of three leaves and a truss, gradually produced more and more flowers and fewer leaves. After reaching a certain distance from the center of the plant each branch stopped growing and formed a final flower cluster. In the years since this first plant was spotted, this trait has been bred into many different tomato varieties which now are called determinate.

Because their growth is limited and predetermined, these plants never get very large. All their flowers bloom within a limited time so that the fruits ripen over a short period, sometimes within as little as ten days. This trait makes them ideal for gardeners who want to process their harvest. You are

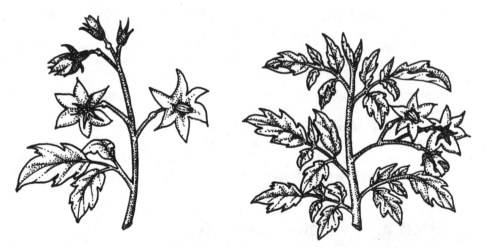

Determinate and Indeterminate Plants: *The terminal buds eventually set fruit in determinate-type plants (left). Once the terminal buds form flowers, the main stem stops growing. At left are shown the last leaf and terminal truss of a determinate plant. In indeterminate plants (right), terminal buds do not set fruit, only leaves and stems. Each branch tip will produce a series of three leaves, then a cluster of flowers, another three leaves, followed by a second set of flowers, and so forth. The vines continue to grow until the tip is killed.*

assured of a large enough batch of ripe tomatoes to work with at one time instead of having to wait for the more dispersed harvest of indeterminate plants. Determinate plants are perfect for people limited to small gardens or tub growing, and they work well for northern gardeners who must contend with short growing seasons.

Staking and Pruning Pointers

When you order your tomato seeds, be sure to check whether the varieties you are considering are determinate or indeterminate, and buy the right sort to suit your needs. If you buy indeterminate varieties, you must give some thought as to how you want to stake and prune your plants, or if you even want to bother with any of that at all. Indeterminate plants will grow and produce without you fussing over them, but there are several advantages to staking that make it an attractive and popular practice. Staked plants take up less space and produce considerably less rotted or slug-ravaged fruit than plants allowed to sprawl along the ground. With staking, each plant gives you less fruit, but since you can space your plants much more closely together you can obtain a higher total yield per square foot of garden space. It's also easier to harvest from neatly staked tomatoes than from a tangled mass of viny growth, for the ripe fruit is easy to see and not hidden away under the leaves.

To stake your tomatoes, drive a strong 5- to 7-foot wooden or metal stake into the ground about 1 foot from each plant at transplanting time. Have some soft twine, pieces of old nylon stocking, or special tomato ties on hand to tie the plant to its support. There are several ways you can prune your plants to make them more manageable. You can prune all but the main stem, tying it at intervals to the stake. This is the classic method of pruning, but it leaves the fruit exposed to the sun, thereby increasing its susceptibility to sunscald and cracking. If you allow the first sucker (one of a number of shoots that appear in leaf axils along the plant) as well as the main stem to grow, then you will end up with two stems to tie to the stake. With this double-stem technique there will be more fruit per plant and more leaves to shield the fruit from the sun. You can even keep three main stems if you like, but then the process of tying and pruning becomes more time consuming, even though the yield will increase. Once you have decided upon which course of pruning you will follow, be diligent in removing all excess suckers, for every sucker will develop into a full-fledged stem when given the chance. (Gardeners in cooler climates should take note that pruning may actually decrease the harvest by reducing the number of photosynthetic leaves. The best course of action is to just keep tying up the new stems.)

Another effective, less labor-intensive way to support tomato vines is to use tomato cages. These cages are available in a variety of designs and materials. Most consist of circles or squares of heavy wire held together by metal

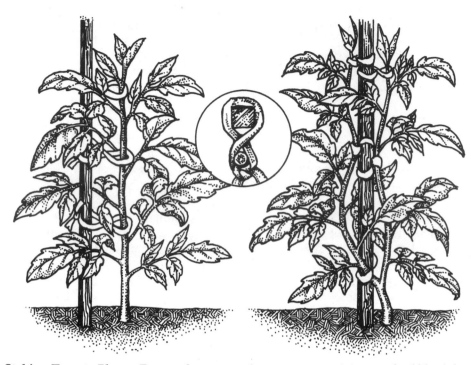

Staking Tomato Plants: *Tomato plants, pruned to one or two main stems, should be tied to stakes for support. Drive a 5- to 7-foot stake into the ground about 1 foot away from each plant. Tie the plants to the stakes with soft twine or pieces of nylon stocking in a figure-8 loop.*

spikes which anchor the cage securely. You can also make your own tomato cages by forming lengths of turkey fencing into cylinders. Simply set one cage over each plant, and as the branches grow, rest them on the horizontal wires. There's no need to prune your plants when you use cages. Since there's ample foliage cover, you'll seldom have problems with sunscald or cracking. Your garden will have a neat and tidy look since the cages contain the plants' growth, and your harvest will be in good shape since the fruits have been held off the ground.

If you grow the smaller, self-contained determinate varieties, you must not prune the vines, for pinching off any of the blossoms will cut into your harvest and you may end up with almost no fruit. Instead, let your determinate plants grow naturally, mulching them generously with clean straw or black plastic to protect the lower fruits from rotting when they touch the ground. If you like, you can tie the branches to a short stake to keep the fruit off the ground. Just remember which of the tomato plants in your garden are determinate varieties so that you won't be tempted to prune them.

From Flower to Fruit

When your tomato plants begin to produce lots of pale yellow flowers, pick one so you can examine how it is put together. At the base of the flower you'll see the green sepals and the yellow petals. Look in the center of the flower for the cluster of yellow stamens that are all fused together. Take your fingernail and pull the stamens apart to expose the small, round, green ovary that lies deep within the flower. This rather insignificant-looking green globe will one day develop into the big red fruit

Attached to the top of the ovary is the style, with its sticky stigma on top. This modern tomato flower differs quite a bit from the original tomato flower, which had a much longer style and a stigma that stuck way out beyond the stamens. Pollen from the anthers of this early flower couldn't reach the extended stigma, so the flower had to be cross-pollinated before fruit would form. But the cultivated tomatoes that we grow nowadays have been bred to self pollinate with a short style that barely extends beyond the stamens. Since the flowers naturally hang downward, plenty of pollen from the anthers drifts to the mouth of each flower and pollinates the stigma when they are only slightly jostled.

Commercial greenhouse growers ensure bountiful pollination by using machines to shake their plants. You can do the trick out in the garden by gently tapping each blossom or by shaking the plant's supporting stake early in the season. (If you're raising an off-season crop in the greenhouse or indoors on a sunny windowsill, the same technique will ensure good pollination in the absence of wind and insects.) Later in the season foraging honey bees will jiggle the flowers by landing on them and loosen pollen grains in the process. The bees, of course, can also cross-pollinate the flowers by bringing pollen from other blossoms. Most commercial varieties now grown, however, have styles so short that they are completely buried within the stamens, making self-pollination almost a certainty and just about ruling out cross-pollination.

When you were looking at the flower you probably got small, sticky clumps of yellow on your fingers. These clumps consist of pollen grains. Each pollen grain which falls on the stigma is able to fertilize only one potential seed within the small, round ovary by the way of the pollen tube (see chapter 2 for more on the mechanics of pollination and fertilization). The ovary houses many young seeds, each waiting to be fertilized by a different pollen grain. After the flower is pollinated, many pollen tubes are simultaneously growing through the style towards the ovary. With tomatoes, the more pollen tubes that grow, the better, for the more seeds that are fertilized, the bigger the resulting fruit will be. Tomatoes with only a few fertilized seeds may be misshapen as well as small.

When you see your tomato plants laden with blossoms early in the season, you naturally begin to imagine a plant just covered with fruits. But all

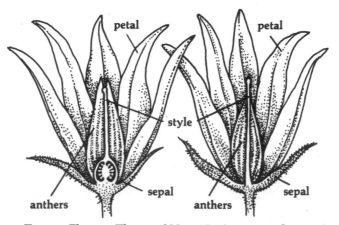

Tomato Flowers Then and Now: *Ancient tomato flowers (right) had a long style with a stigma that protruded well beyond the stamens. These plants had to be cross-pollinated, because pollen from the anthers could not reach the stigma. Modern flowers (left) have a shorter style, so self-pollination can occur freely.*

too often, to your consternation, these early blossoms fall off the plant without even starting to form the anticipated fruit. Unfortunately, there are a number of factors that can lead to blossom drop, and most of them are outside of your control. Speedy fertilization of the flowers within 50 hours of opening is absolutely essential for successful fruit set. The young embryos in the seed formed at fertilization produce auxin which helps the blossoms set. The blossom is joined to the stem by a region of special cells which weaken and separate, causing the flower to fall off if they don't receive auxin within a certain time after the flower opens. Auxin from the young, tiny seeds keeps these cells alive and healthy, allowing the new baby tomato to stay attached to the stem. Low temperatures (below 55°F) slow down the growth of pollen tubes so much that auxin isn't released in time to save the flower from falling off.

Temperatures higher than 74°F at night or over 104°F during the day also make the blossoms fall off by causing the weakened cell layer to develop too fast. Other factors such as inadequate light, an overfertilized soil, or a previous heavy fruit set can also make the blossoms drop off, even if they were successfully fertilized. While you can't do much about the weather or the heaviness of a previous fruit set, you can certainly make sure you plant in a spot that gets plenty of light and in soil that has the right balance of the major nutrients.

The Ripening Process

Forty to sixty days after the blossom opens, the ripe red tomato is ready to pick and enjoy. For the hungry, impatient gardener the wait may seem all too long, but the perfect tomato is the result of many complex processes which do take time. Before it's ready to pick, the tomato must undergo a series of very important changes that transform it from a tiny, hard, dark green ball into a soft and succulent red fruit. About half the ripening process is taken up by the actual growth and enlargement of the fruit. This is accomplished as each cell making up the small green tomato gradually swells to many times its original size. The result of this cellular expansion is the mature green tomato, a full-sized but sour, hard fruit with immature seeds.

You would think that the hardest part was now over for the tomato, because all it needs to do is turn red, soften, and become sweeter. But in reality, all of these processes are very slow and complex. The first hopeful sign of progress is a whitening of the fruit as the green chlorophyll pigment is chemically broken down. Ethylene gas is one factor responsible for chlorophyll breakdown. The tomato hastens its own ripening by producing ethylene gas itself. Commercial growers, recognizing the role of ethylene in ripening, often treat tomatoes artifically with this gas to hasten ripening in storage.

All the colors your tomatoes go through before attaining that luscious, deep red are caused by pigments called carotenoids, named for their presence

Tomato Fruit: *The juicy, mature tomato is actually the enlarged ovary of the flower. The thick, flavorful flesh of the fruit is the ovary wall, which contains cavities called locules that are filled with watery liquid and seeds.*

in the bright orange carrot. The carotenoid which gives tomatoes their lovely red color is called lycopene. If you've ever wondered why some tomatoes are orange or yellow when they are ripe, the answer is easy—they don't have any lycopene.

Once the change in color is underway, the tomato also begins to soften. A hard, green tomato contains a large concentration of pectins in its cell walls. These pectins are much like those present in apples which are used to firm up jams and jellies. As the tomato ripens, enzymes in the fruit break down the pectins making the cell walls softer and less rigid. At the same time, the tiny embryos within the seeds are growing to their final size, and the seed coats are developing and hardening.

The very last stage in ripening is the most important to us, for at this time the sugars and the vitamin C which give the tomato its distinctive sweet-sour flavor are developing. This flavor-enhancing process continues as long as the fruit remains on the vine. Tomatoes picked at the mature green stage will never taste as delicious as vine-ripened fruit, for vitamin C and sugars are actually destroyed during off-the-vine ripening. Once you know this, it's easy to understand why homegrown, vine-ripened tomatoes are so superior in nutrition and flavor to typical store-bought ones.

While harvesting your tomatoes, have you ever paused to wonder why the fruits from the same plant aren't all uniform in size? The final size of each tomato depends on several factors. Fruits formed on the lower, earlier trusses are the biggest, in part just because they are first to form and don't need to compete with other tomatoes for nutrients. Also, how well pollinated the flower was will affect fruit size, for the more seeds that actually form, the larger the tomato will be. The number of locules (the cavities of the fruit that contain the seeds) is also important in determining fruit size. A cherry tomato has only two, while a beefsteak tomato has many.

Extending the Harvest

As the expected first frost date looms near in the North, many gardeners anxiously cover their tomato vines with plastic to prevent them from freezing. This season-extending tactic is fine as long as the covering is taken off during the day. A plant saved from sudden death by an early frost can go on to produce many more ripe tomatoes during the balmy days of an Indian summer. However, once the temperatures start to drop and stay there, it's a mistake to think that you can keep your plants going by keeping them covered day and night into the consistently cold weather.

As the outside temperature drops lower and lower, the temperature under the plastic may not get above 54°F. If the temperature remains below 54°F for a week, any mature green tomatoes on the plants will have an inferior flavor when they do ripen. They will also be more subject to rot. If your tomatoes are almost ripe enough to harvest and the temperature drops below 60°F for more than five or six days, these tomatoes also will have the same problems. If you have a few warm, sunny days interspersed among the cold, cloudy ones and the temperature under the plastic rises much over 86°F, this can spell the ruin of your ripening fruit unless you rush out and open the plastic or uncover the plant. The high humidity levels (close to 100 percent) that occur with the high temperatures under plastic also encourage fungal growth.

Instead of battling the elements for one last harvest of vine-ripened fruit, many gardeners content themselves with house-ripened tomatoes. While the results of indoor ripening are often disappointing, an understanding of the ripening process can help you end up with the best house-ripened tomatoes possible. Whether you pull the vines and hang them upside down in your basement or pick the individual fruits off the vines, you should never store the tomatoes where the temperature is below 54°F. Temperatures lower than this will damage the fruits so much that they will never ripen normally and will have an inferior flavor.

With this 54°F minimum in mind, you can control the speed of ripening by holding the tomatoes at different temperatures. If you want your tomatoes to ripen slowly, keep them between 54° and 61°F; if you want ripe tomatoes as soon as possible, keep them in the ideal ripening range of 61° to 86°F. You can see from these numbers that unripe tomatoes should never be stored in the refrigerator where the temperature usually hovers around 40°F. If you want to stretch out the ripening period, put some tomatoes in a cool, dark closet and keep others at room temperature.

It is just about useless to pick tomatoes which have not reached the mature green stage, for even if they ripen instead of shriveling up, they will be watery and almost flavorless. But do pick all obviously full-sized fruit and any small ones which have begun to whiten. After you've picked all the likely candidates for ripening, sort them out according to their different stages of maturity and store all tomatoes at a similar stage together. For example, this means putting the dark green tomatoes in one box and the light green ones in another. Tomatoes require high humidity to keep their quality—85 percent to 90 percent—so it's a good idea to cover them to keep the circulating air from drying them out. Wrapping will also keep the ethylene gas produced by the fruits close to them and thus hasten ripening.

The best procedure is to wrap each tomato individually in newspaper and store them all in a single layer in a well-ventilated place such as a cardboard or wooden fruit box. If you live in a part of the country where the humidity is fairly high, you can lay them out in a single layer in a cardboard box and cover them with a couple of layers of newspaper instead of wrapping each one. Never store your immature tomatoes in plastic bags, because they are likely to rot before they ever reach a usable stage.

Problems with Tomatoes

Tomatoes are susceptible to many diseases and a few pests. But rarely do such problems become serious for the home gardener, and if they do, you can often turn to resistant tomato varieties as a remedy. The discussion here centers on problems that afflict homegrown tomatoes, in the belief that they are easier to deal with once you understand their causes.

Cracking of fruits: It is very frustrating to see your beautiful, plump, almost-ripe tomatoes develop cracks near the stem end which spoil their beauty and may allow rotting fungi to get inside. If this happens in your garden you're not alone, for most gardeners have had this problem at one time or another. The cracking is caused when water droplets hit a ripe tomato that contains a large amount of sugar. The high sugar content in the cells causes water to be absorbed, which in turn causes swelling and rupturing of some of the cells. All this activity at the cellular level will be visible to you as ugly splits on the smooth surface of the fruit. One way you can avoid such cracking is to avoid watering from above vines that are laden with ripening fruit. It's much safer to use a drip irrigation system or soaker hoses.

Unfortunately, there's not a lot you can do to keep the rain off your tomatoes at this critical time. If you live in an area where rains frequently occur right when most of the tomatoes are ripening, your best bet is to grow varieties that are resistant to cracking, such as Campbell's 17, Marion, Heinz 1350, and Sunripe. Many of the paste-type tomatoes also exhibit a resistance to cracking.

Blossom end rot: A tomato that suffers from blossom end rot certainly seems as if it has been attacked by some awful virus or fungus. In the early stages of this malady, the blossom end (bottom) of the fruit looks water-soaked. The affected area enlarges, sometimes covering half the fruit, before it turns black and leathery. Often the discolored spot is sunken as well, and may reach far into the interior of the fruit.

Despite the unappealing appearance, this common tomato disorder is not caused by any sort of disease organism at all. It basically results from water stress to the plant and is most likely to strike the early fruits of vigorous vines that are suddenly exposed to very hot, dry weather or to water deficiency. Under such stressful conditions, the plants' leaves, in dire need of water, draw it from the far ends of some of the fruits. The fruit cells, deprived of water, dry, shrivel up, and form the blackened area. Many times, a lack of sufficient calcium in the soil is also involved.

There are some simple steps you can take to make sure your tomatoes don't fall victim to blossom end rot. Make sure there is enough calcium available by adding bone meal or wood ashes when you prepare the soil. Avoid using too much high-nitrogen fertilizer, which will encourage rapid leaf growth. And finally, water deeply and regularly, and mulch to conserve soil moisture during hot, dry spells.

Tobacco mosaic virus: This virus can infect not only tobacco plants but tomatoes and many other members of the Nightshade family. Infected plants show yellow mottling of the leaves, which may also curl upward slightly. While the virus doesn't kill the plants, it does reduce their yield.

The virus is spread by various means but often begins when a person who has been smoking touches plants in the garden and leaves behind traces of tobacco which had accumulated on his hands. This is dangerous because much of the tobacco used in cigarettes is contaminated by the mosaic virus. So if you smoke, take preventive measures like washing your hands thoroughly with soap and water or dipping them in milk before you touch your plants (milk inhibits the virus). Likewise, you should never smoke in the garden, and you should ask people who come to admire your handiwork to also refrain from smoking or carelessly discarding their cigarette butts anywhere near the garden.

If mosaic virus does appear in your garden, remove the infected plants right away and be careful not to let them or your infected hands brush up against healthy plants. You can add the plants to the compost pile as long as it is properly constructed and heats up well, since the high temperatures will effectively destroy the virus.

Certain weeds, such as catnip, jimsonweed, nightshade, and plantain, can carry mosaic virus. If you've been having trouble with this disease, keep the tomato patch well weeded and be on the lookout for patches of these weeds that may be growing adjacent to the garden.

Tomato hornworm: Because of the poisonous alkaloids in its leaves, the tomato plant is bothered by few leaf-eating pests. The one notable exception is the tomato hornworm, which is a voracious eater of tomato leaves and can devastate a plant in no time. This big, bright green caterpillar with white bars along its sides and a pointed "horn" at its tail end looks quite alarming (it can be up to 4 inches long) but is actually harmless to human beings.

Several good control methods are available for this pest. If only a few have taken up residence in your garden, an easy and effective method is to simply pick them off by hand. If you see any hornworms with white capsules attached to their backs, don't bother to remove them. These caterpillars have been infested by the *Trichogramma* wasp, an admirable parasite, and will soon die and release many more wasps to kill more hornworms. For a heavier infestation, and in the absence of helpful parasites, the bacterial spray *Bacillus thuringiensis* works well. You can also plant dill as a trap plant; hornworms love to feast away on feathery dill leaves and they are a lot easier to spot there than on the heavy foilage cover of tomato plants.

Tomato Frontiers

Like wild potatoes, some wild tomatoes have hairy leaves with sticky hairs that can trap insect pests like aphids. In at least one wild tomato variety, the sticky substance is poisonous as well and can kill caterpillars that feed on tomatoes. Scientists have isolated the poison and have found that it is not an alkaloid like other deadly nightshade poisons. Since this wild tomato variety crosses readily with the domestic tomato, scientists hope to develop a hybrid which has poisonous leaves as well as good quality fruits. But even if they are not successful with such breeding attempts, the poison itself might be further developed as a natural insecticide for tomato pests.

Since tomatoes are rather particular about the temperatures at which they will set fruit and germinate, scientists are trying to develop varieties that can produce at higher and lower temperatures than present-day tomatoes. A wild tomato from the mountains of Peru offers hope that a more frost-resistant tomato may one day be available. This variety lives about 3,000 feet above sea level where it tolerates light frosts. Through a program of extensive cross-breeding with domestic varieties, a tomato that will survive light frosts may be produced in the not-so-distant future.

Another possibility for expanding the climatic tolerance of tomatoes comes from the seashore. In the Galapagos Islands lives a wild tomato relative that thrives just above the high-tide line. This wild species with its ¼-inch, sickly yellow fruits is a far cry from the domestic tomato, but it can survive irrigation with 100 percent sea water, a great accomplishment for any land plant. This is certainly a valuable feature to incorporate into crops in a world where much land cannot be cultivated because the soil itself is too salty or the only water available for irrigation is salty. Successful crosses of this remarkable plant with cultivated tomatoes have been made and have produced a plant which has bright red, cherry-tomato-sized fruits with a fine flavor. The taste is even said to be better than that of our present garden tomatoes! This new plant will tolerate 70 percent sea water in the experimental plots where it is being grown. Despite the promise this new plant shows, it will be years before it can be made available to the gardening public. In general, it takes 10 to 15 years to develop a variety which is completely reliable when grown from seed and to produce enough certified seed for commercial purposes.

Chapter 13

Peppers: From Sweet Bells to Red-Hot Pods

Vital Statistics

Family:
Solanaceae
Species:
Capsicum annuum
Soil:
Deep, loose, and rich
pH:
5.5–7.0
Soil Temperature for Germination:
60°–95°F; 85°F optimum

Air Temperature for Best Growth:
75°–85°F, daytime; 50°–65°F night-time; lower than 32°F kills the plants
Seed Viability:
2–4 years
Seed Germination:
6–28 days
Seed Planting Depth:
½"

Peppers are one of the most fun and satisfying garden crops to grow. They don't take up a lot of space, and the lovely, compact plants with their shiny, dark green leaves and colorful fruits are attractive enough to grace the flower bed as well as the vegetable garden. There are peppers to suit every taste, from sweet, fruity bells to flaming hot pods that will have you breathing fire. The fruits cover a colorful spectrum, from dark, shiny green gems to bright yellow, orange, or red ones.

Most people think of peppers as a tropical crop best suited to southern climates. But actually, the garden pepper's closest wild relatives live in the Mexican highlands, where daytime temperatures aren't too fiercely hot and nights get quite cool. In the United States, peppers are grown commercially in warm regions—Florida and Southern California—but as a winter crop. In those regions, summers are actually too hot for peppers! Many northern gardeners don't even try to grow peppers because they assume their season is too short and their climate too cool. But with thoughtful variety selection, proper cultural methods, and a little luck, even northern gardeners can harvest a few fat red bells along with many green and yellow fruits.

Although there is no one secret to successful pepper growing, it is critical that you keep your plants healthy and growing at every stage in their development. This is especially important for gardeners working against the seasonal clock, for a setback to the pepper plants can mean no pepper harvest at all or a disappointing yield of sad, bitter, thin-walled fruits. Rapid, continuous growth is essential.

There's a nutritional incentive for you to grow a healthy, prolific crop of peppers. Many people don't realize that peppers contain even more vitamin C than tomatoes—five to ten times as much by weight. As peppers ripen, their vitamin C content increases, which helps impart that lovely fruity flavor to the sweet varieties. A mature pepper can have up to 70 times as much vitamin C as an immature fruit, so health-conscious gardeners will wait to pick the fruits until they are mature. Besides, they taste better then, too!

Why Hot Peppers Are Hot

Like tomatoes and potatoes, peppers are members of the Nightshade family (Solanaceae). Despite the great differences in growth patterns, fruiting habits, and climatic preferences, all garden peppers belong to the same species, *Capsicum annuum*. The tabasco pepper, from which the sauce is made, belongs to a different species, *Capsicum frutescens* (available from some seed companies as the variety Serrano).

The peppery hotness of tabasco and chili peppers that leaves a memorable impression on your taste buds is caused by a group of related chemicals called capsaicinoids. The greatest concentration of these chemicals is in the placenta, the fleshy tissue inside the fruits which supports and nourishes the seeds as they develop. The seeds themselves pick up hotness from the placenta, and the walls of the pepper also contain some capsaicinoids. The degree of hotness is determined by the amount of these chemicals that are present in the pepper. Although you may not suspect it, even the sweetest bell contains some of them. Scientists have determined the relative content of capsaicinoids in eight varieties of peppers, using a quantitative chemical test to compare their hotness. As reported in the 1942 Proceedings of the American Society for Horticultural Science, they ranked the peppers on a scale from 1 to 9, with some interesting results. Oakview Wonder was the mildest, with a rating of 1. Then came Sweet Roumanian at 1.2; Hungarian Yellow Wax, 2.2; Anaheim Chili, 2.8; Long Red Cayenne, 3.5; Floral Gem, 3.8; Red Chili, 5.5; and Argentine Wonder, 8.2. (And we think of Cayenne peppers as being hot!)

After classifying the peppers through this chemical test, the intrepid scientists tasted each variety to see if their sensory rating would correspond to the capsaicinoid level. The tasters found that they perceived no hotness at

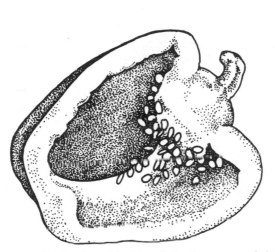

Pepper Fruit: *Capsaicinoids, which give peppers their hot, lively flavor, are primarily concentrated in the placenta, the tissue in the fruit that supports and nourishes the seeds. That's why you should remove the seeds and placenta from a bell pepper before you eat it.*

all in the three peppers with the least capsaicinoid content, and they couldn't distinguish by taste which was which among the four hottest kinds! Cayenne burned the taste buds just as intensely as Argentine Wonder. In cooking, however, these differences do show up; the prudent chef uses a very light touch, indeed, in adding a fiery-flavored pepper like Argentine Wonder to a sauce or soup.

As a matter of fact, cooks must use all hot peppers with an ample measure of caution, for some people are very sensitive to capsaicinoids. The first time Diane tried to roast hot peppers to peel them, her hands began to burn as she was washing the fruit. Her husband took over with no trouble and placed the shiny green culprits under the broiler while she tried to get the irritant off her hands with lots of soapy water. Even then, her troubles were far from over because as soon as the peppers started to roast, her lungs began to burn until she could hardly breathe. She had no choice but to leave the house and stand outside forlornly on the porch while her husband roasted, peeled, and cut up the peppers with no problem at all. Once the air had cleared and Diane rejoined her family, they all ate the peppers diced up in a salad, where they were delicious. Why was Diane able to enjoy her salad thoroughly even though only a short time earlier those innocent-looking green cylinders had threatened to scorch her lungs? There was no magic involved, just the simple fact that cooking deactivates much of the irritating quality of the capsaicinoids.

Some friends of hers had a similarly memorable experience in the kitchen. They naively followed a Chinese recipe calling for 23 dried, hot red peppers to be fried in hot oil. When the peppers hit the oil, the fumes were so strong that everyone had to leave the house for four hours before the irritants had dissipated enough that they could breathe without coughing uncontrollably!

Don't forget our tales of woe if you decide to cook with hot peppers—learn from our lesson rather than repeat it! If your skin even starts to tingle slightly while working with them, wash your hands immediately and don a pair of kitchen gloves before going any further. And if you decide to try a recipe that calls for frying hot peppers, make sure your oil isn't smoking hot when you add the peppers, turn the kitchen fan on high, and open all the windows you can.

There is, of course, a reason for the pepper's hotness. In fact, it performs an important biological function, for it appears to make the germination of pepper seeds possible. The explanation lies in the capsaicinoids' effect on fungi, which are mortal enemies of pepper seeds. While many seeds will germinate within a reasonable time at fairly low temperatures, pepper seeds are somewhat unusual in that they may take a month to germinate at 60°F. This gives soil-dwelling fungi plenty of time to attack and kill the seeds. And under the high temperatures that allow more rapid germination, fungi will also pick up the pace and grow more quickly. Once the seed has germinated and the plant is maturing, fungi can still cause problems. Namely, they can attack the fruits as they are growing, before the capsaicinoid-laced seeds have fully developed inside.

Experiments with the tabasco pepper done by a group of Canadian researchers in 1975 have shown that if fungi attack the young fruits before any capsaicinoids are present, the fruits will form them within 24 hours of the fungi attack. This halts the growth of the fungus, then other defensive chemicals in the fruit get into the act and actually kill off the fungus. The same mechanism is almost certainly at work in our familiar garden peppers (especially in the hotter varieties) protecting them from fungi.

Peppers begin to accumulate capsaicinoids about 20 days after the fruit has set. The amount increases until the fruit is fully ripe. Peppers grown in warm temperatures accumulate more capsaicinoids than those raised in cooler conditions, so if you have an especially hot summer, beware of the potential fieriness of pepper varieties which may have tasted only mildly pungent after a cooler growing season. Long, sunny days and a rich soil can also contribute to hotness. If you pick your hot peppers before they are fully ripe, they will continue to increase in hotness and color if you place them at room temperature in the light.

Pepper Varieties

Peppers come in a more bewildering assortment than just about any other garden crop, with the possible exception of tomatoes. How do you decide

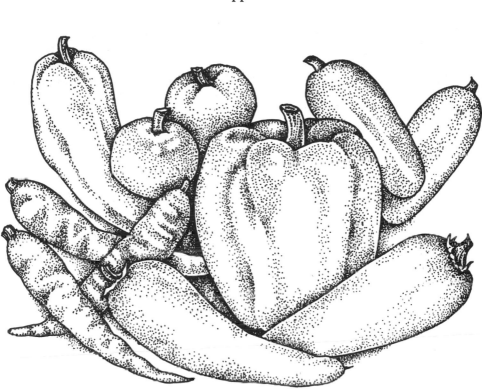

Pepper Possibilities: *The bell pepper in the center is surrounded by (clockwise from upper right) Jalapeño, sweet frying peppers, three cayennes, a poblano, and two round hot peppers.*

what to grow when you have as many as 35 different choices in just one catalog? You might think the easy way out is to buy plants instead of seeds, for no garden store will have 35 different kinds of seedlings, and the selection won't be so overwhelming. But unless you live in a long-season area, you might as well forget about buying pepper plants that will meet your needs, for the variety of plants offered commercially is generally quite limited. You can buy California Wonder bell peppers, Cayenne hot peppers, and, if you are lucky, Jalapeño hot peppers as plants, and that is usually about it. These long-season varieties would certainly be a mismatch for a short-season garden. Small wonder that so many gardeners have given up on peppers!

But no matter where you live, there are pepper varieties offered in seed catalogs which give you at least a fighting chance of growing this tasty crop successfully. While the ever-popular California Wonder takes about 75 days to reach the picking stage, other varieties of bell peppers such as Ace Hybrid and Canape Hybrid take only about 60 days. The key to growing bell peppers successfully if you're faced with a short season is to buy the earliest varieties you can get your hands on. Other good ideas are to plant several varieties and not to be too attached to the idea of nice blocky green bell peppers. Here in Montana, some of our most successful sweet peppers—Cubanelle, Dutch Treat, and Italian Sweet—are not bell shaped at all. Cubanelle is a long, pale green frying pepper which, despite its name, grows quite well where the weather is cool. Dutch Treat is a pretty plant with sweet, aromatic, pointed yellow fruits which form an attractive cluster near the top of the plant. Italian Sweet peppers are long and pointed and have a delightful fruity flavor, even when still green. The walls of the fruit are thin but crisp, and the plants are small and take up little space. Sweet Banana peppers also do well in our climate—so well that the plants are covered with long, slim yellow peppers long before many other varieties have ever begun to form fruits.

Bell peppers, unless the catalog description states otherwise, turn red when ripe. (You must be careful when estimating how soon you will get ripe peppers; days to maturity signify the time from transplanting to mature green pepper stage, omitting the time it takes to start them from seed on one end, and the time it takes for them to fully ripen to the red stage at the other end.) They take less time to reach a usable stage than hot peppers, and there are varieties to suit a wide range of growing conditions. Besides the early ma-turers, there are dwarf and disease-resistant varieties to choose from.

Hot peppers come in many sizes and shapes, too, and it can be fun to experiment with growing a different variety than you usually do. Even if the seed catalog lists a long time to maturity for a hot variety, you still may be able to grow it successfully in a short-season area. For example, the variety Cayenne commonly takes 75 days from the time of transplanting to reach its red, ripe stage, but when picked green, these peppers will ripen quite nicely in the house. Ancho peppers are supposed to take about 80 days, but that is the time they need to reach a red, ripe state. At this point, these fruits are dried, whereupon they can be properly called Anchos. You don't have to wait this long to use them though, for while the glossy fruits are in their dark green immature stage, they can add a delightful, mild zip to many Mexican dishes. Some cooks say that Poblanos, as these immature Ancho peppers are called, are the only variety to use for *chilis rellenos*.

If your summers are long and hot instead of cool and short, you should consider planting your peppers early so that they will mature before the torrid weather descends. If the temperature is consistently above 90°F, peppers won't set fruit. Since hot varieties can stand the heat better than sweet ones, you might also want to concentrate your attention on them. Besides the familiar Cayenne and Jalapeño, there are many interesting hot peppers which differ greatly in size, shape, and degree of fiery flavor. There are the beautiful, dark green Poblanos mentioned above; in long-season areas, these peppers can either be harvested green or allowed to ripen into the deep red Anchos. There is the tiny spherical variety, Pequin, which is among the hottest of peppers, and the little finger-sized variety, Serrano, which has its own special flavor. Even if you live where the heat makes growing bell peppers difficult, you can still have fun trying your hand at different kinds of peppers like these.

Pointers on Seed Storage and Germination

Pepper seeds can last for two to four years if stored in a cool, dry place. However, they seem to be extremely sensitive to temperature and humidity, and old seeds may be slow and uneven in germinating. Even year-old seeds may be unreliable if they have been stored at normal room temperature in their original packet. If possible, plant either fresh seeds or seeds not more than a year old unless you have taken special care to keep your seeds dry (see chapter 1) and have them stored in a cool place. Cool does not mean cold, however. We do not recommend storing pepper seeds in the freezer. While volunteer tomatoes often appear around the edges of our compost piles in the spring, pepper seedlings never come up there spontaneously, so we suspect that the seeds may be killed by freezing winter temperatures. It's best to avoid potential problems and store your pepper seeds in an unheated closet, a cool corner of the basement, or even in the refrigerator.

Another germination problem peculiar to peppers is the possibility of dirty seeds. As we already mentioned, pepper seeds are especially susceptible to fungus infection, even though they contain chemicals which offer them some protection. If seeds are saved from fruits that are cracked or damaged by slugs or other nibbling pests, there's the distinct possibility that fungus spores or bacteria may have entered the fruit and reached the seeds. We have found that seeds from some suppliers, especially small firms which specialize in unusual pepper varieties, are not very reliable. These companies may send generous packets, but we have to plant twice as many seeds to get enough plants for our gardens. This problem could stem from the fact that their seeds may not be as carefully collected and stored as those from the larger suppliers. If you save seeds from your own peppers, make sure they all come from whole, undamaged fruits.

Some gardeners have little or no trouble growing peppers from seeds. They just plant the seeds ½ inch deep in sterile potting soil, water lightly, cover the containers loosely with plastic, set them in a warm place, and wait for the seedlings to emerge in a week or so. We use this simple method for fresh seeds from major suppliers, but for older seeds or those from less reliable firms we recommend one of the following two techniques.

One method is to germinate the seeds between layers of dampened paper towels and then plant them as they germinate. The technique is the same as the one described in chapter 1, in the box on Germinating Seeds between Paper Towels. Place them in a warm place (75° to 85°F) and begin checking for germination after three days. The first sign will be the emergence of the tiny root. As soon as you see that a seed is germinating, remove it from the paper towelling with a toothpick or tweezers (but don't squeeze too hard), plant it ½ inch deep in a sterile potting soil mix, and water thoroughly. With some varieties, you may find that one seed germinates quickly while the others take a long time. Your luck may be very uneven with old seeds, but pregerminating them before planting will at least let you know quickly if they are any good. If none of the seeds from a particular batch have shown signs of germination after ten days, you should replace that batch with fresh seeds of the same variety, if you can.

Another simple method, one that is used by scientists to sterilize and germinate seeds, should also work well for home gardeners. First, boil a pot of water (containing at least eight cups of water) for ten minutes to sterilize it. Then, let it cool to room temperature with the cover on to keep the water as sterile as possible. Place your pepper seeds in a small bag made from a double layer of cheesecloth tied shut with string, and submerge them in a solution of one cup water and ¼ cup liquid household chlorine bleach. Leave the seeds in this solution for ten minutes, swirling the bag around frequently to make sure all the seeds get exposed to the bleach. Then dunk the bag of seeds into a plain cup of sterile water (that has cooled to room temperature) and swirl for a minute. Remove and swirl in another fresh cup of sterile water for a minute. Repeat this procedure for six more rinses in sterile water, then plant the seeds.

Bleach-treated pepper seeds germinate about four days earlier than untreated seeds, and the bleach solution is strong enough to kill any bacteria and fungal spores which may contaminate the seeds. Although no one has proven that their seed coat contains germination inhibitors, a lot of evidence points in that direction; perhaps the faster germination of the bleach-treated seeds is due to the destruction of such inhibitors. In our experience, even soaking the seeds in a few changes of water before planting can hasten germination by a couple of days.

Anything you can do to hurry along germination of pepper seeds is worth the trouble, for they can really be slow to wake up. While peppers can germinate at any temperature from 60° to 95°F, you may have to wait three weeks for them to sprout at 65°F. By that time, if you find that the seeds are no good, you could be out of the pepper-growing business for the entire season. On the other hand, at 85°F, pepper seedlings can be poking their heads up as early as a week after planting. As you can see from this wide range of times to germination, it is especially important to locate a warm place for your pepper seeds to get them off to a quick start (see the discussion on Warm and Cool Places, in the Introduction). To keep from cooling down the soil each time you water the seeds, remember to always use lukewarm water.

How often you water is important, as well. Make sure to keep the seed flats or pots evenly moist, for if germinating pepper seeds dry out, that spells trouble. If they dry out shortly after they've been planted, germination may be thwarted, and at best all you will get is a stalk with the dried-up seed coat on top that never amounts to much of a plant. Inattention to proper watering once the seeds have germinated can have dire consequences, too. Pepper seedlings developing in loose potting soil that's been allowed to dry out will most likely have a hard time shedding the old seed coat. This seed coat will trap the cotyledons at the very stage when they should be spreading out. Sometimes, even when you keep the soil sufficiently moist, the seed coat will be reluctant to come off. When this happens, you can very gently squeeze the old seed to release it from the seed leaves. But too often, this process results in damaged cotyledons. A better solution is to buy a plant-misting bottle and fill it with sterile water. Every day, gently mist your pepper seedlings as they are emerging from the soil. This procedure should keep the seed coats moist enough to come off naturally. Also, make sure you plant your seeds ½ inch deep so that the old seed will be carried through the soil as the seedling pushes its way up. This resistance will help the seedling rub off the seed coat.

Caring for Pepper Seedlings

While exposure to cool nights makes tomatoes bloom earlier than they would otherwise, there's no early stimulus for peppers, for they appear always to start flowering only after nine to eleven nodes have developed on the stem. Cool nights do, however, affect pepper growth in a positive way—they make the plants branch more extensively. Since pepper plants produce flowers at the bases of their branches, the bushier the plant, the more fruits it can yield. However, the cool nights which increase branching also slow the overall growth rate of the plants. So if you live in a short-season area, you may want to avoid exposing the seedlings you're growing indoors to cool nighttime temperatures. In this case it's probably better to trade off the extra bushiness for the continuous growth that warmer temperatures will permit.

If you have a cold frame, you will find that the advantages of growing your plants in direct sunlight out-of-doors will more than compensate for the slower growth caused by the cooler night temperatures. While plants raised in cold frames in Montana are 4 to 5 inches shorter at transplanting time than those grown indoors, they undergo less transplant shock and actually produce more mature peppers by the end of the season than do plants started indoors.

In order to avoid any checks in growth, pepper seedlings should be given their own individual pots to grow in while still small. If you've sown the seeds in a flat, you should transplant them to separate quarters as soon as the first true leaves emerge. You can save yourself a step by starting the seeds in individual pots; just plant two or three seeds per pot and thin to the sturdiest seedling after the plants are up. One friend of ours grows beautiful plants in half-gallon cardboard milk cartons which have been rinsed out, poked with holes for drainage, and completely opened up at the top to leave a nice, roomy, square opening. These milk cartons can be nestled closely together so they don't take up as much room as round pots, and they give the peppers plenty of space to stretch out and establish a healthy root system. Another nice benefit of this arrangement is that when packed tightly together, these straight-sided containers keep the soil temperature from fluctuating drastically when nights are cool.

Peppers are more sensitive than tomatoes to low light intensities, so if you have limited lighting, give your peppers a front-row seat at the south-facing window and put the tomatoes behind them. Peppers grown indoors need a slow, careful hardening-off period to avoid playing havoc with their growth once they're set out in the garden (see chapter 4 for more details on hardening off).

Soil and Growing Conditions

Pepper plants have a fibrous root system. If the topsoil is deep and loose, their roots can reach down as far as 26 inches and grow as far away from the stem as 40 inches in any direction. This extensive root system allows pepper plants to make efficient use of water in the soil, so they do not need to be watered as often as less efficient crops such as cabbage. Peppers do need more water than tomatoes, however; grown side by side, peppers will wilt from lack of water before tomatoes do.

There seems to be some confusion about pepper plants and how much nitrogen they need to grow well. Many gardening books warn you not to plant peppers in soil that has been treated with large quantities of nitrogen-rich fertilizers. They say that high soil nitrogen will result in bushy, fruitless plants. We believe that this advice is aimed chiefly at chemical gardeners working with highly concentrated sources of nitrogen, for we have found that peppers grow best and yield the most fruits earliest in good, rich organic soil. Fertilizing with organic materials high in nitrogen, like composted manure, will not hurt your pepper crop. On the contrary, peppers appear to be quite sensitive to low nitrogen levels, responding with pale leaves and few flowers. Since we live in a region that's only marginally hospitable to peppers, we pamper them by working fresh or composted chicken, rabbit, or sheep manure into the soil in the fall where we plan to plant our peppers the following season. If you follow our lead, don't get too carried away adding poultry manure, since it's very salty and peppers do not like salty soil.

Peppers are also sensitive to low levels of phosphorus in the soil, but they don't display the familiar warning signal of discolored reddish or purple leaves the way tomatoes do; instead, they produce narrow, grayish-green leaves and small, slender fruits. An infusion of a fast-acting fertilizer like wood ashes may supply enough phosphorus to salvage your present crop. Even if it's too late to save them, take the hint from your plants and apply a phosphorus-rich, but slow-acting fertilizer like phosphate rock or bone meal to ensure that there will be enough phosphorus in the soil for succeeding crops. It's interesting to know that like some other plants, peppers form an association with helpful soil fungi which increases their ability to take up phosphorus from the soil (when enough is present in the first place).

When there's not enough potassium available in the soil for your plants, you'll witness a slowdown in their growth and start to see bronzed leaves appear with spots along the veins. The fruits on these potassium-starved plants will be small and few in number. Midway through the season is no time to run up against these kinds of problems since they jeopardize your harvest. The time to make sure your soil has the proper balance of important nutrients is before you plant.

If your soil isn't loose and crumbly deep down, dig up an area about 24 inches wide and 18 inches deep where you plan to plant your peppers, and add well-rotted manure or compost to the soil. Plant your peppers deeply, up to the level of the first leaves. Like tomatoes, peppers will grow lots of new roots along the buried portion of the stem. If you plant them at the same level that they have been growing in their containers, you may find that some plants will topple over from the weight of the fruits later in the season.

The proper planting distance for peppers is not a clear-cut matter. Gardening books generally recommend 18 to 24 inches between plants. This spacing can be misleading, for pepper plants vary greatly in size depending on the variety, and small plants can be spaced closer than 18 inches while large ones may need more than 24 inches. Italian Sweet plants may reach only 12 inches in height and can be planted 10 inches apart, while Ancho forms small bushes, 24 inches or more tall and 24 inches wide, needing over 24 inches between plants. Because plant size varies so much from variety to variety, you must refine the general rule of 18 to 24 inches until it applies to what you observe in your garden. If your plants are cramped for room at a 24-inch spacing, make a notation in your garden journal that next season you'll give that particular variety a wider berth, say 30 inches. If there's room to spare, you'll know next year that you can shrink the 18-inch spacing to 12 inches.

You should be aware that pepper roots are quite temperature-sensitive. Soil temperatures that hover around 85°F will stunt the roots, but so will soil temperatures of 50°F or less. If you garden in a hot, dry area, lay down an organic mulch around your peppers as soon as the soil warms up. This buffer zone will keep the soil temperature from soaring as the temperatures climb higher and higher. If you garden in a cool climate, you can use a black plastic mulch to warm the soil. Dorothy always unrolls a black plastic mulch over the area to be planted and then inserts her peppers in holes about 8 inches in diameter cut out of the black plastic. Plastic may not be organic, but it does warm the soil!

If you have a lot of flat stones around, put them to good use by placing a couple at the base of each pepper plant. During the day, the stones soak up the sun's rays and at night slowly radiate it back into the soil. In this way, they help keep the soil temperature evenly warm in an area with chilly nights. Some ingenious cool-climate gardeners mulch their peppers with aluminum foil, which reflects heat and light up to the branches, thereby channeling more of the sun's energy to the plants to help them grow. If you give this mulch a try, make sure to leave a 4- to 8-inch area around the base of each plant free of foil so that water can penetrate and reach the roots.

Whatever sort of mulch you use, wait until the soil has warmed to about 60°F before planting. Loosening the soil as the last frost-free day approaches will help it to warm up faster. This little bit of handiwork with the shovel or garden fork will allow air to get in and dry out the moisture-laden soil particles. As the soil dries out, it will warm up. You may have to wait until after your tomatoes are in before you plant your peppers, but be patient; jumping the gun may expose your plants to chilly temperatures, with the outcome that their growth is slowed. One year, Dorothy's family had a June vacation planned, and she had to plant her peppers before they left. When they returned home, she ran eagerly to the garden to see how her favorite crop was doing. Much to her disappointment, the pepper plants looked just the same size as they were three weeks earlier when she had planted them with such great expectations! The weather had been cold and rainy, and as a result, the peppers had just sulked the entire time.

Pepper Flowers and Fruiting

If you pause to observe how your tomato and pepper plants are developing in the garden, the differences in their growth habits should soon become apparent to you. The vines of indeterminate tomato plants grow larger as the tip of each branch develops three leaves, a flower cluster, three leaves, a flower cluster, and so on. The plant just keeps on going until some outside force curtails the growth of the branch tips.

Peppers grow and flower in a different way. Only one flower is formed at the tip of a stalk, which is actually a tiny branch of the plant. Then, the axillary buds at the base of the flower branch grow to produce more branches. After forming two leaves and a flower, each of these branches stops growing, then its axillary buds form branches which go on in the same way. The result is a busy plant whose size depends on how long the branches grow between flowers.

When you examine your pepper plants early in the season, you may become encouraged by the sight of flower buds developing low on the plant.

Bushy Pepper Plants: *The growth and flowering habit of pepper plants gives them a bushy appearance. First a flower is produced at the tip of a stalk. The axillary buds at the base of the flower branch grow to produce more branches. Two leaves and a flower follow. The branch will then stop growing while the axillary buds from these branches develop, and each produces another two leaves and a flower.*

Buds mean flowers, which mean fruit. But pepper flowers do not follow the usual pattern of opening, which is, first to come, first to fruit. Even though they are the first to develop, those lower flowers may remain closed until many top flowers have formed and opened.

Like the roots, pepper flowers are a bit touchy about temperature. If nights stay hotter than 83°F, the flowers will fall off before they can open, and your harvest will be nipped in the bud, so to speak. On the other hand, nighttime temperatures in the 40s will also cause the flowers to drop off. The best nighttime temperatures for fruit-setting are between 60°F and 68°F. If your climate is hot, you can still get a good yield of peppers by planting them early so that plenty of fruit is set before the sweltering nights arrive. In cooler climates, gardeners sometimes must wait a long time before they get any peppers. Two summers ago, our nights were cold all through July and, although our pepper plants bloomed profusely, we didn't even see any tiny immature fruits before August. Luckily for us, August and September were warm, so we were eventually able to harvest some fine peppers.

Pepper plants will set fruit when exposed to borderline temperatures around 50°F, but few seeds will be produced. This has important consequences for fruit size, because developing seeds produce the hormone auxin which helps induce the fruit to grow. Fewer seeds means less of this hormone, which ultimately means smaller fruit. You'll also notice that the fruits are shaped abnormally; instead of having straight sides with lobes on the bottom, they will be rounded. You can offset the effects of these low nighttime temperatures and increase fruit size by gently hand-pollinating your pepper flowers with a paint brush. In this way you are encouraging more auxin-producing seeds to form.

Once the fruit has set, high nighttime temperatures (around 68°F) will help the fledgling fruits grow fast and assume a normal shape. Fruit which sets at an optimal nighttime temperature but then must develop further during a cold snap (with temperatures in the 40s) will be longer and more slender than normal.

Picking Peppers at Their Peak

Pepper fruits grow so rapidly during good weather that you can practically see them getting bigger from day to day. Just like tomatoes, peppers should be picked when they are at their ripe, flavorful best. An immature green bell pepper is just not as sweet and fruity as a full-grown one. And the spicy, fiery flavor of hot peppers is enhanced by a long stay on the vine. Many gardening books and articles advise keeping your green peppers picked so the plants don't slow down their production, but this advice should be tempered with the knowledge that the longer a pepper stays on the plant, the better it will taste and the more vitamin C it will contain. If you live in a short-season area, you might as well leave your peppers on the plants as long as possible, for picking them early won't affect your eventual yield. In longer-season regions you should experiment with picking the fruits at different stages until you find out when you like them best.

Left on the plants long enough, peppers will turn red. (A few varieties turn yellow or orange or even almost black.) The ripening process is similar to that in tomatoes—the green chlorophyll disappears and is replaced by red pigments called carotenoids. As with tomatoes, about half the pepper's life is spent in growing to its full size, while the second half is devoted to ripening.

The eventual color of the ripe fruit is affected by temperature. The fullest color develops when temperatures range between 65° and 75°F. When temperatures hover above 80°F during most of the ripening process, the fruit that results will be yellowish-red in color. The other extreme, where temperatures stay below 55°F, tends to hold peppers in their green state by stopping ripening altogether. You can see that peppers, just like tomatoes, should not be left out in the garden under plastic too late in the fall. You're just asking for trouble if you do, for the fruits won't ripen if the temperature is too cold, and the high humidity under the plastic will encourage fungal growth. Once fall settles in and the temperature stays at or below 65°F during the day, you might as well pick your peppers and bring them inside.

Storing the Harvest

Like tomatoes, peppers will continue to ripen after picking. But if you keep them in a warm place that encourages the ripening process, they may turn overripe and undesirable long before you want to use them. Clean, dry peppers will last several weeks in good shape if you store them in an unheated place. Dorothy has had good luck storing them in plastic bags in an unheated, west-facing storeroom. There they lasted more than six weeks, turning red one by one. While green bell peppers keep best at 45° to 50°F, you can store them in plastic bags in the refrigerator for about three weeks. However you store your peppers, you should be vigilant in checking every few days for rotting fruits. Remove and discard these immediately, and if they have contaminated any of the surrounding peppers, wash and dry the remaining fruits before returning them to a clean storage bag.

If you can't find a good place to store peppers in their fresh state, look to your freezer as an alternative. Peppers freeze very well, and although they do lose their firm texture when thawed, they can still be used in chopped form or whole for stuffing with good results. Some people blanch their peppers before freezing, but this isn't necessary. You can chop them coarsely or just cut them into quarters, removing the seeds and veins before freezing. Chili peppers, such as Colorado or Anaheim, are good candidates to be frozen whole for later stuffing. In addition to freezing, drying is another storage option. Thin-walled peppers like Cayenne dry well whole, and thick-walled sweet peppers fare better when chopped into pieces.

Collecting and Saving Pepper Seeds

Peppers must be close to maturity for their seeds to be any good. The way you know the seeds are ripe is to watch the color of the fruit. Red fruit means ripe seeds, and ripe seeds mean good germination rates. To make sure the fruit has ripened sufficiently, you must leave it on the plant for three to six weeks beyond the mature green stage (the point where the pepper's skin changes from matte and slightly wrinkled to darker green and glossy). If you are trying to save seeds and your season ends before the fruits are ripe, you can take them inside and finish ripening them at room temperature. If the peppers had reached the mature green stage by the time you lifted them from the plant, the seeds will develop just fine as the fruits ripen. Once the peppers are fully ripe and have begun to soften, open them up and scrape out the seeds. Dry them thoroughly on paper towels, and store the prepared seeds following the general guidelines given in chapter 1 and the specific instructions for pepper seed given earlier in this chapter under Pointers on Seed Storage and Germination.

Problems with Peppers

Peppers tend to be afflicted by the same sorts of troubles that beset tomatoes. This makes sense, of course, when you realize they belong to the same plant family. We've mentioned a few of the pepper's most frequent ailments here, and where the pest or disease is noted as being common to peppers and tomatoes, refer to Tomato Problems in chapter 12 for some tips on how to deal with these nuisances.

Bacteria, fungi, and viruses: As we've already said, fungi are among the pepper's greatest enemies. Not only do the seeds often fall victim to fungus, but the mature plants can as well, especially if they're grown in a rainy or very humid climate. Fungal and bacterial diseases form sunken, discolored spots on the peppers' leaves or fruits, while virus diseases generally cause a mottled leaf color and bitter, bumpy-looking fruits. If your peppers become diseased, pull up the affected plants right away and discard them in the trash or burn them. Peppers as well as tomatoes can suffer from mosaic virus, so you should observe the same precautions with peppers as with tomatoes if you use tobacco.

Blossom end rot and sunscald: Peppers, like tomatoes, can suffer from blossom end rot. Sunscald occurs when the pepper plant doesn't have enough foliage to cover the fruits. Overexposure to the sun results in discolored areas which become sunken and bleached. Fungi and bacteria can attack through the weakened area, so you should pick and use sun-scalded fruits right away. Some pepper varieties are more susceptible to sunscald than others. A variety such as Dutch Treat, which carries most of its fruit high on the plant above the leaves, may not produce a satisfactory crop in a hot, dry area because of the fruit's susceptibility to sunscald.

Cutworms and hornworms: These voracious insects attack peppers with gusto. Cutworms threaten your crop at the young seedling stage, while hornworms seem to do their dirty work on more mature plants. A cardboard collar slipped around pepper seedlings will be enough to deter cutworms. Treat your hornworm-infested pepper crop the same way you would your tomatoes.

Pepper maggots and pepper weevils: These pests are mainly pepper predators, and only rarely bother other garden crops like eggplants and tomatoes. The pepper maggot is the larva of a small yellow fly with three brown bands across both wings which lays its eggs in the fruit. You can combat this pest by sprinkling talcum powder on the fruits during July and August while the fly is busy laying its eggs. The talcum powder will interfere with the egg-laying process.

The pepper weevil is a small beetle with a long snout. Both the adult and its larva, a ¼-inch white grub with a pale brown head, feed on pepper plants. The grub chews up the buds and fruit from the inside, making them vulnerable to diseases and leaving them misshapen and discolored. The adult beetles eat leaves, buds, and fruits. Pepper weevils live mainly in the southern states and can be controlled by a careful cleanup after harvest in which you remove any plant residue that may harbor eggs. Rotenone can also be used to kill weevils.

Pepper Frontiers

Unfortunately, little research into pepper improvement is being done by North American breeders since peppers are not a major commercial crop in the United States and Canada. What work is being done centers on producing more disease-resistant varieties. Other countries have forged ahead, however, and foreign breeders have developed new varieties which tolerate cool climates (such as Dutch Treat) or which produce an early crop (such as Tokyo Bell). Fortunately for us, these seeds are being sold in North America.

Chapter 14

Cucumbers, Melons, and Squash: Those Rambling Cucurbits

Vital Statistics

Family:
  Cucurbitaceae
Species:
  Cucumis sativus—Cucumbers
  Cucurbita species—Summer and
  winter squash; pumpkins
  Cucumis melo—Muskmelons
  Citrullus lanatus—Watermelons
Soil:
  Rich and loose
pH:
  Close to 7.0; do poorly in acid
  soil

Soil Temperature for Germination:
  65°–100°F; optimum varies
  from 80°–95°F
Air Temperature for Best Growth:
  Cucumbers, squash, pumpkins,
  and muskmelons, 65°–75°F;
  watermelons, 70°–85°F
Seed Viability:
  2–5 years
Seed Germination:
  3–10 days
Seed Planting Depth:
  ½–1"

The Cucurbit family includes many of our most popular, tasty, and colorful vegetables—summer and winter squash, cucumbers, muskmelons (such as cantaloupe), pumpkins, and watermelons. Cucurbits all prefer warm weather, and while northern gardeners have no trouble growing the usual over-abundance of zucchini that plagues gardeners everywhere, one or two muskmelons ripening on a vine can be a major source of pride to a northerner. Unlike the members of the Cabbage family which all belong to one species, the cucurbits belong to several different genera and species, some of them more closely related than others. But even though they look different, all cucurbits have much the same character and require very similar cultural conditions for success.

The versatile cucurbits came originally from a number of different geographic regions and have been cultivated for thousands of years. Cucumbers have been grown for 3,000 years in their native region of India. Watermelons seem to have come from the African deserts, while wild melons are found in the wet tropical regions of Africa. Squash and pumpkins are American natives that have been cultivated for 10,000 years. Mexico and northern South America seem to be their original homelands (a fact that explains the preference of these crops for hot summer weather).

A Nutritional Profile of the Cucurbits

While cucurbits are not among the most nourishing of vegetables, yellow and orange ones do contain large quantities of vitamin A. A half-cup serving of Butternut squash contains 6,500 units of vitamin A, much more than the Recommended Daily Allowance for an adult. The same size serving of Hubbard squash provides 4,800 units and of Acorn, 1,400. Orange-fleshed cantaloupes are also high in vitamin A, but green melons (like honeydew) are not. The seeds of squash and pumpkin, which are delicious either raw or toasted, provide concentrated food in the form of fats and proteins. If you are weight-conscious, you may find the greatest virtue of cucurbits to be their low calorie content. An entire average-sized cucumber has only 45 calories, and a satisfying breakfast of half a cantaloupe (82 calories), a boiled egg (82 calories), and a slice of whole grain bread (61 calories) amounts to only 225 calories.

What's in a Name?

The vast array of squashes and pumpkins all belong to the same genus, and are classified into four distinct species. It's sometimes hard to tell the difference between squashes and pumpkins, but here's how they break down botanically:

Cucurbita maxima—Winter squash
Cucurbita mixta—Cushaw squash
Cucurbita moschata—Winter crookneck squash
Cucurbita pepo var. *pepo*—Field pumpkin, acorn squash
Cucurbita pepo var. *melopepo*—Summer squash

Getting Started with Cucurbits

Cucurbit seeds may stay viable as long as five years when stored properly in a cool, dry place. Since these are tropical plants, it is best not to freeze the seeds. Under poor storage conditions, the seeds will deteriorate quickly and may lose their viability in two years, so take good care of them. Hybrid squash and hull-less pumpkin seeds often have a low germination rate, so it's a good idea to plant more than you need of these types to be on the safe side.

The seeds require very warm soil temperatures for germination—the optimal germination temperature is 95°F. But while such a high temperature allows these warmth-loving plants to germinate quickly, squash seeds may carry the spores of diseases that also grow rapidly at high temperatures, so a lower temperature of 80°F (as listed in the Vital Statistics box) is actually preferable. Muskmelons will emerge in one week at 68°F and in five days at 77°F, while cucumbers will come up within four days if the soil temperature is in the 70's. In many parts of North America, such high soil temperatures are hard to come by early in the season, so planting cucurbit seeds indoors is often a good idea. If they are planted outdoors in cold soil, cucurbit seeds will simply sit there and rot. On the other hand, in southern areas where the soil may be warmer than 80°F, you can plant your cucurbits 1 inch deep. The large seeds contain enough stored food to nourish the embryo until it breaks through the soil surface and puts forth leaves.

Because they grow so quickly and have such sensitive roots, cucurbits should not be started indoors more than two weeks before planting out, and one week is even safer. These plants normally have a long taproot which can be inhibited by confinement in a small pot. When this happens, the plant develops a fibrous root system instead and needs more water throughout the season than a plant with the normal long, penetrating taproot. So, if you start your cucurbits indoors, remember that they may need more water later on than will direct-seeded plants. Each plant should have its own individual pot to grow in. If you use peat pots you must plant the pot along with the seedling (see chapter 4), so the roots are not disturbed during transplanting. Plastic pots are also good for starting cucurbits, for when the soil is just damp, the entire rootball will slide out easily with a minimum of trauma to the roots.

Diane has had consistent success using the following method to start all her cucurbit crops. You may want to try it, too. One week before the average frost-free date, plant two seeds in a narrow, 4-inch-deep plastic pot, water it and put it in a warm place. As the seedlings emerge, use a sharp knife or scissors to cut off the weaker one in each pot at ground level (so that you don't disturb the survivor). Move the pots to a cold frame where they receive full sunlight but are warmer than they would be out in the exposed garden.

As soon as the first true leaves unfold, transplant the seedlings into the garden. The weather should be warm when the plants are set out—reaching

Mini-Greenhouses: *Plastic milk jugs provide a warm, protected mini-greenhouse environment for cucurbits planted outdoors. Cut the bottoms out of 1-gallon milk jugs, and set them over the planting site one week before planting. At sowing time, place the germinated seeds in the prewarmed soil under the jugs.*

a daily average of at least 65°F. Let the soil dry slightly so the soil particles are moist but still cling together, then carefully slide the soil ball out of the pot and place it quickly into a prewatered planting hole in the garden, setting the plant about ½ inch deeper than it was in the pot. After gently filling in the soil around the seedling, water it carefully again with warm water. With this pampered treatment, your cucurbit seedlings will rarely wilt, and they'll get off to a healthy head start.

Cucurbits also thrive when started outdoors in mini-greenhouses. There are several ways to do this, but the basic idea is to provide the young plants with a warm, protected place in which to grow. One way to make a mini-greenhouse is to cut the bottom off a plastic one-gallon milk jug. About a week before planting time, set it over the hill where you plan to plant your cucurbits. This method has worked well for Dorothy. She germinated the seeds between damp paper towels in a warm place indoors and then planted them in the prewarmed soil under the jugs. Young cucurbits can be grown in these mini-greenhouses (also called hot caps) for a few weeks, until they become crowded. On sunny days, the top of the jug can be unscrewed to keep it from getting too hot inside. The cap can be screwed on again at night to hold in the warmth.

If you want to plant directly in the garden but have a spell of cool, unsettled weather, soak your seeds in warm water for 20 hours before planting. Scientists who tried this method with cantaloupe and watermelon seeds found that soaking increased the percent of successful germination when soil temperatures were less than desirable (55° to 65°F) for these crops.

Soil and Growing Conditions

Cucurbits grow very quickly when weather conditions are right for them, but they need a loose, very rich soil to support their rampant growth. The rapid proliferation of cucurbit vines is easy to observe, but the growth of the hidden roots is even more impressive. The taproot of melons and cucumbers can grow an inch a day down to a depth of 4 feet, while the main root of squashes and pumpkins can reach down 6 feet into the earth! Cucurbit roots may extend laterally farther than the vines sprawl and grow 2½ inches in a day. One careful estimate of the total area covered by a large squash root system was 1,000 cubic feet of soil.

The soil must be loose for such rapid root growth to occur. A heavy, compacted or clay soil can prevent cucurbit roots from growing quickly and will thus keep the leafy part of the plant from getting the optimum amount of minerals and water it needs from the soil. The plant will grow more slowly, yield less, and may produce a late crop, which can mean little or no crop in a short-season area. A soil that contains lots of organic matter will not only be sufficiently light and porous, it will also help retain the copious amounts of water these thirsty plants require. Cucurbits need lots of water during their rapid growth period and also during the production of their fruits—just think about how watery watermelons and cucumbers are. If watermelons or squash are water-stressed, they may produce misshapen fruits or not set fruit at all. If your soil lacks adequate organic matter, dig in fresh or composted manure or shredded compost six weeks or more before you plan to plant.

To compensate for poor soil, Dorothy once dug holes about a foot wide and a foot deep and put 6 inches of manure in the bottoms. She then filled the rest of the holes with soil and planted her squash. The plants really took off at first, but in about four weeks the leaves began to turn yellow. She didn't know then that squash roots rambled so far from the plants; her plants had outgrown their enriched hills. All she could do at that point was water the plants with liquid fish emulsion and add compost to the soil around the plants. She did get some fine squash from those plants, but she would have gotten a much better yield if she had dug the holes a lot wider and added manure over a 2- to 3-foot area so that the plants' growth wouldn't have slowed down when they began to flower.

Just as cucurbit seeds need warmth to germinate, so the plants need warm soil in order to grow well. For example, cucumbers need a soil temperature of at least 70°F for good growth; at 60°F or less they grow very poorly. At such low temperatures the cucumber roots are not able to absorb water well. If you water cucumbers with very cold water and thus reduce the soil temperature, you can actually make them wilt! The tips of the developing fruits may dry out, and the leaves and fruits can be discolored or even killed. For this reason, you should always water your cucurbits with lukewarm water in midmorning, as the soil is being warmed by the sun. Watermelons, cucumbers, and muskmelons are all more sensitive to cold soil than squashes are.

Cucurbits are traditionally planted in raised mounds called hills. They grow best this way because the sun warms the elevated soil, which has more surface area than a flat expanse of soil. Commercial melon growers in southernmost California, who raise cantaloupes in the winter, plant the seeds in ridges running from east to west. Because of the increased surface area, the sun warms the ridges better than it would level ground. Another way to keep the soil warm is to use a rock mulch. Once the plants are up and the soil is warmed, place flat rocks all around the plants, leaving a space about 6 inches in diameter around the stems to allow water to get to them. The rocks heat up during the day and radiate their stored warmth slowly back into the soil at night, keeping the soil at a more even temperature than it would have if left uncovered. Black plastic will also absorb the sun's rays and warm the soil, and it has the additional advantage of keeping the fruit clean.

As with other crops, cucurbits should not be planted in the same place in successive years. Not only is there the risk of transmitting diseases, but the fast-growing plants pull so many nutrients from the soil that it needs replenishing after supporting a season's growth.

Cucurbits do not do well in acid soil and should be grown at a pH of 7.0 (neutral) or higher. They are also sensitive to salts in the soil, so you should be careful not to use too much poultry manure when building up your soil. If poultry manure is the only high-nitrogen fertilizer you have available, add it in the fall so that the winter moisture will leach out some of the salt before planting time.

Cucurbit Flowers and Fruiting

There must be thousands of gardeners who had the same experience Dorothy did the first time she grew cucumbers and zucchini. Everyone is so proud of his or her first garden, and she was no exception. She was thrilled when her zucchini and cucumbers began to bloom and confident that it wouldn't be long until her family could taste the fresh, homegrown product. But after blooming enthusiastically, the first batch of flowers of both crops just dropped right off, leaving no trace of any fruit. She was terribly disappointed and worried—what was wrong? Why didn't her plants set fruit? Since she knew something about biology, she was able to figure out the answer later on, when a different-looking sort of flower appeared on her zucchini bushes. Her detective work led her to hypothesize that the plants must have separate male and female flowers. That kind of information is often missing in gardening books, so we'll explain it here in the hope of saving you some needless worry and confusion about your own crops.

All the cucurbit crops except muskmelons have separate male and female flowers, and the first ones to appear are almost always male. There is nothing

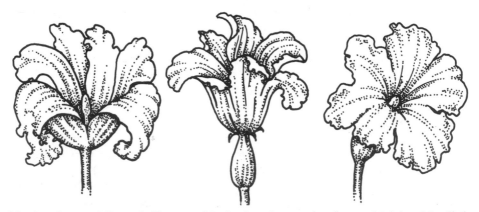

Muskmelon and Squash Flowers: *Muskmelons have perfect flowers (right), while all the other cucurbits have imperfect male and female flowers. The male flower (left) is the first to appear on the plant and has in its center a cluster of anthers laden with pollen. The female flower (center) has an ovary that looks like a miniature fruit where the flower is connected to the plant. A sticky stigma can be found in the middle of the flower.*

you can do about that sequence of events except to be patient and wait until the female flowers appear before you start looking up recipes. Male and female flowers look quite different. The female flowers have an ovary at the point where they attach to the plant. The ovary looks like a miniature fruit. (If you have mixed up your squash seedlings, you'll be able to tell the different kinds apart when the female flowers appear.) If you look into the center of the female flower, you can see the sticky stigma waiting for pollen. The male flower lacks the miniature fruit and has a cluster of fused anthers covered with pollen instead of a stigma inside. The generously big flowers of zucchini are especially good for studying the differences between male and female flowers.

Male and female flowers appear in a regular sequence in cucurbits, but the sequence varies somewhat among the different crops. Long days seem to promote the development of male flowers, which explains why they are the first to appear. In cucumbers and summer squash, female flowers come along after the first few male ones, and the plants will produce flowers of both sexes for the rest of the season. (If you like to eat batter-dipped squash flowers as well as the final product, select only male flowers for eating. It takes only a few male flowers to provide adequate pollen for all the females, but if you pick and eat the female flowers, you are seriously cutting into your harvest of squash.)

In acorn squash the situation is more complicated. The first male flowers do not even open, but these are followed by male flowers which do open.

Then both male and female flowers appear and open, and you can begin to think about harvesting and eating that squash. After these flowers (which can produce fruits) appear, still another sort develops—giant female flowers bloom, accompanied by smaller male flowers which pollinate them to form normal, seeded squash. Finally, at the end of the season female flowers appear that will develop into seedless squash without fertilization. Long days (sixteen hours or more) and high nighttime temperatures (above 80°F) lengthen the male phase, while twelve-hour days and lower nighttime temperatures shorten the male phase and encourage female flowers. While male flowers will predominate in the spring and early summer in northerly areas with long days, summer conditions with shorter days but warm nights will encourage both male and female flowers. Finally, the shorter days and cool nights of autumn will bring on the large female flowers which need no fertilization.

Muskmelons are like other cucurbits in that male flowers appear at first, and when they drop off, the gardener may think that all is lost, especially if he or she is trying to grow melons in the north. Let patience prevail, however, for the first fruiting flowers of muskmelons (which are perfect flowers complete with stamens, stigmas and ovaries, rather than female flowers) generally do not appear until the main branch of the plant is 18 inches long. At this time, side branches sprout from nodes near the base of the main branch. The first flowers on these side branches will be perfect ones. If these flowers are successfully pollinated, the rest of the flowers on the still-growing side branches will be male ones. In this way, the melon plant keeps itself from setting more fruit than it can support. When weather early in the season is good, most muskmelons will be found near the center of the plants. But when early weather is too cool or otherwise unfavorable, each side branch will keep producing perfect flowers until they are pollinated and set fruit, so the fruits will be further out on the branches.

Poor weather affects the pollination of all cucurbits. When it is cold, pollen may not be released from the male flowers; pumpkin and squash pollen is not released at temperatures below 48°F. Watermelons and cucumbers require a minimum temperature of 58°F for pollen release, while the most abundant release of pollen occurs at 65° to 70°F. Muskmelons require a minimum temperature of 65°F to set fruit, their optimum is 68° to 70°F.

Cucurbit flowers are most receptive to pollen right after they open, and it takes 24 to 48 hours for the pollen tubes to grow through the style and complete pollination. If you look carefully at the stigma of a cucumber flower, you can see that it actually consists of three equal parts which meet at the center. If you cut into a cucumber crosswise, you will see three seed chambers; each of these corresponds to one section of the stigma. If one of these stigma sections isn't properly pollinated, the cucumber will be lopsided.

Bees do a very effective job of pollinating cucurbit flowers. Many bees visit the same flower and cover the whole surface of the stigma evenly with

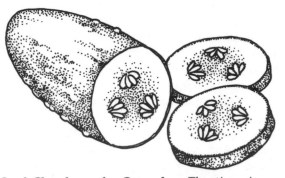

Seed Chambers of a Cucumber: *The stigma in a cu-cumber flower has three equal parts that meet at the center. When the fruit matures, the seeds will be grouped in three separate seed chambers; each chamber corresponds to one part of the stigma.*

pollen. But it takes a lot of bee visits to pollinate a cucurbit flower well. A cantaloupe flower, for instance, must be worked by ten to fifteen bees which leave several hundred pollen grains on the stigma in order to produce a big melon.

If it is cloudy or rainy while your first female flowers begin to bloom and the bees are not out doing their job, you may want to help the crop along by pollinating the flowers yourself. One way to hand-pollinate is to pick a fully open male flower and rub the anther on the stigma of a female flower. (Make sure the pollen can be brushed off the stamen easily—if it's reluctant to come off, the pollen is not yet ready to be released.) Another method is to take a cotton swab or soft paintbrush, pick up a generous quantity of pollen from one or more male flowers, and carefully dust the pollen evenly over the stigma of the female flower. Do as the bees do and spread the pollen evenly over the stigma, for cucurbits, like tomatoes and peppers, grow bigger fruits when they are heavily pollinated. For all cucurbits except cucumbers, you must move from plant to plant, applying the pollen from one plant onto the stigma of a flower on a different plant. The cucumber is the only member of the family that can pollinate its flowers with pollen from the same plant. Even for cucumbers, though, transferring pollen from one plant to another is still more effective.

You can tell within a couple of days whether or not a cucurbit flower has been successfully pollinated. If it has, the blossom withers and then the miniature fruit starts to grow. With summer squash, a properly fertilized fruit will fill out all the way to the blossom end as it grows. If it wasn't fertilized, the blossom end remains smaller than the rest of the squash and becomes shrivelled. After about two days, the little fruit stops growing. Such squashes should be picked off the vine right away, for they drain the plant of energy which could be better invested in well-fertilized fruits.

Cantaloupes and watermelons should also be watched for misshapen fruits. Any fruit that sets will inhibit other flowers from setting fruits—even flowers that have been properly pollinated. So if you leave misshapen fruits on the vine, that is all you're likely to get for a long time. The imperfect fruit can inhibit fruit set from other flowers for as long as several weeks. But if you pick off the bad ones, other flowers will set fruit or those from other already-pollinated flowers will start to develop.

If you think about the size of a cucurbit vine compared to the size of the fruits it produces, you can understand why it is important for the plant to have ways of limiting the number of fruit that it sets. For instance, you might harvest one 50-pound watermelon from a vine that weighs, at the most, 10 pounds. A great deal of energy goes into forming each of those crunchy cucumbers, juicy melons, and succulent squashes. Scientific study has shown that the leaves of cucumber plants with fruits on the vines photosynthesize at a more rapid rate and send out 40 percent more photosynthetic product (sugars) to the rest of the plant than do the leaves of plants without fruits. For this reason, it is especially important to take good care of cucurbit leaves. When you pick the fruits, be careful not to bend the stems (and damage the phloem which carries nutrients to the fruits) or injure the leaves by rough treatment. You should also take care to eliminate any insects which may be munching on your cucurbit leaves. With some crops, a few holes in the leaves make little difference in the eventual yield. But with cucumbers and their relatives, insect damage can significantly inhibit the ability of the leaves to make enough food for the rapidly developing fruits.

If you want to grow really big melons or pumpkins, pick off all but two watermelons or pumpkins or all but three or four cantaloupes per vine. This will channel all of the food energy produced by the leaves into fewer fruits, thus increasing the size of each of the remaining ones.

Saving Cucurbit Seeds

Many people have the idea that cucumbers will cross with cantaloupes or watermelon. This isn't true, for the three crops belong to three different species. You can safely save seeds from standard (nonhybrid) varieties of these crops even if they are growing right next to another. Whereas different species of plants generally will not cross-pollinate, two of the squash species *can* interbreed, greatly increasing your chances of seeing weird hybrids. For this reason, when you save seeds of *Cucurbita maxima* and *C. moscata*, you can never be sure of what will come up.

If you are growing more than one variety of a given species, however, you must separate the plants by at least 200 feet so they will not cross-pollinate. Many varieties within a species can cross-pollinate, resulting in some weird hybrids.

Last year Dorothy's neighbor grew plants from seeds she had saved from her spaghetti squash the year before. The resulting fruits didn't look at all like spaghetti squash; they were bigger and were orange instead of their usual green or the creamy yellow they turn when ripe. Other friends of the neighbor cooked some of this strange squash like winter squash and claimed it was delicious. However, the squash Dorothy was given looked so strange that she put the gift in a cold storeroom, meaning to cook it later. Now and then she'd look at it, wondering what to do. Eventually it was springtime, and she still hadn't faced that squash. It developed some mold on one side, so she decided it was doomed to the compost pile. But when she picked it up to toss it, she discovered that it was completely dried out and hollow, like a giant gourd! After that she didn't feel quite so bad about not getting up the nerve to cook it.

If you do decide to be adventurous and save your own cucurbit seeds, be aware that those of muskmelons, watermelons, winter squash, and pumpkins can simply be saved from the ripe fruits. Cucumbers and summer squash for seed should be allowed to mature on the vines. Remember that by allowing a fruit to mature, you will shut down production of harvestable fruits on that particular plant. When the fruit is mature, cut it open and scoop out the seeds. Mature cucumbers should be golden yellow with no trace of green left; summer squash should be large, hard, and gourdlike—it will take two months after the young, edible stage for the squash to develop mature seeds. Wash the seeds to remove any clinging flesh, dry them on paper towels, and then store in an airtight container in a cool, dry place.

Cucurbit Problems

Cucurbits are susceptible to a great variety of insect pests and diseases caused by viruses, bacteria, and fungi. Not only can the insect pests themselves damage foliage and fruit, they can sometimes also carry the diseases from plant to plant. For organic gardeners plagued with pests, the best solution is to grow resistant varieties (see the chart, Resistant Varieties of Cucurbits). Plant breeders have developed cucurbits resistant to some of the most common diseases: fusarium wilt, verticillium wilt, anthracnose, and powdery mildew. Some of these diseases exist as different strains (called races in seed catalogs), and you may need to know which strains are common in your area. Cucurbit varieties resistant to insect pests also exist. For specific information on pests and diseases, consult *Organic Plant Protection* (see the Bibliography).

Resistant Varieties of Cucurbits

Variety	Disease Resistance*
Cantaloupe (Muskmelons)	
Charantais (cantaloupe)	F, M
Edisto	A, DM, PM
Harvest Queen	F
Vedrantais (cantaloupe)	F, M
Cucumber	
Burpless Hybrid	DM, PM
Marketmore 76	DM, M, PM, S
Poinsett 76	ALS, DM, PM, S
Victory	ALS, DM, M, PM, S
Watermelon	
Charleston Gray	An, F, Sunburn
Crimson Sweet	An, F
Sweet Favorite	An, F

*Disease resistance or tolerance: A = Alternaria; ALS = angular leaf spot; An = Anthracnose; DM = downy mildew; F = Fusarium wilt; M = mosaic; PM = powdery mildew; S = scab.

Note: Disease resistance is not as highly desirable a feature in squash as it is in other cucurbits. So, very little breeding effort has been directed toward creating resistant squash varieties.

Cucumbers

With the possible exception of zucchini, cucumbers are probably the most popular cucurbit with gardeners. Just about everyone enjoys cool, crisp cucumber slices in their salads, and pickles are a favorite home-canned vegetable. With their modest-sized leaves, cucumbers take up less space than many other cucurbits, and gardeners pressed for space can choose to grow the newer bush cucumbers or to trellis the traditional vining kinds.

Cucumber Varieties

Which cucumbers you should grow depends on how you plan to use them. There are special varieties for pickling and others for slicing, as well as all-purpose sorts. Pickling cucumbers must have firm flesh that will hold its color and shape well through processing. These varieties bear an abundance of small fruits at one time so that you don't have to wait forever to gather enough for a batch of pickles. They are specially bred not to wrinkle, bloat, or float when brined. Pickling cucumbers also make fine fresh eating.

Burpless cucumbers are especially good for salads. They are crisp and sweet and don't seem to develop the bitterness that plagues some of the traditional varieties. That bitter flavor is caused by several different chemicals whose production in the fruit is controlled by a whole group of genes, so it is hard for breeders to eliminate the taste from cucumbers. If you have persistent problems with bitterness in your cucumbers, try growing a burpless variety. In addition to enjoying them fresh, you can also use burpless cukes for making cross-cut dill pickles or any other type of sliced or chopped pickles or relishes. If you want to try something a little different, you might grow lemon cucumbers next season. These prickly, round yellow fruits have an especially refreshing lemony flavor which matches their bright color.

For gardeners with limited space or a desire for many cucumbers over a short time span, bush cucumbers are just the thing. These attractive plants have short internodes, so they form an attractive, compact bush with a cluster of pretty yellow flowers rather than a scraggly vine with widely spaced flowers. Bush cucumbers will produce slightly more cucumbers per plant than vine types, and the harvest will be more concentrated, which makes them ideal for pickles.

If you are frustrated by all those early male flowers which fall off without accomplishing anything, then maybe gynoecious cucumbers are for you. These specially bred varieties have an abundance of female flowers which are borne earlier than on conventional cucumbers. Strictly speaking, the term "gynoecious" refers to plants that bear only female flowers, but some cucumber

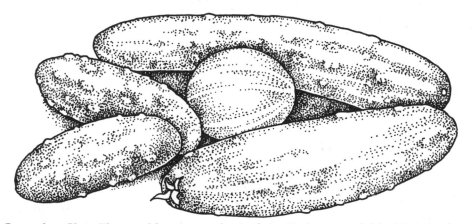

Cucumber Clan: *The round lemon cucumber in the center is surrounded by (clockwise from upper right) burpless, slicing, and pickling cucumbers.*

varieties called gynoecious do have a few male flowers as well. When you receive your packet of gynoecious seeds, you will find some colored seeds in the packet along with them. These are seeds of a pollinator variety that will produce male flowers to pollinate your female vines. The female flowers should bloom early in the season, right along with the male flowers on the pollinator vines, giving you an early and abundant harvest. Some gynoecious varieties produce especially heavily and are ideal for pickle fanciers. Most major seed companies carry a few gynoecious varieties. Some of the more popular ones include County Fair, Gemini, Pioneer, Saladin, Streamliner, Sweet Slice, Triumph, and Victory.

Some cucumber varieties have been developed especially for greenhouse culture. These cucumbers have a special group of genes that direct the fruit to develop even if the flower is not pollinated. Seeds of these varieties are quite expensive, but if you want to grow your cucumbers in a greenhouse or other place where there aren't enough bees to pollinate the flowers, they are worth the investment.

Growing Cucumbers

Because cucumber plants are smaller than some other cucurbits, they can be grown closer together. If you grow vining varieties on the ground, plant them in hills spaced 3 feet apart in all directions, with three plants to a hill. Vining cucumbers can also be planted in rows 3 feet apart, with the plants spaced at 6-inch intervals. Bush cucumbers can be planted in hills 2 feet apart in all directions or in rows 2 feet apart. They also make pleasing container plants and are attractive enough to be used in foundation plantings along the south side of the house.

One of the best ways to grow vining cucumbers is to train them up a trellis. Cucumber vines have grasping tendrils that grow from the leaf axils. When the tendrils are about one-third grown, they become sensitive to contact and will wrap around anything they touch. The tendrils can react quickly, sometimes beginning to twine within twenty seconds after touching a support. If you plant your cucumbers along a trellis, the tendrils will grab hold and the vines will climb up the supports with no further assistance needed.

Trellising is especially recommended in humid regions, for when the vines are growing upwards, air can circulate through them and keep them drier and less susceptible to fungal infection. Trellising also minimizes damage done to plants by hail and heavy rains. Trellised vines take up far less ground space than cucumber hills, and heat-sensitive crops such as lettuce can be planted in the shade produced behind the growing vines.

There are other advantages to growing cucumbers vertically. Trellised cucumbers may bear more abundantly, for all the leaves on the trellis can face the sun more directly. Trellising is also a good way to grow long cucumbers such as the burpless, Japanese, and Armenian varieties. When these varieties are grown on the ground, the fruits often end up curling around because of contact with the soil. On a trellis, they can hang perfectly straight. The fruits of trellised cucumbers are also easier to find than those of ground-grown plants, and damage to the vines during harvesting is minimized.

All these advantages add up to a greater harvest of higher-quality fruits than the traditional hill-planting method produces. When scientists compared trellised plants of the varieties Ashly, Fletcher, and High Mark II with ground-grown ones, they harvested twice as many fruits from the trellised vines. There was a dramatic decrease in scab and soil rot, as well as fewer misshapen culls. Pesticides were used in this study, but organic gardeners will find that it's easier to spot pests such as cucumber beetles on an exposed, trellised vine than on a ground-hugging one. And if you use rotenone or bug-juice sprays, even coverage of trellised vines is easier to accomplish than for hilled plants.

Space plants for trellising 6 inches apart in a straight row, and anchor the trellis at planting time so you won't disturb the roots later.

Harvesting Your Cucumbers

When you pick your cucumbers depends on what you plan to do with them. Pickling cucumbers should be picked when they reach the proper size for their particular sort of pickle. For the crispest pickles, pick the cucumbers young—2- to 3-inch-long fruits no more than two days old will give you the crunchiest pickles. Cucumbers can grow very fast—they may increase in size by 40 percent in only 24 hours—so if you are trying to catch them at a particular size check the vines carefully every day. Cucumbers for fresh eating should be picked before the seeds have developed very far; about 8 to 10 inches is the usual recommended size. Supermarket cucumbers always seem to be full of big, tough seeds, and one of the joys of homegrown fruits is biting into a cool, crisp cylinder that's tender all the way through.

Take a sharp knife with you when you go out to harvest your cucumbers; remember, you do not want to damage the vines. When hunting the harvest among ground-grown vines, be careful not to bend them or you'll damage the phloem pipelines that bring nourishment to the growing fruits. Always remove any overmature cucumbers which have escaped your notice in previous searches, for they will inhibit the setting of new fruits and the vine will waste a lot of energy producing seeds. It is very important to keep cucumber vines well watered throughout their flowering and fruit-producing period for the succulent fruits need plenty of moisture for quick growth.

After harvest, cucumbers should be stored at 45° to 50°F with a relative humidity of 90 to 95 percent. They will keep for fourteen days under these conditions. The refrigerator is really too cold for good cucumber storage; fresh-picked fruits will keep safely only about a week there. Cucumbers held at too cold a temperature for too long will develop water-soaked spots which quickly turn into mushy pits.

Cucumber Frontiers

Unfortunately for us gardeners, cucumber breeders are focusing their attention mostly on problems faced by commercial growers. While they are working on developing more disease-resistant varieties, they concern themselves little with types resistant to insects, for commercial growers rely on chemical pesticides to kill off pests.

A major goal of breeders is to develop cucumbers that produce all their fruits at one time, so the commercial grower can harvest all at once. Such varieties could come in handy for home gardeners with limited space who want to make pickles, for if all the fruits came on at the same time it wouldn't be necessary to accumulate them until there were enough for processing.

At the present time, hybridizing cucumbers requires a lot of painstaking hand pollination, and hybrids are therefore expensive to develop. Breeders are trying to find cheaper ways to produce hybrids.

Summer Squash

Summer squash is a popular home garden crop for it grows rapidly, yields if anything too abundantly, and produces early. In northern areas where no melons and only a limited variety of winter squash can be grown, gardeners can experiment successfully with any of the summer squashes, for these adaptable plants grow well in nearly all climates and thrive in cooler weather than melons. Here in Montana, where even one ripe melon is the sign of a master gardener, everyone seems to have more zucchini in August than can be put to good use.

Squash Varieties

One of the great virtues of summer squash is the size of the plants—all are available as high-quality bush varieties. Instead of having to cope with rambling vines that spread all over the garden, you can work with compact hills of plants that grow predictably. Summer squashes come in a number of shapes and colors. All have a mild, slightly sweet flavor, but their textures vary from the moist, airy yellow squash to the very firm Scallopini.

Several types of summer squash are an attractive bright yellow color. Crookneck has a thin, bent stem end and a warty skin. Its texture is quite loose and a bit watery, but its flavor is good. There are other straight-necked

Summer Squash Selections: *The familiar oblong zucchini on the bottom and unusual round zucchini in the middle are flanked by yellow crookneck. Scallopini, or patty pan, is shown in the upper middle.*

yellow varieties that are otherwise similar to crookneck, but some newer sorts of straight-necked yellow squash (such as Gold Rush) have a taste and texture that is very similar to zucchini. It is fun to grow both yellow and green squashes and serve the slices together as a colorful side dish with a summer meal.

Zucchini itself is the most popular summer squash. Some zucchinis have a light greenish gray skin, while others are a dark, almost black-green. In recent years, summer squashes similar to zucchini but with different shapes have been introduced. One type, Gourmet Globe, is round, which makes it good for scooping out and stuffing. Another, called Scallopini, has a flattened shape with a scalloped edge, like the pale green Peter Pan squash, but has the dark green color of zucchini. Scallopini has very firm but tender flesh and keeps longer in storage than some other summer squashes.

Growing Summer Squash

There is no secret to growing summer squash—just give it good, rich soil, plenty of sunshine, and adequate water, and within two months of planting you will be harvesting abundant quantities of squash. Because of the compact bushy habit of summer squash, its hills can be spaced as close together as 3 feet, with three plants per hill.

Harvesting and Storing Summer Squash

Summer squashes must be watched carefully for their fruits grow very fast. Within four to eight days of pollination, a summer squash is ready to pick, depending on the variety and weather conditions: the warmer it is, the faster it grows. The shriveled petals of summer squash flowers retain excess moisture and are thus an excellent place for fungal growth to start. Since this can spoil the blossom end of the fruit, you should remove the withered petals when the fruit starts to grow. If you have your eye on some developing fruits, check the plants every day, for summer squash grows about ¾ inch each day. A few days of neglect can leave you with a giant on your hands! While many gardeners wait until their summer squashes are 8 or 10 inches long before picking them, the truth is that the earlier you harvest, the firmer and more tender your summer squash will be. Keeping the fruits picked also will keep the plants producing. Always cut the stem cleanly with a sharp knife when harvesting summer squash so as not to damage the fruit or the plant.

Summer squash doesn't keep long in storage, so try to eat or process it for storage as it comes in. If you must store your summer squash for a few days, remove the withered petals if they are still attached to the fruits. If the fruits are dirty, wash them, dry them carefully, and store them in plastic bags. Try not to break the tender skin. They will keep up to two weeks in the refrigerator or three weeks at 45°F at 80 percent humidity. Summer squash can also be dried, and it freezes well although it tends to be limp when thawed.

Winter Squash

There's something especially satisfying about going to the storeroom in the dead of winter and choosing a colorful, sweet winter squash for the evening meal. And while many people are familiar with eating pumpkin seeds (sold in expensive little packets as *pepitas*), not so many know that winter squash seeds taste almost the same and can be munched just like pumpkin seeds after they've been roasted gently in a low oven. The variety of winter squash is dazzling and no wonder—four different plant species produce these versatile fruits!

Winter Squash Varieties

Some multi-purpose varieties of winter squash can be harvested early and used as a summer squash or at the mature stage for winter storage.

Winter Squash: *Clockwise from upper right are shown two spaghetti squash, a butternut, a hubbard, another butternut, and two acorn squash.*

Acorn, Jersey Golden Acorn, and Table Queen are examples of this type of squash. Kuta is a relatively new all-purpose squash that can be eaten as a pale green summer squash when it's 2 to 8 inches long or can be cured for winter storage at a larger size. Kuta grows in bush form to conserve space and may begin to bear as early as 42 days after planting.

Vegetable Spaghetti, also called spaghetti squash, is another variety that can be harvested in the summer, but don't expect to pick any fruits before 70 days of growth. The squash can be picked while still green for immediate use or when mature and yellow for winter storage; it will keep until about New Year's Day. Vegetable Spaghetti is still relatively unfamiliar to many gardeners, but it's gaining friends fast, for it provides a unique eating experience. It is especially popular with dieters, who bake or boil the whole fruit, cut it in half, and scrape out the long, spaghetti-like strands to serve as a low-calorie substitute for pasta.

There are many varieties of vining winter squash—too many to cover here. But a few old favorites can be mentioned—Butternut and Acorn are especially popular, and Buttercup is particularly fine, with delicate, dry flesh and a sweet, rich flavor. Hubbard squash, which comes in several varieties, has also stood the test of time, and its seeds are plentiful, large, and very tasty. All these types also store especially well, often long into spring.

For those of us with small gardens and a yen for winter squash, breeders have developed several fine bush winter squashes in recent years. Sweet Mama Hybrid is a prolific variety with smooth flesh which will keep for four months. Table King and Table Queen are both bush varieties of Acorn squash, while Kindred is a buttercup type. Kindred sometimes sends out runners which make it look like a vining squash, but these can be clipped off to keep the plants under control.

Growing Winter Squash

Bush varieties of winter squash can be grown like bush summer squashes, but the vining kinds need a lot more room. In long-season areas, winter squash and pumpkins can be planted among the corn rows to conserve space. This method won't do in short-season areas, because the vigorous squash vines will take over, robbing the corn of nutrients and sunlight, thereby slowing its growth so that you will harvest little or no corn.

Winter squash is traditionally planted in hills spaced 6 to 8 feet apart. The wider the spacing, the larger the ultimate size of the fruit. So if you want small squashes instead of big ones, plant your hills closer together. Just be sure to give the plants soil with plenty of organic matter, and keep them well watered; more closely spaced plants will need more water than those which are farther apart.

Vining winter squashes can be grown on trellises to save space, for they have branched tendrils that enable them to hang onto a trellis even when laden with fruit. If the fruits get really big, they can be supported in slings made from old sheets which are tied to the trellis supports.

Use your imagination when planting winter squash, for their rampant vines can actually be useful for covering rocky, unlandscaped ground. As long as the roots are anchored in rich, moist soil, the vines can sprawl out anywhere, covering unsightly areas while providing your family with a tasty harvest.

Harvesting and Storing Winter Squash

Winter squash should be allowed to ripen fully on the vine before picking. It may take six weeks for the fruit to mature. Wait until the skin is hard (so you can't pierce it with your fingernail) and the stem becomes tough and woody. Cut the stem as long as possible when you harvest, and *do not* carry the squash by the stem. The stem is very likely to break off, leaving an area vulnerable to attack by bacteria and fungi. If they are dirty, wash the fruits with water or a solution of 1 part household bleach to 3 parts water and dry thoroughly. If the weather forces you to harvest some of your squashes before they are completely mature, plan on eating those first, for they won't keep long. Winter squash can tolerate some chilly weather—in fact, a light frost increases the sugar content. The vines may be killed, but the fruit won't be harmed. A hard frost, however, will reduce the keeping quality, so harvest all your winter squash before this happens.

Many sources recommend curing winter squash before storage, but others say it isn't necessary. If you plan on storing your squash in a place with an unregulated atmosphere, such as your basement, you are better off curing it first. Cure the squash at 80° to 85°F for ten days at a relative humidity of 80 percent, then place in storage. The best storage conditions are a temperature of 50° to 60°F and low humidity. Depending on the variety, your squash should keep for three to eight months. Check them often, and if some fruits of one variety begin to deteriorate, use that kind up as soon as possible. If you notice mold on any of the squash, discard them right away before it spreads to other stored squashes.

The United States Department of Agriculture recommends that winter squash not be cured: in fact, it claims that curing damages Table Queen, changing its color and causing deterioration in the flavor. They say that curing has no effect either way on the storage life and quality of other varieties. They recommend storing Hubbard squashes at 50° to 55°F with a relative humidity of 70 to 75 percent and Butternut and Acorn types at 50°F with 50 percent humidity. The USDA also advises growers to remove the stems of Hubbard squash completely before storing and not to store this variety near apples, for they may cause the squash skin to become yellow.

Squash Frontiers

While most cucurbits require a lot of water to produce well, some wild squashes can grow with surprisingly little water. Squash breeders are trying to incorporate this trait into cultivated varieties without bringing along the bitterness of wild squashes. Seeds of wild squashes are also very high in protein; if this quality could be bred into domestic squashes the seeds of this vegetable could be as valuable a crop as the fruits themselves.

Pumpkins

While we think of pumpkins as a separate sort of vegetable from squash, the fact is that pumpkins actually represent varieties of three of the four squash species! For this reason, most of the recommendations given for winter squash also apply to pumpkins. Pumpkins do not keep in storage as long as some winter squashes, however. Don't worry if you end up having to pick some pumpkins while they are still green; the skin will develop a rich orange color in storage. Despite the poems about frost on the pumpkin, both pumpkins and winter squash should be picked before temperatures go below 30°F, for colder temperatures can damage the fruits.

Pumpkin Varieties

Which pumpkins you grow depends on why you are growing them and on how much space you have in your garden. If you want to make pies, grow one of the Sugar varieties, for these are famous for their fine-textured, sweet flesh. Jack O'Lantern was developed especially for Halloween fun, while Connecticut Field is a large pumpkin which makes good eating and carving. Lady Godiva and Naked Seeded are both varieties which produce hull-less seeds just right for eating. Triple Treat is an all-purpose pumpkin with naked seeds and sweet golden flesh; its rounded shape also make it a good candidate for carving. There are also a few semi-bush pumpkin varieties for the small garden, such as Cheyenne, Spirit Hybrid, and Funny Face Hybrid.

Muskmelons

For most of us, the word "melon" conjures up the image of a juicy watermelon or cantaloupe. But the melon known as cantaloupe in North America is really not a cantaloupe at all; it is properly called a muskmelon. Our muskmelons have a musky aroma which true cantaloupes, Honeydew, Crenshaw, and Casaba melons lack. Real cantaloupes (such as the varieties Charantais and Vedrantais) are rarely grown in America, for their seeds have only recently become available here.

True cantaloupes, muskmelons, and other melons such as Honeydew, Crenshaw, and Casaba, all belong to the species *Cucumis melo*. But there are three subgroups of this species which are nowhere near as different from one another as the varieties of Cabbage family crops. The true cantaloupes belong to the group Cantalupensis. The muskmelons belong to the group Reticulatus, a word which refers to the netting on the skin. The Honeydew, Crenshaw, and Casaba melons belong to the third group, Inodorus, so-called because they lack the powerful muskmelon aroma. Since the three groups are members of the same species, it should be no surprise that, like cabbages and kale, they cross-pollinate freely. Breeders have experimented in recent years with crossing true cantaloupes with muskmelons, for the former have some built-in resistance to mosaic virus and fusarium wilt. Any other varieties whose

Melon Medley: *Clockwise from upper right are shown muskmelon, crenshaw, true cantaloupe, honeydew, another muskmelon, and casaba.*

names begin with "Cha-" or end with "-tais," such as Chaca, are hybrids between true cantaloupes and muskmelons. These melons do well in many areas; we've harvested good crops of Chaca even here in Montana.

Muskmelons are more closely related to cucumbers (*Cucumis sativus*) than to watermelon (*Citrullus lanatus*), which is evident when you look at the plants. The leaves are similar to cucumber leaves in size and shape, and the vines grow in much the same way as cucumber vines. Because of their smaller leaves and shorter vines, muskmelons take up less space in the garden than winter squash or watermelon. And since nothing you can buy in the supermarket matches the flavor of homegrown, vine-ripened muskmelons, you should by all means give them a try.

Muskmelon Varieties

Like so many other crops, muskmelons have recently become a possibility both for northern gardens and small gardens. Chaca, which has rich, juicy, salmon-colored flesh, has a relatively small vine and matures in 75 days; it is resistant to powdery mildew and fusarium wilt, like its European parent. Earli-Sweet Hybrid and Early Northern Queen Hybrid are both ready for picking in 70 days. For people with small gardens, a few compact varieties with small vines are available. Minnesota Midget matures in only 65 days and has vines which only reach 3 feet in length (standard varieties spread 4 or more feet). They produce an abundance of small (4-inch diameter) fruits.

If you live where the growing season is longer, ask your county agent which diseases tend to plague muskmelons in your area, and buy seeds of varieties that are resistant to those diseases or strains of diseases if at all possible. Resistance is especially important in muskmelons, for diseases tend to strike right as the melons are ripening. Infections clog the phloem and interrupt the vital flow of sugars to the fruits, resulting in bland, disappointing melons. A good variety to grow in humid southeastern areas is Edisto, which is resistant to powdery mildew, downy mildew, and alternaria leaf spot. If you live in a southeastern region where mildews and gummy stem blight are a problem, try Gulf Coast or Southland. Western areas tend to be plagued by powdery mildew, but many varieties are resistant to it.

When you first start out with muskmelons, it's a good idea to grow two varieties. If the two varieties have different maturation times, you'll be extending your harvest season. And you will also increase your chances of getting a harvest from healthy plants. If you find that one variety doesn't do well in your garden and the other does, grow the successful one the following year, along with a new choice. After a few years, you should know which melon varieties grow best under the conditions in your garden.

Muskmelon breeders have found genes which confer tolerance to the melon aphid and are working on incorporating this trait into cultivated varieties. But as yet none of these varieties are on the market.

Growing, Harvesting, and Storing Muskmelons

The same advice applies for growing muskmelons as for cucumbers. Like cucumbers and winter squash, muskmelons can be trained to grow up a trellis if the fruits are carefully tied up in slings, so they don't fall off or snap their stems when ripe. The ideal spacing for muskmelons is 18 inches in all directions between plants. This spacing allows the vines to overlap and shade out weeds. While each vine will produce fewer melons, your total yield per garden area will be greater. Trellising the plants will save even more space. Planting in rows with wider spacings will give you more melons per plant but will take up more garden space. Muskmelons can be planted by the traditional hill method if you wish, too. Because the plants love warmth, mulching muskmelons with black plastic and giving them some sort of mini-greenhouse to grow in while they are small will increase your yields significantly.

After your melon plants have set fruit, don't be alarmed if some of the melons shrivel up and disappear when they are about the size of hen eggs. This is the normal response of the plant; it allows only as many melons to grow to full size as it can support. The nutrients present in the excess fruits are reabsorbed by the plant and redistributed to the melons that will mature. Whenever you must handle the vines, do so with special care, for they are even more sensitive to handling than cucumber vines. You don't want to risk injuring the energy-producing leaves or the phloem tissue in the stems.

Most muskmelons are ripe when a crack appears between the stem and the fruit; the fruit is said to have reached full slip when it separates easily from the vine. You'll notice a strong musky odor around the stem end, and the netting will be very pronounced. That is the best time to take the melon inside and eat it, for from the time it is picked, the fruit respires on its own, using up bit by bit the sugars stored in its sweet flesh. Any fruits you don't eat right away should be refrigerated immediately to slow down respiration. They will keep there (preferably at a relative humidity of 85 to 90 percent) for five to fourteen days.

True cantaloupes, Honeydews, Casabas, and Crenshaws do not slip when ripe, and they don't develop the distinctive musky aroma, so it's a bit harder to tell when they are ready to pick. The blossom end of these melons becomes a bit soft when pressed firmly with your thumb at ripening. The skin of Honeydews changes from pale blue-green to a lighter ivory or cream color when the melon is ripe. Hybrids like Chaca should be harvested at half slip, when the stem begins to separate from the fruit. Honeydew, Crenshaw, and Casaba melons should not be stored in the refrigerator, for their flesh is damaged by cold air. Place them at 45° to 50°F if possible, and keep the relative humidity at 85 to 90 percent if you can.

Watermelon

Nothing tastes better on a sweltering August afternoon than a juicy slice of cool, sweet, field-ripened watermelon. For many years, we gardeners found that the luxury of devoting the necessary space to this challenging crop was impossible, or the climate where we lived made growing watermelons a challenge too great to face. But the development in recent years of bush watermelons and early maturing varieties makes this tasty crop at least worth trying in most North American gardens.

Watermelon Varieties

There are dozens of varieties of watermelons, but once you know what sort of fruit you want and what sort of special conditions your garden offers, you can narrow down your choice quite easily. If you hanker after the biggest melons, try Black Diamond (also called Cannonball and Florida Giant). In favorable climates, this variety consistently produces 50-pound melons. If diseases plague watermelons in your area, check with your county agent about which diseases are prevalent and choose resistant varieties.

You can pick between round and cylindrical melons, striped and plain ones, and big and small ones. If you don't like to spit out a lot of seeds, there are several varieties of small-seeded melons, such as Allsweet, to choose from. The ultimate watermelon for seed-haters, though, is the seedless type. This was developed by Japanese breeders through a costly, complex process that involves artificially creating a watermelon which cannot cross with other varieties to produce viable seeds. For this reason, the seeds are very expensive, costing 10 cents or more per seed. While these fruits have no seeds, they do contain some empty white seed coats that can just be swallowed. Only small-seeded watermelons are used in breeding seedless varieties because the larger-seeded types would leave a large empty seed coat that would be as much of a nuisance as a seed.

Seedless watermelons, like gynoecious cucumbers, are sold with extra seeds of a pollinator variety. Plant one pollinator for every five seedless plants, and be sure if you grow a seedless variety to mark which plants are pollinators so you will know which melons are seedless come harvesttime (the pollinator plants will produce melons with seeds).

For gardeners with limited space, bush watermelons such as Sugar Bush are the answer. These plants need only 6 square feet of garden space, and each vine produces two to four small melons, about six pounds each. Northern gardeners can try an early variety such as Northern Sweet, Golden Midget, or the yellow-fleshed Yellow Doll. Watermelon breeders are continuing their search for plants that take up less space and produce smaller, more abundant melons.

Growing, Harvesting, and Storing Watermelons

Watermelons need even more growing room than other cucurbits. They are traditionally grown in hills placed about 10 feet apart, with three plants to a hill, but watermelons can also be grown in rows, placing single plants 6 feet apart in all directions. Bush varieties can be grown in rows with 2½ feet separating the plants or in hills about 5 feet apart. In northern areas, it's a good idea to start the plants indoors as described earlier and to cover the young plants in the garden with hot caps or plastic milk cartons until the weather is warm and settled.

Knowing when a watermelon is ripe takes some practice. When you thump on a melon, it makes a different sound when ripe than when it was unripe. If the melon isn't yet ready to harvest, the sound will be a high-pitched ringing. But when you knock on a ripe melon, you'll hear a hollow thud. The sound of a ripe melon is dull and hollow rather than pingy. After you have experimented with your own melons, you'll learn to distinguish between the two types of sound.

Try to eat your melons soon after they're picked, for watermelons do not store well. If you have to keep them for a while, the best conditions are a temperature of 40° to 50°F at 80 to 85 percent relative humidity. Don't expect to keep them for more than two weeks. Your melons will lose their red color in cold storage, but if you keep them at room temperature for a few days, the redness will intensify.

Glossary

Annual: a plant that completes its life cycle in one growing season.

Anther: the top part of the stamen that contains the pollen.

Apical tip: the region of actively dividing and growing cells at the top of the stem.

Axillary bud: a bud located in the leaf axil (the angle between the leaf and the stem) which serves as a potential growth site.

Biennial: a plant that completes its life cycle in two growing seasons, growing vegetatively the first season, and flowering, fruiting, and dying the second season.

Bolting: elongation of a flowering stem of a plant at the expense of its vegetative growth; generally, a plant at this stage is no longer edible.

Bulb: an underground storage structure composed of a shortened stem surrounded by thick, fleshy leaf bases; the onion is a bulb.

Chlorophyll: the green pigment in plants responsible for trapping the sun's energy and using it to fuel internal chemical reactions.

Chloroplast: a specialized microscopic structure located in the leaf cells that contains chlorophyll and aids in the manufacture of food for the plant.

Cotyledons (also called seed leaves): special leaflike storage organs present inside the seed which nourish the young seedling; cotyledons of many plants, such as beans and tomatoes, can be seen as the first "leaves" on the seedling; they look different from the true leaves.

Cross-pollination: the transfer of pollen from the anther of one plant to the stigma of a flower on another plant.

Determinate growth: a type of growth in which the shoot tip eventually stops stem formation and usually forms a flower; examples include corn and determinate tomatoes such as Nova and Fireball.

Dicot: a plant whose embryo has two seed leaves or cotyledons; an example is the bean.

Dioecious: having separate male and female plants; spinach is an example.

Endosperm: nutritive tissue that develops around the plant embryo in a seed; often used up by the maturing seed in many plants but stays intact in seeds of corn and other cereal plants.

Fibrous root system: a root system lacking one central axis in which the roots branch out in all directions; corn and potatoes are fibrous rooted.

Gynoecious: a plant with only female flowers; this trait appears in some specially bred varieties of cucumbers.

Hardy: term used for plants which are able to withstand temperatures at or below freezing.

Hybrid: offspring produced by crossing two different strains of a particular plant species; seeds saved from a mature hybrid plant will produce plants unlike the parent.

Indeterminate: plant growth habit in which the apical tip continuously forms stem tissue; flowers form from lateral buds; cucumbers and many tomato varieties exhibit this type of growth.

Leaching: the process by which nutrients are carried down through the soil by percolating water, often out of the reach of plant roots.

Monocot: a plant whose embryo has one seed leaf or cotyledon; corn and onions are monocots.

Monoecious: a plant with two types of flowers, male and female; squash and corn are examples.

Node: a region of the stem from which leaves and axillary buds raise.

Open-pollinated variety: a variety of vegetable from which the seeds can be saved; unlike hybrids, seeds from open-pollinated varieties will produce plants that resemble the parents.

Perennial: an herbaceous plant which lives for three or more years.

Phloem: vascular tissue in plants responsible for carrying food from the leaves throughout the rest of the plant; also aids plant structure by providing support for the stem.

Photosynthesis: the conversion of carbon dioxide and water into carbohydrates necessary for plant growth; light energy fuels the conversion which takes place in the chlorophyll-laden tissues of plants; oxygen is released as a by-product.

Pistil: the female organ of a flower which consists of a stigma, style, and ovary.

Rotation: the practice of alternating which crops are grown in the same part of the garden to alleviate pest and disease problems and nutrient drain; crops in the same plant family, those susceptible to the same pest and disease problems, and those that use the same nutrients should be grown in the same part of the garden no more than once every three or four years.

Stamen: the male organ of a flower consisting of an anther and filament.

Stigma: the upper portion of the pistil which receives the pollen grains during pollination.

Stomata: tiny openings in the epidermis of leaves and stems through which carbon dioxide is absorbed and moisture is given off; singular form, stomate.

Taproot: a fleshy main root from which smaller, lateral branches radiate; carrots and beets are taprooted.

Tender: term used for plants which cannot withstand freezing temperatures.

Tuber: an enlarged, fleshy, short underground stem; the potato is a tuber.

Vernalization: the process whereby near-freezing temperatures speed flowering of plants.

Viable: a term, when applied to seeds, that indicates they are capable of germinating.

Xylem: the vascular tissue that transports minerals and water from the roots to the rest of the plant.

Bibliography

Carr, Anna. *Rodale's Color Handbook of Garden Insects*. Emmaus, Pa.: Rodale Press, 1979.

Logsdon, Gene. *The Gardener's Guide to Better Soil*. Emmaus, Pa.: Rodale Press, 1975.

Lorenz, Oscar A., and Maynard, Donald N. *Knott's Handbook for Vegetable Growers*. 2d ed. New York: John Wiley and Sons, 1980.

Mangelsdorf, Paul C. *Corn: Its Origin, Evolution, and Development*. Cambridge, Mass.: Harvard University Press, 1974.

Ryder, Edward J. *Leafy Salad Vegetables*. Westport, Conn.: AVI Publishing Co., 1979.

Simmonds, N. W., ed. *Evolution of Crop Plants*. New York: Longman Inc., 1976.

"Trickle Irrigation Guidelines for the Home Garden." Research Report No. 285, Michigan State University Agricultural Extension Service, July 1, 1975.

Wolf, Ray, ed. *Solar Growing Frame*. Emmaus, Pa.: Rodale Press, 1980.

Yepsen, Roger B., ed. *Organic Plant Protection*. Emmaus, Pa.: Rodale Press, 1976.

Index

---

growth of, 294–95
harvesting of, 295
storage of, 295
varieties of, 293–94
vital statistics, 278

T

Temperature, 2–5, 37–41
average daily, 3
degree days and, 2–3
effect on flowers, 37–41
microclimates and, 3–4
Tomatoes, 245–60
flowering of, 253–55
frontiers, 259–60
growth of, 249–51
harvesting of, 256–57
problems with, 258–59
ripening of, 255–56
seedlings, care of, 248–49
seeds, starting of, 247–49
staking and pruning of,
251–52
varieties of, 246–47
vital statistics, 245

V

Vegetables, 43–45
development of, 44–45
growth of, 43–45
ripening of, 43–45

W

Watermelon, 302–4
growth of, 303–4
harvesting of, 303–4
storage of, 303–4
varieties of, 302–3
vital statistics, 278
Weather, effects on growth,
2–4
Winter squash, 295–98
frontiers, 298
growth of, 297
harvesting of, 297
storage of, 297
varieties of, 295–97
vital statistics, 278

Z

Zea Mays. See Corn